MUIRHEAD LIBRARY OF PHILOSOPHY

An admirable statement of the aims of the Library of Philosophy was provided by the first editor, the late Professor J. H. Muirhead, in his description of the original programme printed in Erdmann's *History of Philosophy* under the date 1890. This was slightly modified in subsequent volumes to take the form of the following statement:

'The Muirhead Library of Philosophy was designed as a contribution to the History of Modern Philosophy under the heads: first of Different Schools of Thought—Sensationalist, Realist, Idealist, Intuitivist; secondly of different Subjects—Psychology, Ethics, Aesthetics, Political Philosophy, Theology. While much had been done in England in tracing the course of evolution in nature, history, economics, morals and religion, little had been done in tracing the development of thought on these subjects. Yet "the evolution of opinion is part of the whole evolution".

'By the co-operation of different writers in carrying out this plan it was hoped that a thoroughness and completeness of treatment, otherwise unattainable, might be secured. It was believed also that from writers mainly British and American fuller consideration of English Philosophy than it had hitherto received might be looked for. In the earlier series of books containing, among others, Bosanquet's *History of Aesthetic*, Pfleiderer's *Rational Theology since Kant*, Albee's *History of English Utilitarianism*, Bonar's *Philosophy and Political Economy*, Brett's *History of Psychology*, Ritchie's *Natural Rights*, these objects were to a large extent effected.

'In the meantime original work of a high order was being produced both in England and America by such writers as Bradley, Stout, Bertrand Russell, Baldwin, Urban, Montague, and others, and a new interest in foreign works, German, French and Italian, which had either become classical or were attracting public attention, had developed. The scope of the Library thus became extended into something more international, and it is entering on the fifth decade of its existence in the hope that it may contribute to that mutual understanding between countries which is so pressing a need of the present time.'

The need which Professor Muirhead stressed is no less pressing today, and few will deny that philosophy has much to do with enabling us to meet it, although no one, least of all Muirhead himself, would regard that as the sole, or even the main, object of philosophy. As Professor Muirhead continues to lend the distinction of his name to the Library of Philosophy it seemed not inappropriate to allow him to recall us to these aims in his own words. The emphasis on the history of thought also seemed to me very timely: and the number of important works promised for the Library in the very near future augur well for the continued fufilment, in this and other ways, of the expectations of the original editor.

H. D. LEWIS

MUIRHEAD LIBRARY OF PHILOSOPHY

General Editor: H. D. Lewis

Professor of History and Philosophy of Religion at the University of London

The Absolute and the Atonement by DOM ILLTYD TRETHOWAN
Absolute Value by DOM ILLTYD TRETHOWAN
Action by SIR MALCOLM KNOX
The Analysis of Mind by BERTRAND RUSSELL
Ascent to the Absolute by J. N. FINDLAY
Belief by H. H. PRICE
Brett's History of Psychology edited by R. S. PETERS
Broad's Critical Essays in Moral Philosophy edited by DAVID R. CHENEY
Clarity is Not Enough by H. D. LEWIS
Coleridge as Philosopher by J. H. MUIRHEAD
The Commonplace Book of G. E. Moore edited by C. LEWY
Contemporary American Philosophy edited by G. P. ADAMS and W. P. MONTAGUE
Contemporary British Philosophy first and second series edited by J. H. MUIRHEAD
Contemporary British Philosophy third series edited by H. D. LEWIS
Contemporary Indian Philosophy edited by RADHAKRISHNAN and J. H. MUIRHEAD 2nd edition
Contemporary Philsophy in Australia edited by ROBERT BROWN and C. D. ROLLINS
The Discipline of the Cave by J. N. FINDLAY
Doctrine and Argument in Indian Philosophy by NINIAN SMART
The Elusive Mind by H. D. LEWIS
Essays in Analysis by ALICE AMBROSE
Ethics by NICOLAI HARTMANN translated by STANTON COIT 3 vols
Ethics and Christianity by KEITH WARD
The Foundation of Metaphysics in Science by ERROL E. HARRIS
Freedom and History by H. D. LEWIS
G. E. Moore: Essays in Rectrospect edited by ALICE AMBROSE and MORRIS LAZEROWITZ
The Good Will: A Study in the Coherence Theory of Goodness by H. J. PATON
Hegel: A Re-examination by J. N. FINDLAY
Hegel's Science of Logic translated by W. H. JOHNSTON and L. G. STRUTHERS 2 vols
A History of Aesthetic by B. BOSANQUET 2nd edition
A History of English Utilitarianism by E. ALBEE
Human Knowledge by BERTRAND RUSSELL
A Hundred Years of British Philosophy by RUDOLPH METZ translated by J. H. HARVEY, T. E. JESSOP, HENRY STURT
Hypothesis and Perception by ERROL E. HARRIS
Ideas: A General Introduction to Pure Phenomenology by EDMUND HUSSERL translated by W. R. BOYCE GIBSON
Identity and Reality by EMILE MEYERSON
Imagination by E. J. FURLONG
In Contact with the Physical World by JOHN PENNYCUICK
In Defence of Free Will by C. A. CAMPBELL

Indian Philosophy by RADHAKRISHNAN 2 vols revised 2nd edition
Introduction to Mathematical Philosophy by BERTRAND RUSSELL 2nd edition
Kant's First Critique by H. W. CASSIRER
Kant's Metaphysic of Experience by H. J. PATON
Know Thyself by BERNADINO VARISCO translated by GUGLIELMO SALVADORI
Language and Reality by WILBUR MARSHALL URBAN
A Layman's Quest by SIR MALCOM KNOX
Lectures on Philosophy by G. E. MOORE edited by C. LEWY
Matter and Memory by HENRI BERGSON translated by N. M. PAUL and W. S. PALMER
Meaning in the Arts by ARNAUD LOUIS REID
Memory by BRIAN SMITH
Mental Images by ALASTAIR HANNAY
The Modern Predicament by H. J. PATON
Natural Rights by D. G. RITCHIE 3rd edition
Nature, Mind and Modern Science by E. HARRIS
The Nature of Thought by BRAND BLANSHARD
Non-Linguistic Philosophy by A. C. EWING
On Selfhood and Godhood by C. A. CAMPBELL
Our Experience of God by H. D. LEWIS
Our Knowledge of Right and Wrong by JONATHAN HARRISON
Perception by DON LOCKE
The Person God Is by PETER A. BERTOCCI
The Phenomenology of Mind by G. W. F. HEGEL translated by SIR JAMES BAILLIE revised 2nd edition
Philosophy in America by MAX BLACK
Philosophical Papers by G. E. MOORE
Philosophy and Illusion by MORRIS LAZEROWITZ
Philosophy and Political Economy by JAMES BONAR
Philosophy and Religion by AXEL HAGERSTROM
Philosophy of Space and Time by MICHAEL WHITEMAN
Philosophy of Whitehead by W. MAYS
The Platonic Tradition in Anglo-Saxon Philosophy by J. H. MUIRHEAD
The Principal Upanisads by RADHAKRISHNAN
The Problems of Perception by R. J. HIRST
Reason and Analysis by BRAND BLANSHARD
Reason and Goodness by BRAND BLANSHARD
Reason and Sceptism by MICHAEL A. SLOTE
The Science of Logic by G. W. F. HEGEL
Some Main Problems of Philosophy by G. E. MOORE
Studies in the Metaphysics of Bradley by SUSHIL KUMAR SAXENA
The Subject of Consciousness by C. O. EVANS
The Theological Frontier of Ethics by W. G. MACLAGAN
Time and Free Will by HENRI BERGSON translated by F. G. POGSON
The Transcendence of the Cave by J. N. FINDLAY
Values and Intentions by J. N. FINDLAY
The Ways of Knowing: or the Methods of Philosophy by W. P. MONTAGUE

MUIRHEAD LIBRARY OF PHILOSOPHY

EDITED BY H. D. LEWIS

BROAD'S CRITICAL ESSAYS IN MORAL PHILOSOPHY

BROAD'S CRITICAL ESSAYS IN MORAL PHILOSOPHY

BY

C. D. BROAD

Trinity College Cambridge

EDITED BY DAVID R. CHENEY

Massachusetts State College at Bridgewater

LONDON . GEORGE ALLEN & UNWIN LTD

NEW YORK . HUMANITIES PRESS INC.

First published in 1971

BRITISH ISBN 0 04 190006 5

U.S.A. SBN 391-000178-7

Printed in Great Britain
in 12 point Fournier type
by Unwin Brothers Limited
London & Woking

EDITORIAL PREFACE

Certainly, there is no need to preface this collection with an estimation of the importance of Professor Broad's philosophical work—besides, it would be presumptuous of me to undertake such. One encounters its influence time and again, and further finds that many contemporary philosophers share an assessment similar to that of G. E. Moore, viz. 'Of all living philosophers, it is Broad's work, next to Russell's and Wittgenstein's, that I have thought it worthwhile to study most carefully.' Though Professor Broad has published numerous books on diverse topics, the greater part of his philosophical papers have made their initial and sometimes sole appearance in journals. To present one's work piece by piece in periodicals has clearly become the fashion of our time, especially for men such as Broad, who declare that they have no philosophical system. However, when a philosopher's sustained efforts, proffered in this manner, attain a certain measure of respect among his peers, a consequence requiring remedy manifests itself, viz. the difficulty of having access to and gaining a full view of the whole of a philosopher's work on a given topic. The remedy is, of course, to publish an edition of collected essays. And recently, the task of bringing Professor Broad's logical papers together was initiated by Professor Hintikka, who edited the volume containing Broad's essays on *Induction, Probability, and Causation* (Synthese Library, 1968). The present collection of papers represents a further endeavour along this line, presenting for the first time in one volume Professor Broad's critical essays on certain issues in philosophical ethics.

As a glance at the contents of this book will show, Professor Broad has expended a considerable proportion of his philosophical efforts in considering the problems of moral philosophy. The products of this side of his philosophical career have a twofold significance: first, for the conspicuous quality of the work itself, and secondly, for the particular influence which it has had. Concerning the latter, Professor Frankena noted in his contribution to *The Philosophy of C. D. Broad*, 'Few if any worthwhile contributions to ethical theory have appeared since 1930 which have not been significantly affected by Broad's writings'. His ethical papers are of two general types, either historical, interpretive essays or critical analyses of moral phenomena. Characterization of the latter set of papers as *critical analyses* rests on the common distinction between speculative and critical philosophy which Professor Broad explicated in his article 'Philosophy' (*Inquiry*, 1958). In that account he comments that the basic character of philosophy in any of its manifestations is 'synopsis,' i.e. the collation of diverse ingredients of human experience with the intent to discern interrelationships among them. This synoptical enterprise takes either of two forms: speculative or critical. The latter involves one or more of the following tasks, 'Analysis of Propositions and Concepts', 'Detection and Formulation of Presuppositions', and 'Critical Appraisal of Presuppositions.' The essays comprising this collection are all of the *critical* sort, in this sense, and conjointly they represent Professor Broad's efforts to analyse and appraise the propositions, concepts, and presuppositions of moral experience. Among these papers, some display a direct endeavour to carry out this project, while the remainder further it through criticism of the attempts of other philosophers to resolve similar concerns with ethics.

This collection presents the whole of Broad's expressed thought on these matters, though two of his critical papers are not included as they tend to duplicate the content of other, included essays. They are: 'Certain Features of Moore's Ethical Doctrines' (*The Philosophy of G. E. Moore*), the content of which is discussed and expanded in Essays V and XV; and 'Imperatives, Categorical and Hypothetical' (*The Philosopher*, 1950), which is an earlier version of Essay XVI. In this regard, it should be noted that the collection contains four papers (IV, VI, VII, and XI) which, subsequent to their original publication, were reprinted along with several other papers on diverse topics in a volume entitled *Ethics and the History of Philosophy* (Routledge and Kegan Paul, 1952), which is now out-of-print.

Further, two additional matters should be noted: first, Essay XII, 'Self and Others', which was Professor Broad's Herbert Spencer Lecture delivered at Oxford in 1953, is published here for the first time; and second, Essay XIV is an excerpt from Professor Broad's reply to his critics' remarks which appeared in *The Philosophy of C. D. Broad* and this selection contains additional comments concerning many of the views which are expressed in Essays I to XIII.

Concerning Broad's historical, interpretive ethical writings, the bulk of this work—with few exceptions—appeared in the widely read volume *Five Types of Ethical Theory*. The exceptions include several book reviews and two papers, one entitled 'Hägerström's Account of Sense of Duty and Certain Allied Experiences' (*Philosophy*, 1951) and another called 'Berkeley's Theory of Morals' (*Revue Internationale de Philosophie*, 1953). These two essays have been reluctantly omitted from the present collection as they are primarily expository, though the interested reader is urged to seek them out, for they provide a recent example of Professor Broad's expositive scholarship.

Though some papers found in this volume originally appeared several decades ago, a perusal of their contents, as well as that of the more recent essays, shows clearly that the topics covered remain living issues in current Ethics. In this respect, it should be noted that the long reign of 'ordinary language philosophy' has in part subsided and in other part simply altered its vision to include philosophical approaches of greater scope. And philosophers of that persuasion are, in fact, increasingly utilizing analytic procedures similar to those which Professor Broad has employed throughout his career as a philosopher. As moral philosophers, in particular, they are recognizing that there is more to Ethics than talk about 'moral talk'. Surely, the advantages of this wider view are emphasized by a reconsideration of Broad's critical ethical papers, which clearly evidence a sensitivity to the full complexity of man's moral experience.

Before concluding these remarks I would like to extend my gratitude to those who have made the job of editing a much easier one than it might have been. In addition to the several original publishers of these essays and to the publishers of this collection, I sincerely thank four persons: Professor H. D. Lewis, Editor of the Muirhead Library, for his invaluable concern and assistance; Professor Ramon M. Lemos, Philosopher at the University of Miami (Florida), for his counsel and encouragement; Liana, my wife, for her loving aid in carrying out the manifold chores of editing this book.

Lastly, my gratitude to Professor Broad can only be acknowledged, though not extended, as his death came on March 11, 1971, not long after the completion of work on this volume and its original preface. In our correspondence concerning this collection, which took place during the last year of his life, he was always kind and immensely helpful at every turn in the process of completing this project. If it were appropriate for an editor to dedicate the final fruit of his labour, I simply do so to the memory of Professor Broad.

D. R. C.

Bridgewater, 1971

PREFACE BY C. D. BROAD

I would begin by expressing my thanks to Professor Cheney, who initiated the idea of publishing a sequence of my various occasional writings on ethical topics. I received the first suggestion in a letter from him dated March 10, 1970. Since then we have had much correspondence on matters of detail, all of it friendly and helpful. I am most grateful to Professor Cheney for all the trouble that he has taken, and for the efficiency with which he has carried out the detailed work involved in getting the various permissions needed to enable these papers to be re-published.

In a letter of June 18, 1970, Professor Cheney informed me that Messrs. Allen & Unwin had agreed to publish the collection as a book in their series *The Muirhead Library of Philosophy*. After this I came in contact by letter with Professor H. D. Lewis of King's College, London, and I would like to thank him for all the help which he has given in his capacity of Editor of that series of philosophical works.

Lastly, in recording my obligations, I would thank all those persons, institutions, and firms of publishers, whose consent has been so kindly given for the reprinting of the various papers contained in the present collection.

It will be noted that the period covered by the 16 papers here reprinted is exactly 50 years, stretching from 1914, when I was in my 27th year, to 1964, when I was in my 77th. This period may be sub-divided into the following five successive sub-sections, viz. (i) before World War I, (ii) during World War I, (iii) between World Wars I and II, (iv) during World War II, and (v) after World War II.

Into sub-period (i) there falls only one of the papers here reprinted, viz. 'The Doctrine of Consequences in Ethics'. Into sub-period (ii) there also falls only one paper, viz. 'On the Function of False Hypotheses in Ethics'. If I am not mistaken, both of these appeared in the long since defunct *International Journal of Ethics*, then under the editorship of the late Professor J. S. Mackenzie (1860–1935). Later, when I had become professor in Bristol, I came to know him personally. I also came to know that extremely original and gifted lady his wife, and her very remarkable brothers and sisters, the Bristol Hughes's.

To the sub-period (iii), i.e. between the two World Wars, belong Papers III, IV, V, and VI. Of these I will mention only the following two. That entitled 'Determinism, Indeterminism, and Libertarianism' was the inaugural lecture which I gave on becoming Knightbridge Professor of Moral Philosophy in the University of Cambridge. This seemed to me to be an appropriate occasion for trying to get my mind clear on a number of inter-related topics which have always been of fundamental importance for ethics.

The other paper belonging to this sub-period which I will mention is that entitled 'Ought we to Fight for our Country in the Next War?' By 1936 it had begun to seem considerably more likely than not that the situation contemplated in the title would become actual in the fairly near future. It was fashionable at that time among left-wing intellectuals to believe, or to talk as if they believed, that the next war in which England would be engaged would be one against Russia, a country which was then supposed in those circles to stand for all that was best and highest in social and political life. And it was common form for those who held such views to say that they would refuse to fight for their country in any such war. A symposium was held at King's College, Cambridge, on the subject in question, and this paper was my contribution to it.

Papers VII, VIII, and IX belong to sub-period (iv), i.e. to the six years of World War II. During nearly the whole of that time I was mainly occupied as Acting Junior Bursar of Trinity College, Cambridge, in the absence of David Hinks, the real Junior Bursar, on important military duties. Of these three papers only the first, viz. 'Conscience and Conscientious Action', was called forth by the circumstances of the war in which England was involved. Tribunals had been set up to deal with the cases of persons who claimed exemption from military service on grounds of conscientious objections to it. This furnished the occasion and the motive for me to reflect more carefully than I should otherwise have done on the notions of 'conscience' and of 'conscientious action', and to publish the results of my reflexions.

The remaining papers, viz. X to XVI, were written and published in the period after World War II. Of these I will comment only on the following, viz. XI and XII, and XVI.

Papers XI and XII, 'Egoism as a Theory of Human Motives' and 'Self and Others', may be said to complement each other in the following way. The first is concerned with what Sidgwick called '*Psychological* Egoism'. The second deals with various topics all of which come under what he called '*Ethical* Egoism'. As regards Paper XVI, 'Obligations, Ultimate and Derived', I would say this. In its original form it dates from 1950. On May 6th of that year I read it to a meeting of the now defunct Philosophical Society of England, and it was afterwards published in their journal *The Philosopher*. Later I re-wrote it in its present form, and I see that the new version was completed on June 23, 1962.

The 50 years covered by these papers have witnessed a very remarkable revival, both in England (more especially in Oxford) and in the USA, of interest in and speculation upon fundamental questions of ethical theory. One might put the fundamental issues which have been discussed in the form of the following question: 'What is expressed by seriously uttering or writing a moral sentence in the indicative, such as, e.g. "Stealing is *wrong*", "He *ought* not to have done that", "To desire the happiness of others is *good*", and so on?' Such sentences, by their verbal form, naturally suggest that a predicate (whether a quality or a relational property) is being ascribed to a certain subject (generally an action or an experience of a certain kind).

One type of answer, and that which was most usual at the beginning of the period, was to take for granted that this *prima facie* appearance is correct. On that assumption one can raise questions as to the nature of the predicate. Is it of a unique and peculiar kind? Or is it analysable into a combination of qualities and/or relational properties which occur severally in *not* specifically moral contexts? In Cambridge this line of thought was followed by G. E. Moore, and in Oxford by H. A. Prichard (a man of immense ability whom I have always regarded as the Oxford Moore) and by W. D. Ross.

A later type of answer has been to contend that the grammatical form of moral sentences in the indicative is fundamentally misleading. According to this view, the utterance of such a sentence does *not* express a judgment ascribing a certain predicate to a certain subject. Any such view as this at once leads to questions of the following kind. Why should what is in fact expressed by uttering a moral sentence in the indicative be literally couched in this misleading grammatical form? If such utterances do not in fact express judgments, what do they in fact express? In what sense, if any, can the notions of *truth* and *falsity* be applied to that which such utterances really express? In what sense, if any, can that which is really expressed by one such utterance stand in *logical relations* (e.g. negation, implication, etc.) to that which is expressed by another such utterance? Very different answers have been given by different thinkers in England and USA who have agreed in accepting the basic negative premiss. Among the most eminent of these writers still living may be mentioned in England Professor R. M. Hare of Oxford, and in USA Professor C. L. Stevenson of Ann Arbor, Michigan. As is usual in philosophy, nothing approaching general agreement has been reached. But alternatives have been suggested and defended which had not before been seriously considered.

I will end this Preface on the following personal note. Experience as a member of many committees in Cambridge and elsewhere has taught me the desirability of retiring before one has become too 'ga-ga' to realize just how 'ga-ga' one is becoming. I am now approaching the end of my 83rd year, and prudence and laziness combine in advising me not to expose myself further in print.

C. D. BROAD
Trinity College, Cambridge
Oct. 16, 1970

CONTENTS

I

THE DOCTRINE OF CONSEQUENCES IN ETHICS (1914)[1]

The opinion that the rightness of an act is in some way connected with the goodness or badness of its consequences is, I suppose, held by everyone in practice and by most moralists in theory. If we only listen to what people *say* instead of also noticing how they act and judge, we might be inclined to underrate the amount of agreement on this point. Nothing is commoner than such phrases as 'you must never do evil that good may come', which, if they mean anything, imply that some acts are wrong, however good their consequences. Yet, in practice, people who quote this maxim and also believe that pain is an evil do not, as they ought to do, shun their dentists as moral lepers. Again, there is no doubt that common sense thinks motives important as well as consequences, but it would reject the Kantian view that they are all-important, and that only one kind of motive is morally valuable.

But at this point agreement ceases. Are consequences the sole relevant factor in judging the rightness of an act; or do other factors enter, and, in particular, are some acts right and some wrong, whatever their consequences? Again, is it the actual or the probable consequences that are ethically relevant? And further, if you decide to include motives in judging the rightness of an act, is the question whether the act is the immediate response of a good nature or results only as the consequence of a moral struggle, of ethical importance? The first two of these questions have been discussed with considerable fulness in recent years by Mr Russell in his *Philosophical Essays*, and by Mr Moore in his little book on *Ethics*. The names of these two

[1] Reprinted from the *International Journal of Ethics*, Volume XXIV, April 1914, by courtesy of the University of Chicago Press.

philosophers are a sufficient guarantee for the ingenuity and subtlety of their arguments; but, since they disagree, one must be wrong, and of course both may be. It will, therefore, be of some interest to take their views as a text for the discussion of the subject of this paper.

I will begin with the points on which Moore and Russell are at one. Both seem to hold that you can only talk of right actions, and not of good ones. 'What is called good conduct,' Mr Russell says, 'is conduct that is good as a means to other things that are good on their own account'. If this be the whole of what is meant by good conduct, it is no doubt well to do as Mr Russell proposes and call it 'right' and its consequences alone 'good', because otherwise 'good' is used in two different senses when we speak of 'good conduct' and of 'good consequences'. Now I cannot help thinking that neither of our authors has given enough attention to the possibility that there may be *good* conduct in their sense of good, as well as right conduct in their sense of right, and that the two need not coincide. This possibility arises in two different ways. In the first place, if other states of mind be intrinsically good or bad, I do not see why volitions should not have intrinsic goodness or badness. I should suppose that most people think that they have, and the question is at least worth discussion. Moore and Russell scarcely touch on this point, but I conclude that their opinion is that they are intrinsically indifferent. Mr Moore says (*Ethics*, p. 185): 'It is contrary to our view that motives can be intrinsically good or bad. But, if it is true, it makes no difference to the rightness or wrongness of an action, but only to the goodness of a total state of affairs.' The latter part of the statement is unquestionably true on Mr Moore's definition of rightness, because that explicitly only refers to consequences and therefore does not include the motive or volition that precedes them, so that the intrinsic value of the latter does not enter into consideration. But this only shows that Moore is consistent with his own definition, not that he means by rightness what other people mean when they understand themselves. But this, I suppose, is what he is trying to show.

We have seen then that it is at least possible that some volition may be intrinsically good, and therefore, since an act is certainly not identical with its own consequences, there may be good acts as well as right ones. But even if Moore be right in thinking that no motive is intrinsically good, it will not by any means follow that the intrinsic value of the consequences $x +$ the volition a will be the same as that of the consequences $x +$ the volition b. For to assert that because a and b are intrinsically indifferent, therefore ax and bx must necessarily have the same intrinsic value would be to forget the Principle of Organic Unities. I do not suppose that Moore or Russell would really deny anything that I have been saying; all that I suggest is that it is of some importance and seems to have been overlooked by them. I do not quite know whether Mr Russell thinks that anything but consequences are good, for he makes the curious statement (*Philosophical Essays*, p. 31): 'I do not wish to deny that right conduct is among the things that are good on their own account, but, if so, it depends for its intrinsic goodness upon the goodness of those other things which it aims at producing.' As it stands, this is surely contradictory; a thing cannot depend for its *intrinsic* goodness on anything else. What I suppose Russell must mean is that it is *not* intrinsically good, but, when added to its consequences, may produce a whole whose intrinsic value differs from that of the whole formed by the consequences only.

So much then for the agreement between Moore and Russell. As some good *consequences* are certainly states of mind, we shall be inclined to suppose that the states of mind that result in consequences may also have intrinsic value; and, even if they have not, the Principle of Organic Unities forbids us to deny the possibility of good conduct differing from right conduct in Moore's sense of the word. I shall return to this question at a much later stage of the paper.

Let us now consider the differences between the two writers. They differ about rightness. Russell has a complicated theory which introduces the probable consequences of actions. Moore's theory is simpler, and, at first sight, much more paradoxical since it makes rightness depend wholly on the actual results of our actions. It further makes much use of the notions of justifiable praise and blame. As a matter of fact, we shall see that really both theories have to introduce probability, and that Russell's view when worked out is much less plausible than it seems at first sight. I will begin by sketching and criticizing Russell's theory.

That act which has as good consequences[1] as any that is open to the agent is called by Russell 'a most fortunate act', and by Moore a 'right act'. But Russell will not admit that a most fortunate act is necessarily a right one. He grants that there is an objective and a subjective sense of right, but holds that even the objective sense is partly subjective, whilst what is most fortunate is quite independent of our knowledge and belief. If the evidence be against an actually most fortunate act being most fortunate, it is objectively wrong to go against the evidence. An objectively right act is what he calls a 'wisest act', i.e. one which is probably a most fortunate act. This theory, he says, has the advantage that it makes unforseen factors irrelevant to rightness and wrongness. Now objectively, of course, a man ought to do what is objectively right; but there is another sense of ought, Russell holds, in which we must say that he sometimes ought to do what is objectively wrong. This second sense of ought, of course, involves another sense of right. A man acts rightly in this sense (or conscientiously, as we may call it) if he does what he judges to be objectively right, after he has reflected with a view to finding out the truth on this point, and not merely with a view to proving one course right. If the act be unimportant, and if it would need much reflection to come to any decision about its objective rightness, it is morally indifferent.

We may admit that this is an ingenious and plausible theory which seems to cover most of the obvious facts. But I think we shall find that it is not nearly so simple as it looks. It is not explicitly remarked by either Moore or Russell that there is a

[1] Russell says '*the* best consequences', and speaks of '*the* most fortunate act'; but Moore rightly points out that two possible acts may have equally good consequences, and that they will then both be right if the consequences are better than those of any possible alternative. I have altered Russell's language to meet this objection.

very close analogy between the three meanings of ought in ethics which between them they use, and three meanings of ought in logic. I believe it will be helpful to develop this analogy a little. When I ask: 'What ought I to believe?' one answer certainly would seem to be: 'What is true'. Now, 'what is true' corresponds here to a most fortunate act in ethics in its complete independence of anyone's knowledge or belief. So this answer corresponds to that which Moore makes to the question: 'What ought I to do?' But there certainly seem to be plenty of cases where in a sense I ought to believe what is actually false. If I believe that all *M* is *P* and that all *S* is *M*, there is certainly a sense in which I ought to believe that all *S* is *P* (or, at any rate, ought not to believe that some *S* is not *P*). Yet if one of the first two beliefs be false, it may very well be the case that what I ought to believe about the relation of *S* and *P* is false, and what I ought not to believe is true. Nor is it relevant to answer: You ought not to have believed, e.g. that all *M* is *P*, since that is false. Even if this be so (and to assert it is to beg the question as to whether there are not several meanings of ought in logic), yet we must still ask: What ought I to believe, granted that as a matter of fact I have this belief, which, of course, I do not know to be false so long as I have it? The answer: You ought to believe, or perhaps I should rather say, you ought not to disbelieve what logically follows from what you do believe, corresponds rather closely with Russell's objective sense of ought and right. Then, finally, it might be suggested that you ought to believe what you *think* logically follows from what you do believe. If you really think that *A* propositions can be simply converted and believe that all *S* is *P*, then you ought not to believe that some *P* is not *S*. This seems to correspond to subjective rightness in ethics.

I think, then, we may fairly suggest that Russell's theory of the different meanings of right in ethics can probably be reduced to considerations involving the different meanings of ought in logic + what seems to be a purely ethical meaning of ought which appears equally in both his senses. The ethical common meaning is involved in the statement: I ought ethically always to do that action which I ought logically to judge a most fortunate action of those possible to me. Russell's two meanings of ought are syntheses of this common third ethical meaning with the two logical senses of the word. Russell's qualification about reflecting with a view to finding out what is objectively right is involved in the logical sense of ought; for you have no right in any logical sense to believe what is not self-evident and what you have not investigated with a desire to reach the truth, whatever it may prove to be.

What is objectively right, then, on this theory is what, on my information, has probably at least as good consequences as any other action open to me. The mixture of the objective and subjective here is nothing specially ethical, but is what is involved in all applications of probability. The point is simply this. Any proposition, whether about goodness or anything else, is either true or false. But, relative to various selections of other propositions, this proposition will have different degrees of probability. So far, all is perfectly objective; the probability of one proposition, relative to any definite selection of others, is as independent of anyone's knowledge or belief about it as its truth or falsehood. When the individual mind enters, it is simply as a selective agent. Any particular mind believes some proposition and not others; and is acquainted with some and not with others; and relative to those which it believes, any given proposition has a certain probability, whether this particular mind or any other knows its value or not. It is necessary to add, however, that whilst there is not ambiguity, and nothing subjective, in the probability of a proposition relative to any definite selection of others, there is some vagueness as to what Russell supposes to be included in the selection involved in his theory of objective rightness. This is really an important matter. Does objective rightness depend on the probability of the consequences relative to all the propositions that the agent believes; or to all those that he believes and the contradictories of those that he disbelieves; or to all the true propositions that he believes and the contradictories of all the false ones that he disbelieves; or what precisely is the principle of selection? It seems to me that Russell has talked cheerfully about *the* probabilities of propositions without remembering that all probabilities are relative to selections of propositions, and that it is vital to state what selection he considers relevant in defining rightness. When this fact is taken into account, the distinction between objective and subjective rightness on Russell's theory becomes a somewhat subtle one, though I grant that it remains. My doubt is whether it corresponds to any distinction involved in the various ethical judgments of commonsense which led Russell to his theory of objective rightness. Let me elaborate this point a little.

On Russell's theory it is clear that of precisely similar acts performed by A and B, under circumstances agreeing in all respects but in the knowledge or beliefs of the agents, one can be *objectively* right and the other objectively wrong. For, since the probability of the consequences is relative to different selections of propositions in the two cases, it will in general be different. Now, of course, we all admit that difference of knowledge may alter the *subjective* rightness of acts performed under otherwise precisely similar circumstances; but I do very much doubt whether any judgment of common sense implies that what is *objectively* right for A can be objectively wrong for B. Still I do not wish dogmatically to assert that there is not an ethical sense of right and ought different from what Russell calls subjectively right and from what he calls most fortunate. My lingering doubt in his favour is due to the fact that there does seem to me to be such an intermediate meaning of right and ought in the logical sense, and that Russell's objective rightness seems, as I have said, to correspond to this.

I said that the logical sense of ought that corresponds to Russell's objective rightness is that you ought to believe or at least not to disbelieve what logically follows from what you do believe and from the contradictories of what you disbelieve. It is clear that this does not imply that what you believe is true, or what you disbelieve false; for otherwise this kind of logical rightness would not be (as it certainly is) compatible with its being right to believe what is false, and to disbelieve what is true. Now the probability of one proposition relative to others seems to me to be as much a matter of pure logic as its being implied by them. Hence, we must include in this logical sense of right that it is right to attribute to any proposition that degree of probability that it actually has, relative to the propositions that you believe and to the contradictories of those that you disbelieve. If my analogy between this logical sense of ought and Russell's objective rightness be accepted, we have now made a beginning of answering the question—which, as we saw, he left unanswered—as to what precisely is supposed to be the selection of propositions; relative to which the probability involved in objective rightness is to be reckoned. The relevant propositions are roughly those which the agent believes and the contradictories of those which he disbelieves, irrespective of whether what he believes is true or what he disbelieves is false. But some modification must be made in this.

This distinction between the use of a proposition as a premise and as a principle is familiar to logicians. When I argue in accordance with Barbara and justify my procedure by pointing this out, I do not use Barbara as a premise, but as a principle. Now, for logical rightness we must qualify what I have already said by adding that it is only the truth or falsity of a man's beliefs in propositions which he uses as premisės that is irrelevant to his logical rightness; we must assume that his beliefs in all propositions that he uses as principles are actually ture. This is, of course, simple enough when we are dealing with certain inference; but it is less easy to see what is a premise and what a principle when we come to deal with probability. In the first place, it is clear that the purely formal laws connecting the probability of a complex proposition, conjunctive or disjunctive, with that of its separate elements must be taken as principles and not as premises. I must also never count among the premises, relative to which I reckon the probability of a proposition, propositions about its probability relative to the other premises. Such propositions are principles not premises, and my belief in them must be true if I am to be logically right. For, otherwise, the true probability of anything relative to my state of information, would depend on my belief about the true probability, and this would make the whole notion purely subjective, which it is not. And this is supported by the analogy with certain inference, since to be logically right there, I must not have false beliefs as to whether one proposition implies another or not, and the case of implication is one where the probability of what is implied relative to what implies it is 1.

We now see what is the logical sense of rightness that we take to correspond with Russell's objective ethical rightness. Does his ethical objective rightness involve anything further than that it is objectively right to do what it is logically right to believe to be a most fortunate action? There are great difficulties and ambiguities in the notion of a probably most fortunate action which I will deal with later, but at present the question is where precisely the ethical element enters, and whether it introduces any new question of principle. It is, of course, clear that to reach judgements, about the probable goodness of anything, there must be some premises about values believed, as well as premises about facts. Can these ethical premises be treated as precisely on a level with the factual ones or not; i.e. is it only the question whether we believe or disbelieve the ethical premises that is relevant to objective rightness, or is the truth or falsehood of our beliefs and disbeliefs here of importance? I am inclined to think that there is a difference between the two kinds of premises in this respect.

Suppose, for instance, that a person is an ethical hedonist, i.e. that he believes as one of his ethical premises that the goodness of any state of affairs is directly proportional to the amount of pleasure in it and to that alone. Relative to this proposition, an act that will probably produce more pleasure on the whole will probably have better consequences than one that will probably produce less pleasure. But, supposing that ethical hedonism is false, are we to say that the man's act is objectively right, if he is right about the probability of its pleasurable consequences? If, for example, one is logically justified by one's factual premises in holding that pushpin will probably give more pleasure on the whole than poetry, and if one is logically justified on one's ethical premises in holding that more pleasurable states are always better than less pleasurable ones, is it objectively right to prefer pushpin to poetry, even though your ethical belief be false? I do not think this can be maintained, and therefore there must be an important distinction between the positions of ethical and of factual beliefs in the matter of objective rightness. Let us, then, sum up the results of our attempts to clarify Russell's notion of objective rightness, as far as they have yet appeared. An act is objectively right if it is probably a most fortunate act relative to (*a*) the propositions about matters of fact which the agent believes, and the contradictories of those which he disbelieves, independently of whether they be true or false; (*b*) to true ethical premises, whether he believes them or not; and (*c*) to true principles of inference and probability, whether he believes them or not. Subjective rightness depends wholly on what people believe or disbelieve, and not at all on what is true, while Russell's objective rightness depends, partly, on what people believe, whether it be true or not, and, partly, on what is true, whether people believe it or not.

But we are by no means at the end of our difficulties. Russell does not seem to have remarked that the notion of a probably most fortunate act remains ambiguous even after you have defined the selection of propositions, relative to which its probability and that of alternative acts are to be reckoned. The fact is that the question of probability enters twice, and Russell has not distinguished its two appearances. It is not clear whether the objective rightness of an act depends on the actual value of its probable consequences, or the probable value of its actual consequences, or the probable value of its probable consequences. All that we are told is that it does not depend on the actual value of its actual consequences. I submit that *until* the theory that objective rightness depends on probable consequences decides between these three alternatives, it cannot be satisfactory, and that *when* it is faced by them, it loses some of its original plausibility.

We must devote a moment to the consideration of these alternatives. So far as I can see, the most plausible view for Russell to take would be that rightness depends on the probable value of probable consequences. For if either the actual goodness or the actual consequences be relevant, it is difficult to see why both should not be; and this he denies. If, however, we work out the implications of this theory, we shall see that it is less simple than it looks. Suppose that an agent has two actions, X and Y, open to him. Suppose, further, that relative to the propositions that the agent believes and disbelieves, the most probable consequences of X and A, and that their probability is p. Let the most probable consequences of Y be B, and let their probability by q. Further, let the most probable measure of the goodness of A be x, and the most probable measure of the goodness of B be y. Now suppose that $p < q$ and $x > y$. What then is objectively right? Ought the man to choose the act whose most probable consequences are less probable, but most probably more good, or the one whose most probable consequence is more probable, but most probably less good? It is useless to say that the question is merely academic, since the calculations cannot be made, for it is quite irrelevant to objective rightness whether anyone actually makes the calculations or not. The difficulty is one of principle, and, unless the theory can remove it, it has not produced an unambiguous definition of what it means by objective rightness.

Of the two remaining alternatives, it seems to me that it is more plausible to suggest that objective rightness depends on the actual value of probable consequences than on the probable value of actual consequences. It is, in fact, clear that the latter is not what Russell means, since he congratulates his theory on making objective rightness independent of unforeseeable circumstances, i.e. of true propositions about matters of fact which are not included in the selection believed by the agent at the time of decision. Let us, then, take the view that an act is objectively right whose most probable consequences would be actually at least as good as the most probable consequences of any other act open to the agent. Unfortunately, there is much the same ambiguity here as we noticed above. If I can perform either X or Y, and the most probable consequence of X is A and of Y is B, it will not, in general, be true that the probability of X

being followed by *A* is the same as that of *Y* being followed by *B*. If the probability of the most probable consequence of *X* be p, and that of the most probable consequence of *Y* be q, when $p > q$, whilst the value *A* is x and that of *B* is y where $x < y$, which act is objectively right? We could only avoid this ambiguity by introducing the notion of expectation, i.e. the product of the probability of an event by the actual or most probable measure of its goodness if it takes place. We might then say that an act is objectively right if the expectation of goodness is, relative to the selection of propositions already defined, at least as great as the expectation of goodness of any other act possible to the agent. But does this really seem plausible? I think it is open to two objections: (1) I see no reason to think that the notion of mathematical expectation is really a measure of anything in the world. Suppose it is true that there is something called 'logical expectation', and that it is a function of the probability of an event and of the most probable measure of its goodness, is there the slightest ground for thinking that this function is the product of the two? Is it not merely another case of that unjustifiable simplification which in the Hedonic Calculus assumes: (*a*) that there is such a thing as quantity of pleasure, and (*b*) that it must be measured by the time integral of the intensity of a pleasure? (2) Is the definition of objective rightness which we have reached as a matter of fact what anyone means by rightness? I quite agree with Mr Russell that all ethical phrases are used ambiguously by common sense, and, therefore, whenever we try to give a strict meaning to them, we shall meet with verbal paradoxes. Still, we must not get entirely away from common sense, but try to be clear as to the various separate concepts which it verbally confuses. It is because of certain judgments of common sense that Russell introduced his theory of objective rightness, and it is a real objection to it that it is not only infected with all the doubt and vagueness that attach to the notion of expectation, but also seems hardly to correspond to any of the senses of rightness which common sense vaguely recognizes. If, then, any plausible alternative can be offered, I shall be inclined to prefer it.

Let us then leave Russell's theory about objective rightness and consider Moore's. This theory makes objective rightness turn solely on the actual goodness of actual consequences, whether they are probable relative to the agent's information or not. It has then to deal with the apparent paradox that, whilst unforeseen circumstances may cause the actual consequences of an act to be utterly different from what could have been expected, we do not blame a man because what he has done, on the logically justifiable expectation of its having good results, turns out to have bad ones. Moore's answer is that the paradox arises from confusing what is right to do with what is right to praise, or holding that it is only right to praise right actions and only right to blame wrong actions. This supposition is not necessarily true. A's praise or blame of B's act is a second act, and, like all others, its rightness or wrongness must be judged by its own consequences and not by those of B's act. It will be right for A to praise B's act if the consequences of doing so are at least as good as those of blaming it or saying nothing, no matter what the consequences of B's act may prove to be.

This theory seems to be very plausible, and I think Moore is right in saying that much of the paradox is merely apparent. It is, therefore, worth while to consider the question of praise and blame more closely. The words praise and blame are somewhat ambiguous, and it is important to distinguish three elements: (1) the judgment that an act is right or wrong, (2) certain peculiar feelings of approbation and disapprobation, and (3) the expression of such judgments and feelings. This ambiguity leads to an ambiguity in the question: Am I right in praising some acts that are really wrong, and blaming some that are really right? This may mean: (1) Ought I to believe that some wrong actions are right, and that some right actions are wrong? (2) Ought I ever to have the feeling of approbation to a wrong action, and that of disapprobation to a right one? and (3) Ought I to assert what I believe, and state what I feel in such cases? In my opinion, 'ought' has a different meaning in each of these questions. The first means: Am I ever logically justified in holding that an action is probably wrong when it is actually right, or probably right when it is actually wrong? The answer is clearly in the affirmative. I ought logically to believe probable on my information what actually is probable, but this may be the opposite of what is actually true.

It is perfectly clear that in the second question 'ought' cannot have this meaning. I am under no *logical* obligation to have any particular kind of feeling in given circumstances. But it is also clear that it cannot simply have the meaning that it is right for me to have such and such a feeling in Moore's sense of right. In the first place, for an act to be right in Moore's sense, it must be voluntary, whilst, whether I have a certain feeling under certain circumstances, is largely independent of my will. Further, rightness for Moore depends on goodness of consequences. Now my unexpressed feelings (using expression in a sense wide enough to include a frown and a philippic) have few consequences outside myself. I admit that they may be important; but what I want to suggest is that there is undoubtedly a sense of rightness in which it may be said that a certain feeling is the right one to have, under certain circumstances, no matter what the consequences may be. Take, for instance, the emotion of sorrow on the death of a friend. It is not a voluntary product, and therefore not right or wrong in Moore's sense. But if it could be right or wrong in this sense, it would almost certainly be wrong, for it is difficult to see what good consequences can come from sorrow at what cannot be altered. Nevertheless, there is a perfectly definite sense in which we should say that sorrow is the right, and hilarity the wrong emotion under the circumstances. And this is a new use of right and wrong. Sorrow is not good, nor are its consequences as a rule good, but it may be right. There is, of course, a connection between this sense of right and wrong and goodness and badness. What is called right or wrong here is a feeling in connection with a situation. I think this sense of right might be defined as follows: The feeling x is right in the situation y, when the complex xy is intrinsically better than x alone, and at least as intrinsically good as the complex formed by y and any other feeling that can be directed toward it. *Can* is not used here in the sense of 'can if one will'. In certain circumstances I ought to have certain feelings, whether I could have them by willing or not.

Our second question, then, comes to this: Is the feeling of approbation ever the right feeling (in this new sense) to have toward acts that are wrong in Moore's sense, and that of disapprobation the right feeling to have toward one that is right in his sense? Here again the answer is in the affirmative, but needs some qualification. The sort of feelings that are right or wrong are those directed to an object, as, for instance, sorrow is always sorrow *for* something, and approbation approbation *of* something. And feeling can only be directed to objects as they are known or believed to be by the person who has the feeling, not to aspects of the objects about which he knows nothing or is misinformed. Thus, the right feeling toward an act may very well alter as time goes on and more is known about its consequences; there is, of course, nothing paradoxical about this, because at each different stage of knowledge and belief the feeling is really directed to something different. Further, in practice, our feelings are never toward an act alone, but we have a total feeling that depends on two factors: (1) on our belief in its rightness in Moore's sense, and (2) on the moral qualities of the agent which we infer from the act. As far as I can see, the right feeling toward any act that exhibits conscientiousness is *pro tanto* approbation, though we may believe that the results of the act will be so bad that our total feeling ought to be condemnatory. The following, then, seems to be the answer to our present question: An act which is wrong in Mr Moore's sense ought to meet with feelings of approbation by anyone who believes that the intrinsic value of the whole, formed by the consequences and the moral qualities which the choice of the act exhibits in the agent, is at least as great as that of the whole formed by any alternative act + the moral qualities that it would have exhibited. It may thus be right for us to feel approbation for an act that is not merely wrong in Moore's sense, but is believed to be wrong by us. The moral quality that seems most to add to the values of such wholes is conscientiousness, so that it is often right to approve an act that is wrong and is believed to be wrong, because it has been conscientiously performed. Of course, it is open to anyone to say that here we really have two different feelings, one directed to what we believe to be the rightness or wrongness of the act, and the other to what we believe to be the moral qualities that it exhibits in the agent. I somewhat doubt personally whether, when two objects are so closely connected as an act and the volition that produces it, you can analyse the total feeling directed towards them into two feelings, one directed to each object; but the point is not of great importance for the present purpose.

Finally, we come to the third meaning of 'ought' involved in Moore's theory in the question: Ought I to assert what I believe and state what I feel about the rightness of acts? Here, of course, the meaning of ought corresponds to Moore's general meaning of right. The question is: Will the consequences of stating my belief that an act is right, and showing my approbation of it, have at least as good consequences as any alternative action even when as a matter of fact my belief is false? The answer, of course, is that it probably is sometimes objectively right to praise an objectively wrong act, and vice versa. But if Moore means to offer as a definition of subjectively right acts that they are those which it is objectively right to praise, the definition will hardly do. In the first place, it will clearly follow that the extreme doubt that attaches, on his theory, to whether any particular act is objectively right will now equally infect the question whether it is subjectively right, since the subjective rightness of *all* acts will depend on the objective rightness of a certain class of acts. Moreover, it is easy to imagine acts which it is almost certainly objectively right to praise, and almost certainly subjectively wrong to do. If my friend and I were in the hands of a cruel despot with a taste for flattery, it might very well be objectively right for me to praise his wicked acts in order to save myself and my friend from his cruelty; but this would not make his wicked acts even subjectively right if he believed he was doing wrong.

Let us, then, go a little further into the question of praise and blame for ourselves, since neither Moore nor Russell have descended to detail. Before we go any further it will be well to compare Moore's and Russell's views about probable goodness for a moment; for it is becoming evident that Moore's view is going to introduce probability as well as Russell's, though in a different way. The difference is this: On Russell's view, a probably most fortunate act is an actually right one; on Moore's view, a probably most fortunate act is a probably right one. And this, being quite general, applies, of course, to acts of praise and blame. Now, I think there is some risk of the inconsistency of using Russell's definition of rightness for acts of praise and blame, and Moore's for other acts, and defining subjective rightness by a mixture of the two. This inconsistency must, of course, be avoided if we want to find the real consequences of both views. The consequences of applying Russell's definition are somewhat complicated. We will consider them first.

It might seem at first sight that, on Russell's definition, it will always be right for me to praise what it is right for me to do. For to say that the act x is right for A to do is to say that it is a probably most fortunate act on his information. Now, praise of such acts will certainly tend to make other people perform them, and it seems as if it must be right for A to make other people cause results which it would be right for him to cause himself. But this does not by any means follow: x may be that action which, on A's information, is probably the most fortunate of any that are open to him, but it does not follow that it is probably the most fortunate of any that are open to B; for B may have alternatives open to him which A has not. Hence A's praise of what it would be right for himself to do may cause B to choose an alternative which, on A's information, is not the probably most fortunate one open to B. There is, too, another consequence that is worth mentioning. Suppose that B has only the same alternatives open to him as A, but different information from A; then, on B's information, x may not be the probably most fortunate act open to him, though it is on A's information. Hence A's praise of what it would be right for himself to do may cause B to do what is wrong for him to do.

Let us now apply Moore's theory of rightness to the question of praise and blame. I do not see how we can dispense with the notion that there is a definite sense in which it is right to do what we believe to be objectively right, by means of any considerations about praise and blame. I take it that Moore is trying to make us believe that the notion of subjective rightness can be resolved into that of objective praiseworthiness. This might mean one of two things. It might mean that the two notions are really identical, that the second is an analysis of what people mean by the first; or that, whilst they are genuinely different notions, they have precisely the same extension. The first alternative, of course, implies the latter part of the second. It seems to me that inspection shows that the first alternative is false; if we can further prove that the second is wrong, we shall have an additional refutation of the first. It seems to me that when I have done my best to determine which alternatives open to me are objectively right, I can well admit that I may be mistaken, and yet be certain that it is right for me to do one of these alternatives. And I certainly do not seem to mean by this that it will always be objectively right for me to praise myself or for other people to praise me. For one thing, I do not generally think about praise or blame at all when I think about rightness; and for another, I can no more be certain about the effects of praise and blame than about those of any other action. Further, the sense of rightness which we are trying to analyse is, I think, essentially connected with conscientiousness. Now, I grant that on Moore's theory it is probably objectively right for me to praise what it is probably objectively right for me to do, because I shall thus tend to cause actions that are probably right. But the probable rightness of my praise is independent of the motives of the actions praised, since it merely depends on the probable goodness of their consequences, and this is unconnected with their motives. Thus, the probable rightness of praising an action has no immediate connection with its motive. On the other hand, whilst I should call an action subjectively right that was done conscientiously, it is not clear that it would ever be probably right for me to praise it on this ground. By praising it I might promote conscientiousness; but if it is probably an objectively wrong action, I should also probably be praising objectively wrong acts. I could avoid this difficulty, of course, by praising the motive and blaming the action; but it is not at all clear to me that, on Mr Moore's theory, it is ever probably right to praise conscientiousness. If it be probably right to praise conscientiousness, it must be because that quality is either good in itself, or adds to the goodness of other wholes, or is likely to have good results. Now, I understand Moore to hold that motives have no intrinsic value, which cuts out the first alternative. As far as I know, he has not expressed any opinion about the second alternative. Finally, I do not see the least reason to suppose that conscientiousness is more likely to produce objectively right acts, on his theory, than any other motive. No doubt, it involves that you have done your best to find out what is right and are going to act on your conclusions; but, since the rightness of your action is at the mercy of all that is going to happen in the universe throughout all future time, there is no reason to expect better results from conscientious acts than from the most stupid and biased ones. I conclude, then, that, since the notion of subjective rightness is essentially bound up with conscientiousness, whilst the rightness of praise and blame is directly connected with consequences and not with motives, and further since there is no ground for supposing that it is ever probably right to praise conscientiousness rather than other motives, the notions of subjective rightness and of objective praiseworthiness cannot coincide either in meaning or in extension.

It remains for me, after these criticisms, to see whether anything positive can be said. I agree with Russell that it is neither important nor possible that the terms which we use should always exactly coincide in extension with those used by common sense. All that is important is to recognize clearly every different notion that is involved in the judgments of common sense; to give separate names to them and use them consistently; and, where possible, to analyse them and determine their mutual relations. It may also be necessary for us to recognize notions which common sense does not, and to determine their relations to those which it does. Let us then consider the notions with which we have to deal.

In the first place, Moore's notion of rightness, which is the same as Russell's 'most fortunateness', is a perfectly definite concept which anyone is at liberty to use. My only objection to it is that it involves a somewhat arbitrary cut out of a wider notion, a cut which, I think, is made at a different point from any at which common sense makes one. What I mean by the wider notion is the intrinsic value of the whole universe, past, present, and future. Moore and Russell cut this in two at a voluntary decision between alternatives, and consider that rightness is only concerned with the states of the universe, after this decision. They then further cut the total state of the universe, after the decision, into the part that is and the part that is not a consequence of the decision, and they connect rightness only with the former of these two fractions. We are not told precisely how this second decision is made; but I think the consequences of an act are taken to be everything in the universe that would not be the same, whether the act had been done or not. There is some ambiguity in this, however. Do you mean the same in fact or in value? If you mean in value, you cannot safely take in less than the total future state of the universe as the consequence of any act, because its value will be different according as the act is done or not, provided that the doing or withholding of the act makes a difference to any part of it. This is evidently not what is meant. What is involved is only those facts that would have been different as facts if the action had not been done, and the value of the whole thus formed.

From each of these two ways of cutting up the universe there follows a result that has not, I think, been noticed. It is that a most fortunate act may make the total state of the universe worse than a less fortunate one. If I do *x* I may make the total future state of the universe better than if I do *y*; but the Principle of Organic Unities precludes us from asserting that, because the state of the universe, after a moment *t*, is intrinsically better if I do *x* than if I do *y*, therefore its total state, before and after *t*, is better. For, if two wholes consist of a common part and two different parts, it does not follow that that which has the better part is as good as that which has the worse one. So much for the results of the cut in time. But it follows for similar reasons that the cut in the future states of the universe makes it possible that the total future state itself may be worse through a right act than through a wrong one. The consequences of *x* may be better than those of *y*; but the whole made by the consequences of *x* and the rest of the future states of the universe may be worse than the whole made by the consequences of *y* and the other future states of the universe. These possibilities will equally arise wherever you make the cut. Since it seems paradoxical to say that a most fortunate act may make the total state of the universe worse than a less fortunate one, I shall define a most fortunate act as one such that, if it be performed, the total state of the universe will be at least as good as if any other act open to the agent were performed. It follows that motives will be relevant to the question whether an act is most fortunate, for they are parts of the universe that precede the act and make their contribution to the total value. I think, further, that it has considerably more claim to be called a right act than what Moore calls a right act. By this I simply mean that, whilst it shares with Moore's meaning of right the objection (if it be an objection) that rightness and wrongness then depend on unforeseeable circumstances, yet it is closer to one part of what common sense means by rightness than Moore's definition. Suppose we put aside the question of unforeseeable circumstances by considering the acts of an omniscient God, a conception familiar enough to common sense. Common sense would say that all God's acts are right and that they all produce the greatest possible good on the whole, and it would hold that the two statements are necessarily connected. But with Moore's definition we have seen that there is no necessary connection between them, and the question could arise whether God ought to do what is right or what makes the total state of the universe as good as possible. Since it seems clear that he ought to do both, it looks as if the two notions must coincide in the case of an omniscient God at any rate, i.e. when we leave out of account the question of intellectual limitations. I suggest, then, that the places where Moore and Russell make cuts in the total state of the universe are really arbitrary and do not correspond to any distinction involved in the judgments of common sense, nor, so far as I can see, to any that is of ethical importance.

I shall, therefore, define an objectively right action as one such that, if it be done, the total value of the universe will be at least as great as if any other possible alternative had been done by the agent. I have now to consider how far this agrees with, and how far it differs from, the meaning of the word involved in the judgments of common sense. It agrees, as we have seen, entirely when intellectual limitations are set aside. It also allows of agreement in the matter of motives. Common sense attaches a very great weight to motives, though not, I think, an exclusive one. This is quite in accordance with our theory. The fact that an agent does a certain act from a certain motive may be so valuable as to outweigh the badness of its consequences in Moore's and Russell's more restricted sense of that word. The total state of the universe may be much better if I do an action which will have very bad effects from a sense of duty, than if I do an alternative which will have much better effects from a desire to give pain. On the other hand, it is always possible to imagine consequences so bad that no goodness of motive will balance them. This seems to me in complete accord with common sense. Torquemada's actions were almost certainly wrong, in spite of the goodness of his motives, because of the extreme badness of their effects in Moore's and Russell's sense; Pitt's action in financing the early stages of the revolutionary war by loans may have been right because of the goodness of his motives, in spite of the considerable badness of the results.

Thus, motives actually enter into objective rightness on our definition, as I think they do for common sense. But I do not maintain that this sense of rightness completely agrees with all usages of the term by common sense, or that it furnishes a complete account of the common sense attitude toward motives. There may be marginal cases where common sense judges an action to be right even though it thinks it probable that, when both motive and consequences are taken into consideration, the total state of the universe is worse than if the agent had chosen another alternative. In such cases, however, I think it would tend to say, not that the action was right, but that it was right of the agent to do the action. Thus, common sense might well say that Torquemada's actions were wrong in spite of the goodness of his motives, but that it was right for Torquemada to do them. It is not consistent in its use of the terms, but I think it is quite clear what is meant. To say that Torquemada's actions were wrong does not merely mean that the consequences apart from the motive were bad, but that the bad consequences plus the good motive were bad. To say that Torquemada was right to do them is to pass a judgment on Torquemada's motives in abstraction from the total results of his act. As a matter of fact, the two judgments are likely to be made together; they much more often agree than conflict; and they both involve motives, the one partially and the other exclusively. It is not, therefore, surprising that common sense is liable to confuse them.

Common sense calls an action right for the person who does it, when it approves of the motive; and it will be well worth while to consider motives for a moment. In the sense in which I am using the term, we cannot say with Russell that a motive is simply the cause of a decision. Probably all decisions have causes, but they have not all motives. When I say that I do an action because I judge it to be right, I do no doubt imply that my belief is a part of the cause of the decision; but I am not clear that this is all that I mean by the phrase 'because of' here. Anyhow, motives are a special class of causes of decisions of which the following things can be said: (1) They involve beliefs in the qualities or effects of the act which they cause to be chosen, and (2) the belief has to be quite explicit, and has to be explicitly recognized as in some sense the last and completing factor in the cause of the decision. Now, there is one kind of belief to which common sense attaches very great ethical importance as a motive, viz. the belief in the objective rightness of the action. Common sense considers it a supreme excellence of character when beliefs in the rightness of acts are habitually causes of deciding to do the acts. And it marks its approval by saying that it is always right for a man to act from this motive even though the action be wrong. The excellence of this motive will indeed often make actions done from it *objectively* right, in spite of the badness of their effects; but even when the effects are too bad for the goodness of the motive to counterbalance them, common sense will still say that it was *right for* the man to have acted as he did. And this sense of rightness is peculiarly connected with this kind of motive. Thus, common sense, as distinct from Kant, recognizes that some actions are better when they spring from other motives or from no motive at all; it is better, for instance, other things being equal, to be kind to people because you like to see them happy than because you judge that it is right to make them happy; but, if the act is judged to be objectively wrong, in a particular case, it will be said to have been right for the man who did it because he thought it right, and not for the man who did it from a direct desire to give happiness. We rightly prefer the action of a man who spoils his children because he likes to see them happy to that of one who spoils them because he is a conscientious hedonist; but we should say that the action was right for the second and wrong for the first.

It is clear that this sense of rightness corresponds closely with Russell's subjective rightness. But there is one point where I think Russell makes subjective rightness too subjective. He says that it is subjectively right to do what is conscientiously believed to be objectively right, but that does not imply that to be subjectively right a man must hold Russell's theory as to what is meant by objective rightness. This, I think, is a mistake due to natural modesty. If Russell's theory of objective rightness be true, then a man is not subjectively right if he means something else by objective rightness, and does what he judges to be objectively right on his own definition. In fact, a man is not subjectively right unless he holds true views as to the *meaning* of objective rightness. He may be as mistaken as he likes as to whether an act really has the necessary qualities for making it objectively right, but unless there be agreement as to what these qualities are, there is nothing in common to those beliefs, by agreeing in which men are called subjectively right. You cannot avoid this by saying that it is subjectively right to do that for which you have a feeling of approbation. When feeling of approbation and judgment of objective rightness go together, this is true; but, when they diverge, it is not even subjectively right to act for the feeling and against the judgment. Thus, it is always the judgment that is relevant to subjective rightness; and, therefore, if there is to be a definite common meaning for subjective rightness, there must be a definite common meaning for objective rightness. Thus, Russell ought only to call a man subjectively right in his conscientious actions if the man attaches the same meaning as he himself does to objective rightness.

The upshot of the discussion, then, is as follows: (1) I consider Moore's definition of objective rightness and Russell's definition of a most fortunate act too narrow. They make an arbitrary cut in the whole universe and lead to paradoxes which make us think that they cannot be a part of what common sense means by rightness. (2) I do not think that subjective rightness has any very close connection with the objective rightness of praise or blame, but that it is particularly connected with those motives which are called conscientious, taken in abstraction from the rest of the act. (3) But Russell's definition of subjective rightness is too subjective; for any agreement about subjective rightness involves an agreement about the meaning of objective rightness. (4) There is a special sense of rightness which applies to feelings as directed to situations. (5) I doubt whether common sense means by objective rightness what Russell does, and I hold that his account remains obscure, partly because you cannot talk of *the* probability of a proposition, and partly because of the ambiguity of the phrase 'a probably most fortunate act'. (6) My definition of objective rightness agrees with common sense in making motives an actual and important factor in it; and I think that the difficulty about the attitude of common sense to wrong acts done through ignorance of unforeseeable circumstances is met by the view that it is subjectively right for the agent to do what he judges to be most probably objectively right on his information. (7) But finally the existence of three logical senses of right and ought does make it just possible that there is an ethical sense of right corresponding to Russell's objective rightness, though the difficulty as to what precisely is meant by a probably most fortunate act infects this possible meaning with ambiguity.

II

ON THE FUNCTION OF FALSE HYPOTHESES IN ETHICS (1916)[1]

The title of this paper is obscure, but the question which it proposes to discuss is important; it is closely connected with an ethical principle which is perhaps more often explicitly used in the reasonings of daily life than any other. This principle or mode of argument I call the *Principle of False Universalization.*

A man proposes to himself a certain course of action and debates whether it be right or wrong. At a certain stage he will say to himself, or, if he be discussing the matter with a friend, his friend will say: Suppose *everybody* did what you propose to do. The consequences of this hypothesis will then be considered, and, if they be found to be bad, the man will generally consider that this fact tends to prove that his proposed action is wrong. I think the principle is nearly always used negatively, i.e. to condemn a proposed course of action. We do not in general argue that a proposed action must be right because if everybody did likewise the result would be excellent. How far there is anything to be said for this distinction we may see in the course of our discussion.

Everybody is familiar with this kind of reasoning; everybody seems to think that it is valid and important; and, as we know, something very like it was regarded by Kant as *the* fundamental law of ethics. Yet people have not noticed how extremely paradoxical it is, and what curious and interesting questions it raises on the border line between ethics and logic. The paradox is this. We are asked to believe that the rightness or wrongness of many of our actions depends on the probable consequences, not of what we judge to be true, but of what we know to be false. For,

[1] Reprinted from the *International Journal of Ethics,* Volume XXVI, April 1916, by courtesy of the University of Chicago Press.

in practically every case where we consider what would happen if everybody acted as we propose to act, we know as surely as we can know anything that is not *a priori*, that by no means everybody will act this way. E.g. a man says: I should intensely dislike to be married and don't intend to marry. His friend replies: But suppose everybody refused to marry, would not the results be very bad? If the man agrees that the results would be very bad he will be inclined to think that this is *pro tanto* an argument against the rightness of his refusal to marry. Yet both he and his friend are perfectly well aware that the hypothesis which they are supposing is false; they know quite well that as a matter of fact there is not the least prospect of everybody refusing to marry or even of so many people remaining unmarried as to lead to the consequences which they agree would be bad if they actually existed.

It might of course be said that the paradox only arises when you consider that the rightness or wrongness of actions depends on their actual or probable consequences, and that it is avoided if you suppose that it depends wholly on their own intrinsic qualities. So long as we believe that probable consequences are relevant in deciding the rightness or wrongness of an action, the particular circumstances under which the action is to be performed must be taken into account, since its probable consequence will largely be determined by them. And a very important circumstance must be the question whether other people are or are not going to do similar actions. Hence, if probable consequences are to be considered at all, we cannot and ought not to be guided by a false account of the circumstances; and the hypothesis whose consequence we are asked to consider in the method of false universalization is admittedly a false account of the circumstances in which our proposed action would take place. If we had only to consider the intrinsic quality of the action this difficulty would vanish. For, since we are not to consider circumstances at all, the mere fact that the universalization gives a false account of them need not trouble us. But, as against this, two things must be said: (1) It is thoroughly unreasonable to suppose that the goodness or badness of an action is entirely independent of its probable consequences, and no one but a moralist riding a theory to death would maintain this view for an instant. (2) Such a view can hardly be held consistently by persons who support the method of false universalization. For they are admittedly asking us to consider and appraise consequences; and they can hardly take up the extraordinary position that it is only the consequences of what we know to be false that are ethically relevant, while the consequences of what we believe to be true are wholly unimportant.

And, as a matter of fact, except in the case of false universalization, it would commonly be held that it is only the probable consequence of what is believed to be true that is ethically relevant. To be guided by the probable consequences of what is known to be false would, in most cases, be regarded as absurd and immoral. A man who proposed to establish a system of communism would not be held to have justified himself if he merely said: Consider how excellent the consequences of my system would be if no one were guided by selfish motives. Yet the hypothesis that no one is guided by selfish motives is not more obviously false than the hypothesis that no one is prepared to marry. But, seemingly, the admitted falsity of the former hypothesis makes its consequences ethically irrelevant, while the admitted falsity of the latter does not. There is a real paradox here, and it leads us to the general question: Is the goodness or badness of the consequences of admittedly false hypotheses ever relevant in deciding rightness or wrongness of a course of action; and, if so, what is the distinction between those false hypotheses whose probable consequences are relevant and those whose probable consequences are not?

We may usefully begin by considering cases where the employment of false hypotheses is obviously justifiable, and gradually working up to the more difficult and paradoxical examples of its use which we have just been illustrating. The first and simplest use is for the avoidance of personal prejudice. We feel inclined to perform a certain action and are not sure whether it is right. We then say: Suppose Smith were in my circumstances and did the action that I propose to do, what should I think of him?

If, when we try to envisage this false hypothesis, we find that we should strongly condemn it, we may be fairly sure that our own proposed action is wrong and that our tendency to approve it in ourselves is due to mere personal prejudice. This obviously justifiable and extremely useful employment of false hypothesis raises no theoretical difficulties. We are not supposing that our act takes place under circumstances different from the actual in any relevant respect; we are supposing that its consequences are the same and that the only difference in circumstances is that it is performed by Smith and not by me. And it is essential that no other differences should be introduced. If I introduce considerations about Smith's particular situation, or consider any difference between him and me other than the fact that he differs numerically from me, my judgment based on contemplating his action can no longer be applied straightway to mine. And the reason is that the action will now have been performed under different circumstances and will therefore probably have different consequences from my own proposed act. If the question is: Ought I to buy a motor-car? and I find nothing to disapprove when I contemplate the hypothesis of Smith buying a motor-car, this will have no bearing on the rightness of my proposed action if one of the differences that I have taken into consideration is that Smith's income is twice mine. The essential limitations then of this use of false hypotheses are such that it throws no light on the question of false universalization; for it differs just in the circumstances which make false universalization so paradoxical.

Another use of false hypothesis is where we decide on the right course of action by considering what somebody whose moral character we admire would probably do if placed in our position, e.g. some evangelical Christians claim to solve moral problems by considering: 'What would Jesus do?' No special logical difficulty is involved here, and the method is simply of the following type: I cannot see by direct inspection or by reasoning what is the right course of action here. I can be sure that if Jesus were in my situation His action would be the right one, and I am well enough acquainted with the character of Jesus to be tolerably certain what course of action He would take. I shall therefore be safe in following that course of action. Whatever we may think of the practicability of such a method, there is nothing recondite in it; it is of the same logical type as looking up a recipe in cookery book fortified by the knowledge that Mrs Beeton was a better cook than I am. We are not, as in the method of false universalization, considering the results of an action done under circumstances that we know not to exist. We suppose that Jesus is in exactly the same position as we are and make abstraction of all differences between Him and us except the difference that He knows what is right and will certainly do it, while we are weak in insight and in performance. If we take into account other differences, we cannot reasonably argue from what Jesus would do to the rightness of a similar action on our part. A being who could raise the dead would e.g. be justified in performing certain operations for which a human doctor could justly be blamed. It is perhaps worth while to notice that these considerations wreck the method in practice. To obtain useful ethical conclusions about our own actions, we need to regard Jesus simply as differing from us in insight and good-will. But, to obtain conclusions as to His probable course of action in given circumstances, we must argue inductively from what we know about His recorded actions; and these are the actions of a being differing from us in innumerable other respects beside the two mentioned.

These two examples of false hypothesis then throw very little light on the particular problem that interests us, viz. that of false universalization. But we can now pass to certain genuine cases of false universalization where the logical principles involved are easy to recognize. We will discuss these before passing to the most difficult and paradoxical uses of this principle. The use that we have now to consider may be described as the use of the principle of false generalization as a moral microscope.

The result of one man's action may be very small, and it may be impossible for him to see by contemplating it alone whether it be good, bad, or indifferent. But he may be able to see that a great number of such actions would produce a result of the same kind as a single one but of much greater magnitude, and that this result would be unmistakably good or bad. If he has reason to suppose that the goodness or badness of the results of a large number of similar actions is the sum of the goodness or badness of the results of the separate actions, he will be able to conclude as to the moral quality of his own proposed action though it was not obvious on mere inspection. It is clear that if such an argument be ever applicable, the falsity of the hypothesis is irrelevant. We are admittedly capable of estimating the goodness or badness of merely hypothetical states of affairs. This being granted, the general line of argument runs as follows: If the complex *C* existed it would be good (or bad). Now the complex *C* contains a part *c* precisely similar to the results of a certain contemplated action. We have reason to believe that *C* could not be good (or bad) unless *c* were itself good (or bad). Hence we can come to a conclusion about the moral quality of our proposed action even though this be too small to reveal itself to mere inspection.

The nerve of the argument obviously is the condition that a complex shall be known to be so related to one of its parts that the former cannot be good (or bad) unless the latter has the corresponding moral predicate. Unfortunately, the principle of organic unities makes it extremely difficult to be certain in any particular case that this relation subsists between the value of a whole and that of one of its parts. It seems most plausible to suppose that this relation holds for those complexes which consist of a number of precisely similar parts. And these are the cases contemplated when the principle of false universalization is used as a moral microscope. The appeal to everybody is here, strictly speaking, rhetorical; all that is really necessary is to consider the results of a fairly large number of people performing actions precisely like the one under discussion. And the argument, if *ever* valid, is subject to great limitation and doubt. We must take the results of our act quite in abstraction before hypothetically multiplying them, and this is liable to be overlooked if we bring in the notion of other agents performing precisely similar acts. To take a typical instance. I walk through a field and pluck an ear of corn. Is this right, wrong or indifferent? If I now say:

Suppose a million people walked through and each plucked an ear, the results would be very bad, I must of course make abstraction of the effects of a million people merely walking through. My walking through may have done no damage whatever, but it would be physically impossible for a million people to walk through without doing grave damage. It is better, therefore, not merely to drop the reference to everybody, but also to drop the reference to agents altogether and to consider nothing but the hypothetical multiplication of results like the result of my action.

But, even when this is done, it seems to me that the argument from the damage done by a million ears being plucked to that done by the plucking of one is most precarious. The consequences that have to be considered cannot be the mere separation of the ears from the stalk; this, like all physical events, is in itself morally indifferent. We obviously have to go further and consider the effects on the state of mind of the owner of the field and of others. Now it seems perfectly possible that no one's state of mind is in the least better or worse for the plucking of one ear and yet that it may be very much the worse for the plucking of a million. There is absolutely no logical reason against this and it seems to me to be true. The most probable account of the matter is that the plucking of a certain finite number n (varying of course with the circumstances) is absolutely indifferent, while the plucking of any greater number leads to consequences which get worse as the number gets greater. It is no objection to this view that we cannot state exactly what the number n is; for it is no objection to any theory that it does not presuppose omniscience in its supporters. I think we may put the objection to the moral microscope as follows: If you merely consider physical consequences, they have no moral value and therefore cannot help you to decide any moral question. If you go on to consider psychical consequences, then there seems hardly any reason to believe that the psychical consequences of a large number of precisely similar physical events form a whole consisting of a number of similar parts and itself similar to its parts, or a state differing *only* in magnitude from that produced by each physical event separately. And it is not at all clear to me that if two psychical states differ only in their intensive magnitude and the one with the greater intensive magnitude be good (or bad) the one with the less intensive magnitude must have the same ethical quality but to a smaller degree.

I conclude then that both on practical and ethical grounds it is most unlikely that you can ever safely argue from the goodness or badness of the effect of a number of precisely similar acts to the rightness or wrongness of a single act of the class. And, unless this can be done, the moral microscope can have no valid practical use.

But we now come to a class of cases where the principle is used, but where the moral microscope explanation, even if it be valid, can hardly be the full explanation. And these are just the most paradoxical and perhaps the commonest instances of the use of the principle of false universalization. The cases that we have to consider are the following: A certain good can only be produced by the co-operation of a number of people. The acts of these people need not, of course, and in general will not be *precisely* similar; all that is important is that they resemble each other in the fact of co-operating to this end. The use of the principle that we have now to consider is to prove to people that they ought to co-operate. A man is supposed to admit that the results obtained by the action of a certain group are good, and that they can only be obtained by co-operation. He refuses, however, to co-operate. People then say: But suppose everybody refused to co-operate, this good would be unobtainable. The refuser will generally be inclined to admit that this is a powerful argument against the rightness of his refusal. We may note further that this line of argument is only employed as a rule when the part contributed to the whole good by each member of the group is very small. We can reinforce this point by a negative instance. Suppose my friend discusses with me the propriety of murdering his wealthy uncle Joseph who has remembered him in his will. Unless I am a Kantian or suspect my friend of being one, I shall not consider it appropriate to point out to him that, if everyone murdered his wealthy uncle from whom he had expectations, a deplorable insecurity would prevail among a deserving class of men and an excuse would be provided for them to leave their money to missionary societies.[1] I should rather insist on the loss of well-being to Uncle Joseph himself, and the probable detection and execution of my friend without the enjoyment of his legacy. And this is because the murder of Uncle Joseph would be in itself an act fraught with appreciably evil consequences, and because for considerable evil to be wrought in this direction the co-operation of many uncle-murderers is not essential.

This fact that the argument is only used where the contribution of each member of the group is necessarily small suggests that the moral microscope plays at any rate some part in these instances. An abstention from joining a group is of course from an ethical point of view just as much an action as joining it. And it may be said that the argument is to show that A's abstention must be wrong though its badness is not obvious on inspection, because a large number of precisely similar abstentions would have admittedly bad results.

But it is surely easy to see that this argument is here a very feeble one. It is quite true that A's abstention *would* have bad consequences if it took place together with the abstention of a great many other people. But it does not in the least follow that it *will* have any bad consequences if it take place together with but few other abstentions. Now in judging of the rightness or wrongness of a proposed action it is admitted that we ought in general to take into account the circumstances under which it is to be performed. If a doctor is considering whether he ought to administer chloroform to a patient, it is his duty to consider the particular state of that particular patient's heart, and he will justly be blamed if he omits to do so. Similarly it is impossible to see why A should not have the right and indeed the duty to consider the actual fact that most people have joined the group when he debates on the rightness or wrongness of his joining. It is in fact easy to produce cases where refusal to consider the

[1] Though of course a strict Kantian could not use even as suitable an argument as this.

actual facts about the number of people who have joined will apparently lead A to make a wrong decision. Let us suppose that a group g is co-operating to produce a certain result. Let us suppose that n people have joined the group and let us further suppose that, however great n may be, the joining of the group by an $n + 1$th individuals entails certain sacrifices on him. It is probably reasonable to suppose (*a*) that the sacrifices made by each individual are lessened as the number of members increases but that the rate of decrease diminishes as n grows greater; (*b*) that the amount of good produced by the group (apart from the sacrifices) increases as n increases, but that after a certain point the rate of increase diminishes as n grows greater.[1] If now we call $s(n)$ the total sacrifices made where there are n members and $g(n)$ the total good produced by their efforts (apart from the sacrifices) it is quite likely that a point will be reached where

$$g(n + 1) - s(n + 1) < g(n) - s(n)$$

When this point is reached it would seem to be the duty of people to refuse to join the group, and if they let themselves be guided by the mere fact that $g(0) = 0$ and decide to join, they will presumably decide wrongly. Here again the fact that n cannot exactly be determined is merely of practical interest; probably in most cases upper and lower limits could be given for it. We see then that if moral microscopic considerations be the only ones involved in these applications of the principle of false universalization there is no reason to suppose that the argument to the action of any given person is *ever* valid, and strong reason to believe that after a certain point it will lead to wrong decisions. And in actual fact we notice that the moral microscope is not the main use of the principle in these examples. Suppose that A is told that he ought to co-operate with a certain group because

[1] This hypothesis is unduly favourable to the argument which we are criticising. There are many groups where efficiency would after a certain point continually diminish as n increased. E.g. our drains would be less well cleaned if millions of people were persuaded by the principle of false universalisation to join the group of drain-cleaners. And this would follow from the mere undue increase in numbers in the group, quite apart from the other obvious loss to the general good by this withdrawal from their other occupations.

he approves of the end that can be obtained by their efforts, and is reminded that if everybody refused to co-operate the end could not be obtained. If he replies that the end will be obtained whether he co-operates or not and that therefore the hypothesis is as idle as the hypothesis that the moon is made of green cheese, the reply will probably be: But is it fair that other people should do all the work and that you should share in the profits? This seems to be the natural development of the argument from false universalization in the examples that we are considering where it is clear that the moral microscope is an insufficient explanation. Let us consider it as carefully as possible.

The argument, I think, runs somewhat as follows. You admit that a certain good result can only be obtained by the co-operation of a number of people. Further, this co-operation involves certain sacrifices on the part of all the co-operators. Lastly, the good aimed at is one which, from the nature of the case, must be enjoyed by all the members of a certain class whether this class be identified with the group of producers or not. The enjoyers may not all be producers and the producers may not all be enjoyers. E.g. if any good results come to the victors in a war they will be of such a kind—national prosperity, feeling of national pride, etc.—that they will *ipso facto* be enjoyed by many members of the victorious nation independently of whether they helped to produce them or not. On the other hand, it is quite certain that many of the producers cannot be enjoyers, because they will be dead or injured for life. A feeling of national pride is e.g. a very poor compensation for the loss of both eyes and a leg. Now it may be true that just the same good will be produced whether you co-operate or not, but there is no relevant difference between you and those who join which entitles you to the halfpence without the kicks and them to the certainty of kicks and the possibility of no halfpence.

In fact the argument turns upon distribution. What I mean is this. The possession of certain things and the existence of certain states of mind is intrinsically good. And it is the duty of everyone to aim at what he believes will be the best possible state of affairs on the whole. But the goodness or badness of a complex state of affairs is not a function merely of the goodness or badness of its parts. A certain set of goods distributed in one way between a number of people may constitute an intrinsically better state of affairs than the same set distributed differently. And the appeal to 'fairness' seems to rest on the principle that the best possible state of affairs is reached when the group of producers and that of enjoyers is as nearly identical as possible. In fact common sense would probably go further than this and say that the best possible result was reached when (*a*) producers and enjoyers are identical and (*b*) the share in the good produced that falls to each producer is proportional to his sacrifice in producing them. So the argument from fairness really is that the group of producers and the group of enjoyers have no *a priori* or natural identity; that it is morally desirable that they should be as nearly identical as possible; and that the only way to secure this is for all enjoyers so far as possible to become producers, even though the total product is not thereby increased.

This argument sounds plausible, and I believe that it is in some sense true. But it contains a number of unanalysed difficulties, and it is important to try and determine its limitations. At the very outset a serious difficulty meets us. We have seen that it is almost certain that a point will be reached where, if we disregard questions of distribution, the extra sacrifice due to an additional member joining the group will more than counterbalance the extra benefit due to his action. When we take distribution into account we can see that this limit may very well need to be overstepped in some measure; we can even see that a better total state may be produced by a smaller amount of goods better distributed than by a larger amount worse distributed. But it seems very difficult to deny that there may be a limit beyond which good distribution is too dearly purchased. I imagine that the remark *fiat justitia ruat cœlum* would be the denial of this possibility. But I am not sure that anyone would maintain this maxim unless he felt confident that the world is so constituted that the heavens never will fall if justice be done. Now, whether this confidence be justified or not—I myself see no justification for it—it is a metaphysical proposition and not a proposition of pure ethics. We must therefore, I think, be prepared to admit in theory that there may come a point where it is better that some people should refuse to co-operate although this involves an imperfect distribution, than that they should by co-operating produce a much smaller net-balance of goods though perfectly distributed. Once more it is no objection to say that it is totally impossible to determine exactly where this point comes in any particular case. This is quite true, but it is too common a difficulty in ethics to worry us, and we know that we are lucky in ethical questions if we can state upper and lower limits that are not too ridiculously far apart. Where right ends and wrong begins between these limits, it is utterly impossible to say.

We may now ask ourselves the question: Is there any necessary connection between the method of false universalization and the argument from fairness? We have indeed seen that the former tends to pass into the latter when its more obvious incoherences are pointed out, but *need* we pass to the argument from fairness by way of the argument from false universalization? I think we may say that, so far as we have yet dealt with the argument from fairness, it has no logical connection whatever with the argument from false universalization. The only connection is that both arguments attempt to show that everyone in a certain group should join a certain other group. The argument from false universalization does this by pointing to the evil consequences of no one joining this group, and it is of course a necessary step in the argument from fairness that it shall be admitted that certain good will result if this group be formed and will not result if it be not formed. But this is the only use that the argument from fairness makes of the argument from false universalization; it merely takes over one of the premises of that argument. Its own peculiarity is that it supplies two further premises, one factual and one ethical, which the argument from false generalization does not use. These are (*a*) the factual premise that the goods are of such a kind that they must be enjoyed by a group not necessarily identical with the group of producers and (*b*) that the best distribution is one in which the producers and enjoyers of a certain good are identical.

We must now notice a special difficulty which affects the argument from false generalization. Let A and B be two groups each enjoying a certain good. Let the sole threat to A's good be the existence of a subgroup β in B and the sole threat to B's good be the existence of a subgroup α in A. (E.g. let the good be national prosperity. A and B are two prosperous nations, and the prosperity of A is only threatened by the armed forces (β) of B, while the prosperity of B is only threatened by the armed forces (α) of A.) A citizen of A refuses to join his army and is told that if everyone did as he proposes to do the prosperity of A will be lost. But this depends on whether he means: I don't intend to joint the army of A or I don't intend to join the army of A or of B. If he means the latter, it is clear that the very best results would follow if everyone followed his example, for then both A and B would necessarily retain their prosperity. And if the employer of the argument from false universalization appeals to the fact that other people certainly will join B's army he is (*a*) contradicting his own hypothetical premises and (*b*) laying himself open to the retort that other people will also certainly join A's army. Since it may fairly be assumed that a person who refuses to join his own army intends *ipso facto* to refuse to join any other, his position is absolutely unassailable by the weapon of false universalization alone. But it is clear that the argument from fairness, if it applies at all, would apply here, too; and therefore we can reinforce our conclusion that there is no essential connection between the two arguments.

Is there then no valid use for the principle of false universalization in ethics? I think there is at least one, though it is a very modest one. It can be used to refute a certain kind of mistaken judgment about the rightness of a suggested act. Suppose that certain acts are very unpleasant to everyone and entail very real sacrifices from which everyone shrinks. Suppose further that the performance of such acts by a certain number of persons is essential to the attainment of a considerable good or the avoidance of a considerable evil. If now a man says: I will not act thus *because* I dislike the sacrifice then it is open to us to point out to him that, if this be his sole ground, it is just as valid a ground for all other people, since by hypotheses they all dislike the sacrifice. If then he is right in refusing to do the act, all other people will also be right in refusing on the same ground. But the result will be that a great good will be lost or a great evil suffered. Now it cannot be the case that the result of a number of right actions can be a state of affairs which can be foreseen to be worse than if people had acted differently. Hence we can conclude that these actions could not all be right. But if his ground for supposing that *his* action was right were valid all these actions would be right. We therefore are forced to conclude, not that his action was wrong (for that does not follow at all), but that at any rate his reasons for supposing it to be right were unsound.

We must now notice the extreme limitations of this use of the principle. (1) It does not prove that *all* the people who abstained acted wrongly; it only proves that some acted wrongly and it offers us no means of deciding which. To decide which one acted wrongly we should have to consider the details of each man and the circumstances under which he made his decision. To decide whether *all* acted wrongly we should have to introduce the principle of fairness, and, as we have seen, it does not necessarily follow from this that all who abstained must have acted wrongly. (2) The argument only holds where the dislike of the sacrifice may be assumed to be nearly equal in everybody. If a man refused to marry because he strongly disliked the idea of marriage you could not prove him to be wrong by the principle of false universalization; for he might justly say that most other people do not dislike marriage so strongly as he does and therefore his objection could not be universalized. Other people whose dislike was weaker or non-existent could have no ground to conclude that an abstention in them would be right because an abstention in him was right. (3) This brings us to an exceedingly difficult point where even this modest use of the principle threatens to be wrecked. Suppose the dislike of a sacrifice were about equally strong in everyone. We must admit that some people succeed much better than others in overcoming such dislikes from a sense of duty and other motives. Might not a man argue thus? I am not going to do this action because I dislike it and my dislike is stronger than my sense of duty. But this does not prove that it will be right for others to abstain who have the same dislike but a stronger sense of duty. Hence there is no contradiction between my judgment: This abstention is right in me with my weak sense of duty, and the fact that if all other people whose dislike of the sacrifice is as great as mine were to abstain a great good would be lost or evil produced. For if other people accept my principle it will only justify them in abstaining provided their sense of duty is as weak as mine; and this by hypothesis is not the case. The fact is that you cannot disprove by the method of false universalization the judgment: My sense of duty is so weak compared with my dislike of the necessary sacrifices that I do right in abstaining from the action.

Indeed, paradoxical as such a judgment seems and greatly as it might be abused, it is not in general refutable. In the first place you certainly cannot say that the actual strength of my desire to do what I believe to be right is *never* a relevant factor in deciding on my proper conduct. For (*a*) it is certainly clear that the actual strength of *other men's* desire to do what they believe to be right is a very relevant factor in deciding what I ought to do. Most people believe that it is wrong to read private letters, but I know that their desire to do what they believe to be right is very liable to be overcome by their curiosity. And this is a relevant factor in my decision that I ought to keep important private letters under lock and key. But further (*b*) a man's knowledge that his own desire to keep sober because he believes sobriety to be right is very liable to be overcome by his desire to be drunk when he tastes alcohol is a relevant factor in judging whether he ought or ought not to be a total abstainer. These of course are cases where of two alternatives *a* and *b*, *a* would have better consequences if it were not that it presents a temptation where my sense of duty is weakest, and that the total consequences will be worse if *a* be performed and the temptation be succumbed to than if *b* be peformed. And it may be admitted that this does not correspond accurately to the situation that led to this discussion.

We may state that situation as follows: *a* and *b* are two alternatives open to me, and I believe that *a* will have better consequences than *b*. *a* presents no *especially* dangerous temptation, the only temptation that it presents to my weak sense of duty is the temptation of not completing it. *b* does not present this temptation so strongly.[1] Is the weakness of my sense of duty a relevant factor here? It seems to me that it very well may be. It is no doubt true to say that we are here turning our attention from the probable consequences of our actions to the probability of our performing an action. But, since the consequences will not follow unless we do the action, the probability of the consequences must depend on the probability that we shall carry the action through, and this depends on the strength of my sense of duty as against the particular sacrifices that the action involves. If the consequences of *a* be better than those of *b* and those of *b* better than those of the absence or partial completion of *a*, and if the weakness of my own sense of duty in the fact of the special sacrifices involved in *a* make it more likely that I shall complete *b* than *a*, it is my duty to choose *b* rather than *a*; and the relevant factor is the weakness of my sense of duty. We see then how very limited is that principle which some men seem to have thought the basis of ethics.

There remains, however, one further question to discuss. We have all along assumed that the rightness or wrongness of an action depends wholly on its actual or probable consequences. Now this seems to me not to be true. It is quite certain that its rightness is a function of the goodness of its probable consequences, but, as I have tried to prove in an earlier paper,[2] its rightness is not entirely determined by this. The rightness seems to be a function of the intrinsic goodness of its motive and of the goodness of its probable consequences. Moreover, it is certain that in many judgments when we appear to be judging

[1] An example would be the case of a man who was considering whether he ought to enlist in view of the fact that his sense of duty might not be strong enough to prevent him from running away in battle.

[2] 'The Doctrine of Consequences in Ethics', *International Journal of Ethics*, xxiv, 293.

about the rightness or wrongness of an act we are really judging simply about the goodness or badness of a motive. It is therefore necessary for the sake of completeness to ask whether the principle of false universalization is of any use as a means of judging about motives. It might conceivably have either of two uses. It might (*a*) help us to recognize what our motives are, which is of course an essential preliminary to passing any reasonable judgment of value upon them. Or (*b*) it might help us to judge whether our motives once recognized are good or bad. Moreover, while it is certain that motives have value as means, it seems to me possible that they have intrinsic value, and tolerably certain that they can alter the intrinsic value of wholes consisting of themselves and their consequences. So that (*b*) divides into three questions. Does the principle help us to judge the goodness of a motive (i) as a means, (ii) as an end, or does it enable us to see (iii) whether its presence adds to or lessens the intrinsic value of a whole composed of itself and a certain set of consequences?

(*a*) If I propose to perform a certain act and then am asked to contemplate the hypothesis that everyone acts as I propose to do, it will be necessary for me to be quite clear how I *do* propose to act and why. I shall have every reason to try and be clear on this point because otherwise the universalization will not be fair. Hence if I am challenged to make the universalization, and especially if I object to the way in which my interlocutor makes it for me, I shall have a very good chance of recognizing what my motive really is.

(*b*) i. The principle of false generalization may very well show me that my motive is (in a certain special sense which we will explain in a moment) bad as a means. It will not indeed prove to me that my motive in my circumstances leads to worse results than a different motive; but it may show me that it is bad as a means in the sense that it would be very unfortunate if it were at all a common motive with people. Now this does not prove that it actually leads to bad results in *any* case, for you cannot argue from the fact that the *coexistence* of this motive in a great many people would lead to bad results that its existence in any particular person will lead to bad results. Thus it is only in a very special and not very useful sense that the principle will show that a motive is bad as a means. It is very easy to commit a gross fallacy here. This is to confuse the two statements 'the motive *m* frequently leads to bad results' and 'the frequency of the motive *m* would lead to bad results'. From the former we could conclude that any particular instance of the motive is likely to lead to bad results; from the latter we can conclude nothing of the sort. And it is only the latter that could be proved by the principle of false universalization.

(*b*) ii and iii. I think that the principle has very little direct connection with the intrinsic goodness of motives or with the goodness which their presence adds to or subtracts from that of other wholes. But there is a rather roundabout connection of the following kind. There happens to be one motive—the desire to do what is believed to be right and reasonable as such—which is (*a*) intrinsically good and (*b*) adds to the goodness of a great many (though not I think of all) sets of consequences produced by it. Now it is on the whole true of the world as at present constituted that this motive also has beneficial results in the great majority of cases, and that the results of everybody acting from it would be very beneficial. (This would of course be false if the world were so constituted that the more people tried to judge dispassionately about the goodness of the results of certain actions the more they were likely to be mistaken. But there seems no reason to take such a depressing view as this.) Hence if it can be shown that the results of a number of people acting as I propose to act from my motives would be worse than if they acted differently there is at least a strong presumption that my motive is not the desire to do what *is* right and reasonable. Of course even if my motive were a different one it need not be a bad one. But at least the argument supplies some presumption that my motive does not belong to the most important class of motives which are recognized to be intrinsically good and to add greatly to the goodness of the wholes that are connected with them as consequences.

Such then are the modest and doubful functions of the principle of false universalization. Most of its alleged uses we have seen are sheerly fallacious; and often where we cannot prove a fallacy we can see that there is very likely to be one and can produce no clear case where it is quite certain that no fallacy lurks. The most important use is to lead us to the principle of fairness, and yet there seems to be very little logical connection between the two; so that is it rather a matter of psychology than of logical necessity that the principle of fairness is generally introduced by that of false universalization. And the principle of fairness itself bristles with difficulties which I have barely touched, but to which I hope to return in a later paper.

III

ANALYSIS OF SOME ETHICAL CONCEPTS (1928)[1]

In this paper I propose to take certain notions which we constantly use in our judgements of right and wrong, good and bad, and to analyse them so far as I can and bring out their connexions with each other. The subject is, of course, rather a hackneyed one; but I cannot help thinking that there still remains a good deal which may profitably be said about it. I do not suppose for a moment that my analysis is adequate, and it may well be in part positively mistaken. But I am inclined to think that it may be useful as a beginning of a more adequate and more correct analysis.

The concepts that I propose to consider are Intention, Action, Motive, Conscientious Action, and Rightness. In the course of the discussion I shall try to explain what is meant by 'mixed' and 'pure' motives, and I shall also try to bring out the relations of rightness to motive and intention and consequences.

The various subjects which I shall treat are very closely bound up with each other, so that it is more or less arbitrary which we begin with. But, on the whole, I find it most convenient to start with the notion of 'intention'.

Intention

Whenever a man is called upon either to act or to abstain from action he is in presence of a highly complex total situation, composed of pre-existing persons, institutions, and things, in various relations to each other and to himself. Action is always taken or abstained from by the agent in view of the given situation, as he then believes it to be. Now, in considering what he

[1] Reprinted from the *Journal of Philosophical Studies* (*Philosophy*), Volume III, July 1928, by courtesy of the editors.

should do, the agent will always have to consider, not merely the situation as it is at present, but how it is likely to develop (*a*) if he abstains from interfering with it, or (*b*) if he interferes with it in various alternative possible ways. If he does anything at all, he *must* modify the present situation in one way, and he may (and generally will) also modify it in another way. He will inevitably modify it to the extent that his action is added to it as a new factor which immediately enters into various relations with the pre-existing factors. And he may, and generally will, also modify it further in so far as his action constitutes a cause-factor which makes the future development of the situation different from what it would otherwise have been. I will distinguish these two cases as 'non-causal' and 'causal' modification, respectively.

At this stage a little simple symbolism will be helpful. Let us denote the situation at the moment of acting or abstaining from action, as it appears to the agent, by s_0. And let us denote the successive phases which the agent believes that the initial situation would pass through if he abstained from action by s_1, s_2 . . . We will denote the whole series $s_0 s_1 s_2$ . . . by σ, and we will call it 'the apparent unmodified series'. Suppose now that, instead of leaving the situation s_0 to develop by itself, the agent were to make a certain change x in his body or mind or both. Then he would envisage a modified series, which might be denoted by (xRs_0) $s_1^x s_2^x$ . . . Here (xRs_0) symbolizes the non-causally modified initial situation, consisting of s_0 and x, which the agent believes to be related by the relation R to each other. And s_1^x, etc., symbolize the phases corresponding to s_1, etc., causally modified as the agent believes they would be by the presence of the cause-factor x in the initial phase. Such a series may be denoted by σ_x, and we will call it 'the apparent series as modified by x'.

At the moment of descision, then, the agent contemplates a set of apparent series, which appear to him to be mutually exclusive and collectively exhaustive of the possibilities open to him. This set consists of σ, the apparent unmodified series, and of one or more apparent modified series, σ_x, σ_y, etc. Suppose, now, that, on the whole, he likes one of these more or dislikes it less than any of the others. We will call such a series 'the preferred apparent series'. Then the agent's 'total intention' may be defined as the preferred apparent series.

Action

Now it is a true, but analytical, proposition that the agent will try to actualize that apparent series which, on the whole, he prefers to all the rest that he believes to be open to him. If this should happen to be the unmodified series σ, we say that he 'intentionally abstains from action'. If it should happen to be the modified apparent series σ_x, we say that he 'performs the action x in order to realize the intention σ_x'. So an action is a change which the agent makes in his body or mind or both, because on the whole he prefers the apparent series whose initial phase contains this change to any of the alternative apparent series which seem to him to be possible.

Motive

We have seen that, if the agent decides to act at all, he will choose that action x which initiates that apparent modified series σ_x which, on the whole, he prefers. We have now to consider why σ_x should be preferred on the whole to σ and to σ_y. It is evident that there are in general three relevant factors, viz. (1) the intrinsic qualities which the agent believes x to have, (2) the relation R in which the agent believes x to stand to the apparent initial situation s_0, and (3) the causal modifications which the agent expects x to produce in the subsequent developments of the initial situation. It will be well to say something about each of these factors.

(1) There is not much to be said about the intrinsic qualities of the action. An important quality is its immediate pleasantness or painfulness. If it be believed that x is intrinsically pleasant, this will be *pro tanto* a cause for preferring it to inaction; and if x be thought to be intrinsically pleasanter than y, this will be *pro tanto* a cause for preferring x to y.

(2) The relation in which an action is believed to stand to the initial situation is extremely important. It will be noticed that

actions are classified and named, from a legal or an ethical point of view, very largely from their relations to the situation in which they occur, and very little from their intrinsic qualities or their consequences. Consider, e.g., an act of sexual intercourse of a man with a woman. The intrinsic qualities of such an act are presumably the same whether the woman be his wife, his daughter, an unmarried woman who is not a blood-relation, or another man's wife. But, according to which of these relational properties it has, it is classed as legal cohabitation, incest, simple fornication, or adultery, respectively. And it is obvious that such non-causal relational properties would have often a most important influence in determining whether a man would decide to do such an act or not.

(3) It would be admitted by everyone that the nature of the consequences which an act is expected to have is a very important factor in determining whether the agent will prefer it to another act. Utilititarians hold that nothing else is *ethically* relevant. But at present we are discussing psychology and not ethics. And it is perfectly certain that the agent is in many cases *in fact* determined by what he believes about the intrinsic qualities of an act or its relations to the initial situation, and not merely by what he believes about its consequences. It is, e.g., quite certain that many men would choose the act x and reject the act y simply because they believed y to be an act of ingratitude to a benefactor, although they believed that y would be intrinsically pleasanter than x, and that the consequences of y would be no worse than those of x.

Now it is evident that the three factors may not all point in the same direction. It is rarely, indeed, that I prefer x to all other alternatives for its intrinsic qualities, for its relation to the initial situation, and for its consequences. It may well happen that I prefer x in one respect, y in another, and z in the third. What I prefer on the whole is then nearly always a compromise reached by weighing the attractive and repulsive aspects of these three factors against each other and against the corresponding three factors in the other alternatives. Nor is this the end of the complications. Each factor may itself have several aspects, and some of these may be attractive and others repulsive. I might think that a certain action is at once intrinsically pleasant and intrinsically ignoble. Again, an act may be attractive in virtue of some of its relational properties and repulsive in virtue of others. E.g. suppose a person who had done me a kindness in the past were applying for a post for which I was an elector. To vote for him might attract me as an act of gratitude, and repel me as an act of injustice to another candidate, and as an act of bad faith to the institution which was trusting me as an elector. It is still more obvious that I may like some of the consequences that I expect to follow from an act and dislike others of them. Thus the final preference is doubly a compromise. It is a compromise as between the three factors as wholes, and, with regard to each factor, it is a compromise between its attractive and its repulsive aspects.

We can now begin to attempt a definition of 'motive'. We shall find that it is not at all a simple matter to do this. We may say at once that, even if all actions have causes, it is certain that some actions do not have motives. This is obvious in the case of impulsive actions. But it is true also of intentional actions. Suppose the agent contemplates certain alternatives, σ, σ_x, σ_y, as wholes, without explicitly analysing out certain aspects of each and comparing them in respect of these aspects. And suppose that he then directly prefers σ_x as a whole to the others as wholes. Then I should say that the act x was done intentionally, but without a motive. We say that an action has a motive only when the agent explicitly considers the various alternative series as having certain aspects, compares them with respect to these aspects, and finally prefers the series which contains this action to all the rest *because of* the aspects which he believes it to have as compared with the others.

Let us begin with the simplest possible case. Suppose the agent likes the alternative σ_x as a whole, and dislikes or is indifferent to all the other alternatives. Suppose there are certain aspects in σ_x which he finds attractive, and certain others which he finds repulsive. I will call each such aspect 'an intrinsic motive-factor in σ_x'. Those which attract him I will call 'positive', and those which repel him I will call 'negative'. The resultant of all these factors, positive and negative, in σ_x I will call 'the intrinsic resultant motive of σ_x'. In the case supposed, the intrinsic resultant motive of σ_x is positive, and the intrinsic resultant motives of all the other alternatives are either negative or zero. In this case, and in this case only, we can identify the intrinsic resultant motive of σ_x with what I will call 'the total motive for choosing σ_x'.

But this extremely simple case seldom arises. The agent may dislike all the alternatives, and simply choose the one that he dislikes least. Or he may like several of the alternatives, and choose the one that he likes the best. To deal with these more complicated cases a more elaborate analysis is needed. It is evident that here the total motive of choice is essentially connected with the *relative* attractiveness and repulsiveness of the chosen and the rejected alternatives.

Now to choose the alternative σ_x is evidently precisely equivalent to preferring σ_x to σ, preferring σ_x to σ_y, and so on for all the other alternatives. Conseqently the total motive for choosing σ_x must be composed of the resultant motive for preferring σ_x to σ, the resultant motive for preferring σ_x to σ_y, and so on. Thus the fundamental conception to be analysed and defined is 'the resultant motive for preferring a certain alternative to a certain other alternative'.

It is clear that any two alternative apparent series, σ_x and σ_y, will have a good deal in common. For they all start with the same apparent intial phase s_0, and they continue as alternative apparent developments of it. The differences between σ_x and σ_y can be brought under three heads: (1) Factors present in σ_x and absent in σ_y. (2) Factors absent in σ_x and present in σ_y. (3) Generic factors common to σ_x and σ_y, but present in different specific forms in each. Now the positive motive-factors for preferring σ_x to σ_y can be brought under three corresponding headings: (1) Positive motive-factors present in σ_x and absent in σ_y. (2) Negative motive-factors absent in σ_x and present in σ_y. (3) Generic characteristics common to σ_x and σ_y, but present in σ_x in a specific form which the agent prefers to the specific form in which they are present in σ_y. The negative motive-factors for preferring σ_x to σ_y can obviously be brought under the same three headings by simply interchanging σ_x and σ_y everywhere in each of the above three statements. I will call the resultant of all the positive and all the negative motive-factors for preferring σ_x to σ_y 'the resultant motive for preferring σ_x to σ_y'. And I will call the whole composed of all the resultant motives for preferring σ_x to the other alternatives 'the total motive for choosing σ_y'.

The total motive for choosing the alternative that actually is chosen is thus in general doubly complex. In the first place, it is composed of as many resultant motives of preference as there are other alternatives. Secondly, though each of these as a whole is positive, each is in general the resultant of several motive-factors, some positive and some negative.

We can now deal with a notion which is of considerable importance in ethics, viz. that of 'purity' and 'mixture' of motive. We do not call a man's motive 'mixed' merely because of the first kind of complexity, which is inevitable whenever there are more than two apparent alternatives open to him. Purity and mixture are primarily bound up with the second kind of complexity, viz. the internal complexity of each resultant motive of preference. The best way to approach the subject seems to be the following: Suppose that the resultant motive for preferring σ_x to σ_y consists of the two positive factors *a* and *b*, and of the negative factors *u*, *v*, and *w*. Then, keeping the negative factors fixed, we can consider the following alternatives: (1) *a* in the absence of *b*, and *b* in the absence of *a*, might each be sufficient to make the agent prefer σ_x to σ_y. (2) *a* in the absence of *b* might be sufficient, but *b* in the absence of *a* might be insufficient, to produce the result. (Of course the converse of this might hold, but this would only be another instance of the same possibility.) (3) Neither *a* in the absence of *b* nor *b* in the absence of *a* might be sufficient. To take a concrete example. A man might prefer σ_x to σ_y, both because he believed that the action *x* would be intrinsically pleasanter to himself than the action *y*, and because he believed that the total consequences of *x* would be pleasanter for other men than those of *y*. In such a case, if the negative factors remained constant, there would be the following three types of possible alternative: (1) That he would still have preferred σ_x on account of the superior pleasantness of *x* to *y*, even though he had not believed that the consequences of x for others would be pleasanter than those of y; and, conversely, that he would still have preferred σ_x on account of the superior pleasantness of its consequences for others, even though he had not believed that x would be intrinsically pleasanter for himself than y. (2) The first clause of (1) might be true, and the second clause false; or conversely. (3) Both clauses of (1) might be false. It may be that both factors are necessary and neither is sufficient to determine his preference.

Suppose now that condition (2) is fulfilled. Suppose, *i.e.*, that among the positive factors in the resultant motive for preferring σ_x to σ_y there is one and only one which would suffice to determine the agent to prefer σ_x to σ_y even in the absence of all the other positive factors and in the presence of all the negative factors. Then I will call this factor 'the sufficient motive-factor for preferring σ_x to σ_y'. And I shall say that the resultant motive for preferring σ_x to σ_y is 'unmixed'. When this condition is not fulfilled, I say that the resultant motive for preferring σ_x to σ_y is 'mixed'. Now this mixture may take two forms, according to the different ways in which the above condition may fail to be fulfilled. (i) There may be *more than one* sufficient motive-factor in the resultant motive. I say then that the resultant motive is 'alternatively mixed'. (ii) There may be *no* factor in the resultant motive which would suffice, in absence of the other positive factors and in presence of the negative factors, to determine the preference. I say then that the resultant motive is 'conjunctively mixed'.

So much for resultant motives of preference; we can now deal with the total motive of choice. If the total motive for choosing σ_x is to be unmixed, it is a necessary condition that each of the resultant motives for preferring σ_x shall be unmixed. But this is not sufficient. Suppose that the fact that I believed x to be intrinsically pleasanter than y was the sufficient motive-factor for making me prefer σ_x to σ_y. And suppose that the fact that I believed that the consequences of x would be better than those of z for others was the sufficient motive-factor for making me prefer σ_x to σ_z. Then it would hardly be said that my total motive for choosing σ_x was unmixed. So the second necessary condition is that the sufficient motive-factor for preferring σ_x should be the same in all the resultant motives of preference which together make up the total motive for choosing σ_x. Thus the statement that the motive for choosing σ_x is unmixed would seem to mean that each of the resultant motives for preferring σ_x is unmixed, and that the sufficient motive-factor is the same in each of them. When this condition is fulfilled the common sufficient motive-factor maybe called 'the sufficient motive-factor for choosing σ_x'.

Conscientious Actions

We are now in position to analyse the notion of 'conscientious action'. I call x a 'conscientious action' if and only if the sufficient motive-factor for choosing the alternative σ_x is the belief that σ_x is on the whole *better* than any of the other alternatives. It is evident that many actions are not conscientious in this sense. Some, as we have seen, have no motive. Some have mixed motives. And, even when there is one motive-factor which is the sufficient motive-factor for choosing σ_x this may not be the belief that σ_x is is *better* on the whole than the other alternatives.

I call a conscientious action 'imperfect' if it is based on either inadequate knowledge or mistaken belief. Of course, the inadequacy of the knowledge is relevant only if it leads to mistaken belief. We must begin by distinguishing between (1) factual imperfection and (2) ethical imperfection. The most important respects in which a conscientious action may be factually imperfect would seem to be the following: (1, 1) The agent's knowledge of the initial situation s_0 will always be incomplete, and his beliefs about it may be in part positively mistaken. And incomplete knowledge of the situation may lead to mistaken beliefs about it. (1, 2) The agent's knowledge of the nature of the action may be incomplete, and his beliefs about it may be in part mistaken. (1, 3) The agent's beliefs about the relation of the action to the initial situation may be mistaken. It is at this point that *incomplete* knowledge of the situation or of the intrinsic nature of the action is first specially likely to lead to positive error. It was incomplete knowledge of the situation which led Œdipus to marry a woman who was in fact his mother. And incomplete knowledge of the intrinsic nature of his action might lead an extremely strong man to do in play an action which seriously injured a friend. (1, 4) The agent's beliefs about the future developments of the initial situation, if left to itself or modified by various alternative actions, will always be based on incomplete knowledge and will generally be partly mistaken. Any mistake or inadequacy at the earlier stages will be very likely to entail error here. One's predictions are always at the mercy of unforeseen accidents, and some of these accidents might have been foreseen if one's knowledge of the initial situation had been wider or deeper.

There would seem to be at least two distinct ways in which a conscientious action could be ethically imperfect. (2, 1) The agent may, either wittingly or unwittingly, judge in accordance with some general ethical principle which is in fact false. Suppose, e.g., that the agent were, wittingly or unwittingly, an ethical hedonist. Then he will judge one alternative to be better or worse than another simply and solely according to whether it contains a greater or less balance of pleasure for sentient beings as a whole. Now suppose, for the sake of illustration, that hedonism is a mistaken ethical theory. Then it may be that the intrinsic nature of the action, or its relation to the initial situation, or other characteristics in the consequences beside pleasantness and painfulness, are ethically relevant. If so, the agent may be mistaken in thinking that σ_x is the best alternative open to him, even though he makes no factual mistake. (2, 2) Even if the agent estimates the relative values of the various alternatives in accordance with correct general principles, and has true beliefs about all relevant matters of fact, he may still be mistaken on points of ethical detail. A man might believe that deception is bad, and that pain is bad. And he might hold that these two evils are commensurable, so that there is a degree of pain which it is right to spare a man by lying to him, if it can be spared him in no less objectionable way. Suppose now, for the sake of illustration, that this general principle is true. It might still be the case that the agent honestly judged that a certain lie was justified to spare a certain amount of pain, when it would really have been justified only in order to spare a much greater amount of pain. Under this head we must include what might be called 'moral insensitiveness'. This would consist in failure to see that a certain characteristic was either positively good or positively bad when it was in fact one or the other; or, again, in failing to see that there was any difference in value between two characteristics which do in fact differ in value.

Now it is plain that we attach *some* value to conscientiousness in all circumstances. Even when we disapprove an action on the whole, we do regard the fact that it was conscientiousness as a plea in mitigation of our judgement of the agent. Nor is it difficult to see why we attach this very high value to conscientiousness. As rational and moral beings we want the best alternative possible to be chosen as often as possible when men have to make decisions. And it seems reasonable to believe that, on the whole, the tendency to choose the alternative which seems to be best, because it seems to be best, will more often issue in the choice what actually is best than will any other motive. This is quite compatible with the recognition of three facts which certainly must be recognised: (1) That some of the worst actions that have ever been committed have been conscientious actions. (2) That, in some cases, we think better of a man for acting impulsively, or for acting with intention but no motive, than we should have thought of him had he acted conscientiously. (3) That, in some cases, we think better of a man for acting from some other motive than the belief that the alternative which he is choosing is on the whole the best of those open to him. The first case illustrated by the conscientious persecutor, such as Torquemada. The second is illustrated by comparing the case of a man who helps a parent or benefactor deliberately and from a sense of duty but with reluctance, and that of another man who does the same act with pleasure from an impulse of personal affection. Each is felt to be deserving of praise. But the praise is for different qualities, and, on the whole, we tend to prefer the latter to the former. The third case may be illustrated as follows. In considering which is the best on the whole of the alternatives open to one, it is certainly necessary to take into account and give due weight to the effect of the action on one's own future happiness as well as its effect on the happiness of others. Yet, in some cases, we prefer the man who considers only the happiness of others, though we acknowledge that he 'ought to' have given due weight to his own.

Two comments must be made on the above. Whilst we do admire spontaneous generosity to relatives, friends, and benefactors, we recognize that actions determined by it tend to be unduly restricted and capricious in range and often harmful to the person whom the agent intends to benefit. I think it would be fair to say that we admire the agent more for acting in this way than for acting conscientiously only when we think that his action is in fact the same as that which a conscientious person would have have done in the same situation. When this condition is not fulfilled, our admiration for the agent is very much qualified. Secondly, we have to remember that the tendency to underestimate the value of one's own happiness is much less common than the tendency to underestimate the value of the happiness of others. When so many men are too prudent to be benevolent enough, it is not unreasonable to give special admiration to the few who are too benevolent to be prudent enough. We acknowledge, on reflection, that they are faulty; but we say that their fault is 'on the right side', and that it would be desirable to have more people with this fault when there are so many with the opposite fault.

We must now consider the various kinds and degrees of blame which attach to an agent in respect of a conscientious action which is imperfect. (1) No blame attaches for unavoidable limitations of knowledge about matters of fact, or for positively mistaken beliefs on such matters which arise wholly from these limitations. At most we say the action 'turned out luckily or unluckily'. (2) We do blame the agent for positively mistaken beliefs about matters of fact not based on unavoidable limitation of knowledge. We say that he showed himself 'unintelligent' and that his action was 'unwise' or 'ill-judged'.

We come now to conscientious actions which are ethically imperfect. Here is the first point to notice is that the common distinction between 'intellectual' and 'moral' defects is unsatisfactory. Ignorance or false belief about the relative values of things is at once a moral and an intellectual defect. The proper distinction is between moral and non-moral defects. Each of these in turn is subdivided into cognitive, conative, and emotional defects. It is a cognitive moral defect to be unable to see the good points in the character of a personal enemy, to overestimate the value of one's own happiness as compared with that of others, and so on. The typical conative moral defect is expressed in Horace's lines: *Video meliora, proboque; deteriora sequor*. It is an emotional moral defect to feel the wrong kind of emotion, or too strong an emotion, or too weak an emotion, in a given situation. Of course, the three kinds of moral defect are very closely connected. Emotional moral defects are often important factors in determining intellectual or conative moral defects. What the heart does not trouble about the eye often fails to see.

Cognitive moral defects, as we have noticed, may consist of holding mistaken ethical principles or of making mistakes on points of ethical detail. The former notion needs a little further elucidation. We must distinguish carefully between the principles in accordance with which a man really acts and those which he explicitly formulates. Most people never explicitly formulate general ethical principles at all. And those who do may be quite mistaken in thinking that these are the principles in accordance with which they act. A man may think he is an egotistic ethical hedonist; but an intellectual observer may see that egotistic hedonism is not the principle in accordance with which he acts as a rule. Merely to formulate one's principles wrongly is a non-moral cognitive defect. When we have reason to believe that a man's ethical principles are not only inadequate but possibly false, we regard him as 'corrupt' or 'bad at heart' or 'having the lie in the soul'; even though he never formulates these principles, or formulates principles which we believe to be true and adequate. And this is the most damning judgement that can be passed on any agent; it is far more serious than the judgement that he often makes mistakes on points of ethical detail. A man who honestly 'can't see' that anything is of value but his own pleasure, and who acts on this principle, has an intellectual defect which is, perhaps, quite independent of his will. But anyone with this intellectual defect is *ipso facto* a thoroughly bad man morally. He is plainly far worse than a man who honestly rejects this principle, but habitually overestimates the value of his own pleasure as compared with that of others.

Rightness

I very much doubt whether 'rightness' can be defined. I am almost certain that it cannot be defined in non-ethical terms. And I see no reason to think that it can be defined in terms of other ethical concepts, such as 'good'. At any rate, I do not know, and cannot think of, any satisfactory definition. Still, there are some very important facts which can be stated about rightness.

(1) The fundamental fact seems to me to be that rightness is a relational characteristic, and not a pure quality. When I say that x is right I am saying something about its relations to certain other terms. Rightness is a species of fittingness or appropriateness, and a term which is 'fitting' must be fitting *to* something. The above is, I believe, a true statement about rightness, but it is not a definition of it. For, so far as I can see, rightness is a quite unique kind of appropriateness, just as red is a quite unique kind of colour.

'But', it might be objected, 'are not some actions *intrinsically* right, and others *intrinsically* wrong?' To this I answer that 'intrinsically right' must mean 'fitting to all situations', and 'intrinsically wrong' must mean 'unfitting to all situations'. When this is recognized it becomes very hard to believe that any type of action is intrinsically right, though it may still be plausibly maintained that some types of action are intrinsically wrong. And I am inclined to think it is the latter proposition only which most people who profess to believe in intrinsically right actions are really concerned to maintain.

(2) It is important to notice that rightness and wrongness are not confined to actions. They apply also to emotions; and the doctrine that they are relational properties is strongly supported by considering their application to emotions. An emotion is felt when and only when a certain situation, real or imaginary, is contemplated, and when this contemplation is charaterized by a certain emotional quality. Now the very same emotional quality which is appropriate to a certain kind of contemplated situation

is inappropriate to one of a different kind. It is right to contemplate sorrowfully the undeserved misfortunes of a good man, and it is wrong to contemplate them joyfully. But it is right to contemplate with satisfaction the just punishment of a criminal, though it may also be right to contemplate with regret the existence of criminals. I know of no emotional quality which is appropriate to every kind of contemplated situation, and I doubt if I could mention any emotional quality which is inappropriate to every kind of contemplated situation.

(3) Suppose that *w* is a whole, composed of two interrelated parts *a* and *b*. Then (i) what is appropriate to *a* without *b* may be inappropriate to *b* without a, and conversely. (ii) What is appropriate to *a* without *b* or to *b* without *a* might be inappropriate to the whole *w* which is composed of *a* and *b*. And the converse may hold. Suppose, e.g., that *a* were a pleasurable emotion in X, that *b* were a painful sensation in Y, and that the whole *w* were X's pleasurable contemplation of Y's painful sensation. Then the emotion appropriate to *a* alone would be that of sympathetic pleasure, the emotion appropriate to *b* alone would be that of sympathetic sorrow, and the emotion appropriate to W would be that of moral indignation.

Similar remarks apply even in cases where we can hardly talk of a whole composed of several interrelated parts. A situation *s* may have many different characteristics. The emotion appropriate to it when it is regarded as having one selection of these characteristics might be quite inappropriate to it when it is regarded as having another selection of those characteristics, or when it is regarded as having all of them. Lastly, one emotion may be appropriate to *s* when *s* is regarded only as having a certain generic characteristic *g* in some form or other, and a quite different emotion may be appropriate when *s* is regarded as having this generic characteristic in a certain specific form *g*. It may be right to feel disgust towards a man if I know merely that he is a homicide. But if I know that his homicidal acts have taken the specific form of killing murderers in the course of his official duties as hangman, I ought not to feel disgust towards him.

(4) It is necessary to draw a distinction between what I will call

'formal' and 'material' rightness. I use these terms because of the close analogy between the present distinction and the familiar distinction of formal and material correctness in logic. A conclusion is said to be formally correct if it really does follow from the premises, whether the premises be themselves true or false. It is said to be materially correct if, in addition to this, the premises be themselves true. It is not even formally correct if it involves any *logical* mistake; but it is not rendered formally incorrect by any purely *factual* mistake. Now an action or emotion is formally right if it is appropriate to the situation as it appears to the agent, no matter what *factual* mistakes he may have made, provided only that he has made no *ethical* mistake. It is materially right if, in addition to this, no relevant factual mistake or omission has been made. A factual mistake or omission is relevant provided that the emotion or action which would have been appropriate if this mistake or omission had not been made is the same as that which is appropriate to the situation as it appears to the agent.

It is very important to be clear as to just how much and how little subjectivity is involved in the notion of formal rightness. (*a*) In a most vital sense formal rightness is not subjective at all. If the action or the emotion x is formally right for Smith in a given apparent situation, the same action or emotion is formally right for *anyone* to whom the factual characteristics of the situation appear as they do to Smith. (*b*) The only subjectivity is that the factual characteristics of the same situation may appear differently to different observers, and that what would be appropriate if the situation were as it appears to A may be different from what would be appropriate if the situation were as it appears to B.

Rightness and Motive

I am inclined to agree with Mill that the motive of an action is irrelevant to its rightness or wrongness, though highly relevant to the goodness or badness of the agent. This view is, I think, strongly supported by considering the rightness and wrongness of emotions. It is admitted that the emotion that we feel in a given situation is independent of our volition at the time. Volition may control the expression of emotion, and it may prevent us from acting impulsively on the emotion; but that is all that it can do in the matter. Hence there can be no question of motive in connexion with emotions. Yet we unhesitatingly say that one emotion is right and another wrong in a given situation. And it seems to me that I mean exactly the same by 'right' and 'wrong' when I apply these terms to emotions as when I apply them to actions. I mean in both cases a certain kind of appropriateness between that which is called 'right' and the situation. And the casual antecedents of the event which is called 'right' seem to be equally irrelevant in both cases. Nor does it seem to be in opposition to common sense to say that so-and-so 'acted rightly, but from a bad motive' on a certain occasion.

The doctrine just stated is quite compatible with the view, which appears to me true, that the motive of an action may make a great difference to its *goodness*. To be done from a certain motive is a relational property of an action, and, like any other property, it may effect the goodness of the action. Of two otherwise similar actions, done in similar situations with different motives, one will be no *more right* than the other, but one may be much *better* than the other. I should say that the *goodness* of an action is in fact a function of its own rightness or wrongness and of its motive. We must notice that, owing to the Principle of Organic Unities, a motive which had no intrinsic value might add very greatly to the value of an action or detract very greatly from it. Consequently, even if it be denied that any motive has any intrinsic value, it will not follow that the motive of an action can make no difference to its goodness. Again, an action of the type *A* might be better when done with a motive of the type *a* than when done with a motive of the type *b*, whilst the converse may be true of an action of the type *B*. It seems to me, e.g., that some types of action are better when done on conscientious motives than when done from personal affection, whilst others are better when done from personal affection than when done from conscientious motives.

It is plainly possible that an action might be formally and even materially *right*, and yet be on the whole *bad* in consequence of its motive. Whether any action which is not at least *formally right* can be rendered *good* on the whole by its motive seems to me much more doubtful. It is logically possible that this might happen, but I feel very doubtful whether one can produce any plausible instance of such action.

We might define 'the ideal action' in a given situation as that action which is (*a*) materially right, and (*b*) is done from that kind of motive which adds most to the value of that kind of action. We may define 'the formally ideal action' by substituting 'formally' for 'materially' in the first part of the above definition.

Rightness and Intention

It is plain that the rightness of an action in a given situation depends on two factors which may vary independently, viz. (*a*) its non-causal relations to the initial situation, and (*b*) its effects on the later developments of this situation. The former factor may be called 'immediate fittingness'. The latter may be called 'utility', provided we clearly understand that this is to include effects on *all* characteristics that give value to the future developments, and not merely effects on *happiness*.

Some moralists seem to have maintained that the rightness of an action depends only on its immediate fittingness. Others have certainly maintained that the rightness of an action depends only on its utility. The first alternative, if it has ever been really held, is plainly false. The second, even when 'utility' is interpreted in the wide way in which I am interpreting it, seems also to be inadequate. It is, I think, impossible to avoid flagrant conflicts with common sense unless we make the rightness of an action depend on both these factors. Now, of course, the two factors may point in different directions. The action which is most immediately fitting to a given initial situation may have less utility than an action which is less immediately fitting. And the action which has most utility may be less immediately fitting to the initial situation than one which has less utility. Now the right action is that which fits the *total* situation, i.e. the initial situation and its future developments, best on the whole. Hence, in many cases the right action is necessarily a compromise between what is most fitting immediately and what has most utility.

Naturally a distinction must be drawn between formal and material immediate fittingness and between formal and material utility. The action which is formally most fitting to a given initial situation is that which is most fitting to the situation as the agent at the time believes it to be, assuming that he makes no mistake on any relevant matter of pure *value*. His beliefs may, however, be inadequate or mistaken on relevant matters of *fact* about the situation, the action, and their factual relations. A similar definition can be given for the formally most useful action. What is formally right is the best possible compromise between what would be formally most fitting immediately and what would be formally most useful.

It seems to me very doubtful whether rules can be given for striking the right balance between immediate fittingness and utility, when the two conflict. I suggest that here probably we come, as in the end we always come, to direct judgements which cannot be brought under rules. Doubtless individual skill and delicacy differ here innately, as they do in artistic and athletic activities; and doubtless innate skill can be improved by training and practice, or spoiled by misuse.

IV

DETERMINISM, INDETERMINISM, AND LIBERTARIANISM (1934)[1]

The Implications of Obligability

We often make retrospective judgements about the past actions of ourselves or other people which take the form: 'You ought not to have done the action *x*, which you in fact did; you ought instead to have done the action *y*, which in fact you did not'. If I make such a judgement about a person, and he wants to refute it, he can take two different lines of argument. (1) He may say: 'I could have done *y* instead of *x*, but you are mistaken in thinking that *y* was the action that I ought to have done. In point of fact, *x*, the action that I did, was the one that I ought to have done. If I had done *y*, I should have done what I ought not to have done'. (2) He may say: 'I could not help doing *x*', or he may say: 'Though I need not have done *x*, I could not possibly have done *y*'.

If the accused person makes an answer of the first kind, he is admitting that the alternatives 'ought' and 'ought not' apply to the actions *x* and *y*, but he is objecting to my applying 'ought' to *y* and 'ought not' to *x*. He is saying that 'ought' applies to *x*, and 'ought not' to *y*. It is as if two people, who agree that *x* and *y* are each either black or white, should differ because one holds that *x* is black and *y* white whilst the other holds that *x* is white and *y* black. If the accused person makes an answer of the second kind, he is denying the applicability of the alternatives 'ought' and 'ought not'. If he says: 'I could not help doing *x*', he assumes that his critic will admit that niether 'ought' nor 'ought not' has any application to an action which the agent could not help doing. If he says: 'Though I need not have done *x*, yet I could not

[1] Reprinted from *Determinism, Indeterminism, and Libertarianism*, Cambridge: the University Press, 1934, by courtesy of the publishers.

possibly have done *y*', he assumes that his critic will admit that neither 'ought' nor 'ought not' has any application to an action which the agent could not have done. It is as if one person should say that *x* is black and *y* is white, and the other should answer that at least one of them is unextended and therefore incapable of being either black or white.

Obligability Entails Substitutability

Now we are concerned here only with the second kind of answer. The essential point to notice is that it is universally admitted to be a *relevant* answer. We all admit that there is some sense or other of 'could' in which 'ought' and 'ought not' entail 'could'. We will now try to get clear about the connexion between these two notions.

Judgements of obligation about past actions may be divided into two classes, viz. (1) judgements about actions which were actually done, and (2) judgements about conceivable actions which were not done. Each divides into two sub-classes, and so we get the following fourfold division. (1. 1) 'You did *x*, and *x* was the action that you ought to have done'. (1.2) 'You did *x*, and *x* was an action that you ought not to have done'. (2.1) 'You did not do *x*, and *x* was the action that you ought to have done'. And (2.2) 'You did not do *x*, and *x* was an action that you ought not to have done.' Now both judgements of the first class entail that you could have helped doing the action which you in fact did. If the action that you did can be said to be one that you ought to have done, or if it can be said to be one that you ought not to have done, it must be one that you *need not* have done. And, since you actually did it, it is obviously one that you *could have* done. Both judgements of the second class entail that you could have done an action which you did not in fact do. If a conceivable action which you did not do can be said to be one which you ought to have done, or if it can be said to be one that you ought not to have done, it must be one that you *could have* done. And, since you actually failed to do it, it is obviously one that you *need not* have done.

It is worth while to notice that the common phrases: 'You

ought to have done so and so' and 'You ought not to have done so and so' are generally equivalent to our judgements (2.1) and (1.2) respectively. The former is generally used to mean: 'You did not do so and so, and that was an action which you ought to have done'. The latter is generally used to mean: 'You did so and so, and that was an action which you ought not to have done'. But we often need to express what is expressed by our judgements (1.1) and (2.2). We often want to say that a person did what he ought on a certain occasion, and we often want to say that a person avoided doing something which he ought not to have done on a certain occassion. For this is exactly the state of affairs which exists when a person has in fact done an unpleasant duty in face of a strong temptation to shirk it by lying.

Now the importance of this connection between 'ought' and 'ought not', on the one hand, and 'could', on the other, is very great. People constantly make judgements of obligation of the four kinds which we have distinguished, and such judgements have constantly been made throughout the whole course of human history. Every single one of these judgements has been false unless there have been cases in which actions which *were* done could have been left undone and actions which *were not* done could have been done. And these judgements would all have been false in principle, and not merely in detail. They would have been false, not in the sense that they asserted 'ought' where they should have asserted 'ought not', or *vice versa*. They would be false in the sense that nothing in the world has ever had that determinable characteristic of which 'ought to be done' and 'ought not to be done' are the determinate specifications. They would be false in the sense in which all judgements which predicted redness, blueness, etc., of any object would be false in a world which contained no objects except minds and noises.

It will be convenient to call an action 'obligable' if and only if it is an action of which 'ought to be done' or 'ought not to be done' can be predicated. It will be convenient to call an action 'substitutable' if, either it was done but could have been left undone, or it was left undone but could have been done. We may then sum up the situation by saying that an action is obligable if and only if it is, in a certain sense, substitutable; that, unless all judgements of obligations are false in principle, there are obligable actions; and therefore, unless all judgements of obligation are false in principle, there are actions which are, in this sense, substitutable.

Various Senses of 'Substitutable'

This is one aspect of the case. The other aspect is the following. There are several senses of 'could' in which nearly everyone would admit that some actions which were done could have been left undone, and some actions which were left undone could have been done. There are thus several senses of 'substitutable' in which it would commonly be admitted that some actions are substitutable. But, although an action which was *not* substitutable in these senses would *not* be obligable, it seems doubtful whether an action which was substitutable *only* in these senses *would be* obligable. It seems doubtful whether an action would be obligable unless it were substitutable in some further sense.

At this stage two difficulties arise. (i) It is exteremely difficult to grasp and express clearly this further sense of 'substitutable', i.e. this further sense of 'could' in which an action that was done could have been left undone or an action which was not done could have been done. Many people would say that they can attach no meaning to 'substitutable' except those meanings in which it is insufficient to make an action obligable. (ii) Even if this other meaning of 'substitutable' can be grasped and clearly expressed, many people would say that no action is substitutable in this sense. They would claim to see that no action which has been done could have been left undone, and that no action which was not done could have been done, in that sense of 'could' which is required if an action is to be obligable.

Now anyone who holds these views is in a very awkward position. On the one hand, it is not easy to believe that every judgment of obligation is false, in the sense in which every judgment ascribing colour to an object would be false in a world containing only minds and noises. On the other hand, it is highly depressing to have to admit that there is a sense of 'could' which you can neither grasp nor clearly express. And it is equally unsatisfactory to have to believe that some actions *are* substitutable in a sense in which it seems to you self-evident that no action *could be* substitutable.

There are two problems to be tackled at this point. (i) To try to discover and state the sense of 'substitutable' in which being substitutable is the necessary and sufficient condition of being obligable. And (ii), if we can do this, to consider whether any action could be substitutable in this sense.

Voluntary Substitutablilty

Let us begin by considering an action which has actually been performed. In some cases we should say that the agent 'could not have helped' performing it. We should certainly say this if we had reason to believe that the very same act would have been performed by the agent in these circumstances even though he had willed that it should not take place. It is obvious that there are actions which are 'inevitable', in this sense, since there are actions which take place although the agent is trying his hardest to prevent them. Compare e.g. the case of a conspirator taken with an uncontrollable fit of sneezing.

Next consider a conceivable action which was not in fact performed. In some cases we should say that the agent 'could not possibly' have performed it. We should certainly say this if the act would not have taken place in these circumstances no matter how strongly the agent had willed it. It is obvious that there are conceivable acts which are 'impossible' in this sense, since there are cases where such an act fails to take place although the agent is trying his hardest to bring it about. Compare e.g. the case of a man who is bound and gagged, and tries vainly to give warning to a friend.

We will call acts of these two kinds 'not voluntarily substitutable'. It is plain that an act which is not voluntarily substitutable is not obligable. No one would say that the conspirator ought not to have sneezed, or that the bound and gagged man ought to have warned his friend. At most we may be able to say that they ought or ought not to have done certain things in the past which are relevant to their present situation. Perhaps the conspirator ought to have sprayed his nose with cocaine before hiding behind the presumably dusty arras, and perhaps the victim ought not to have let himself be lured into the house in which he was gagged and bound. But these are previous questions.

We see then that to be voluntarily substitutable is a *necessary* condition for an action to be obligable. But is it a *sufficient* condition? Suppose I performed the action *a* on a certain occasion. Suppose that I should not have done *a* then if I had willed with a certain degree of force and persistence not to do it. Since I did *a*, it is certain that I *did not* will with this degree of force and persistence to avoid doing it. Now suppose that at the time I *could not* have willed with this degree of force and persistence to avoid doing *a*. Should we be prepared to say that I ought not to have done *a*?

Now take another case. Suppose that on a certain occasion I failed to do a certain conceivable action *b*. Suppose that I should have done *b* if I had willed with a certain degree of force and persistence to do it. Since I did not do *b*, it is certain that I *did not* will with this degree of force and persistence to do it. Now suppose that at the time I *could not* have willed with this degree of force and persistence to do *b*. Should we be prepared to say that I ought to have done *b*?. It seems to me almost certain that, under the supposed conditions, we should not be prepared to say either that I ought not to have done *a* or that I ought to have done *b*.

Consider e.g. the case of a man who gradually becomes addicted to some drug like morphine, and eventually becomes a slave to it. At the early stages we should probably hold that he could have willed with enough force and persistence to ensure that the temptation would be resisted. At the latest stages we should probably hold that he could not have done so. Now at every stage, from the earliest to the latest, the hypothetical proposition would be true: 'If he had willed with a certain degree of force and persistence to avoid taking morphine, he would have avoided taking it'. Yet we should say at the earlier stages that he ought to have resisted, whilst, at the final stages, we should be inclined to say 'ought' and 'ought not' have ceased to apply.

Primary and Secondary Substitutablity

An action which was in fact done, but would not have been done if there had been a strong and persistent enough desire in the agent not to do it, will be called 'primarily avoidable'. Suppose, in addition, there could have been in the agent at the time a desire of sufficient strength and persistence to prevent the action being done. The the action might be called 'secondarily avoidable'. If this latter condition is not fufilled, we shall say that the action was 'primarily avoidable, but secondarily inevitable'. Similarly, an action which was not in fact done, but would have been done if there had been in the agent a strong and persistent enough desire to do it, will be called 'primarily possible'. Suppose, in addition, that there could have been in the agent at the time a desire of sufficient strength and persistence to ensure the action being done. Then the action may be called 'secondarily possible'. If this latter condition is not fulfilled, we shall say that the action is 'primarily possible, but secondarily impossible'. An action will be called 'primarily substitutable' if it is either primarily avoidable or primarily possible. It will be secondarily substitutable if it is either secondarily avoidable or secondarily possible. In order that an action may be obligable it is not enough that it should be primarily substitutable, it must be at least secondarily substitutable.

We are thus led on from the notion of voluntarily substitutable *actions* to that of substitutable *volitions*. Suppose that, on a certain occasion and in a certain situation, a certain agent willed a certain alternative with a certain degree of force and persistence. We may say that the volition was substitutable if the same agent, on the same occasion and in the same circumstances, could instead have willed a different alternative or could have willed the same alternative with a different degree of force and persistence. Now there is one sense of 'could' in which it might plausibly suggest that many volitions are substitutable. It seems very likely that there are many ocassions on which I *should* have willed otherwise than I did, *if* on previous occasions I had willed otherwise than I did. So it seems likely that many volitions have been voluntarily substitutable.

It is necessary to be careful at this point, or we may be inadvertently granting more than we are really prepared to admit. Obviously it is often true that, if I had willed otherwise than I did on certain earlier occasions, I should never have got into the position in which I afterwards made a certain decision. If e.g. Julius Caesar had decided earlier in his career not to accept the command in Gaul, he would never have been in the situation in which he decided to cross the Rubicon. This, however, does not make his decision to cross the Rubicon substitutable. For a volition is substitutable only if a different volition could have occurred in the agent in the *same* situation. Again, it is often true that, if I had willed otherwise than I did on certain earlier occasions, my state of knowledge and belief would have been different on certain later occasions from what it in fact was. In that case I should have thought, on these later occasions, of certain alternatives which I did not and could not think of in my actual state of knowledge and belief. Suppose e.g. that a lawyer has to decide what to do when a friend has met with an accident. If this man had decided years before to study medicine instead of law, it is quite likely that he would now think of, and perhaps choose, an alternative which his lack of medical knowledge prevents him from contemplating. This, however, does not make the lawyer's volition in the actual situation substitutable. For, although the external part of the total situation might have been the same whether he had previously decided to study medicine or to study law, the internal part of the total situation would have been different if he had decided to study medicine, instead of deciding, as he did, to study law. He would have become an agent with different cognitive powers and dispositions from those which he in fact has. No one would think of saying that the lawyer ought to have done a certain action, which he did not and could not not contemplate, merely because he would have contemplated it and would have decided to do it if he had decided years before to become a doctor instead of becoming a lawyer.

Having cleared these irrelevances away, we can now come to the real point. A man's present conative-emotional dispositions, and what we may call his 'power of intense and persistent willing', are in part dependent on his earlier volitions. If a person has repeatedly chosen the easier of the alternatives open to him, it becomes increasingly difficult for him to choose and to persist in pusuing the harder of the two alternatives. If he has formed a habit of turning his attention away from certain kinds of fact, it will become increasingly difficult for him to attend fairly to alternatives which involve facts of these kinds. This is one aspect of the case. Another, and equally important, aspect is the following. If a man reflects on his own past decisions, he may see that he has a tendency to ignore or to dwell upon certain kinds of fact, and that this had led him to make unfair or unwise decisions on many occasions. He may decide that, in future, he will make a special effort to give due, and not more than due, weight to those considerations which he has a tendency to ignore or to dwell upon. And this decision may make a difference to his future decisions. On the other hand, he may see that certain alternatives have a specially strong attraction for him, and he may find that, if he pays more than a fleeting attention to them, he will be rushed into choosing them, and will afterwards regret it. He may decide that, in future, he will think as little as possible about such alternatives. And this decision may make a profound difference to his future decisions.

We can now state the position in general terms. Suppose that, if the agent had willed differently on earlier occasions, his conative-emotional dispositions and his knowledge of his own nature would have been so modified that he would now have willed differently in the actual external situation and in his actual state of knowledge and belief about the alternatives open to him. Then we can say that his actual volition in the present situation was 'voluntarily avoidable', and that a volition of a different kind or of a different degree of force and persistence was 'volutarily possible'. An action which took place was secondarily avoidable if the following two conditions are fulfilled. (i) That this action would not have been done if the agent had willed with a certain degree of force and persistence to avoid it. (ii) That, if he had willed differently in the past, his conative-emotional dispositions and his knowledge of his own nature would have been such, at the time when he did the action, that he would have willed to avoid it with enough force and persistence to prevent him doing it. In a precisely similar way we could define the statement that a certain conceivable action, which was not done, was secondarily possible. And we can thus define the statement that an action is secondarily substitutable.

Can we say that an action is obligable if it is secondarily substitutable, in the sense just defined, though it is not obligable if it is only primarily substitutable? It seems to me that the same difficulty which we noticed before reappears here. Suppose that the agent could not have willed otherwise than he did in the remoter past. It is surely irrevelant to say that, *if* he had done so, his conative dispositions *would* have been different at a later stage from what they in fact were then, and that he *would* have willed otherwise than he then did. One might, of course, try to deal with this situation by referring back to still earlier volitions. One might talk of actions which are not only primarily, or only secondarily, but are tertiarily substitutable. But it is quite clear that this is useless. If neither primary nor secondary substitutability, in the sense defined, suffice to make an action obligable, no higher order of substitutability, in this sense, will suffice. The further moves are of exactly the same nature as the second move. And so, if the second move does not get us out of the difficulty, none of the further moves will do so.

Categorical Substitutability

The kind of substitutability which we have so far considered may be called 'conditional substitutability'. For at every stage we have defined 'could' to mean 'would have been, if certain conditions had been fulfilled which were not'. Now I have concluded that merely conditional substitutability, of however high an order, is not a sufficient condition for obligablity. If an action is to be obligable, it must be *categorically* substitutable. We must be able to say of an action, which was done, that it could have been avoided, in some sense of 'could' which is not definable in terms of 'would have, if'. And we must be able to say of a conceivable action, which was not done, that it could have been done, in some sense of 'could' which is not definable in terms of 'would have, if'. Unless there are some actions of which such things can be truly said, there are no actions which are obligable. We must therefore consider whether any clear meaning can be attached to the phrase 'categorically substitutable', i.e. whether 'could' has any clear meaning except 'would have, if'. And, if we can find such a meaning, we must enquire whether any actions are categorically substitutable.

Various Senses of 'Obligable'

Before tackling these questions I must point out that the words 'ought' and 'ought not' are used in several different senses. In some of these senses obligability does not entail categorical substitutability.

(i) There is a sense of 'ought' in which we apply it even to inanimate objects. It would be quite proper to say: 'A car ought to be able to get from London to Cambridge in less than three hours', or: 'A fountain-pen ought not to be constantly making blots'. We mean by this simply that a car which did take more than three hours would be a poor specimen of a car, or would be in a bad state of repair. And similar remarks apply to the statement about the fountain-pen. We are comparing the behaviour of a certain car or fountain-pen with the average standard of achievement of cars or fountain-pens. We are not suggesting that *this* car or *this* pen, in its present state of repair, unconditionally could go faster or avoid making blots. Sometimes when we make such judgements we are comparing an individual's achievements, not with those of the *average* member, but with those of an *ideally perfect* member, of a certain class to which it belongs. We will call 'ought', in this sense, 'the comparative ought'. And we can then distinguish 'the average-comparitive ought' and 'the ideal comparative ought'.

(ii) Plainly 'ought' and 'ought not' can be, and often are, used in this sense of human actions. But, in the case of human actions, there is a further development. Since a human being has the power of cognition, in general, and of reflexive cognition, in particular, he can have an idea of an average or an ideal man. He can compare his own achievements with those of the average, or the ideal, man, as conceived by him. And he will have a more or less strong and persistent desire to approximate to the ideal and not to fall below the average. Now it is part of the notion of an ideal man that he is a being who would have a high ideal of human nature and would desire strongly and persistently to approximate to his ideal. Obviously it is no part of the notion of an ideal horse or an ideal car that it is a being which would have a high ideal of horses or cars and a strong and persistent desire to live up to this. When we say that a man ought not to cheat at cards we often mean to assert two things. (*a*) That the average decent man does not do this, and that anyone who does falls in this respect below the average. And (*b*) that a man who does this either has a very low ideal of human nature or a very weak and unstable desire to approximate to the ideal which he has. So that, in this further respect, he falls below the average.

Now neither of these judgements implies that a particular person, who cheated on a particular occasion, categorically could have avoided cheating then; or that he categorically could have had a higher ideal of human nature; or that he categorically could have willed more strongly and persistently to live up to the ideal which he had. For an action to be obligable, in this sense, it is plain enough that it should be secondarily substitutable, in the sense already defined.

The Categorical Ought

Some philosophers of great eminence, e.g. Spinoza, have held that the sense of 'ought' which I have just discussed is the only sense of it. Plainly it is a very important sense, and it is one in which 'ought' and 'ought not' can be applied only to the actions of intelligent beings with power of reflexive cognition, emotion, and conation. I think that a clear-headed Determinist should hold either that this is the only sense; or that, if there is another sense, in which obligability entails *categorical* substitutability, it has no application.

Most people, however, would say that, although we often do use 'ought' and 'ought not' in this sense, we quite often use them in another sense, and that in this other sense they entail categorical substitutability. I am inclined to think that this is true. When I judge that I ought not to have done something which I in fact did, I do not as a a rule seem to be judging merely that a person with higher ideals, or with a stronger and more persistent desire to live up to his ideals, would not have done what I did. Even when this is part of what I mean, there seems to be something more implied in my judgement, viz. that I *could* have had higher ideals or *could* have willed more strongly and persistently to live up to my ideals, where 'could' does not mean just 'would have, if'. Let us call this sense of 'ought' the 'categorical ought'. It seems to me then that we must distinguish between an action being obligable in the comparative sense and being obligable in the categorical sense; and that, if any action were categorically obligable, it would have to be categorically substitutable.

Analysis of Categorical Substitutability

We can now proceed to discuss the notion of categorical substitutability. It seems to me to involve a negative and a positive condition. I think that the negative condition can be clearly formulated, and that there is no insuperable difficulty in admitting that it may sometimes be fulfilled. The ultimate difficulty is to give any intelligible account of the positive condition. I will now explain and illustrate these statements.

Suppose that, on on a certain occasion, I willed a certain alternative with a certain degree of force and persistence, and that, in consequence of this volition, I did a certain voluntary action which I should not have done unless I had willed this alternative with this degree of intensity and persistence. To say that I categorically could have avoided doing this action implies at least that the following negative condition is fulfilled. It implies that the process of my willing this alternative with this degree of force and persistence was not completely determined by the nomic, the occurrent, the dispositional, and the background conditions which existed immediately before and during this process of willing. In order to see exactly what this means it will be best to contrast it with a case in which we believe that a process is completely determined by such conditions.

Suppose that two billiard-balls are moving on a table, that they collide at a certain moment, and that they go on moving in modified directions with modified velocities in consequence of the impact. Let us take as universal premises the general laws of motion and of elastic impact. We will call these 'nomic premises'. Let us take as singular premises the following propositions. (i) That each ball was moving in such and such a direction and with such and such a velocity at the moment of impact. We will call this an 'occurrent premise'. (ii) That the masses and coefficients of elasticity of the balls were such and such. We will call this a 'dispositional premise'. (iii) That the table was smooth and level before, and after the moment of impact. We will call this a 'background premise'. Lastly, let us take the proposition that the balls are moving, directly after the impact, in such and such directions with such and such velocities. Then this last proposition is a *logical consequence* of the conjunction of the nomic, the occurrent, the dispositional, and the background premises. That is to say, the combination of these premises with the denial of the last proposition would be *logically inconsistent*. It is so in exactly the same sense in which the combination of the premises of a valid syllogism with the denial of its conclusion would be so.

The Negative Condition

We can now work towards a definition of the statement that a certain event *e* was completely determined in respect of a certain characteristic. When we have defined this statement it will be easy to define the statement that a certain event was not completely determined in respect of a certain characteristic. I will begin with a concrete example, and will then generalize the result into a definition.

Suppose that a certain flash happened at a certain place and date. This will be a manifestation of a certain determinable characteristic, viz. colour, in a certain perfectly determinate form. It may, e.g. be a red flash of a certain perfectly determinate shade, intensity, and saturation. We may call shade, intensity, and saturation the three 'dimensions' of colour, and we shall therefore symbolize the determinable characteristic colour by a three-suffix symbol C_{123}. When we want to symbolize a certain perfectly determinate value of this we shall use the symbol C_{123}^{abc}. This means that the shade has the determinate value a, that the intensity has the determinate value b, and that the saturation has the determinate value c. Each *index* indicates the determinate value which the dimension indicated by the corresponding *suffix* has in the given instance.

Now the statement that this flash was completely determined in respect of colour has the following meaning. It means that there is a set of true nomic, occurrent, dispositional, and background propositions which together entail the proposition that a manifestation of colour, of the precise shade, intensity, and saturation which this flash is manifested, would happen at the place and time at which this flash happened. To say that this flash was *not* completely determined in respect of colour means that a there is *no* set of true nomic, occurrent, dispositional, and background propositions which together entail the proposition that a manifestation of colour, of the precise shade, intensity, and saturation which this flash manifested, would happen at the place and time at which this flash happened.

There are two remarks to be made at this point. (i) It seems to me that the second statement is perfectly *intelligible*, even if no such statement be ever true. (ii) It is a purely *ontological* statement, and not in any way a statement about the limitations of of our knowledge. Either there is such a set of true propositions, or there is not. There may be such a set, even if no one knows that there is; and there may be no such set, even if everyone believes that there is.

We can now give a general definition. The statement that a certain event e was completely determined in respect of a certain determinable characteristic C_{123} is equivalent to the conjunction of the following two propositions. (i) The event *e* was a manifestation of C_{123} in a certain perfectly determinate form C_{123}^{abc} at a certain place and date. (ii) There is a set of true nomic, occurrent, dispositional, and background propositions which together entail that a manifestation of C_{123} in the form C_{123}^{abc} would happen at the place and date at which *e* happened. The statement that *e* was *not* completely determined in respect of C_{123} is equivalent to the conjoint assertion of (i) and denial of (ii).

The next point to notice is that an event might be partly determined and partly undetermined in respect of a certain characteristic. As before, I will begin with a concrete example. Our flash might be completely determined in respect of shade and saturation, but not in respect of intensity. This would be equivalent to the conjunction of the following two statements. (i) That there is a set of true propositions, of the kind already mentioned, which together entail that a flash, of precisely the shade and saturation which this flash had, would happen at the place and date at which this flash happened. (ii) There is no such set of true propositions which together entail that a flash, of precisely the insity which this flash had, would happen at the time and place at which this flash happened. We thus get the notion of 'orders of indetermination' in respect of a given characteristic. If an event is undetermined in respect of one and only one dimension of a certain determinable characteristic, we say that it has 'indetermination of the first order' in respect of this characteristic. If it is undetermined in respect of two and only two dimensions of a certain determinable characteristic, we say that it has 'indetermination of the second order' in respect of this characteristic. And so on.

It is obvious that there is another possibility to be considered, which I will call 'range of indetermination in respect of a given dimension of a given characteristic'. Suppose that our flash is undetermined in respect of the intensity of its colour. There may be a set of true propositions, of the kind mentioned, which together entail that a flash, whose intensity falls within certain limits, would happen at the time and place at which this flash happened. This range of indetermination may be wide or narrow. Complete determination in respect of a given dimension of a given chracteristic is the limiting case where the range of indetermination shuts up to zero about the actual value of this dimension for this event. Thus the 'extent of indetermination' of an event with respect to a given characteristic depends in general upon two factors, viz. (i) its order of indetermination with respect to the dimensions of this characteristic, and (ii) its range of indetermination with respect to those dimensions for which it is not completely determined.

We can now define the statement that a certain event *e* was completely determined. It means that *e* has zero range of indetermination for every dimension of every determinable characteristic of which it is a manifestation. The statement that a certain event *e* was *not* completely determined can now be defined. It means that *e* had a finite range of indetermination for at least one dimension of at least one of the characteristics of which it was a manifestation.

And now at last we can define 'Determinism' and 'Indeterminism'. Determinism is the doctrine that *every* event is completely determined, in the sense just defined. Indeterminism, is the doctrine that some, and it may be all, events are not completely determined, in the sense defined. Both doctrines are, *prima facie*, intelligible, when defined as I have defined them.

There is one other point to be noticed. An event might be completely determined, and yet it might have a 'causal ancestor' which was not completely determined. If y is the total cause of z ,and x is the total cause of y, I call both y and x 'causal ancestors' of z. Similarly, if w were the total cause of x, I should call y, x, and w 'causal ancestors' of z. And so on. If at any stage in such a series there is a term, e.g. w, which contains a cause-factor that is not completely determined, the series will stop there, just as the series of human ancestors stops with Adam. Such a term may be called the 'causal progenitor' of such a series. If Deteriminsm be true, every event has causal ancestors, and therefore there are no causal progenitors. If Indeterminism be true, there are causal progenitors in the history of the world.

We can now state the negative condition which must be fulfilled if an action is to be categorically substitutable. Suppose that, at a certain time, an agent deliberated between two alternatives, *a* and *b*, and that he actually did *a* and not *b*. Suppose that the following conditions are fufilled. (i) The doing of *a* by this agent at this moment was completely determined. (ii) The total cause of *a* being done contained as cause-factors a desire of a certain strength and persistence for *a* and a desire of a certain strength and persistence for *b*. (iii) These two desires were not completely determined in respect of strength and persistence. (iv) The range of indetermination was wide enough to include in it, as possible values, so strong and persistent a desire for *b* or so weak and fleeting a desire for *a* as would have determined the doing of *b* instead of the doing of *a*. Conditions (iii) and (iv) are the negative conditions which must be fulfilled if *b* is to be categorically substitutable for *a*. They amount to the following statement. It is consistent with (*a*) the laws of nature, including those of pyschology, (*b*) the facts about the agent's dispositions and the dispositions of any other agent in the world at the moment of acting, (*c*) the facts about what was happening within and without the agent at that moment, and (*d*) the facts about the general background conditions at that moment, that the strength and persistence of the desires mentioned in (ii) should have any value that falls within the range mentioned in (iv).

Before we go further there is one point to be mentioned. Strictly speaking, what I have just stated are the negative conditions for *primary* categorical substitutability. For I have supposed the incomplete determination to occur at the *first* stage backwards, viz. in one of the cause-factors in the total cause of the action *a*. It would be quite easy to define, in a similar way, the negative conditions for secondary, or tertiary, or any other order of categorical substitutability. All that is needed is that, at *some* stage in the causal ancestry of *a*, there shall be a total cause which contains as factors desires of the agent answering to the conditions which I have stated. That is to say, all that is necessary is that *a* shall have a causal ancestor which is a causal progenitor, containing as a factor an incompletely determined desire of the agent's.

We come now to the final question. Supposing that this negative condition were fulfilled, would this *suffice* to make an action categorically obligable? It seems to me plain that it would not. Unless some further and positive condition were fulfilled, all that one could say would be the following: 'The desire to do *a* happened to be present in me with such strength and persistence, as compared with the desire to do *b*, that I did *a* and avoided *b*. The desire to do *b* might have happened to be present in me with such strength and persistence, as compared with the desire to do *a*, that I should have done *b* and avoided *a*'. Now,if this is all, the fact that I did *a* and not *b* is, in the strictest sense, an *accident*, lucky or unlucky as the case may be. It may be welcomed or it may be deplored, but neither I nor anything else in the universe can properly be praised or blamed for it. It begins to look as if the categorical ought may be inapplicable, though for different reasons, both on the hypothesis that voluntary actions have causal progenitors and on the hypothesis that none of their causal ancestors are causal progenitors.

The Positive Condition

Let us now try to discover the positive conditions of categorical obligability. I think that we should naturally tend to answer the sort of objection which I have just raised in the following way. We should say: 'I deliberately identified myself with my desire to do *a*, or I deliberately threw my weight on the side of that desire. I might instead have made no particular effort in one direction or the other; or I might have identified myself with, and thrown my weight on the side of, my desire to do *b*. So my desire to do *a* did not just happen to be present with the requisite strength and persisistence, as compared with my desire to do *b*. It had this degree of strength and persistence because, and only because, I *reinforced* it by deliberate effort, which I need not have made at all and which I could have made in favour of my desire to do *b*.' Another way of expressing the same thing would be this: 'I forced myself to do *a*; but I need not have done so, and, if I had not done so, I should have done *b*.' Or again: 'I might have forced myself to do *b*; but I did not, and so I did *a*.'

It is quite plain that these phrases express a genuine positive experience with which we are all perfectly familiar. They are all, of course, metaphorical. It will be noticed that they all attempt to describe the generic fact by metaphors drawn from specific instances of it, e.g. deliberately pressing down one scale of a balance, deliberately joining one side in a tug-of-war, deliberately thrusting a body in a certain direction against obstacles, and so on. In this respect they may be compared with attempts to describe the generic facts about time and change by metaphors drawn from specific instances, such as flowing streams, moving spots of light, and so on. The only use of such metaphors is to direct attention to the sort of fact which one wants one's hearer's to contemplate. They give no help towards analysing or comprehending this fact. A metaphor helps us to understand a fact only when it brings out an analogy with a fact of a *different* kind, which we already understand. When a generic fact can be described only by metaphors drawn from specific instances of itself it is a sign that the fact is unique and peculiar, like the fact of temporal succession and the change of events from futurity, through presentness, to pastness.

Granted that there is this unique and peculiar factor of deliberate effort of reinforcement, how far does the recognition of it help us in our present problem? So far as I can see, it merely takes the problem one step further back. My doing of *a* is completely determined by a total cause which contains as factors my desire to do *a* and my desire to do *b*, each of which has a certain determinate strength and persistence. The preponderance of my desire to do *a* over my desire to do *b*, in respect of strength and persistence, is completely determined by a total cause which contains as a factor my putting forth a certain amount of effort to reinforce my desire for *a*. This effort-factor is not completely determined. It is logically consistent with all the nomic, occurrent, dispositional, and background facts that no effort should have been made, or that it should have been directed towards reinforcing the desire for *b* instead of the desire for *a*, or that it should have been put forth more strongly than it actually was in favour of the desire for *a*. Surely then we can say no more than that it just happened to occur with a certain degree of intensity in favour of the desire for *a*.

I think that the safest course at this stage for those who maintain that some actions are categorically obligable would be the following. They should admit quite frankly what I have just stated, and should then say: 'However paradoxical it may seem, we do regard ourselves and other people as morally responsible for accidents of this unique kind, and we do not regard them as morally responsible, in the categorical sense, for anything but such accidents and those consequences of them which would have been different if the accidents had happened differently. Only such accidents, and their causal descendants in the way of volition and action, are categorically obligable'. If anyone should take up this position, I should not know how to refute him, though I should be strongly inclined to think him mistaken.

This is not, however, the position which persons who hold that some actions are categorically obligable generally do take at this point. I do not find that they ever state quite clearly what they think they believe, and I suspect that is because, if it were clearly stated, it would be seen to be impossible. I shall therefore try to state clearly what I think such people want to believe, and shall try to show that it is impossible. I suspect that they would quarrel with my statement that, on their view, the fact that one puts forth such and such an effort in support of a certain desire is, in the strictest sense, an accident. They would like to say that the putting forth of a certain amount of effort in a ceratin direction at a certain time *is* completely determined, but is determined in a unique and peculiar way. It is literally determined *by the agent or self*, considered as a substance or continuant, and not by a total cause which contains as factors *events in* and *dispositions of* the agent. If this could be maintained, our puttings-forth of effort would be completely determined, but their causes would neither be events nor contain events as cause-factors. Certain series of events would then originate from causal progenitors which are continuants and not events. Since the first event in such a series would be completely determined, it would not be an accident. And, since the total cause of such an event would not be an event and would not contain an event as a cause-factor, the two alternatives 'completely determined' and 'partially undetermined' would both be inapplicable to it. For these alternatives apply only to events.

I am fairly sure that this is the kind of propositon which people who profess to believe in Free Will want to believe. I have, of course, stated it with a regrettable crudity, of which they would be incapable. Now it seems to me clear that such a view is impossible. The putting-forth of an effort of a certain intensity, in a certain direction, at a certain moment, for a certain duration, is quite clearly an event or process, however unique and peculiar it may be in other respects. It is therefore subject to any conditions which self-evidently apply to every event, as such. Now it is surely quite evident that, if the beginning of a certain process at a certain time is determined at all, its total cause *must* contain as an essential factor another event or process which *enters into* the moment from which the determined event or process *issues*. I see no *prima facie* objection to there being events that are not completely determined. But, in so far as an event *is* determined, an essential factor in its total cause must be other *events*. How could an event possibly be determined to happen at a certain date if its total cause contained no factor to which the notion of date has any application? And how can the notion of date have any application to anything that is not an event?

Of course I am well aware that we constantly use phrases, describing causal transactions, in which a continuant is named as the cause and no event in that continuant is mentioned. Thus we say: 'The stone broke the window', 'The cat killed the mouse', and so on. But it is quite evident that all such phrases are elliptical. The first, e.g., expresses what would be more fully expressed by the sentence: 'The coming in contact of the moving stone with the window at a certain moment caused a process of disintegration to begin in the window at that moment'. Thus the fact that we use and understand such phrases casts no doubt on the general principle which I have just enunciated.

Let us call the kind of causation which I have just described and rejected 'non-occurrent causation of events'. We will call the ordinary kind of causation, which I had in mind when I defined 'Determinism' and 'Indeterminism', 'occurrent causation'.

Now I think we can plausibly suggest what may have made some people think they believe that puttings-forth of effort are events which are determined by non-occurrent causation. It is quite usual to say that a man's putting-forth of effort in a certain direction on a certain occasion was determined by 'Reason' or 'Principle' or 'Conscience' or 'The Moral Law'. Now these impressive names and phrases certainly do not denote events or even substances. If they denote anything, they stand for propositions or systems of propositions, or for those peculiar universals or systems of universals which Plato called 'Ideas'. If it were literally true that puttings-forth of effort are determined by such entities, we should have causation of events in time by timeless causes. But, of course, statements like 'Smith's putting-forth of effort in a certain direction on a certain occasion was determined by the Moral Law' cannot be taken literally. The Moral Law, as such, has no causal efficacy. What is meant is that Smith's *belief* that a certain alternative would be in accordance with the Moral Law, and his *desire* to do what is right, were cause-factors in the total cause which determined his putting forth of effort on the side of that alternative. Now this belief was an event, which happened when he began to reflect on the alternatives and to consider them in the light of the moral principles which he accepts and regards as relevant. And this desire was an event, which happened when his conative-emotional moral dispositions were stirred by the process of reflecting on the alternatives. Thus the use of phrases about action being 'determined by Moral Law' may have made some people think they believe that some events are determined by non-occurrent causation. But our analysis of the meaning of such phrases shows that the facts which they express give no logical support to this belief.

Libertarianism

We are now in position to define what I will call 'Libertarianism'. This doctrine may be summed up in two propositions. (i) Some (and it may be all) voluntary actions have a causal ancestor which contains as a cause-factor the putting-forth of an effort which is not completely determined in direction and intensity by occurrent causation. (ii) In such cases the direction and the intensity of the effort are completely determined by non-occurrent causation, in which the self or agent, taken as a substance or continuant, is the non-occurrent total cause. Thus, Libertarianism, as defined by me, entails Indeterminism, as defined by me; but the converse does not hold.

If I am right, Libertarianism is self-evidently impossible, whilst Indeterminism is *prima facie* possible. Hence, if categorical obligability entails Libertarianism, it is certain that no action can be categorically obligable. But if categorical obligability entails only Indeterminism, it is *prima facie* possible that some actions are categorically obligable. Unfortunately, it seems almost certain that categorical obligability entails more than Indeterminism, and it seems very likely that it entails Libertarianism. It is therefore highly probable that the notion of categorical obligability is a delusive notion, which neither has nor can have any application.

V

IS 'GOODNESS' A NAME OF A SIMPLE NON-NATURAL QUALITY? (1934)[1]

As is well-known, Professor Moore in his *Principia Ethica* claimed to show that an affirmative answer must be given to the question which forms the title of this paper. There has been a great deal of discussion on the subject during the thirty-one years which have elapsed since the publication of *Principia Ethica*, and it seemed to me that it might be worth while to review the question on the light of our present knowledge and beliefs.

(1) *Statement of Moore's Theory*

I shall begin by stating in my own way what I understand to have been Moore's theory at the time when he wrote *Principia Ethica*. The theory may be summed up in the following six propositions: (i) When we use a sentence like: 'That experience is good', we are often, if not always, expressing a judgement in which we ascribe a certain characteristic to the experience. So the word 'good' is often, if not always, used *as a name of a characteristic*. (ii) The word 'good' is, of course, highly ambiguous. In some of its senses it undoubtedly stands for complex characteristics which can be analysed. When used in any of these senses the word can be defined. In these senses some other word or phrase, such as 'benefic' or 'contributively good' or 'instrumentally efficient', can be substituted for 'good' without loss or gain of meaning. (iii) There is, however, another sense of the word, which is presupposed in some or all of these definable senses of it. This we will call the 'primary sense'. In this sense 'good' stands for a characteristic which is *simple and therefore analysable*.

[1] Reprinted from the *Proceedings of the Aristotelian Society*, Volume XXXIV, 1933-34, by courtesy of the Editor of the Aristotelian Society.

Consequently the word 'good', in this primary sense, cannot be defined. (iv) It follows at once that the characteristic for which it stands cannot be a *relational property*, i.e. a characteristic of the form: 'Having the relation R to so-and-so'. For, obviously, all relational properties are complex, and are analysable into a relation and term. (v) The characteristic is a pure *quality* and not a pure relation. (vi) The characteristic is of a peculiar kind, which Moore calls *non-natural*'.

I think that these are the essential points of the theory. They are not all separately stated by Moore, but those which are not stated are clearly implied.

(2) *Discussion of the Theory*

I will now take the six points in my statement of the theory in order, and consider the arguments for and against them.

(2.1) *Is 'Goodness' a Name of a Characteristic?* Moore always assumes that 'good' is used as a name of some characteristic or other in sentences like: 'This experience is good'. He evidently thought that this would be admitted by everyone, and that the only question is about the nature of this characteristic or these characteristics.

Now it has been pointed out by Mr Duncan Jones that it is not safe to let this assumption pass without question. Certainly the sentence: 'This is good' is of the same grammatical form as many sentences which undoubtedly do state that a certain thing has a certain characteristic. It is, e.g., of the same form as: 'This is square', and there is no doubt that anyone who utters the latter sentence is intending to convey the belief that a certain particular has a certain characteristic of which 'square' is a name.

But we must remember that a sentence, which is grammatically in the indicative mood, may really be in part interjectional or rhetorical or imperative. It may be in part the expression of an emotion which the speaker is feeling. In that case to utter the sentence 'That is good' on a certain occasion might be equivalent to uttering a purely non-ethical sentence in the indicative, followed by a certain interjection. It might, e.g., be equivalent to saying: 'That's an act of self-sacrifice. Hurrah!'. Similarly, to utter the sentence 'That is bad' on a certain occasion might be equivalent to saying: 'That's a deliberately misleading statement. Blast!'. Again, a sentence may be used to evoke a certain kind of emotion in the hearer. In that case to utter the sentence 'That is good' might be equivalent to uttering a purely non-ethical sentence in the indicative in a pleasant tone and with a smile. To utter the sentence 'That is bad' might be equivalent to shouting a purely non-ethical indicative sentence at the hearer with a frown. Here the use of ethical words 'good' and 'bad' is merely a stimulus to produce certain emotions in the hearer, as smiling at him or shouting at him might do. In this case the sentence might be called 'rhetorical'. Lastly, such sentences may be used to command or to forbid certain actions in the hearer. To utter the sentence 'That is good' might be equivalent to uttering a purely non-ethical indicative sentence followed by a sentence in the imperative. It might e.g., be equivalent on a certain occasion to: 'That's an act of self-sacrifice. Imitate it!'. To utter the sentence: 'That is bad' on a certain occasion might be equivalent to saying: 'That's a deliberately misleading statement. Don't do that again!'.

On this view, words like 'good' and 'bad' do not *mean* anything in the sense in which words like 'white' and 'square' do. There are no characteristics of which they are names. A person who utters sentences in which they occur as grammatical predicates is not using them to convey the belief that a certain subject has a certain peculiar characteristic of which the grammatical predicate is a name. And a person who hears such sentences and understands them is being exhorted or commanded or emotionally stimulated, but is not receiving any special kind of information about the subject of the sentence. If this be so, Professor Moore's theory breaks down at the first move, and so too do the theories of most of his opponents.

Mr Duncan Jones points out that his theory fits in with two very important facts: (i) It explains why all attempts to define ethical words in purely non-ethical terms seem unsatisfactory. Suppose you substitute a sentence containing only non-ethical words for one that contains an ethical word. Then the interjectional, rhetorical, or imperative force which the original sentence derived from the ethical word in it, has vanished. You feel that something is missing, and you are quite right. Suppose you have never doubted that ethical words are names of characteristics. Then you will explain this feeling of 'something missing' by saying that the proposed analysis of an ethical characteristic into purely non-ethical characteristics has missed out some essential logical constituent of the ethical characteristic. (ii) Attempts to define one ethical word, e.g. 'good' partly in terms of another ethical word, e.g. 'right', do not always seem unsatisfactory. It is not, e.g., obviously inadequate to define 'a good experience' as 'an experience which can rightly be desired'. Nor, on the other hand, is it obviously inadequate to define 'right conduct' as 'conduct which is conducive to good consequences.' Now the theory can explain this fact too. Both the original sentence and the proposed equivalent now contain ethical words. Both have therefore interjectional, rhetorical and imperative force. Now it is possible that two different sentences, both of which have this kind of force, may produce precisely similar effects, as evokers of emotion or as commands, in all people of a certain community who may hear them. Suppose you have never doubted that ethical words are names of characteristics. Then you will think that the more complex of two such sentences states the analysis of the ethical characteristic which is named by the ethical word in the simpler of the two sentences. And so you will think that some ethical characteristics can be analysed in terms of other ethical characteristics and of non-ethical characteristics.

I think that this theory may be further supported by reflecting on how we learn ethical words as children. I suspect that, for a small child, 'good' and 'right' acts are practically co-extensive with those which its mother or nurse names in a certain tone and with a smile or which she exhorts it to do. And 'bad' or 'wrong' acts are practically co-extensive with those which its mother or nurse names in a certain other tone and with a frown or which she forbids it to do. Very soon the ethical words aquire the same rhetorical or imperative force as the tone of voice or the facial expression or the explicit command or forbidding. It may be noted that many words are 'amphibious' in character, i.e. partly non-ethical and partly ethical. Compare, e.g., the two sentences: 'That is a statement made with the intention of producing a false belief', and 'That is a lie'. The first is in purely non-ethical terms. The second has for its grammatical predicate the amphibious word 'lie' which is partly non-ethical and partly ethical. Now it is quite certain that the second sentence does commonly express or stimulate an emotion which the first does not. And it is plausible to hold that this is the *only* difference between the first, which is purely non-ethical, and the second, which is partly ethical.

It seems to me then that Mr Duncan Jones's theory is quite plausible enough to deserve very serious consideration. It would have to be refuted before we could be sure that the question: 'Are the characteristics denoted by ethical names analysable or unanalysable?' is a sensible question. If this theory were correct the question would be like asking whether unicorns are or are not cloven-hoofed.

Henceforth, we will suppose, for the sake of argument, that words like 'good' and 'bad' are names of characteristics. We may agree that when 'good' is used in the sense of 'benefic' or of 'contributively good', it stands for a characteristic which is complex. And we will assume that, when 'good' in these senses is defined, the definition always involves the word 'good' in another sense, which may be called the *primary* one.

(2.2) *Is the Characteristic which 'Good' Denotes Analysable?* The next question is this: 'Assuming that the word 'good', in the primary sense, is a name of a characteristic, is there any reason to believe that this characteristic is unanalysable?'. It seems to me quite clear that there is no means of *proving*, with regard to any characteristic, that it is unanalysable. At most we might be able to show that no analysis so far proposed is satisfactory; and even this is not always so easy as one might think, for the question involves some very fundamental and difficult logical points which I will now try to state.

Suppose a person raises the question whether the characteristic of which a certain word *n* is a name is simple or complex, and whether, if it is complex, a certain proposed analysis of it is correct or not. Plainly, in *some* sense of the phrase, he must 'know what the word *n* means'. For, otherwise, he does not know what he is asking his question about. Equally plainly this cannot be the same as 'knowing the analysis, if any, of the characteristic which *n* stands for'. If he knew this in knowing what the word *n* means, the question whether the characteristic is simple or complex, and what is its correct analysis, if it is complex, could never arise for him. So the question presupposes at least the following three propositions: (i) That there is a certain one characteristic which the person who asks the question is thinking of whenever he uses the word *n* in certain kinds of context. (ii) That, whether this characteristic be in fact simple or in fact complex, he can think of it without *ipso facto* knowing that it is simple or knowing that it is complex. (iii) If it be in fact complex, he can think of it without *ipso facto* knowing its correct analysis. In practice a further assumption is, I think, always made. It is assumed (iv) that all or most other people who speak the language of the questioner correctly are thinking of the same characteristic as he is thinking of whenever they use the word *n* in the same kinds of context.

Now it might be extremly difficult to justify assumptions (i) and (iv) in many cases. Can I be sure that there is any *one* characteristic of which I am thinking whenever I use the word 'good' in the primary sense? May there not be, as Mr Braithwaite has suggested, a whole lot of characteristics, such that I am sometimes thinking of one and sometimes of another of them when I use the word 'good' in the primary sense? Again, can I be sure that, when other people use the word 'good' in certain contexts they are always or generally thinking of the characteristic which I am thinking of when I use the word in such contexts? The only evidence that can be produced is consistency or inconsistency of usage. Do I sometimes call certain things 'good' and at other times call precisely similar things 'bad' or 'indifferent'? Do other people agree among themselves and with me in the things that they call 'good' and in the things that they call 'bad', and in the things that they call 'indifferent'? If there is great inconsistency in applying the words 'good' and 'bad', there is at least a presumption that conditions (i) and (iv) are not fulfilled. Now there certainly is a considerable amount of inconsistency.

We will suppose, however, that this difficulty can be overcome, and that we can satisfy ourselves that conditions (i) and (iv) are fulfilled. We will now concentrate our attention on conditions (ii) and (iii). There are several grave logical difficulties which I could raise at this point; but I propose to waive them and to pass straight to the following question: 'Supposing that you can think of a certain characteristic *c* without *ipso facto* knowing whether it is simple or complex, and without *ipso facto* knowing its correct analysis if it be complex, how are you to set about answering the question whether it is simple or complex? And, if it is complex, how are you to decide whether a certain proposed analysis of it is right or wrong?'.

Suppose it is suggested that the characteristic is analysable into the characteristics *c*1, *c*2 and *c*3. Then (*a*) we can reject this suggestion at once if we can think of anything which has *c* and lacks either *c*1 or *c*2 or *c*3. And we can reject it at once if we can think of anything which has *c*1 and *c*2 and *c*3 and lacks *c*. (*b*) Suppose that, after applying this test, we are left with one or more suggested analyses of *c*. We can next proceed as follows. Granted that I know of nothing which has *c* and lacks any of the characteristics *c*1, *c*2 and *c*3, and that I know of nothing which has *c*1, *c*2 and *c*3 and lacks *c*, can I conceive that there *might be* such a thing? If I can, I can reject the proposed analysis of *c* into *c*1, *c*2 and *c*3. For a characteristic and its analysis would be *necessarily* co-extensive. The equivalence of their extensions would not be just a contingent fact, like the fact that chewing the cud and having cloven hoofs are co-extensive. (*c*) Suppose that we are left with one or more suggested analyses of *c* which pass this test and can be seen to be *necessarily* co-extensive with *c*. There might be several such. The property of being circular, e.g., is necessarily co-extensive with an enormous number of other complicated sets of characteristics. For there are enormous numbers of complicated properties which we can prove *must* belong to all circles and *cannot* belong to anything but circles. So we are finally faced with the following question: 'If we know of only one set of characteristics which is necessarily co-extensive with *c*, how can we tell whether this set is or is not an analysis of *c*? And, if we know of several such sets of characteristics, how can we tell which, if any, of them is the *analysis* of *c*, and which of them are necessarily and reciprocally but *synthetically* connected with *c*?'. Suppose, e.g., that it seemed evident that anything that was good would necessarily be a fitting object of desire, and that anything which was a fitting object of desire would necessarily be good. How could we tell whether being a fitting object of desire is the *analysis* of being good, or whether it is just a complex characteristic which is necessarily and reciprocally but *synthetically* connected with goodness?

It seems to me that, at this stage, further argument would be impossible. All that an objector can say is: 'I feel that your proposed analysis of goodness misses out something which I have in mind when I use the word *good*'. Or, 'I can't believe that when I use the word *good* I am thinking of anything so complicated as I should be thinking of if your proposed analysis of goodness were correct'. Now suppose that another person does not feel that the suggested analysis misses out anything that *he* has in mind when *he* uses the word 'good'. And suppose that he thinks that what he has in mind when he uses the word 'good' may easily be as complicated as it would be if the suggested analysis were correct. We are assuming that the parties have somehow persuaded themselves that they are both thinking of the same characteristic whenever either of them uses the word 'good' in similar contexts. What further argument is possible between them?

The actual situation is not, however, quite like this. I think it is true to say that all reasonably simple analyses of goodness in purely non-ethical terms seem to most people to miss out something. (Cf., e.g., 'to be good' means 'to be generally desired as an end'). And all analyses of goodness in purely non-ethical terms, which avoid this defect, seem to most people to be too complex to be correct analyses of what they have in mind. (Cf., e.g., 'to be good' means 'to be something which a man would approve of himself or another for desiring'.) It is only certain definitions which are partly in ethical and partly in non-ethical terms that might seem to many people to avoid both defects. (Cf., e.g., 'to be good' means 'to be a fitting object of desire'.) Now how much weight ought to be attached to a fairly *general* feeling that suggested analyses of goodness in purely non-ethical terms either miss out something which we have in mind or are too complex to be correct analyses of what we have in mind?

I think that we commonly make the following assumptions without ever stating them clearly. It is assumed that, if I have thought of a certain characteristic *c* often enough to have associated a name with it, then any proposed analysis of it which is felt by me to be either inadequate or unduly complex is very probably incorrect. It would be admitted that a proposed analysis might *in fact* be incorrect even though I *did not* feel it to be inadequate or unduly complex. But it would be held that, if I *do* feel it to have either of these defects, then it probably *is* defective. And, if most people who have frequently thought of a certain characteristic agree in feeling that a proposed analysis of it is inadequate or unduly complex, it would be held to be practically certain that the proposed analysis is defective.

Now, as regards this general principle, there are two things to be said: (i) I am not much impressed with the importance of a widespread feeling that a proposed analysis is unduly complex. We are assuming, it must be remembered, that a person can think of a characteristic without *ipso facto* knowing its analysis if it has one. Now it seems difficult to suppose that one can estimate the *degree* of internal complexity of a characteristic when one does not know whether it is simple or complex, and does not know its analysis if it has one. (ii) More weight should, I think, be attached to a widespread feeling that a proposed analysis is inadequate. This fact has to be accounted for somehow. The most obvious explanation is that the analysis really does omit some logical constituent of the characteristic, or that it analyses, not *this* characteristic, but some other which is allied to it. Unfortunately this is just the place where Mr Duncan Jones's suggestion becomes highly relevant. It may be that the explanation is simply that the name of the original characteristic has acquired a certain interjectional, rhetorical or emotional force which is lacking in the phrase that expresses the analysis. We feel the lack of this, and we conclude that the analysis is inadequate.

(2.3) *Can Goodness be a Relational Property?* The fourth point in my statement of Professor Moore's theory was that, if the characteristic denoted by 'good' be simple, it cannot be a relational property. It must be either a pure quality or a pure relation. This is quite obvious; but, in order to show that goodness *is* either a quality or a relation, it would be necessary to add the premise that the characteristic denoted by 'good' *is simple.* I have tried to show that this has not been proved, and that there is no conceivable way of proving it. The utmost that has been shown is that all analyses *in purely non-ethical terms*, which have so far been suggested, seem to most people to be either inadequate or unduly complex. For reasons which I have given, I do not think that this proves conclusively that none of these proposed analyses is correct; and, even if they all were incorrect, it would would still be possible that there might be a correct analysis in purely non-ethical terms which no one happens to have suggested. Again, it would still be possible that there might be a correct analysis, partly in ethical and partly in non-ethical terms. There is not even a presumption against this, since certain proposed analyses of this kind do not seem to most people to be obviously inadequate or obviously too complex. It seems to me then that no good reason has been produced for holding that the characteristic denoted by 'good', in the primary sense, cannot be a relational property.

(2.4) *Can Goodness be a Pure Relation?* The fifth point in the statement was that 'good', in the primary sense, is not the name of a relation, and must, therefore, be the name of a quality. I think it is obvious that 'good' is not the name of a relation. If it denotes a characteristic at all, the characteristic which it denotes is either a quality or a relational property. So, if one could show that it denotes a simple characteristic, we could admit at once that it denotes a simple quality. The only remark that I wish to make at this point is the following. It does seem to me conceivable that the relation denoted by 'better than' might be more fundamental than the characteristic denoted by 'good'. It might be that the former is simple and unanalysable, and that the latter is complex and definable in terms of the former. The suggestion would be that 'good' is always an abbreviation for 'good of its kind', and that 'good of its kind' means 'better than the average member of its proximate species'. This would make 'good' a name of a relational property of a peculiar kind, in which the relation is that denoted by 'better than'. If it could be shown that 'good', in the primary sense, does not denote a relational property at all, this suggestion could be dismissed at once. But I suspect that some people, who think they have proved this, have not considered the possiblity that 'good' might denote a relational property in which the relation is that denoted by 'better than'. Perhaps they would not be so sure that 'good' might not denote a relational property of this peculiar kind, even though they were convinced that it could not denote a relational property in which *any other* was involved.

(2.5) *Is Goodness a Non-natural Characteristic?* The last point in Professor Moore's theory is that 'good', in the primary sense, is a name of a 'non-natural' characteristic. Two questions at once arise: (i) What exactly is meant by the distinction between a 'natural' and a 'non-natural' characteristic? (ii) What connection if any, is there between the doctrine that 'good', in the primary sense, denotes a characteristic which is simple and unanalysable, and the doctrine that it denotes a characteristic which is non-natural? We will take these two questions in turn.

(i) We will begin with complex characteristics. A complex characteristic is natural if it can be analysed into a set of simple characteristics every one of which is natural. A complex characteristic is non-natural if its analysis involves at least one simple characteristic which is non-natural. Thus the question at once arises: 'What is meant by calling a simple characteristic *natural* or *non-natural*?'.

Unfortunately we shall get very little light on this question from Professor Moore's published works. The only place, so far as I know, in which it is explicitly discussed is *Principia Ethica*, pp. 40 to 41. We are there told that a 'natural object' is any object that is capable of existing in time, e.g. a stone, a mind, an explosion, an experience, etc. All natural objects have natural characteristics, and some natural objects also have non-natural characteristics. We are told that each natural characteristic of a natural object could be conceived as existing in time all by itself, and that every natural object is a whole whose parts are its natural characteristics. We are told that a non-natural characteristic of a natural object is one which *cannot* be conceived as existing in time all by itself. It can be conceived as existing only as the property of some natural object. Now it seems to me that *every* characteristic of a natural object answers Professor Moore's criterion of non-naturalness, and that no characteristic could possibly be natural in his sense. I do not believe for a moment that a penny is a whole of which brownness and roundness are parts, nor do I believe that the brownness or the roundness of a penny could each exist in time all by itself. Hence I should have to count brownness, roundness, pleasantness, etc., as *non-natural* characteristics if I accepted Profesoor Moore's account of the distinction. Yet he certainly counts them as *natural* characteristics.

I think that Professor Moore is intending to explain the distinction between natural and non-natural characteristics in the very difficult essay entitled *The Conception of Intrinsic Value*, in his *Philosophical Studies*. So far as I can understand his doctrine in that essay, it may be summarized as follows: (*a*) The characteristics of any thing *T* may be first divided into two great classes, viz., those which do, and those which do not, 'depend solely on the *intrinsic nature* of *T*'. (*b*) Characteristics of a thing *T* which depend solely on its intrinsic nature may be sub-divided into those which are, and those which are not, 'intrinsic characteristics' of it. Consider, e.g., an experience which has a certain perfectly determinate kind and degree of pleasantness. Suppose that it also has a certain perfectly determinate kind and degree of goodness. Then, if I understand him aright, Moore would say that both its pleasantness and its goodness are characteristics which depend solely on its intrinsic nature. He would say that its pleasantness is an intrinsic characteristic of it. And he would say that its goodness is not an intrinsic characteristic of it. (*c*) Although he does not explicitly say so, I think that he would identify the non-natural characteristics of a thing with those which *are* determined solely by its intrinsic nature and yet *are not* intrinsic. The natural characteristics of a thing would be those which are either intrinsic or are not determined solely by its intrinsic nature.

Unhappily Moore gives no clear account of this distinction between the intrinsic and the non-intrinsic characteristics which depend on the intrinsic nature of a thing. All that he says is this. A complete enumeration of the intrinsic characteristics of a thing would constitute a *complete* description of it. A description of a thing can be complete even if it does not include characteristics of it which, though determined solely by its intrinsic nature, are not intrinsic characteristics. E.g. a pleasant experience, which is also good, could not be completely described if its pleasantness were not mentioned. But it could be *completely* described without its goodness being mentioned.

I find it most difficult to follow or to accept this. I am inclined to think that the fact which Moore has in mind is that goodness, in the primary sense, is always dependent on the presence of certain non-ethical characteristics, which I should call 'good-making'. If an experience is good, this is never an ultimate fact. It is always reasonable to ask: 'What *makes* it good?'. And the sort of answer that we should expect to get would be: 'Its pleasantness', or: 'The fact that it is a sorrowfully toned awareness of another's distress', or something of that kind. We might, therefore, distinguish the characteristics of a thing into two classes, viz. *ultimate* and *derivative*; and goodness will certainly fall into the class of derivative characteristics. Now there is a sense in which one might say that a thing could not be completely described if any of its ultimate characteristics were omitted, but that it could be completely described without mentioning any of its derivative characteristics. In describing a circle, e.g., it is not necessary to mention any of the innumerable properties which follow of necessity from its definition together with the axioms of Euclidean geometry.

But, although this analogy may throw some light on what Professor Moore had in mind, it certainly does not help us to understand what is meant by saying that goodness is a non-natural characteristic and that pleasantness, e.g., is a natural characteristic. For it is surely quite as evident that pleasantness and unpleasantness are derivative characteristics as that goodness and badness, in the primary sense, are so. If an experience is pleasant, it is always reasonable to ask: 'What *makes* it pleasant?'. And the sort of answer that we should expect is: 'Its sweetness' or: 'The way in which various sounds are combined in it', or something of that kind. So, if pleasantness is to be counted as a natural characteristic, it is impossible to identify the non-natural characteristics of a thing with the derivative subclass of those of its characteristics which depend solely on its intrinsic nature.

It seems impossible, then, to extract from Professor Moore's writings any satisfactory account of his distinction between 'natural' and 'non-natural' characteristics. And yet we all recognize fairly well what he is talking about when he makes this distinction. I suggest that the best plan is to start with an *epistemological* description of the term 'natural characteristic'. I propose to describe a 'natural' characteristic as any characteristic which either (*a*) we become aware of by sensing sensa which manifest it or by introspecting experiences which manifest it; or (*b*) is definable wholly in terms of such characteristics and the notions of cause and substance. I think that this covers every characteristic which would be universally admitted to be natural. It would cover, e.g., yellowness, both in the sense in which it is ascribed to sensa and in the sense in which it is ascribed to physical things. It would also cover pleasantness, fearfulness, intelligence, etc. And it would leave the question whether goodness is a natural or a non-natural characteristic open to discussion. We will therefore take this as our description of a 'natural characteristic' for the rest of the argument.

(ii) We are now in a position to deal with our second question.

What connection, if any, is there between the doctrine that 'good', in the primary sense, denotes a characteristic which is simple, and the doctrine that it denotes a characteristic which is non-natural?

It is plain that our epistemological description at once plunges us into questions about how we become aware of the characteristic called 'goodness', assuming that there is such a characteristic. (*a*) It seems to me quite obvious that it is not manifested to us by any of our senses, as, e.g., yellowness, sweetness, squeakiness, etc., are. It is evident that, when 'good' is used in its primary sense, it does not denote a characteristic of which we could become aware by sight or touch or taste or smell or hearing, or any other sense which we have or conceivably might have. It is doubtful whether goodness, in this sense, can belong to the sort of objects that can be sensed or perceived. And, even if it can and does, it is certain that we do not perceive with our senses the goodness of such objects. At most we perceive with our senses certain natural characteristics which are good-making, e.g., certain combinations of colour, of sound, of taste, etc.

(*b*) It seems equally clear that no simple characteristic which we can discover by introspecting our experiences can be identified with goodness. We become aware through introspection of experiences which are pleasant or unpleasant, toned with desire or aversion, and so on. We thus become aware of the psychological characteristics of pleasantness, longingness, etc., and their opposites. Now it is true that goodness, in the primary sense, *can* belong to experiences. Indeed, some people would hold that, in this sense, it can belong to nothing else. Yet I think that a moment's reflection will convince one that by calling an experience 'good' we do not *mean* that it is pleasant or approving, or that it has any of the other simple psychological qualities of which we become aware through introspecting our experiences. If anyone is tempted to identify goodness with one of these simple psychological qualities, I think that he does so through a confusion. What he really believes is that there is one and only one good-*making* quality of an experience, e.g. pleasantness. He then fails to notice the distinction between *goodness itself* and the one and only good-making quality and so he thinks he believes that 'good' and 'pleasant', e.g., are just two names for a single characteristic. And, since pleasantness certainly is a natural characteristic, he will think he believes that 'good' is the name of a natural characteristic. I do not think that the belief that one means the same by 'good' and 'pleasant', e.g., would survive for a moment after the distinction between goodness itself and a good-making characteristic had been pointed out to one. And similar remarks would apply to any other simple psychological characteristic denoted by 'good'.

We come, therefore, to the following hypothetical conclusion. *If* the word 'good', when used in its primary sense, denotes a simple quality, then that quality is almost certainly *not* one which we become aware of either by sensing sensa which manifest it or by introspecting experiences which manifest it. It is, therefore, not a natural characteristic, as described by us. So, with our description of 'natural characteristics', there *is* an important logical connection between proving that 'good' is the name of a *simple quality* and proving that it is the name of a *non-natural* characteristic.

This, however, does not settle the question whether 'good' is the name of a non-natural charateristic. For I do not think that it has been proved or could be proved, that 'good' is the name of a simple quality. Indeed, I am now going to argue that there are considerable epistemological difficulties in holding that 'good' is the name of a simple quality. Is there any way of becomimg aware of a simple quality belonging to particulars, *except* by sensing or introspecting particulars which manifest this characteristic to one? Many people would say that there plainly is no other way. If they are right, it follows that we could not possibly have an intuitive idea of goodness if goodness were a non-natural characteristic. For, if goodness were a *simple* non-natural characteristic, the consequence would follow at once; and, if it were a complex characteristic which contains one or more non-natural characteristics in its analysis, the consequence would follow at the second move. We could not have an intuitive idea of such a complex characteristic unless we had such ideas of its simple non-natural components; and, if the epistemological principle be accepted, we could not have intuitive ideas of these components.

Now, although this epistemological principle does seem to me highly plausible, I am not prepared to accept it (or any other epistemological principle) as self-evident. I am therefore not prepared to conclude that no characteristic of which I can have an intuitive idea could be non-natural. But I do think it important to point out the following hypothetical fact. *If* goodness is a non-natural characteristic, then anyone's intuitive idea of this characteristic must be an *a priori* notion, or must contain *a priori* notions as elements. For an *a priori* notion just is an intuitive idea of a characteristic which is not manifested in sensation or introspection and is not definable wholly in terms of such characteristics. Anyone who holds that goodness is a non-natural characteristic and that he has an intuitive idea of it is therefore committed to the view that there are *a priori* notions and that his notion of goodness is one of them. Now anyone who holds that goodness is a simple characteristic will be almost compelled to hold that it is non-natural. Therefore anyone who holds that goodness is a simple characteristic and that he has an intuitive idea of it will be almost compelled to hold that there are *a priori* notions and that his notion of goodness is one them.

There is one other epistemological point to be noticed. Suppose that a person regards goodness as a non-natural characteristic, and admits that it is always dependent on the presence of certain natural characteristics which are good-making. Then, if he holds that the connection between a good-making characteristic and the goodness which it confers is *necessary*, he will be obliged to hold that there are *synthetically necessary* facts and that he knows some of them. He will therefore be obliged to admit that he can make *synthetically a priori* judgments. The necessary connection between those natural characteristics of a thing which are good-making and the goodness which their presence necessarily confers on the thing cannot be analytic.

For this would involve that the *non-natural* characteristic of goodness is contained as a factor in the analysis of a purely *natural* good-making characteristic, and this would be self-contradictory.

Now people think it self-evident that all necessary connection must be analytic and that there can be no synthetic *a priori* judgments. I do not find this principle in the least self-evident myself; but it is worth while to point out that anyone who does so will be compelled to hold either (*a*) that goodness is a natural characteristic, or (*b*) that the connection between the goodness of a thing and its good-making characteristics is purely contingent and is known only empirically. He might, of course, combine both views, as Hume did.[1]

[1] *Editor's Note:* The criticisms proffered in this essay are futher developed in Selection 14 of this volume ('G. E. Moore's Latest Published Views on Ethics'), pp. 324-350.

VI

OUGHT WE TO FIGHT FOR OUR COUNTRY IN THE NEXT WAR? (1936)[1]

The question before us is of the general form: 'What ought such and such people (e.g. males of military age) to do under such and such circumstances (e.g. when their country is involved in a war)?'. I shall first point out the general conditions which govern all attempts to answer such questions.

Any argument on the subject will have to use premises of two utterly different kinds, viz. *purely factual* and *ethical*. An ethical proposition is one which involves the notion of good or bad, right or wrong, ought or ought not. A purely factual proposition is one which involves no such notions. That deliberate homicide is wrong is an ethical proposition, true or false. It is a purely factual proposition that, if a man is shot through the heart, he will almost certainly be dead very soon afterwards.

Now the purely factual premises are of two kinds, viz. (i) Statements of alleged particular facts about the past or the present. These may be called *instantial premises*. And (ii) statements of alleged general laws or tendencies. These may be called *nomic premises*. An example of the first kind is the proposition that Japan has spent such and such a proportion of her revenue on her navy for the past ten years. An example of the second is the proposition, true or false, that an increase of armaments tends to produce a war. Now everyone admits that what a person ought or ought not to do at a given moment depends *either* on his present state and circumstances and his past history *or* on the probable consequences of the various alternative actions open to him at the time; and most people believe that it depends to some extent on *both*. In order to conjecture the probable consequences of various alternative actions which might be done in a given

[1] Reprinted from the *Hibbert Journal*, Volume XXXIV, April 1936, by courtesy of the Trustees of the Hibbert Trust.

situation it is always necessary to use both kinds of factual premise. Therefore everyone would admit that factual premises of the instantial kind are needed, and the vast majority of people would admit that factual premises of the nomic kind are also needed, if we are to have any rational argument about such questions as we are asking.

But it is equally certain that ethical premises are also needed in any argument about an ethical question. Now ethical propositions are of two kinds, which I will call *pure* and *mixed*. It is always difficult to be sure that a given ethical proposition is pure, but it is easy to give examples of ethical propositions which are certainly mixed. Suppose I assert that a classical education is a good thing. I mean (*a*) that it is likely to produce in those subjected to it certain experiences and dispositions, which could be described in purely psychological and non-ethical terms; and (*b*) that such experiences and dispositions are good. The first of these two constituents of the original proposition is a purely factual statement of the nomic kind. The second is an ethical proposition. Whether it is *purely* ethical is another question. But, at any rate, the original proposition is certainly a mixed ethical one, and its ethical component is certainly a nearer approximation to a purely ethical one. When mixed ethical propositions are used as premises in ethical arguments they are always liable to lead to mistakes and misunderstandings. If we are to avoid these, it is essential that we should split up such propositions, so far as we can, into their purely ethical and their purely factual components. For two disputants who agree about one of the components may differ about the other; and, if they fail to recognize and distinguish the two, they are bound to be at cross-purposes and to produce crooked answers.

There is another important division of ethical propositions which cuts across the division into pure and mixed. Ethical propositions are of three kinds, which may be expressed respectively by sentences of the three forms:

'You *ought* (or ought not) to do so-and-so in such and such circumstances';

'Such and such an action would be *right* (or wrong) in such and such circumstances'; and

'Such and such an experience or state of affairs would be *good* (or bad.)'.

For the present purpose I shall group the first two together under the name of *judgments of obligation*. I shall call the third kind *judgments of value*. Now this brings us to a fundamental difference of opinion which it is essential to notice if we are to have any intelligent discussion on such questions as we have before us.

Some people hold that there is one and only one *ultimate* obligation, and that this involves an essential reference to *value*. According to them the one ultimate obligation is to secure the increase and to prevent the decrease of the present amount of good, and to secure the dimunition and check the increase of the present amount of evil. All other obligations, such as the duty to keep one's promises or to obey the laws of one's country, are derivative from this one. They are obligations if and only if they are, in the actual circumstances, the most efficient way of fulfilling the one ultimate obligation to conserve and increase good and to check or diminish evil. Otherwise they are wrong. I shall call this the *teleological theory of obligation*.

This theory can, of course, take many different forms. I shall not attempt to distinguish more than two of them, which I will call the *universalistic form* and the *restricted form*. According to the universalistic form of the theory a person has no special obligation to produce good and diminish evil in one person or community rather than in another. Suppose you have two alternative courses of action open to you. By one of them you will improve the condition of your own countrymen, and by the other you will improve the conditions in another country instead. Then it is your duty, on this view, to avoid the former action and to do the the latter, provided that the improvement which you will effect in the foreign country is in the least degree greater than that which you would effect in your own country.

According to the *restricted* form of the teleological theory your ultimate obligation still is to conserve and increase good and to check and diminish evil. But you have a stronger obligation to increase the good and diminish the evil in certain persons and communities, to which you stand in certain special relations, than you have towards other persons and communities to which you do not stand in these relations. On either form of the theory the one and only ultimate obligation is that of *beneficence*. On the universalistic form of it there is only the general obligation to be as beneficent as you can in the circumstances in which you are placed. On the restricted form of it the appropriate strength and direction of the obligation of beneficence is in part determined by the special regulations in which the agent stands to certain individuals, institutions, and communities.

Now many people would reject the teleological theory of obligation. They would hold that there are *many* ultimate obligations, and that they do not all involve an essential reference to value. They admit that I am under a general obligation to be beneficent to human beings as such; and they assert that I am also under more special and stringent obligations to be beneficent to my parents, my benefactors, my fellow-countrymen, and so on. But they say that there are many other obligations which are not reducible to beneficence at all, whether general or special. E.g. if a person asks me a question to which I know the answer, the mere fact that I am in this state and that he and I are in this situation gives him a claim on me to receive a *true* answer. On this view there is an obligation of truth-speaking which is not reducible to any obligation of beneficence and which may conflict with one's general or special obligations of beneficence. And there may be other obligations, e.g. an obligation to obey the laws of one's country, which may conflict with the obligation of truth-speaking and with the special and general obligations of beneficence. I propose to call this theory the *pluralistic theory of obligation*.

On the pluralistic theory a person who is called upon to act in one way or another, or to abstain from action, in a given situation many be subject to many different and conflicting claims or obligations of varying strength, arising out of various factors in his past history and various relations in which he stands to various persons, institutions, and communities. Whichever alternative he chooses he will fufill some of these component obligations, and in doing so he will necessarily break others which conflict with the former. In such cases the right action is the one which makes the best compromise between several conflicting claims, when due weight is given to their number and their relative urgency. But no general principles can be suggested for deciding what is the best compromise.

Now I cannot attempt here to decide between the universalistic form of the teleological theory, the restricted form of it, and the pluralist theory. I will content myself with two remarks about them. (i) *Prima facie* the pluralistic theory is in accord with common sense, and the universalistic form of the teleological theory is flagrantly at variance with common sense. And, if we reject the universalistic form of the teleological theory, it seems doubtful whether we can consistently rest in the restricted form of it. It looks as if the restricted form were an unstable compromise between the pluralistic theory and the universalistic form of the teleological theory. (ii) However this may be, it is essential to be clear in one's own mind as to which theory one is going to assume before one can argue intelligently about the question at issue. Facts which might prove conclusively, on the universalistic form of the teleological theory, that a man ought not to fight for his country might lead to no such consequence if one held that a citizen is under a special obligation of beneficence to his own nation. And their force would be still further diminished if one held that a man is under a strong direct obligation to obey the laws of his country, good or bad, simply because he is a citizen of it.

It remains to say something about the other kind of ethical propositions, viz. judgments of value. Here again there is a profound difference of opinion on a fundamental question. Some people hold that there is one and only one kind of subject of which the adjectives 'intrinsically good' and 'intrinsically evil' can properly be predicated, viz. experiences. And they hold further that there is one and only one characteristic of experiences which makes them good or evil. I will call this the *monistic theory of value.* It might conceivably take many different forms, according to what characteristic of experiences was held to be the one and only good-making or bad-making characteristic. But in practice, I think, nearly everyone who holds the monistic theory of value assumes that the one and only good-making or bad-making characteristic of experiences is their hedonic quality in its two opposed forms of pleasantness and unpleasantness. So, for the present purpose, we may identify the monistic theory of value with the *hedonistic theory of value.*

On this theory, whenever we call a community or an institution or a person or a disposition or an action 'good' or 'bad' we are making a mixed ethical statement. Suppose, e.g., that we call a certain person 'good'. We mean simply and solely to assert the two following propositions. (*a*) That his nature is such that he tends in most circumstances to have, or to produce in others, experiences which are predominantly pleasant. And (*b*) that such experiences are, for that reason and to that extent, good.

Now many people would unhesitatingly reject the hedonistic theory of value in whole or part. Some would hold that persons can be good or evil in the same ultimate sense in which experiences can be. Some would go further, and would hold that this is true also of certain collective wholes, composed of intimately interrelated persons, e.g. nations. Again, even those who hold that nothing but experiences can be intrinsically good or evil may hold that there are other good-making and bad-making characteristics of experiences beside their pleasantness and their unpleasantness. Anyone who holds any of these views may be said to accept the *pluralistic theory of value.*

Once again I shall not attempt to decide between the rival theories. I will content myself with the following remarks. (i) *Prima facie* the hedonistic theory is flagrantly at variance with common sense. The common sense view is *prima facie* that persons, at any rate, can be intrinsically good or evil as well as experiences, and that there are many characteristics beside pleasantness and unpleasantness which make experiences intrinsically good or bad. (ii) If a pluralistic theory of value is admitted, a person who accepts the teleological theory of obligation is faced at the second move with the same kind of problem as faces an adherent of the pluralistic theory of obligation at the first move. He will not, indeed, have to try to find the best compromise between a number of ultimate and conflictng obligations of various degrees of urgency. But he will have to aim at producing the best compromise between a number of ultimate kinds of value and disvalue. He may, e.g., have to weigh the net value of a state of heroic self-sacrifice accompanied by misery and intellectual stupidity against that of a state of clear-sighted and cool selfishness accompanied by comfort. And no general principle can be offered for conducting the comparison. The only person who can avoid such difficulties is one who combines the universalistic form of the teleological theory of obligation with the hedonistic theory of value. And both the elements in this combination seem *prima facie* far too simple to be true. (iii) Whatever may be the truth about these rival theories of value, this at least is certain. It is essential to be clear in one's own mind as to which theory one is going to assume before one can argue intelligently about the question at issue. Facts which might prove conclusively, on the hedonistic theory of value, that a man ought not to fight for his country might lead to no such consequence if it were held that heroic self-sacrifice gives value to the persons who practise it just as pleasantness gives value to pleasant experiences. And their force might be still further diminished if it were held that a nation is a persistent collective entity of a peculiar kind, with a characteristic value or disvalue of its own which is determined by the actions and dispositions of its citizens.

This completes what I have to say about the general conditions which govern all rational discussion about such questions as we have before us. I will summarize them as follows. (i) The factual and the ethical premises must be clearly distinguished; any mixed ethical premises must be analysed into their purely factual and their purely ethical components; and the instantial and the nomic factual premises must be separately stated. (ii) The theory of obligation which is being assumed by any disputant must be explicitly stated. We must know whether he assumes the pluralistic theory or the teleological theory. And, if he assumes the latter, we must know whether he assumes the universalistic or the restricted form of it. (iii) The theory of value which is being assumed by any disputant must be explicitly stated. We must know whether he assumes the hedonistic theory or the pluralist theory. And, if he assumes the latter, we must know whether he holds that only experiences can have intrinsic value or disvalue, or that only experiences and persons can have it, or that experiences and persons and societies can have it. Unless these conditions are fulfilled, there can be no rational *argument;* there can only be emotional hot air emitted in argumentative form.

When these conditions have been fulfilled I do not believe that there is much room for argument on such questions except on the purely factual side. We may be able to alter a man's opinions about the probable consequences of fighting or refusing to fight when his country is involved in war, by showing him particular facts which he had overlooked, or by convincing him, from empirical evidence, of laws or tendencies which he had not suspected. But there are no arguments by which we can alter his opinions as to what circumstances do and what do not impose obligations on him, or as to the kinds of thing which can have intrinsic value or disvalue, or as to the characteristics which do and those which do not confer intrinsic value or disvalue on the things which possess them. If he is a pluralist about obligation, we cannot by argument alter his opinions about the relative urgency of the various conflicting obligations which he believes to be incumbent upon him. If he is a pluralist about value, we cannot by argument alter his opinions as to the various degrees of goodness or badness conferred by the various characteristics which he believes to be good-making or bad-making. We can clear up confusions and indicate possible sources of prejudice; but, when we have done this, we have done all that argument can accomplish in such matters, and, if we still differ, we must agree to do so.

My next business is to try to restate the question in a perfectly clear and concrete form. I shall assume that the war in question is an important one, in the sense that there is real uncertainty as to whether England will win or lose it, and that the loss of it would certainly entail on England such disastrous consequences as accrued to the defeated nations after the war of 1914 to 1918. I shall assume that conscription is in force. And I shall assume that 'we' means persons liable under the act to military service, and not exempted by the authorities because of special usefulness in some other form of war work, such as munition-making. The question is whether such persons, in such circumstances, ought to obey this law or to refuse to obey it. Of course a very similar question would arise for those specially skilled persons, such as research chemists, who would be exempted from military service in order to apply their special skill to other forms of war work. Ought they to refuse both to fight and to exercise their abilities in arming those who are fighting?

Now I have no idea what is the right answer to this question, and, if I had, I should not be able to prove it to people who accepted different ethical principles and premises from those which I accept. I am not sure indeed that it is the kind of question to which there is an answer, even laid up in heaven, as Plato might say. I shall therefore content myself with making a few remarks which are, I think, relevant to it.

(1) There are three and only three cases in which no difficulty can arise. (i) A person may be persuaded that the war in which his country is engaged is the least evil alternative open to it in the circumstances, and he may hold that he has a direct or derived obligation to obey the laws of his country. Such a person will presumably hold that he ought to fight if he is ordered to do so. (ii) A man may hold that there is a direct obligation not to take or help in taking human life, and that this is so urgent that it overrides all other obligations, direct or derivative, which conflict with it. Such a man will have no difficulty in deciding that he ought not to fight, no matter how good the cause may be and even if he admits that war is the only way to bring about a great good or avoid a great evil. (iii) A man may hold that there is a direct obligation to obey the laws of his country, and that this

is so urgent that it overrides all other obligations which may conflict with it. Such a man will have no difficulty in deciding that he ought to fight, no matter how bad the cause may be and even if he thinks that war is an inefficient means of securing good or avoiding evil. Both these opinions seem to me absurd. I do not believe that there is any one obligation which is of such unique urgency that it overrides all other obligations, direct or indirect, that may conflict with it. Therefore the only case that seems to me to be of interest is that of a man who holds that war in general, or this war in particular, is wrong, and who does not hold that there is an overwhelming obligation either to refrain from taking human life or to obey the laws of his country.

(2) The following fact is very important, and is liable to be overlooked. If one believes that war in general, or a certain particular war, is wrong, this may be a conclusive reason for trying to prevent one's country from getting into it and for trying to get one's country out of it if it has entered upon it. But, except on the universalistic form of the teleological theory of obligation, it is *not* a conclusive reason for refusing to fight for your country when, in spite of your efforts, it is engaged in war. There is nothing particularly paradoxial in this. If one is a member of an ordinary partnership or committee, it is often one's duty loyally to help in carrying out a policy which one believes to be wrong and which one has conscientiously opposed while it was still under discussion. No doubt, if the conflict is too extreme, it becomes one's duty to dissolve the partnership or to resign from the committee. But it is just at this point that the analogy breaks down. For you cannot really do anything analogous to resigning from your country. If you are to go on living in England at all during the war, you will be dependent for your food and for such protection as you enjoy on the army, the navy, and the air-force; i.e. on the fact that there is a majority of persons of military age whose consciences are less sensitive than yours or work in a different way. Plainly there is a *prima facie* obligation not to put yourself in this situation of one-sided dependence on what you must regard as the wrong actions of people who are less virtuous or less enlightened than yourself.

This complication would be avoided if the conscription law imposed the death penalty for refusal to undertake military or other war service. I am inclined to think that this ought to be done, and that really conscientious objectors to military service should welcome it.

(3) Refusal to fight in a war is one of those actions whose effects vary very greatly with the proportion and the distribution of those who practise them. If a *majority* of persons of military age in *both* belligerent countries simultaneously refused to fight, it would be an extremely good thing, since it would automatically bring the war to an end without either victory or defeat. If a considerable proportion of such persons in England refused to fight, whilst few if any in the enemy country did so, the result would be the defeat of England. Under the conditions of modern war a complete and early defeat might be better for the defeated country than victory after prolonged fighting. But it is not worth discussing either of these alternatives, because it is as certain as anything of this kind can be that nothing like them will in fact be realized. The actual situation will certainly be that only a quite negligible proportion of those liable to military service, either in England or in any country with which England is likely to be at war, will refuse to fight. The intending refuser can safely assume that, if he refuses, he will be a tiny minority, and that his action will make no appreciable difference to the duration or the outcome of the war.

Now there are two remarks to be made about this. (i) It is a mistake to suppose that, because refusal *would be* right if most people in both countries were going to refuse, therefore it *will be* right in the actual case where only very few people in either country will refuse. No legitimate inference can be made to what is right in the actual case from what would be right in the widely different hypothetical case. The rightness or wrongness of an action depends, *inter alia*, on the circumstances in which it is done; and one extremely relevant circumstance in the present case is the extent to which other people will perform similar actions.

(ii) Since the large-scale effects of refusing to fight are likely to be negligible, the individual who is debating whether he ought to refuse can confine his attention to the probable effects on himself and his circle of friends and relations when considering the utility or disutility of refusal. This is, no doubt, a great convenience for him. But he will have to reflect that he owes this convenience, as he will owe his food and protection, to the fact that he can count on most other people doing what he judges to be wrong and deciding to fight. Unless he holds the universalistic form of the teleological theory of obligation and the hedonistic theory of value, he may suspect that it is not altogether fitting that his honour should be rooted in the fortunate dishonour of most of his contemporaries.

In conclusion I would make one remark to those who are convinced that they ought not to fight for their country in the next war or are not convinced that they ought to. They can avoid most of their difficulties by suicide; and on the whole, this is the course which I should recommend to those of them who do not think that there is an overwhelming obligation not to take one's own life. Of course it is possible that we survive the deaths of our present bodies, and it is alleged that the position of the suicide in the next life is less eligible than that of the non-suicide. But there is no conclusive evidence for the first proposition, and no evidence at all that the position of the suicide is worse than that of the victim of any other form of violent death. The next life, if there be one, must be bad indeed if it is worse than this life will be in time of war. And the gas in your oven is no less deadly and far more merciful than that which you will encounter on the battle-field or in the streets of your own town if it should be bombed.

VII

CONSCIENCE AND CONSCIENTIOUS ACTION (1940)[1]

At the present time tribunals, appointed under an Act of Parliament, are engaged all over England in dealing with claims to exemption from military service based on the ground of 'conscientious objection' to taking part directly or indirectly in warlike activities. Now it is no part of the professional business of moral philosophers to tell people what they ought or ought not to do or to exhort them to do their duty. Moral philosophers, as such, have no special information, not available to the general public, about what is right and what is wrong; nor have they any call to undertake those hortatory functions which are so adequately performed by clergymen, politicians, leader-writers, and wireless loudspeakers. But it *is* the function of a moral philosopher to reflect on the moral concepts and beliefs which he or others have; to try to analyse them and draw distinctions and clear up confusions in connection with them; and to see how they are interrelated and whether they can be arranged in a coherent system. Now there can be no doubt that the popular notions of 'conscience' and 'conscientious action' are extremely vague and confused. So I think that, by devoting this paper to an attempt to elucidate them, I may succeed in being topical without being impertinent.

I shall begin by trying to describe what I understand by 'conscience', in the widest sense of the word. I have no doubt that it is often used in certain narrower senses, which I shall indicate in due course. I think that failure to recognize this ambiguity often leads to misunderstandings and disputes which are mainly verbal.

[1] Reprinted from *Philosophy*, Volume XV, April 1940, by courtesy of the editors.

All civilized languages which I know or have heard of contain adjectives like 'right' and 'wrong', 'good' and 'evil', or their equivalents. This shows that human beings from the earliest times have had certain experiences which they took to be cognitions of acts, intentions, motives, etc., as having certain characteristics, viz. *moral* ones, which can take opposed forms. Again, restrospection assures most of us that we too have had such experiences when we have contemplated certain actions, dispositions, or characters, whether our own, or those of other real people, or those of fictitious persons in novels or plays. I am not at present concerned with the question whether there really are moral characteristics and whether we really do cognize them. I am concerned only with the plain psychological and historical fact that most of us, and most of our human predecessors back into prehistoric times, have had experiences which they took to be cognitions of such characteristics in acts, dispositions, characters, etc. I shall call these experiences 'ostensibly moral cognitions'.

It is an equally plain psychological fact that, when a human being contemplates an action or disposition or character in which these moral characteristics seem to him to be present, he is liable to feel certain kinds of emotion which he would not otherwise feel. All languages have words like 'remorse', 'feeling of guilt', 'feeling of obligation', 'moral indignation', and so on; and most of us know what such words indicate from our own experiences of such emotions. I propose to call these 'morally directed emotions'.

Here I must interpolate some remarks in order to ward off possible misunderstandings. We must notice that nothing ever has or could have *only* moral characteristics, any more than a word could have *only* meaning without any particular sound or visible form. Anything that has moral characteristics will also have certain non-moral ones; and, what is more, its moral characteristics will always depend upon certain of its non-moral ones. If I am told that a certain act was wrong, it is always sensible for me to ask: 'Why? What *made* it wrong?'. And the answer that I expect would be an indication of some characteristic which can be full described and understood without the use of any moral term, e.g. that it was an intentionally misleading answer to a question, that it was an intentional infliction of unnecessary pain, and so on. I propose to call these non-moral characteristics on which moral characteristics depend 'right-making', 'good-making', and so on.

Now emotions may be and often are felt towards acts, experiences, etc., in respect of their non-moral characteristics. Suppose, e.g. that a friend grants me a favour unfairly at the expense of another person because he likes me and does not like him. I shall tend to view this act with a non-morally directed emotion of complaisance in respect of its non-moral characteristic of being an act of special love and favour towards myself. But I shall tend also to view it with a morally-directed emotion of disapproval in so far as it is an act of unfairness towards my rival. It is, I think, quite possible to feel a non-morally directed dislike for an act in respect of those very right-making characteristics which give it a rightness which calls forth one's moral approval. Our attitude towards certain acts of stern justice towards their sons by typical Roman fathers is of this mixed kind.

It follows from all this that we may often think that we are feeling an *unmixed* morally directed emotion, when what we are really feeling is a mixture of morally and non-morally directed emotion. And we may sometimes mistake a purely non-moral emotion, such as fear of discovery and punishment or malice, for a morally directed emotion, such as remorse or righteous indignation. But the possibility and even the frequency of such mistakes has no tendency to show that there are not specifically moral emotions. The very fact that we recognize that we are liable to make these mistakes, strongly suggests that there are specifically moral emotions.

Lastly, it is an equally plain psychological fact that the belief that a certain course of action would be right does exercise a certain attraction or compulsion on most people and thus provides them with a motive-component for doing it. Still more obvious is it that the belief that a certain course of action would be wrong exercises a certain repulsion or inhibition on most people and thus provides them with a motive-component against doing it. Sometimes every other feature in alternative *a* is such as would make one prefer it to *b*. To do *a* might benefit me and other people, and to do *b* might injure me and other people. But to do *a* would involve breaking a promise which I gave, after due consideration, to a person who is now dead and therefore cannot release me. If I believe that it is wrong to break a promise given under those conditions, this one feature in *a* may make me reject it and choose *b*. I am not at present considering such cases from an ethical point of view; all that I am concerned with here is the psychological fact that they happen and are perfectly familiar. All civilized languages have words like 'ought', 'duty', 'obligation', etc. All these words refer to the fact that the supposed rightness of an action gives rise to a motive-component for doing it, and that the supposed wrongness of an action gives rise to a motive-component against doing it, and that these specifically *moral* motive-components may conflict with others which arise from one's belief about the non-moral characteristics of the action. I shall refer to these psychological facts as 'moral motivation'.

Here again we must notice that non-moral motive-components, based on the attractiveness or repulsiveness which an action derives from the non-moral characteristics which we believe it to have, will generally co-exist and co-operate with components of moral attraction and moral repulsion. In consequence of this a person may often think that he is being moved by purely moral motives when really his total motive for choosing or rejecting an alternative contains both moral and non-moral motive-components. And we may sometimes mistake a purely non-moral motive, such as desire for comfort or safety, for the moral motive of desire to do what is right as such. But the possibility and even frequency of such mistakes has no tendency to show that there is not moral motivation.

We may sum up these facts by saying that the vast majority of sane adult human beings are capable of ostensibly moral cognition, of morally directed emotion, and of moral motivation.

Now every such person is also capable of *reflexive* cognition, i.e. of contemplating himself, his experiences, dispositions, intentions, motives, and actions, from various points of view. To say that a person 'has a conscience', when this phrase is used in its widest sense, is equivalent to asserting the following three closely connected propositions about him. (1) That he has and exercises the cognitive power of reflecting on his own past and future actions, and considering whether they are right or wrong; of reflecting on his own motives, intentions, emotions, dispositions, and character, and considering whether they are morally good or bad; and of reflecting on the relative moral value of various alternative ideals of character and conduct. (2) That he has and exercises the emotional disposition to feel certain peculiar emotions, such as remorse, feeling of guilt, moral approval, etc., towards himself and his own actions, dispositions, etc., in respect of the moral characteristics which he believes these to have. (3) That he has and exercises the conative disposition to seek what he believes to be good and to shun what he believes to be bad, as such, and to do what he believes to be right and avoid what he believes to be wrong, as such.

I propose to describe this as 'the phenomenological sense' of the phrase 'having a conscience'. I think that the most sceptical of speculators about morals would hardly deny that most people nowadays and throughout the course of history have 'had a conscience', in this phenomenological sense. Let us consider where ethical scepticism would be relevant to this question. The most radical form of scepticism would deny that adjectives like 'right', 'morally good', 'obligatory', etc., really stand for characteristics. Its advocates would allege that sentences in which such words occur as grammatical predicates are really interjections or commands masquerading as statements about certain peculiar characteristics of actions, dispositions, persons, etc. If so, those experiences which seem to most people to be cognitions of moral characteristics cannot really be so; for there will be no such characteristics to be cognized. But it can hardly be denied that there are experiences which *seem* to be cognitions of moral characteristics. If there were not, it is impossible to see why moral sentences in all languages should have been couched in the indicative form with a moral adjective as grammatical predicate. So I do not think that such an ethical sceptic, if he knew his business, would attempt to deny that there are *ostensibly* moral cognitions, and this is all that is involved in the cognitive part of the definition of 'having a conscience', in the phenomological sense of that phrase.

If there are no ethical characteristics, it cannot be their presence in the actions, etc., which we contemplate, that moves our emotions. But that would not affect our definition. Granted that a person believes that there are moral characteristics, and believes that such and such of them are present in certain objects which he contemplates, there is no reason why this belief (however false or baseless it may be) should not evoke in him specifically moral emotions towards those objects. The ethical sceptic will, indeed, have to regard those emotions rather as a disbeliever in ghosts might regard the fear which a superstitious person would feel in a room which he believes to be haunted. But any reasonable person would admit that, even if ghosts do not exist, a specific kind of fear is felt by persons who believe in ghosts when they are in places which they believe to be haunted. What is more, a disbeliever in ghosts might himself feel such a fear in such circumstances, though he would judge it to be unreasonable. Similarly an ethical sceptic might himself continue to feel morally directed emotions, though he would have to regard them as unreasonable. And he should have no difficulty in admitting that most human beings do so. Therefore this kind of ethical sceptic need not deny that the emotional condition for having a conscience, in the phenomenological sense of that phrase, is fulfilled by most people.

Precisely similar remarks apply to the question of moral motivation. We are moved by our *beliefs* about the characteristics of things, regardless of whether those beliefs be true or false, well or ill founded. Since it can hardly be denied that most people believe themselves to be aware of moral characteristics in the actions, dispositions, etc., which they contemplate, the doctrine that all such beliefs are in principle mistaken is quite consistent with the contention that most people are susceptible to moral motivation.

An independent attack could, no doubt, be made on the applicability of the second and third clauses in our definition of 'having a conscience'. It might be contended that, whether we cognize moral characteristics or not, our beliefs in the presence of such characteristics never evoke any specific emotion and never influence our actions. Our emotions, it might be said, are evoked and our actions are influenced *only* by what we believe about the *non-moral* characteristics of what we are contemplating. But we proceed either to deceive ourselves or to try to deceive others about the direction of our emotions and the nature of our motives.

I think that this kind of scepticism is usually based on some general theory of human action, such as psychological hedonism, which would rule out the possibility of specifically moral emotion and motivation. I need only say that all such general theories rest on certain rather subtle verbal confusions, and may safely be rejected. A more empirical basis for such scepticism is the admitted mixture of non-moral emotions and motives with moral ones, and the admitted possibility of mistaking one of the former for one of the latter in any particular case. As I have already said, it does not seem to me that the facts about mixture and about mistakes and sophistications are adequate to support the sweeping negative conclusions which have been based on them, in face of the strong *prima facie* evidence for moral motivation and moral emotion.

I see no reason, then, to qualify my assertion that, in the phenomenological sense of the phrase, practically every sane adult human being 'has a conscience', whatever may have been the case with himself as an infant or with his prehistoric ancestors. Of course an individual may happen to live in an environment in which his conscientious dispositions are hardly ever excited or are constantly suppressed. They may then atrophy or become warped, as any other set of dispositions would be likely to do under similar circumstances.

We must now notice some important negative facts about

having a conscience, in the sense defined. (1) To say that a person has a conscience, in this sense, neither entails nor excludes that this person holds any particular theory about the nature of goodness or rightness or moral obligation. It neither entails nor excludes that he holds any particular theory about what makes good things good or right acts right. And it neither entails nor excludes that he holds any particular theory about the nature and sources of our moral knowledge and belief. A plain man, with no theories on any of these subjects, can have a conscience and act conscientiously. So too can persons who hold the most varied theories on these points; a man can be a conscientious Utilitarian, a conscientious Intuitionist, a conscientious Hegelian, or what not. All that is necessary is that he shall believe that, in some way or other, he can form a reasonable opinion about the rightness or wrongness, goodness or badness, of various courses open to him, and that his opinions on such matters shall be capable of evoking his emotions and influencing his decisions.

(2) The fact that most people have consciences, in the sense defined, does not, so far as I can see, establish or refute any particular ethical theory. This is, of course, quite a different point from the one which we have just been discussing. It is one thing to say, e.g. that a person could equally well have a conscience whether he accepted or rejected Utilitarianism. It is quite another thing to say that a person could equally well have a conscience whether Utilitarianism be true or false. I assert that, on my definition of 'having a conscience', both these statements are true, and that they would be equally true if any other ethical theory were substituted for Utilitarianism.

Now there is no doubt that the phrase 'to have a conscience' has often been used in a narrower sense than this. I propose now to consider the more important of the narrower senses in which it has been used. In order to do this I must begin with a very brief account of the moral situation in which we appear *prima facie* to find ourselves. It is roughly as follows.

We seem to be under an obligation to do what we can to maintain and increase the amount of good and to diminish the amount of evil, of every kind, in the lives of other persons whom we can affect appreciably by our actions. Let us call this a 'teleological obligation'. *Prima facie* it seems that we have other obligations, not derivable from it, which limit it and may conflict with it, e.g. the mere fact that a person has made a promise seems to be enough to impose on him an obligation to keep it unless the promisee should release him. This obligation appears to be independent of any good that may be produced or evil that may be averted or diminished in others by keeping the promise. We seem to be under an obligation to keep it even when we have strong reason to believe that the consequences would be better for all concerned if we were to break it. Again, there seem to be non-teleological obligations which bear upon the direction and range of our teleological obligations. Granted that one has a duty to do good to others, it seems obvious to most people that a man has a more urgent duty to do good to his parents or his benefactors than to complete strangers.

Now there seem to be a number of non-teleological obligations, e.g. to answer questions truly, to keep one's promises, and so on. And they are liable to conflict, not only with our teleological obligations, but also with each other. E.g. a person may have made a certain promise and he may afterwards be asked a certain question. And it may be impossible to keep the promise and answer truly. In order to keep the promise he must tell a lie, and in order to answer truly he must break the promise. The only remaining alternative is to refuse to answer the question; but in many cases refusal to answer would, for all practical purposes be equivalent to answering in a certain way and betraying a confidence which one had promised to keep.

Now there is an important epistemological difference between teleological and non-teleological obligations. Suppose I am in a situation where several alternative actions are open to me, and that I am trying to fulfil the teleological obligation to produce as much good or as little evil as I can in others. In order to discover my duty I shall have to consider elaborately the probable remote consequences of the various alternative courses of action. Now this involves a great deal of wholly *non-moral* reflection on the properties of things, the dispositions of persons, the laws of nature, and so on. The conclusions of such reflections will generally be highly uncertain, and one's capacity to conduct them successfully will depend on the extent of one's knowledge about non-moral facts and the degree of one's capacity for reasoning about physical, psychological, social, economic, and political matters. The *moral* insight that is needed will be concerned only with estimating and comparing the goodness and badness of the consequences which one thinks it likely that the various alternative courses of action would produce. Suppose, on the other hand, I am in a situation where non-teleological obligations are predominant, such as truth-telling and promise-keeping. Then in most cases the ascertainment of the relevant non-moral facts is perfectly simple and straightforward and can be performed without any expert knowledge or technical skill and instruction. If one has made a promise and is asked a question, there is generally not the least difficulty in being certain as to what answers would be lies and what answers would be breaches of promise. Here, then, almost the whole of the cognition involved is specifically *moral*; it is concerned with seeing that making a promise, as such, imposes an obligation to keep it; that answering a question, as such, imposes an obligation to answer it truthfully; and with estimating the relative urgency of these two obligations in cases where they conflict.

It is not surprising, therefore, that many people should be inclined to use the word 'conscience' in such a way that conscience, on its cognitive side, is confined to the task of intuiting non-teleological obligations and estimating their relative urgency.

Suppose we take 'conscience' in this narrower sense. Then it will follow that, if Utilitarianism be true, no one has a conscience. For the essence of Utilitarianism is that there are no non-teleological obligations. And, if there are none, no one can intuit them and estimate their relative urgency; though non-Utilitarians may mistakenly think that they do so. According to the Utilitarian, what makes it obligatory to keep a promise is not the mere fact that the promise has been made. What makes it obligatory, when it is so, is that we are under the obligation to produce as much good and as little evil as possible by our actions, and that experience has shown that promise-keeping on the whole leads to better consequences than promise-breaking. And similar remarks apply, *mutatis mutandis*, to all the alleged non-teleological obligations.

I am not at present concerned to discuss the truth or falsity of Utilitarianism, so I will confine myself to the following three remarks.

(i) In deciding what he ought to do in any situation, a Utilitarian would have to consider carefully, not only what the consequences of various alternative actions would probably be, but also what kinds and amounts of good and evil would attach to each of these consequences if it were realized. It seems inconvenient to use the word 'conscience' in such a way that intuition and comparison of *goods and evils* would not be a function of conscience, whilst intuition and comparison of *non-teleological obligations* would be so.

(ii) Suppose that Utilitarianism is false, and that there are non-teleological obligations. It can hardly be denied that there is *also* the teleological obligation to produce as much good and as little evil as one can. The mistake of Utilitarianism would be to hold that this is the *only* obligation, and to fail to see that there are others, equally fundamental, which limit it and may conflict with it. Truth-speaking and promise-keeping will be duties not reducible to beneficence, but beneficence will still be one duty among others. Therefore, in deciding what one ought to do in a given situation, it will often be necessary to consider the relative urgency of the teleological obligation of beneficence and certain non-teleological obligations, such as truth-telling and promise-keeping. In order to estimate the urgency of the obligation of beneficence it will be necessary to enter into precisely the same kind of calculations as Utilitarians consider to be necessary in every case, since this urgency will plainly depend on the nature and amount of good to be produced or evil to be averted by one's actions. It seems to me that it would be highly inconvenient to use the word 'conscience' in such a way that it was part of the function of conscience to compare the urgency of various non-teleological obligations, but was no part of its functions to compare the urgency of non-teleological obligations with that of teleological ones or to compare that of two or more teleological ones with each other.

(iii) Nevertheless, the considerations which have now been brought to our notice do suggest that the following explanatory sentences should be added to our definition of 'having a conscience'. We must distinguish between the *purely factual* and the *purely ethical* considerations which are involved in any attempt to decide what we ought to do in a given situation. Both factors enter in all cases. The purely factual elements are generally (though by no means always) obvious, even to quite ignorant and simple people, when only non-teleological obligations are in question; but, when teleological obligations have to be seriously considered, they may be highly complex and uncertain and may demand technical knowledge and skill of an advanced kind. Now conscience, as such, is concerned directly only with the purely ethical factors. The operation of forecasting the consequences of various alternative actions, as distinct from estimating the goodness or badness of these consequences, could be performed as well or better by a person who had no conscience. But, although this intellectual process cannot itself be assigned to conscience, it is an essential condition without which conscience cannot do its own proper work in situations of any complexity. A person who is trying to find out what he ought to do is not using his conscience properly if he fails to inform himself as fully and accurately as possible of all the relevant facts, or if he omits to apply his utmost care and skill to the task of forecasting the remote and the indirect consequences of the alternatives under consideration.

When the word 'conscience' is used in such a way that conscience, in its cognitive aspect, is confined to intuiting and balancing non-teleological obligations, I shall say that it is used 'in the intuitional sense'. I have now tried to show that this is an inconveniently narrow sense. But the word is often used in senses which are even narrower than this, and I will now consider some of them.

It is held by some people that certain kinds of non-teleological obligations are so urgent that a person ought not under any conceivable circumstances to do an action which would infringe any of them. This claim has been made, e.g., for the obligation to answer a question truthfully if at all. Now it seems to me that the word 'conscience', and phrases which contain it, are often used in such a way as to imply that a person cannot have a conscience unless he holds this opinion, and that his conscience is in operation only on occasions when his action or his refusal to act is based on his belief that one of these unconditional obligations is involved. I should consider it most undesirable that the word should be used in this narrow way. For the opinion in question is almost certainly mistaken; and, even if it were true, it has been rejected by many people who, in any ordinary use of language, have been scrupulously conscientious, such as John Stuart Mill. It would plainly be unfortunate to use the word 'conscience' in such a way that no one could be said to have a conscience unless he were mistaken on an important point of moral theory, and that no one could be said to be following his conscience except when he was under the influence of this delusion. The utmost that can be granted to the intuitionist is that we can see directly that certain relationships, as such, impose certain component obligations on us, and that some of them are so urgent that any act which would conflict with any of these has a very strong tendency to be wrong. In certain cases this is true, not only of all the *actions* open to one, but also of the only remaining alternative, viz. *refusal to act*. If we care to say that, in such cases all the alternatives are wrong, we can do so; but we shall then have to admit that we ought to choose that alternative (be it one of the actions or refusal to act) which is the *least wrong*. And in complex cases there is not the faintest reason to believe that we have intuitive knowledge as to which one this is.

It remains to notice one further narrowing of the word 'conscience'. Sometimes it is used in such a way that a person would be said to be following his conscience only in so far as he bases his decision about what he ought to do on some alleged divine revelation. In many cases, I think, this amounts to little more than the previous usage decorated with theological frillings. The pronouncements of conscience about what is unconditionally wrong are regarded as, in some sense, the voice of God speaking in and to the individual; and so the agent can take them to be infallible without arrogating too much for himself. In other cases, however, the situation is quite different. Certain actions are regarded by the individual as unconditionally right or unconditionally wrong, not because he sees this for himself by direct inspection, but because he believes that God has given a ruling on the matter either in inspired writings or in the traditions of a divinely founded and directed Church.

I will now leave the notion of conscience, and pass to that of a conscientious action. Conscience, as I have defined it, is a system of cognitive, emotional, and conative *dispositions*, and it is only when these dispositions are in operation that we have conscientious action.

The question whether an action is conscientious or not is mainly a question about the agent's motives in doing it. We must clear up the notion of motive a little before we can give a satisfactory definition of 'conscientious action'. Suppose that an agent is contemplating a certain possible course of action in a given situation. He will have various beliefs and expectations about its qualities, its relations, and its consequences, e.g. he may believe that it would be unpleasant to himself, that it would please his mother, and that it would be a breach of a promise made to his father, and so on. Some of these beliefs and expectations will attract him towards doing the action, some will repel him from doing it, and others may leave him unmoved. I call any belief about an action which attracts one towards doing it a 'motive-component *for* the action', and any belief about it which repels one from doing it a 'motive-component *against* the action'. Suppose that a certain action is in fact chosen and performed. Then I say that the agent's 'total motive *in* doing the action' was the resultant of all the motive-components for doing it and all the motive components against doing it. And I say that he did it '*because of*' the former, and '*in spite*' of the latter.

Now suppose that there were several components for doing a certain action, and several against doing it, and that it was in fact done because of the former and in spite of the latter. Let us call the former *a*, *b*, and *c*, and the latter *u*, *v*, and *w*. Now consider, e.g., the component *a*. We can ask ourselves the following question about it. Would *a* have been sufficient, in the absence of *b* and *c*, to induce the agent to do this action in spite of the components *u*, *v*, and *w* against doing it? Or did the component *a* need to be supplemented by *b* or by *c* or by both in order to overcome the influence of *u*, *v*, and *w*? If and only if the first alternative is true, we can say that *a* was 'a *sufficient* motive-component for doing the action'. Next we can raise the following question. Would *bc* have been sufficient, in the absence of *a*, to induce the agent to do the action in spite of the components *u*, *v*, and *w* against doing it? Or did *bc* need to be supplemented by *a* in order to overcome the influence of *u*, *v*, and *w*? If, and only if, the second alternative is true, we can say that *a* was 'a *necessary* motive-component for doing the action'. Lastly, suppose that *a* had been the only component for doing the action. Then we could say that 'the action was done *purely* from the motive *a*'.

We can now apply these general considerations to the particular case of conscientious action. An action is conscientious if the following conditions are fulfilled. (i) The agent has reflected on the situation, the action, and the alternatives to it, in order to discover what is the right course. In this reflection he has tried his utmost to learn the relevant facts and to give each its due weight, he has exercised his judgment on them to the best of his ability, and he has striven to allow for all sources of bias. (ii) He has decided that, on the factual and ethical information available to him, the action in question is probably the most right or the least wrong of all those which are open to him. (iii) His belief that the action has this moral characteristic, together with his desire to do what is right as such, was either (*a*) the *only* motive-component for doing it, or (*b*) a *sufficient and necessary* motive-component for doing it. If the first alternative is fulfilled, we can say that his action was '*purely* conscientious'. If the second is fulfilled, we can say that it was '*predominantly* conscientious'. The following would be an example of a predominantly conscientious action. Suppose that a person, after reflection, decides that the right action for him is to undertake military service. Suppose that the two motive-components which induce him to undertake this action, in spite of fear, love of comfort, etc., are his belief that it is right, together with his desire to do what is right as such, and his dislike of being thought cowardly by his friends. Then the action is predominantly conscientious if (*a*) his desire to do what is right, as such, *would* have sufficed to overcome his fear and his love of comfort even in the absence of his dislike of being thought cowardly, whilst (*b*) his dislike of being thought cowardly *would not* have sufficed to overcome those motive-components in the absence of his desire to do what is right, as such. In such a case we can say that the non-conscientious component for doing the action which the agent believes to be right is indeed present but is superfluous and insufficient. It would be absurd to refuse to call the action 'conscientious' merely because a superfluous and insufficient non-conscientious motive-component for doing it happened to co-exist with the sufficient and necessary conscientious motive-component for doing it.

We come now to a much more difficult and doubtful case. Suppose that the agent's belief that the action is right, together with his desire to do what is right as such, is sufficient, but not necessary, to induce him to do it, in spite of the components against doing it. This would be illustrated by our old example if we varied it in the following way. We must now suppose that the agent's dislike of being thought cowardly *would* have sufficed to overcome his fear and his love of comfort and *would* have induced him to choose the course of action which he believes to be right, even if his belief that it is right and his desire to do what is right, as such, had been absent. The situation may be described as follows. The non-conscientious motive-component for doing the action is still superfluous; but now we must say that the conscientious component for doing it is equally superfluous. Each is sufficient, and therefore neither individually is necessary; all that is necessary is that one or other of them should be present. If you confine your attention to the *sufficiency* of the conscientious motive-component, you will be inclined to say that the action *is* conscientious; if you attend only to the *superfluity* of this component, you will be inclined to say that it is *not* conscientious.

We pass now to another difficult and doubtful case. Suppose now that the agent's belief that the action is right, together with his desire to do what is right as such, is necessary but not sufficient to induce him to do it in spite of the components against doing it. This would be illustrated by the following modification of our old example. We must now suppose (*a*) that the agent's belief that it is right for him to undertake military service, together with his desire to do what is right as such, would not have sufficed, in the absence of his dislike of being thought cowardly, to overcome his fear and his love of comfort; and (*b*) that the latter motive-component, in the absence of the former, would also not have sufficed to overcome his fear and his love of comfort. Each of the two motive-components for doing the action is now necessary, and therefore neither of them individually is sufficient. If you confine your attention to the *indispensability* of the conscientious motive-component, you will be inclined to say that the action *is* conscientious; if you attend only to its *insufficiency*, you will be inclined to say that it is *not* conscientious.

I will group together purely and predominantly conscientious actions, in the sense defined above, under the name of '*fully* conscientious actions'; and I will group together the two doubtful cases, which we have just been discussing, under the name of '*semi-conscientious* actions'. The two kinds of these can then be distinguished as (i) actions in which the conscientious motive-component is sufficient but superfluous, and (ii) actions in which the conscientious motive-component is indispensable but inadequate.

If a person does an act which he believes to be less right or more wrong than some other act open to him at the time, he does it in spite of his desire to do what is right, as such. Any action of this kind may be called '*contra-conscientious*'.

It is plain that a great many of our deliberate actions are neither fully conscientious, nor semi-conscientious, nor contra-conscientious; for many are done without considering them and the alternatives to them from the standpoint of rightness and wrongness. Such actions may be called '*non-conscientious*'. A non-conscientious action may be such that, if the agent had considered it and the alternatives to it from the standpoint of rightness and wrongness, he would have judged it to be the most right or the least wrong of the alternatives open to him. And it may be that he would then have done it for that reason alone or for that reason combined with others which are superfluous and insufficient. If both these conditions are fulfilled, we may say that this non-conscientious action was '*potentially* conscientious'. In a similar way we could define the statement that a certain non-conscientious act was '*potentially* contra-conscientious'.

I have now completed the task of analysis and definition, and I will conclude my paper with a few remarks about conscientious action, as defined above. (1) There is a very important sense of 'ought' in which it is true to say that a person ought always to do the alternative which he believes, at the time when he has to act, to be the most right or the least wrong of all those that are open to him. (There are, undoubtedly, other senses of 'ought' in which this would not be true; but we are not concerned with them here.) For this sense of 'ought' to be applicable it does not matter how ignorant or deluded the agent may be about the relevant facts, how incompetent he may be to make reasonable inferences from them, nor how crazy or perverted his judgments about right and wrong, good and evil, may be. But, the more fully this is admitted, the more obvious does the following complementary fact become. The most right or the least wrong act open to other individuals or to a society, in certain cases, may be to prevent a conscientious individual from doing certain acts which he ought, in this sense, to do, and to try to compel him to do certain acts which he ought, in this sense, to refrain from doing. Moreover, if other individuals or the authorities in a society honestly believe that the most right or the least wrong action open to them is to treat a certain conscientious individual in this way, then they *ought*, in the very same sense, to do so. What is sauce for the conscientious goose is sauce for the conscientious ganders who are his neighbours or his governors. This fact is often obscured because many people inadventently or dishonestly confine their attention to cases, such as the trial of Socrates or of Christ, in which subsequent generations have held that the individual was not only conscientious but also correct in his ethical opinions, whilst the tribunal which condemned him was either not conscientious or was mistaken in its ethical opinions. It may be salutary for such persons to widen their purview by envisaging the case of a high-minded Indian civilian conscientiously securing the capture and execution of a high-minded Thug for conscientiously practising murder.

(2) It is sometimes said that, when an individual sets up his conscience against the general opinion of his society or of mankind, he is claiming 'moral infallibility'. If he knows his business, he is doing nothing of the kind. In order for it to be his duty, in the present sense, to do a certain alternative, all that is necessary is that he should think it *probable*, after considering the question to the best of his ability, that this alternative is more right or less wrong than any of the others which are open to him. Since he has to enact one of the alternatives, it does not matter in the least whether this probability is high or low. Nor does it matter whether the difference in rightness or wrongness is great or small. In considering the question, it is his duty to give full weight to the fact that most members of his society or most of the human race have formed a certain opinion about it. If he is a wise man, he will attach very great weight to this fact. But if, in spite of having done so, he comes to a contrary opinion, he ought, in the present sense, to act upon it, no matter how far short of complete conviction his opinion may fall.

(3) The last remark that I have to make is this. A *purely* conscientious action, in the sense defined above, must be a very rare event. It is hardly credible, e.g. that either undertaking or refusing military service could be a purely conscientious act, in

that sense; for everyone fears death and wounds and everyone dislikes to be thought cowardly.

Now the definitions of 'predominantly conscientious' act, and of the two kinds of 'semi-conscientious' act, all have the following peculiarity. They all involve the notion of what *would* have happened if certain conditions had been other than they in fact were. This notion of the consequences of unfulfilled conditions always enters whenever the question of sufficiency and dispensability is raised. It follows that an individual can seldom be rationally justified in feeling a very strong conviction that an action of his was conscientious; for, in order to decide this question, he has to form an opinion as to how he would have acted in the *absence* of certain motive-components which were in fact *present*. It seems to me that *a fortori* it must be almost impossible for anyone to decide rationally as to whether another person's action is conscientious or not.

If I am right in this, the Tribunals have been given a task which is, from the nature of the case, incapable of being satisfactorily performed. This, so far as it goes, is a strong ground against allowing exemption from military service on grounds of conscience and against setting up Tribunals at all. There are, no doubt, other reasons which point in the opposite direction; and Parliament has decided that, in the present state of public opinion in England, the balance of advantage is in favour of allowing exemption on such grounds, and has therefore set up Tribunals to consider claims. It only remains for us to watch with sympathy and interest the efforts of these well-meaning men to deal with questions to which God alone can know the answer.

VIII

CRITICAL NOTICE OF JULIAN HUXLEY'S *EVOLUTIONARY ETHICS* (1944)[1]

This little book contains the *Romanes Lectures*, delivered in the Sheldonian Theatre on June 11, 1943, together with 13 pages of notes.

The contents may be divided into the following five main sections. (1) A theory of the development of conscience in the individual from infancy. (2) An account of the chief features of evolution in general. (3) An account of the evolution of moral codes and of their correlation with different stages in the evolution of societies. (4) An attempt to show that objective moral standards can be based on a study of the characteristic features of evolutionary change. (5) A statement of the chief peculiarities of a code of morality based on a study of evolution.

I propose first to state the various parts of the theory as fairly as I can, and then to make some comments and criticisms.

(1) *Development of Conscience in the Individual*

The theory which Professor Huxley puts forward is based on the speculations of certain psychoanalysts. So far as I can understand it, it may be stated as follows.

At about the second year of its post-natal life a baby begins to draw a distinction between itself and the outer world. At this stage the focal point of the latter for the baby is its mother or any other person, such as its nurse, who has constant charge of it. This individual is recognized by the baby as another *person*, and it views her under two aspects, viz. (i) as a source of satisfaction, peace, and security, and (ii) as an authority who has

[1] Reprinted from *Mind*, Volume LIII, October 1944, by courtesy of the editors.

Evolutionary Ethics was published in 1943 by the Oxford University Press.

and exercises the power to thwart certain of its impulses. The baby's cognition of its mother under the former aspects is toned with affection; its cognition of her under the latter is toned with hostility.

Hostile emotion towards the mother, and the associated hostile wishes and actions, become the objects of a new kind of emotion in the baby. To this second-order and reflexive emotion Professor Huxley gives the name 'feeling of guilt'. Emotions, wishes, and tendencies towards action which are the objects of guilty emotion tend to be either relegated to the background of consciousness or wholly repressed into the unconscious. There they continue to exist and to be the objects of guilty emotion, and thence they continually seek an outlet. Generally they can find one only in disguised forms; but from time to time they emerge more or less openly in the form of rage and violence against the mother.

The process described above is useful to human beings for the following reason. Young children are faced with many kinds of conflict to which other young creatures are not exposed. Owing to their lack of experience they cannot solve them rationally. Now it would be highly detrimental to the development of the individual if the conflicting impulses merely inhibited each other and led to a complete deadlock, or if they just alternated with each other on equal terms leading to endless vacillation. The attachment of a feeling of guilt to some and not to others of the conflicting impulses, and the consequent fairly complete suppression or repression of the former, ensures that these two disadvantages will be avoided.

After the capacity to feel guilty emotion has once been brought into activity over the conflict between love and hate of one's mother that kind of emotion can be directed to one term in *any* conflict of impulses, and it will then lead to the same kind of results in the way of suppression or repression. This, however, is subject to one limitation. Such an extension of the guilty emotion from a person's hostility towards his mother to certain of his other impulses will take place only when the latter are viewed by him in relation to some person or institution for which he feels love or respect. This latter feeling may be either unmixed or blended with other emotions into some complex sentiment, such as awe, patriotism, self-respect, etc.

Professor Huxley envisages another way of dealing with conflicting impulses, which becomes available to an individual only when he has acquired adequate experience. This is described as solving such conflicts 'rationally'. It is not clear to me what Professor Huxley considers this process to be, or how he supposes it to be connected with the 'proto-ethical mechanism' which he has been describing. Does this mechanism merely set the stage and prepare certain of the conditions without which no *persistent* action of any kind, and therefore no deliberately planned action, can take place? Or is there some more detailed connection between the proto-ethical mechanism and the deliberate subordination and co-ordination of impulses in pursuance of a course of action inspired by moral ideals and limited by moral principles?

(1.1) *Healthy and Unhealthy Development of Conscience.* The processes which have been described above may go on in a 'healthy' way or may be subject to various 'unhealthy' aberrations. In the former case, we are told, 'the feeling of rightness reflects, though in an embryonic form, a morality which is objectively right'. It can then be 'developed by reason and aspiration into a conscience which is indispensable as a moral guide'. In the latter case, however, the patient will develop a conscience which is described as 'distorted and unrealistic'. He may also develop (what is not the same thing) 'distorted and unrealistic' beliefs about the nature of conscience. It is not clear to me whether these two very different pathological results are held by Professor Huxley to be invariable concomitants.

(1.11) *Healthy Development.* About the 'realistic' conscience which develops when the process goes on healthily we are given the following information. It is 'normal' and 'healthy' to feel *some* degree of guilty emotion towards one's hatred of those 'whom we must at all costs love'. In particular it is said to be 'perfectly realistic to feel *some* guilt at hating one's beloved mother'.

A distinction is drawn between 'internal' and 'external'

realism. The former consists in not feeling excessive guilt and in not compensating for it in certain pathological ways to be described later. It seems to be identified (p. 23) with a satisfactory adjustment between the individual's conscience and the moral standards current in the society in which he lives. But these standards may themselves be 'unrealistic'; and in that case the individual's conscience, if adjusted to them, will lack *external* realism. The latter is said to be relative to (i) the general state of knowledge and belief in a given society at a given time, and (ii) to its 'intellectual and moral climate, and the quality of the human beings who live in it'. Since both these factors gradually change, a set of moral standards which have been externally realistic may, unless they change concomittantly, become unrealistic.

(1.12) *Unhealthy Forms of Development*. The following are said to be typical unhealthy ways of development from the infantile proto-ethical stage:

(i) Instead of, or in addition to, the baby feeling guilty emotions towards its hostility to its mother, it may feel such emotions towards those of its impulses by checking which its mother incurred its hostility. In that case those impulses may be repressed instead of, or in addition to, its feelings of hostility towards its mother.

(ii) The repressed guilt-laden hatred, originally felt towards the mother for checking a certain impulse, may be extended or diverted to that impulse itself. If both the first and the second of these unhealthy developments should take place in an individual, he will feel towards certain of his impulses both a transferred emotion of *guilt* and a transferred emotion of *hatred* which will itself be the object of a guilty feeling.

(iii) Whilst it is 'normal and healthy' and 'perfectly realistic' to feel *some* degree of guilt towards one's hatred of those whom 'one must at all costs love', the degree of guilt felt may be too great. It is then described by Professor Huxley as 'an excessive load which does not correspond with any reality'. This may lead to a sense of unworthiness and self-hatred which Professor Huxley describes as 'quite irrational'.

(iv) It is alleged that when the degree of guilt felt is excessive the following further distortions are liable to ensue. (*a*) Suppose that the inordinate feeling of guilt has arisen through being afflicted with a fussy or domineering parent. Then the patient will be apt to model his dealings with himself on his parent's dealings with him, and thus to develop a finicky and over-severe conscience. (*b*) Another alternative, which may be either combined with or substituted for the first, is to model one's idea of God on one's early experiences of one's parents. God is then liable to be regarded as a fussy and domineering person, of irresistible power and super-human knowledge, mainly occupied in forbidding one to do what one would like to do. God will then be hated, but the hatred will be the object of a strong guilty feeling and will be largely repressed. (*c*) A person may get rid of an excessive load of guilt by thinking of himself as the innocent victim of unforunate circumstances, of wicked and hostile individuals, or of an oppressive society.

(v) When a person's conscience has developed, whether healthily or unhealthily, he will find himself condemning some of his impulses and approving others of them. Now he may not be able to face the fact that he has certain strong impulses of which he strongly disapproves. He may then come to ignore their presence in himself and to imagine them to be present to a marked degree in certain other individuals or classes. His disapproval of such impulses, which prevents him from acknowledging their presence in himself, is then turned upon these other persons, who thus act as scapegoats or whipping-boys. He may then feel it to be his duty to loose upon them, for their supposed moral defects, those impulses of cruelty and aggression in himself which he would otherwise have disapproved and kept in check.

(1.2) *Inferences from the Above Theory of Conscience*. From the psycho-analytic theory of the development of conscience in the individual as he grows up Professor Huxley draws the following conclusions:

(i) There are no innate moral principles or concepts. What is innate in a child is the tendency to love its mother in respect of most of her dealings with it and to hate her in respect of those of her acts which check its impulses; the tendency to feel guilty about this hostility and not about this love, and to repress or suppress the former and not the latter; and the tendency to extend the feeling of guilt to one member of other pairs of conflicting impulses. The kinds of action which eventually come to be regarded as right or wrong depend wholly on the individual's environment and are very largely determined by the influence of his mother. Even the general capacity to develop a conscience of some kind or other will not be fulfilled if the circumstances are unfavourable. It is asserted, e.g., that persons who have had no mother or mother-substitute between the ages of one and three years from birth fail to develop a moral sense of any kind.

(ii) The psycho-analytic theory is alleged to provide an explanation for what Professor Huxley calls the 'absolute, categorical, and other-worldly quality' of moral obligation. He asserts that this quality becomes attached to moral obligation through the following causes. (*a*) The fact that thoughts, emotions, and wishes to which the feeling of guilt is attached tend to be repressed into the unconscious, and do not merely take turns on an equal footing with their opposites in occupying consciousness or issuing in overt action. (*b*) The fact that the occasion on which guilt is first felt is that on which the infant discovers with a shock that there is a world outside himself which is not amenable to his wishes. It is alleged that a baby is originally in a state of 'magic solipsism', and that what first awakens it from this is the intrusion of the external world in the form of its mother demanding control over its primitive impulses.

(2) *General Account of Evolution*

The main points in Professor Huxley's general account of evolution may be summarized as follows:

(i) It is a process of change which is 'creative' in two senses. (*a*) New and more complex levels of organization are successively reached. (*b*) New possibilities for further development are opened up.

(ii) The growth in complexity of organization is in general gradual, but there are occasional sudden and rapid changes to new and more comprehensive types of organization. After any such critical point there are new emergent qualities and new methods of further evolution. The two most important critical points known to us are (*a*) the change from inorganic to living matter, and (*b*) the change from pre-human to human life. After each turning-point the *area* of further evolution tends to be restricted to those creatures which have taken the new turning and their descendants, but the *tempo* of evolution among them tends to be greatly accelerated.

(iii) Living beings are highly complex and unified material systems with the power to produce offspring which predominantly resemble their parents but have variations which may themselves be handed on. At their highest levels living organisms have a very considerable degree of self-regulation, they become to a large extent independent of variations in their environment, and they acquire appreciable powers of controlling it. At this end of the biological scale the presence of a mind something like the human mind is apparent for the first time.

(iv) At the level of life a new method of evolution emerges, viz. natural selection between competing variants. This greatly accelerates the process, and it is still further hastened by the development of bisexual reproduction with Mendelian recombination of genes.

(v) Purely organic evolution merges into evolution which is social and is to some extent deliberately controlled. This becomes possible when speech and conceptual thinking have developed. Then and not till then the results of experience become transmissible, tradition becomes cumulative, and deliberate training becomes possible. This leads to a new type of organization, viz. that of a self-perpetuating society of conscious individuals, and it becomes possible to take deliberate control of further evolution.

(vi) A line of evolution may be said to be 'progressive' so long as there remains a capacity to reach a higher level of organization along that line which will not itself cut out the possibility of still further advance. In organic evolution this requires all-round flexibility as opposed to one-sided specialization. The latter leads to a blind alley, and thereafter only minor variations are possible. Professor Huxley says that all the main lines of purely organic evolution seem to have ended in such blind alleys a very long time ago. The field of further evolution on earth has now been restricted to one species, viz. men; and in them it is social and thought-determined, not blindly biological. But the possible tempo has been enormously increased.

(vii) Professor Huxley asserts that, after the level of social and thought-determined evolution has been reached, two important new features emerge: (*a*) Many of the experiences which now become available for the first time have 'intrinsic value'; and (*b*) it becomes possible to 'introduce faith, courage, love of truth, goodness—moral purpose—into evolution'. (I am not at all sure what Professor Huxley understands or wishes his readers to understand by either of these statements.)

(3) *Evolution of the Moral Codes of Societies*

The moral standards prevalent in various societies and at various stages of a single society are roughly correlated with the stage reached by the society in its evolution. But Professor Huxley mentions, and tries to account for, certain exceptions to this general rule. He says that careful study of a number of primitive communities has shown that there is no close correlation between, e.g., the degree of competitiveness or of co-operation enjoined by the moral code of such a community and the prevalence of competition or co-operation in the life of it. Similar facts, he says, have been observed about peaceableness and aggressiveness. It appears that peaceableness may be morally approved in a community which is predominantly aggressive, and aggressiveness in one that is predominantly peaceable.

He tells us that a more detailed study of such facts discloses that all such societies are primitive, small, culturally isolated, and on the same general level of social evolution. Now it is found that small and isolated species of fairly simple plants or animals are liable to develop and propagate variations which are not specially adapted to their circumstances and their mode of life. The reason alleged is that, in the absence of severe competition, random variations have a fair chance of surviving even when they are not useful.

Suppose, however, that we confine our comparisons to communities which are either (i) at quite different levels of culture, or (ii) highly advanced but on very different lines of development. Then, he says, we shall find that there is a high positive association between those types of character and action which are morally approved in a community and those which are favourably relevant to its chief functions.

Professor Huxley distinguishes the following main levels:
(i) *Pre-agricultural Societies*. Here morality is chiefly concerned with the propitiation of supposed supernatural beings, the harnessing of supposed magical forces, and the solidarity of the group. The principal subjects of moral approval and disapproval are acts and sentiments connected with totem and taboo, and the acts which are approved or disapproved are viewed mainly in the light of their supposed magical efficacy.
(ii) *Early Civilized Societies*. Here the chief subjects of moral approval or disapproval are those which are concerned with class-domination and the rivalries of groups. Moral codes tend to be regarded as expressions of the will of God, and morality is closely connected with religion.
(iii) *Later Civilized Societies*. The most important development here is the appearance for the first time of a set of moral principles which are supposed not to be restricted in their application to the members of a certain community as a whole or to those of a certain group within it, but are held to apply to every human being as such. Professor Huxley asserts that the first known appearance of such a universalistic moral code was in about 500 BC. Such a code has generally been thought of as fixed for all time and independent of local and temporal variations in circumstances. Professor Huxley thinks that this attitude has been fostered by the uncritical use of certain abstract nouns, such as *The Good*, which are really nothing but 'convenient pigeon-holes for a variety of qualities which have *nothing in*

common but a certain emotive quality' (my italics). He also considers that the belief in the immutability of the principles of universalistic morality has been buttressed by regarding them as expressions of the immutable will of God.

In all advanced societies there have been several more or less distinct moral codes which partly conflict and partly support each other. Among these Professor Huxley enumerates the following: (*a*) An official code imposed by a ruling class to ensure the stability of their own position; (*b*) the working code of the ordinary citizen; (*c*) the codes of certain oppressed classes or minorities, seeking consolation or revolutionary change; (*d*) a code concerned with securing personal salvation as an escape from inner conflict or outer violence and misery; (*e*) the code of an 'impossible perfection'; and (*f*) what he calls 'the true ethics of disciplined and developed goodness and sainthood'. Professor Huxley alleges that there is nothing common and peculiar to all these except that they are concerned with 'the labels of rightness and wrongness'.

(4) *Evolution as a Clue to an Objective Moral Standard*

Professor Huxley says that we are left with the following problem: 'How can we be sure that the objects to which our moral sense affixes the labels of felt rightness and wrongness are *in fact* right and wrong?'. So far we have been told only of the adaptation of particular moral codes to particular kinds of society. Is there any criterion for judging whether the labels 'right' and 'wrong' are *correctly* attached? Again, have we any right to say that one adaptation or one society is *better than* another? He asserts that a study of the course of evolution provides answers to such questions and enables us to discover 'independent ethical standards' in three different but interconnected regions, viz. nature as a whole, human society, and the human individual.

So far as I can see, Professor Huxley bases his moral code on certain ultimate judgments of value. I will collect at this point his main statements on this topic.

(i) Men find that some of the possibilities which are realizable at the human level of evolution 'have value in and for themselves'.

(ii) Among these they assign a higher value to those which are either (*a*) 'more intrinsically or permanently satisfying', or (*b*) 'involve a greater degree of perfection'.

(iii) Those evolutionary trends which are likely to lead to such intrinsically valuable possibilities being realized are judged to be 'the most desirable direction of evolution'.

(iv) It is said to be evident 'on evolutionary grounds' that the individual is 'higher than the state or the social organism'. Again, we are told that 'the rightly developed individual is, and will continue to be, the highest product of evolution'. It is explained that the phrase 'rightly developed', in this context, is to cover both (*a*) the full all-round development of a person's powers, and (*b*) the one-sided development of any special capacity in which he is capable of excelling. Professor Huxley realizes that there may be a conflict between developing a certain talent to the utmost and performing one's ordinary duties towards one's family, colleagues, country, etc. He does not explicitly mention, what is equally obvious, that there may be a conflict between all-round self-development and the cultivation of a particular talent to the highest degree of which it is capable.

The ground which is given for holding that an individual is higher than any social group is that the 'possibilities which are of value for their own sake . . . are not experienced by society as a unit'.

(v) In a group of individuals it is desirable that there should be the maximum of variety that is compatible with the unity of the group as a whole. 'It is not uniformity which our evolutionary analysis shows to be right', says Professor Huxley, 'but the maximum of variety-in-unity'.

Professor Huxley's main pronouncements about what is *right* may be summarized as follows:

(i) The most fundamental proposition seems to be that it is right to 'aim at whatever will promote the increasingly full realization of increasingly high values'.

(ii) There is also a principle of equality. It is right that there should be universal equality of opportunity for development. This is said to follow from the fact that 'the right development of an individual is an evolutionary end in itself'. But there appears to be an independent argument for it which would make it a derivative principle, viz. that equality of opportunity leads to the maximum of variety.

(iii) It is right (*a*) to realize new possibilities in evolution, especially those which are intrinsically valuable; (*b*) to respect human individuality and to encourage its further development; and (*c*) to construct such a social organization as will best subserve (*a*) and (*b*).

From these principles Professor Huxley draws the conclusion that the right course at any moment will be a compromise between one which would wholly sacrifice future possibilities of further development to the fullest realization of existing possibilities and one which would wholly sacrifice the latter to the former. Social organization should be designed to encourage change in desirable directions, but at any moment there will be an optimum rate of change in those directions.

(5) *Special Features of Evolutionary Ethics*

Professor Huxley realizes that a good many more or less educated persons in England and the United States and the Dominions might be prepared to assent, with minor qualifications, to most of what he has said about the sort of things which have value and the sort of actions which are right. But they might be inclined to ask: Is not this just the ethics of 'Christianized Liberalism'? What has the appeal to evolution done for us?

There would seem to be two different questions here. (i) Has the appeal to evolution provided any reason, which was not already available, for accepting the judgments of value and of obligation enumerated above? (ii) Does it provide us with any new or modified judgments of value or of obligation?

To the first question Professor Huxley answers that the study of evolution has provided an *inductive basis* for what had already been guessed by religious moralists, viz. a universalistic morality based on the ultimate and intrinsic value of human personality.

In considering the second question Professor Huxley enumerates what he takes to be the main points of likeness and the main points of unlikeness between the evolutionary moral code and that of 'Christinized Liberalism'. He says that the only likenesses are the following: (i) That both codes are in principle *universalistic*. I take this to mean that each requires that any two persons shall be treated alike unless it can be shown, to the satisfaction of an unbiased third party, that there are such differences between themselves or their circumstances that better results on the whole are likely to follow from treating them differently. (ii) That both take the value of the *individual* to be primary and paramount. (iii) The two codes will further resemble each other in any principles which follow from (i) or (ii) or the conjunction of both of them.

The main differences between the two systems of morality are said to be the following: (i) The moral standards or criteria of 'Christianized Liberalism' are accepted on authority or on the grounds of an alleged revelation, and are therefore fixed once and for all. Those of the evolutionist can be modified and developed. (ii) The moral standards of the evolutionary system are 'dynamic', whilst those of its rival are 'static'. This seems to mean that the moral code of 'Christianized Liberalism' takes the nature of human individuals and human societies to be now fixed and henceforth susceptible only of minor fluctuations, and legislates only for the relations of such individuals in such societies. The moral code of the evolutionist is concerned, not only with this, but also with the rights and wrongs of *processes of change* which carry individuals and societies from one stage of evolution to another.

From these primary differences Professor Huxley claims to derive the following secondary ones. The evolutionist will lay more stress than the 'Christianized Liberal' on (i) the obligation to plan for *social change*; (ii) the value of *knowledge* as a means to controlling future evolution; (iii) the value of *art*, both as introducing new possibilities of intrinsically valuable experience and as providing the chief means by which emotional, as distinct from intellectual, experiences may be shared; and (iv) certain kinds of *personal religion* as opening the way to attaining certain kinds of 'satisfying experience and desirable being'. On the other hand, we are told, the evolutionary code condemns practices aimed at securing salvation in a supernatural other life, in so far as these may retard or oppose 'right social change'.

(6) *Comments and Criticisms*

I hope that the above is a fair and a reasonably complete synopsis of the main points in Professor Huxley's theory. I shall now proceed to make some comments and criticisms upon it.

(6.1) *Development of Conscience in the Individual.* I will begin with one general remark. Of all branches of empirical psychology that which is concerned with what goes on in the minds of babies must, from the nature of the case, be one of the most precarious. Babies, whilst they remain such, cannot tell us what their experiences are; and all statements made by grown persons about their own infantile experiences on the basis of ostensible memory are certainly inadequate and probably distorted. The whole of this part of psychology therefore is, and will always remain, a mere mass of speculations about infantile mental processes, put forward to explain certain features in the lives of grown persons and incapable in principle of any independent check or verification. Such speculations are of the weakest kind known to science.

The next general remark that I would make is this. The connection between the psycho-analytic and the evolutionary part of Professor Huxley's theory is by no means clear. The former is concerned entirely with conation and emotion, the latter professes to supply a criterion for judging what is really right and really wrong, i.e. it is concerned with cognition. How are the two inter-related? I will try now to clear this up.

There is evidently a close positive association between what a person calls 'right' and what he feels morally obliged to do and guilty in omitting to do, and between what he calls 'wrong' and what he feels morally obliged to avoid and guilty in doing. A person tends to feel *guilty* (as distinct from merely apprehensive, embarrassed, disgusted, etc.) when and only when he knows himself to be acting or wishing or feeling, or believes himself to have acted or wished or felt, in a way which he would call '*morally wrong*'. Conversely, a person tends to call an act or wish or feeling of his 'morally wrong' only if his contemporary awareness or his subsequent memory of it is qualified by a feeling of *guilt* (as distinct from one of mere apprehension, embarrassment, disgust, etc.).

Now, it might be held that when a person calls an act or experience of his 'wrong' he is either (*a*) merely expressing his feeling of guilt, as a person who is angry might express that feeling by exclaiming 'Blast!'; or (*b*) merely stating the fact that he is feeling guilty, as a person might state that he is feeling angry by uttering the sentence, 'I am angry'. I will call these two alternatives respectively the *interjectional* and the *autobiographical* analysis of what a person is doing when he calls one of his own acts or experiences 'wrong'.

It is quite clear that Professor Huxley could not consistently accept either of these analyses. For, in the first place, he asks: 'How can we be sure that the objects to which our moral sense affixes the labels of felt rightness and wrongness are *in fact* right and wrong?'; and he claims that a study of the course of evolution provides an answer to such questions. Plainly the question would be meaningless and the answer ridiculous if, when a person calls one of his actions 'right' or 'wrong', he is only expressing a certain emotion towards it or is only stating that he is feeling such an emotion towards it. On the first alternative the speaker is not expressing an opinion at all, and so there can be no question of his being correct or incorrect in calling the action 'right' or 'wrong'. On the second alternative he is making an autobiographical statement about this own present feeling towards the action. Such a statement is hardly likely to be false unless he is deliberately lying; and, if it can reasonably be questioned, it is plain that a study of the course of evolution is completely irrelevant to testing its truth or falsehood.

Secondly, Professor Huxley evidently holds that the emotion of guilt is *appropriate* to some kinds of action or experience and inappropriate to others, and that it may be felt in an *ordinate* or an inordinate degree towards those objects to which it is appropriate to feel it. For he says that guilt is an appropriate emotion for a person to feel towards his hatred of his 'beloved mother', and more generally towards his hatred of those whom 'he must at all costs love'. And he tells us that, whilst it is 'perfectly realistic to feel *some* degree of guilt at hating one's beloved mother', it is possible to feel a degree of guilt which is 'excessive', which 'does not correspond to any reality', and which is 'quite irrational'. From this I conclude that he holds that it is appropriate to feel guilt towards those, and only those, of one's actions and experiences which are 'in fact' wrong; and that there is some proper proportion between the degree of wrongness and the degree of guilt felt.

It seems certain then that Professor Huxley must hold that, when a person utters the sentence, 'So-and-so is wrong', he is not just expressing an emotion but is making a judgment; and that in this judgment he is ascribing to so-and-so a predicate which has no special reference to his present feelings towards so-and-so.

I suppose, therefore, that the connection between the psycho-analytic and the evolutionary part of the lecture must be this. The former claims to explain how a person comes to attach feelings of guilt of such and such degrees to such and such of his actions, desires, and feelings; and to show what function this attachment of guilt performs in his general development. The conclusion of it is that a feeling of guilt may become attached to anything, wrong or right or indifferent, and that its intensity need bear no proportion to the degree of wrongness of the actions or experiences to which it becomes attached. A person will be inclined to believe that those and only those of his actions and experiences to which he has attached a feeling of guilt are wrong, and to believe that the degree of wrongness of each is measured by the intensity of the guilty feeling which he has attached to it. But in believing an action or experience of his to be right or wrong he is ascribing to it a certain predicate which has no special reference to his feelings towards it. Whether or not it has this predicate, and the degree to which it has it if it has it at all, are questions which can be decided only by criteria which are elicited in the evolutionary part of the lecture by a study of the course of evolution.

If this account of Professor Huxley's theory as a whole be correct, we must notice that one important question concerning the development of conscience is ignored by it. How does the individual acquire the notions of right and wrong? According to the evolutionary part of the theory when a person calls one of his actions or experiences 'right' or 'wrong' he is not just talking about his own emotions. He is ascribing to that action or experience (whether correctly or incorrectly) a predicate whose presence or absence can be tested by an objective evolutionary test. If so, he must have an *idea* of that predicate; and nothing that has been said in the psycho-analytic part of the theory about the emotion of guilt and its gradual transference from hatred of the mother to other acts and experiences takes us a step towards explaining the origin of that idea. It is obvious that no theory which is entirely in terms of a person's emotions will explain how he comes to attach to the words 'right' and 'wrong' a meaning which is not definable in terms of his emotions.

It is no reproach to a theory that it does not explain everything; but it is very important that it should not be thought to explain more than it does. Therefore I shall state explicitly what seem to me to be two presuppositions of the present theory. (i) It presupposes that the notions of right and wrong are either innate or are acquired by the individual in some way which it does not explain. (ii) It presupposes that a person has a tendency (*a*) to ascribe wrongness to those and only those of his actions and experiences towards which he feels an emotion of guilt, and (*b*) to ascribe to an act or experience a degree of wrongness which is measured by the intensity of the guilty emotion which he feels towards it.

I think that the theory can be illustrated by means of an analogy with the emotion of fear. The theory maintains that the native and primary object of a person's guilty emotion is his hostility to his mother. We are told by psychologists that the native and primary object of fear in infants is sudden loud noises. The guilty emotion may be extended or diverted from a person's hostility towards his mother to any of his other acts or experiences, right, wrong, or indifferent. Similarly, fear may be extended or diverted to almost any object, whether dangerous, harmless, or beneficial. Therefore the fact that a person feels guilty about x and not about y, though it will certainly tend to make him *believe* that x is wrong and that y is not, is no guarantee that these beliefs are correct. And the fact that he feels more guilty about x than about z, though it will certainly tend to make him *believe* that x is more wrong than z, is no guarantee that this is true. Similarly, a person may be frightened of x and not of y, and may be more frightened of x than of z. This will certainly tend to make him think that x is dangerous and that y is not, and that x is more dangerous than z. But it may in fact be the case that y is dangerous and x is not, or that z is more dangerous than x. It might be held to be 'reasonable' that a person should feel fear only towards what is really dangerous, and that the intensity of his fear should be proportionate to the real degree of danger. Similarly, it is in some sense 'reasonable' that a person should feel guilt only towards those of his acts and experiences which are really wrong, and that the intensity of his guilty feeling should be proportionate to the real degree of their wrongness.

Perhaps this notion of 'reasonableness' or 'appropriateness' might be analysed somewhat further on the following lines. Professor Huxley might say that the emotion which the average baby feels towards the average mother in respect of the vast majority of her dealings with it is *love*. It is only in respect of a special class of occasional acts, viz. those which check certain of its impulses, that the average baby feels hatred and hostility towards the average mother. Therefore love is the 'normal' emotion for a baby to feel towards its mother, in the sense that it is the emotion which is habitually felt. Hatred towards its mother is 'abnormal', in the sense that it is opposite in kind to the emotion which is normally felt by it towards the same object and that it is felt only on certain isolated special occasions.

Professor Huxley might add that love, and the actions which

spring from it, are more conducive to the harmonious development of the individual and the stability of society than are hate and the actions which spring from it. A human being is at first wholly dependent on its mother; throughout a long childhood he remains predominantly dependent on her and on others; and throughout his whole life he will be largely dependent on the good-will of his fellows. He will not receive such support for long, and he will be incapable of benefiting from it, unless he is on the whole docile, co-operative and friendly. Now, unless certain of his impulses are checked at an early age, and unless he largely represses his instinctive reactions of hostility against those who check them, he will become an object of disgust and enmity to those with whom he has to live. To say that a guilty feeling is 'appropriate' to a person's hostility towards his mother and 'inappropriate' to his love for her might mean that (*a*) it tends to repress anything to which it is attached, and (*b*) the repression of the former is, whilst that of the latter is not, conducive to the harmonious development of the individual and the stability of society.

Finally, Professor Huxley might give the following account of the distinction between a 'reasonable' and an 'unreasonable' degree of guilty feeling. He might compare the feeling of guilt to a medicine which tastes nasty and has various collateral ill-effects on general health. The feeling is unpleasant in itself and depressing and cramping in its effects. It will be too weak if it is not strong enough to repress the hostility to the mother. But, if it is present in more than the minimal degree needed for that and similar purposes, it will hamper rather than forward the all-round development of the individual and his adjustment to society. So the 'right' or 'reasonable' degree of guilty feeling is the smallest dose that suffices for the function which Professor Huxley ascribes to it.

I will end this part of my comments with the following observations. Any theory which claims to trace the development of conscience in the individual is faced with at least two questions: (i) How does the individual acquire the *notions* of moral rightness and wrongness, goodness and badness, etc.? (ii) How does he come to *apply* these notions to the particular objects to which he does eventually apply them, i.e. to count such and such actions as right, such and such others as wrong, and so on? I have tried to show that the psycho-analytic theory supplies no answer to the first question. So far as it goes, moral rightness and wrongness, goodness and badness, might be simple, unanalysable characteristics, and the disposition to form concepts of them might be innate in the human mind. In that case the only answer that could be given to the first question would be to describe the conditions which are severally necessary and jointly sufficient to stimulate this innate disposition into activity and cause the individual actually to think of these characteristics. But, even on this supposition, there might be no innate *moral principles* and even no innate *moral biases*. A person might be equally ready to attach the notion of right or wrong, good or evil, to anything; and the particular ways in which he did in fact come to apply them might be wholly determined by the conditions to which he was subjected in early childhood.

Now, as we have seen, Professor Huxley does hold, on the basis of the psycho-analytic theory, that there are no innate moral principles. For, if I have interpreted him correctly, he holds that an individual's earliest judgments of right and wrong are completely determined by and moulded upon his feelings of guilt, and that the extension of his feelings of guilt from his hatred of his mother to any other of his acts or experiences is entirely determined by the influences which are brought to bear on him in early childhood. Professor Huxley does not explicitly consider the possibility of what I have called 'innate moral bias'. By this I mean the possibility that the human mind may be so constituted that attempts to make a person feel guilty about certain kinds of act or experience might 'go against the grain' and seldom be wholly successful, whilst attempts to make him feel thus about certain others kinds of act or experience might 'go with the grain'. There is some *prima facie* evidence for this, but I do not know whether it would survive critical investigation.

I think that Professor Huxley's conclusions about how an individual comes to have the beliefs which he does have about what is right and what is wrong might be compared in certain respects to the known facts about the development of intelligible speech as a person grows up. The power to speak is not innate in human beings; but the power to acquire that power may fairly be said to be innate, since the vast majority of men do learn to speak whilst no other creatures can be taught to do so. Nevertheless, a child will not acquire the power to speak unless it is surrounded by other persons who talk to it, listen to it, and train it. Again, the particular language which a child will first talk if it ever learns to speak at all depends entirely on the particular way in which it is conditioned by those who train it in its early years. Of course other languages may be learned deliberately in later life; but, if so, they will probably be spoken with the 'accent' of the language which was first acquired spontaneously in infancy.

On Professor Huxley's theory the contents of different moral codes might be compared to different languages, or perhaps more profitably to the characteristic grammatical structures of different groups of languages, e.g. Indo-European, Semitic, Chinese, etc. In this connection it is worth remarking that the grammatical rules which a person follows correctly but unwittingly in speaking his native tongue may be of extreme subtlety, as becomes apparent when they are formulated by grammarians and have to be learned and applied deliberately by a foreigner. There is obviously some analogy to this in the highly complex rules of totem and taboo which anthropologists laboriously elicit from the practices of certain primitive communities.

(6.2) *The Notions of 'Internal' and 'External Realism'*. So far as I can see, the essential points here are the following: A person's conscience is internally realistic if (i) he feels guilty about those and only those of his acts and experiences which are *commonly believed* to be wrong in the society in which he has to live, and (ii) if the intensity of the guilty emotion which he feels towards any act or experience is roughly proportionate to the degree of wrongness which is *commonly ascribed* in that society to acts or experience of that kind. Thus internal realism is necessary and sufficient to ensure a satisfactory adjustment between an individual's conscience and the moral code prevalent in the society in which he lives.

Now, whether an act of a certain kind is really right or wrong will largely depend on the nature of the effects which acts of that kind are likely to produce either severally or collectively. And these effects in turn will depend, not only on the nature of the act, but also on the circumstances, both material and mental, in which it is done.

Suppose, now, that a person judges a certain act to be *right*. Then it may be that, *if* it would have the effects which he believes that it would have, it *would* be right. In that case I shall say that his judgment is 'ethically reasonable', even if he is mistaken about the effects that it will have. On the other hand, it may be that, if it would have the effects which he believes it would have, it *would not* be right but would be indifferent or wrong. Then I shall say that his judgment that it is right is 'ethically unreasonable', even if he is correct in his beliefs about the effects of the action. If he is correct in his judgment about the circumstances in which an act is done and the effects which it will have, I shall say that he is 'factually correct'; if not, I shall say that he is 'factually incorrect'. It is plain then that, if a person makes the judgment, 'So-and-so is right', there are four possibilities, viz. (i) that he is being ethically reasonable and factually correct, or (ii) ethically reasonable but factually incorrect, or (iii) ethically unreasonable but factually correct, or (iv) ethically unreasonable and factually incorrect. Similar remarks apply, *mutatis mutandis*, if a person makes the judgment, 'So-and-so is wrong'.

Now, there is no doubt that what Professor Huxley calls 'external realism' is closely connected with what I have called 'ethical reasonableness'. If a person makes a moral judgment which is ethically reasonable I shall describe it as 'realistic relative to his factual information', no matter whether that information is adequate, correct or incorrect. If, in addition, his relevant factual information is adequate, and correct, I shall describe his moral judgment as 'absolutely realistic'.

It is evident that the moral code of a society might not be realistic even in relation to the factual information which is common in that society. It may never have been so. And, even if at some time in the past it was realistic in relation to the relevant factual information then available, it may have ossified at that stage, whilst the relevant factual information available has since been extended and corrected. I have no doubt that a great deal in the current moral code about sexual matters is unrealistic, from the one cause or the other, in relation to the relevant factual information at present available.

Even if the moral code of a society were completely realistic relative to the factual information which is common in that society at a given time, it might not be absolutely realistic; for that information might be either inadequate or inaccurate. And, even if it were absolutely realistic at a certain time, there is no guarantee that it would remain so. For conditions might change, and similar acts performed in widely different conditions might have consequences which were good in one set of conditions and bad in the other.

Obviously the ideal position for an individual is that he should live in a society whose moral code is absolutely realistic, and that his conscience should be fully adjusted to it. But neither of those conditions will ever be completely fulfilled. Suppose that one had to train a child who one knew would be obliged to live in a society whose moral code was largely unrealistic. Then one would have to compromise between the two evils of giving him a conscience adjusted to the society in which he is to live and therefore largely unrealistic, or a conscience which is highly realistic and therefore largely out of adjustment to the society in which he is to live. This is by no means a merely academic problem for an intelligent and well-intentioned parent or teacher who has to compromise as best he can between producing contented philistines or embittered prigs.

(6.3) *Objective Rightness and Wrongness.* Professor Huxley's theory of the nature of rightness is a particular form of a very ancient and familiar doctrine, viz. Utilitarianism. For it takes intrinsic value as the primary notion in ethics, and it makes the definition or the criterion of the rightness of an act to be its tendency to produce or to conserve or to increase what is intrinsically valuable. There is, so far as I can see, no special connection between this account of rightness and the theory of evolution. Utilitarianism was put forward, elaborated, criticized, and defended long before the theory of evolution was thought of, and all the best arguments for it are quite independent of that theory and of the facts on which it is based.

In my opinion the only relevance of the facts of evolution to Utilitarianism is the following. The most serious rival to Utilitarianism is what I will call 'Intuitionism'. This is the theory that the rightness or wrongness of certain kinds of act, e.g. promise-keeping, lying, etc., depends, not on their tendency to produce consequences which are good or bad, as the case may be, but on their intrinsic nature as acts. E.g. this theory holds that the non-ethical characteristic of being an act of promise-keeping necessarily involves the ethical characteristic of being right, and that the non-ethical characteristic of being an act of deliberate deception necessarily involves the ethical characteristic of being wrong, just as the property of being an equilateral triangle necessarily involves that of being an equi-angular triangle. Such a theory of the nature of the connection between rightness or wrongness, on the one hand, and the various right-making or wrong-making characteristics, on the other, is generally combined with the *epistemological* theory that such connections are immediately obvious to careful inspection, i.e. that they not only *are* intrinsically necessary but also can be *seen* to be so by any rational being who reflects on the terms. Now anything that tended to weaken this theory would *pro tanto* strengthen Utilitarianism which is its most formidable rival. I suspect that the only relevance of the psycho-analytic account of the development of conscience to the Utilitarian part of Professor Huxley's theory is that, if it were true, it would cut away the grounds for the rival doctrine of Intitutionism. On the psycho-analytic theory it would be very improbable that a person really does see any necessary connection between the nature of certain acts, such as promise-keeping or lying, and their rightness or wrongness; and there would be a psychological explanation of the fact that many people are inclined to think that they do so. But, for reasons which I have given, I consider that the evidence for this theory of conscience is too weak to make it a strong weapon against Intuitionism.

Professor Huxley enunciates the general principle of Utilitarianism in the formula that it is right to 'aim at whatever will promote the increasingly full realization of increasingly high values'. But, as Bentham saw, and as Sidgwick insisted, the general principle needs to be supplemented by some principle about *distribution*. For our acts contribute not only to produce good and bad experiences and good or bad individuals, but also to determine *which* individuals shall have good experiences and which shall have bad ones. It will be remembered that Bentham formulated the distributive principle, 'Everyone to count for one and no-one to count for more than one', whilst Sidgwick enunciates several principles of impartiality in the distribution of goods and evils. Professor Huxley also has a principle of equality. He says that it is right that there should be universal quality of opportunity for development.

He alleges that this follows from the fact that 'the right development of an individual is an evolutionary end in itself'. I do not see that the addition of the adjective 'evolutionary' to the substantive 'end-in-itself' adds any weight to this argument. I am not sure that the conclusion is true, and I do not see precisely how it follows from the premise. It is plainly conceivable that circumstances might exist in which if equal opportunities were given to all members of a society none of them could develop very far; whilst, if the opportunities given were distributed most bountifully among those who had the greatest innate capacity, much greater aggregate development would result. It is certainly not obvious to me that, in such circumstances, opportunities for development ought to be distributed equally. And I should like to see the steps by which it is supposed to follow from the premise that the right development of an individual is an end in itself. I suspect that some additional premises would be needed, and that they would not be particularly plausible if they were brought into the light.

Whether the argument in support of the principle of equality of opportunity from the premise that an individual is an end-in-itself be valid or invalid it is not a Utilitarian argument. But Professor Huxley does also support the principle on Utilitarian grounds. He says that equality of opportunity leads to maximum variety, and he holds that a group of inter-related individuals is in the best state possible when there is in it a 'maximum of variety-in-unity'. It seems to me quite uncertain whether equality of opportunity for development would necessarily lead to the maximum variety possible with a given amount of resources. If the available resources were small, there could be only very slight development for anyone if the opportunities were equal, and this would seem to involve a fairly uniform low level of attainment. If the same resources were distributed unequally, e.g. if they were used to enrich a small class of aristocrats with a taste for being patrons of art and learning and sport, it is quite likely that far greater variety would result.

(6.4) *Intrinsic Values.* Utilitarianism, which is a theory about the nature and criteria of *rightness and wrongness*, does not logically entail any particular theory about *intrinsic goodness and badness.* But it presupposes some view or other on this latter subject. So we must now consider Professor Huxley's opinions about intrinsic value.

In Section 4 above I have collected all that I could find of Professor Huxley's views on this topic. I will begin by remarking that there are three main questions which may be asked about intrinsic value. (i) What is the right analysis of statements of the form 'So-and-so is intrinsically good (or bad)'? Do they, as their grammatical form suggests, express judgments in which the speaker ascribes a predicate to a subject? Or is this a delusion, and do they merely express a certain emotion which the person who utters them is feeling? Again, if they do express judgments, what is the nature of the predicate which they ascribe to a subject? Is it simple and unanalysable? If not, how should it be analysed and defined? (ii) If intrinsic value or disvalue be a predicate, of what kinds of subject can it be intelligibly predicated? Or if the Interjectional Analysis be correct, towards what kinds of object can the emotion be felt which is expressed by sentences which *seem* to ascribe intrinsic value to a subject? (iii) If intrinsic value or disvalue is a predicate, what are the non-ethical characteristics of a subject which make it intrinsically good or bad, as the case may be? Or, if the interjectional analysis be correct, what are the non-ethical characteristics of an object which call forth the emotion which is expressed by sentences which *seem* to ascribe intrinsic value to a subject?

(i) I think it is certain that Professor Huxley holds that such sentences as 'So-and-so is intrinsically good (or bad)' do express judgments in which a predicate is ascribed to a subject, and do not merely express an emotion which the speaker is feeling. But I have no idea whether he thinks that the characteristic denoted by the phrase 'intrinsically good (or bad)' is simple or complex. And I have no idea what he thinks to be the correct analysis of it if it be complex.

(ii) It seems certain that Professor Huxley holds that intrinsic value can be predicated intelligibly of (*a*) certain experiences, and (*b*) human individuals. I am not sure whether he holds that it can also be predicated of (*c*) certain groups of inter-related human beings.

Some of his statements, if taken literally, seem to imply that he holds (*c*). He says, e.g., that the individual is 'higher than the state or the social organism'. Now, if such a comparison can be made at all, it implies that both an individual and a society can have intrinsic value. What precisely it means is not clear to me. Does it mean that the value of *any* individual is greater than that of *any* human society? Or does it mean that the value of the *best* individual is greater than that of the *best* society? Whatever it may mean, two reasons are given for it. One is that individuals have experiences, whilst no group of individuals can literally have an experience; and that certain experiences are of very great intrinsic value. The other is that the conclusion is evident 'on evolutionary grounds'.

I find all this very unsatisfactory. Consider the following three questions. (*a*) Can intrinsic value be predicated intelligibly of certain groups of inter-related individuals? (*b*) If it can, can the value of such a group and that of an individual be intelligibly compared in respect of magnitude? (*c*) If so, is the value of any individual, however bad, necessarily greater than that of any group, however good? Or is the value of the best possible individual necessarily greater than that of the best possible group? The mere fact that only an individual can literally have experiences and that certain experiences have very great intrinsic value, does not seem to me to settle any of these questions. And, if there be 'evolutionary grounds' for answering the third question affirmatively in either of its forms, I have failed to discover them in Professor Huxley's lecture and I am quite unable to imagine for myself what they may be.

(iii) About the non-ethical characteristics whose presence confers intrinsic value on the things which possess them Professor Huxley's views seem to be as follows:

(*a*) He does not explicitly enumerate the characteristics which he thinks confer intrinsic value on *experiences*. He contents himself with mentioning certain experiences which are commonly held to be intrinsically valuable, e.g. certain æsthetic and religious experiences. But he does mention two characteristics which he thinks confer a higher value on an experience the more fully and intensely they are present in it. These are the property of being 'intrinsically or permanently satisfying' and that of 'involving a degree of perfection'.

I do not clearly understand what is meant by 'perfection' in this context. It seems tautologous, and is certainly not illuminating, to say that the more perfection an experience has the more valuable it will be. The notion of being 'intrinsically or permanently satisfying' also needs a great deal of further analysis and elucidation. The first move would be to attempt to draw and justify a distinction between what 'really would satisfy' a person and what he 'thinks he wants'. At the next move we should have to raise the question whether a stupid or a cruel or a lustful person might not get 'real' satisfaction from experiences which we should hesitate to call intrinsically good. All these questions have been commonplaces of ethical discussion for some two thousand years, and I cannot see that any fresh light has been thrown on them by reference to evolution.

(*b*) Intrinsic value is conferred on an individual by a combination of the fullest all-round development of his powers with the special development of any particular talents in which he is capable of excelling. This, again, is a form of a very ancient and familiar doctrine. It goes back to Plato and was put forward in England in the nineteenth century by moralists of the school of Green and Bradley and Bosanquet under the name of 'self-realization'. Its strong and weak points have been very fully canvassed, and I do not think that evolution has anything fresh to add to the discussion.

(*c*) If Professor Huxley does hold that intrinsic value can be significantly ascribed to certain groups of individuals, it is plain that he thinks that what gives intrinsic value to such a group is a combination of individual variety with collective unity.

It is useful in this connection to bear in mind McTaggart's distinction between the value *in* a group and the value *of* a group. I think it is quite possible that, if the distinction were put to him, Professor Huxley would deny that there is goodness or badness *of* a group, and would say that variety-in-unity is important only as making for maximum goodness *in* a group, i.e. for making it consist to the greatest possible degree of good individuals enjoying good experiences.

(6.5) *The Relevance of Evolution to Ethics*. There are two questions to be discussed, and it is important to be clear about the connections and disconnections between them. (i) What bearing, if any, has knowledge of the facts of evolution on the question of what is *intrinsically good or bad?* (ii) What bearing, if any, has it on the question of what is *right or wrong?*

It is important to notice that, even if such a knowledge had no bearing at all on the first question, it would almost certainly have a bearing on the second. This would be so even if Utilitarianism were false, but it is more obviously so if it is true. The reason is as follows. On any theory of right and wrong which is worth consideration *one* of our duties, and a very important one, is to produce as much good and as little evil as we can. If Utilitarianism is true, this is our *only* ultimate duty and all our other duties can be derived from it. If Utilitarianism is false, we have other duties not derivable from this which may conflict with and limit it, but it will remain an urgent obligation. Now, in order to decide whether the effects of an action will be good or evil we must first know *what* its effects will be. This is a factual and not an ethical question, and the answer to it depends on the circumstances in which the action is done and the relevant laws of nature. It is plain that knowledge of the laws of evolution may be highly relevant in attempting to foresee the large-scale and long-term consequences of certain types of action. Such knowledge may also suggest possibilities which would not otherwise have been contemplated, and it may rule out as causally impossible certain results at which it might otherwise have seemed reasonable to aim. I do not think that any moralist would deny that evolution has this kind of relevance to the question of what is right or wrong.

If knowledge of the facts of evolution had a bearing on the question of what is intrinsically good or bad, it would have an additional relevance to the question of what is right or wrong. This would be the case on any view of rightness and wrongness which makes beneficence to be one of our duties, and it would be most obvious on the Utilitarian view which makes beneficence to be our only fundamental duty. For, on the present hypothesis, a knowledge of the facts of evolution would help to tell us, not only *what* the effects of certain actions would be, but also whether such and such effects, if they were produced, would be *intrinsically good or bad.* So the question that remains is whether knowledge of the facts of evolution has any bearing on the question of what is intrinsically good or bad.

It is plain that Professor Huxley thinks that it has an important bearing on this question, but I find it extremely hard to see why he does so. Perhaps I can best bring out the difficulty that I feel in the following way. Take the things which Professor Huxley considers to be intrinsically good, and imagine him to be confronted with an opponent who doubted or denied of any of them that it was intrinsically good. How precisely would he refute his opponent and support his own opinion by appealing to the facts and laws of evolution? Unless the notion of value is surreptitiously imported into the definition of 'evolution', knowledge of the facts and laws of evolution is simply knowledge of the *de facto* nature and order of sequence of successive phases in various lines of development. In this way we may learn that certain lines of development have stopped short, in the sense that a point has been reached after which the successive phases in this line have shown no further increase of complexity-in-unity. By comparing and contrasting such lines with others which stopped short at a more complex stage or which have not yet done so at all we may be able to infer some of the necessary conditions for continued growth of complexity-in-unity in the successive phases of a line of development. This much could be discovered and understood by an intelligent being who had never had the faintest notion of intrinsic value or disvalue; and this is *all* that a knowledge of the facts and laws of evolution, considered as a part of natural science, amounts to.

If, then, Professor Huxley is to support his own views about the intrinsic value of so-and-so and to refute those of an opponent by appealing to the facts and laws of evolution, there must be a suppressed premise in the argument. This premise must be some such proposition as 'states of affairs which have more complexity-in-unity are as such intrinsically better than those which have less complexity-in-unity', or (what is by no means the same) 'processes of change in which there is increase of complexity-in-unity in the successive phases are intrinsically better than those in which there is stability or diminution in this respect'. (Professor Huxley might prefer the latter as more 'dynamic', since it ascribes intrinsic value, not to the separate phases, but to the process of change itself in which they occur.) At any rate he must use *some* 'mixed' premise, connecting certain *purely factual* characteristics, which are all that a study of evolution can possibly reveal to us, with the *value-characteristics* of intrinsic goodness and badness. I must confess that this seems to me to be so obvious a platitude that I am almost ashamed to insist upon it; but it seems that it is still liable to be ignored.

Now, whatever may be the evidence for such a mixed premise, it is quite plain that it must be something different from the evidence for the facts and laws of evolution. For the premise required asserts a connection between certain of those facts and laws and something else, viz. intrinsic value or disvalue, which forms no part of their subject-matter. Therefore, whilst I agree that a knowledge of the facts and laws of evolution might have considerable and increasing relevance to the question whether certain acts would be right or wrong, since it might help us to foresee the large-scale and long-range consequences of such acts, I am unable to see that it has any direct bearing on the question whether certain states of affairs or processes or experiences would be intrinsically good or bad.

IX

SOME REFLECTIONS ON MORAL-SENSE THEORIES IN ETHICS[1] (1945)

During the long vacation of 1944 I spent such time as I could spare from my other duties in reading with some care Richard Price's book *A Review of the Principal Questions and Difficulties in Morals*. This was first published in 1758, and it reached a third edition in 1787. Price died soon afterwards, viz. in 1791. Until Ross published his book *The Right and the Good* in 1930 there existed, so far as I know, no statement and defence of what may be called the 'rationalistic' type of ethical theory comparable in merit to Price's. Price was thoroughly well acquainted with the works of other great English philosophers and moralists, such as Locke, Berkeley, Hume and Butler, and he develops his own views in conscious opposition to those of Hutcheson, the founder of the so-called 'moral-sense' type of ethical theory.

I had thought at one time of writing a critical account of Price's doctrines. But, when I began to do so, I soon found that it would be more profitable to treat independently and in modern terminology some of the questions with which Price was mainly concerned. Therefore my further references to Price will be only occasional and incidental; but I wish to make it plain that his book is the background of my paper, and that reading the former was the stimulus to writing the latter.

The topic with which I shall be primarily concerned may be called the 'epistemology of moral judgments'. This subject is of considerable interest in itself, and I think that it has been very inadequately treated by most writers on ethics. But it is important also for another reason. Questions of epistemology and of logical analysis are interconnected, and the answer which we give to a

[1] Reprinted from the *Proceedings of the Aristotelian Society*, Volume XLV, 1944-45, by courtesy of the Editor of the Aristotelian Society.

question of the one kind may have an important bearing on that which we should be inclined to give to a question of the other kind, e.g. I should be prepared to argue that, if ethical terms, such as *right* and *good*, are simple and non-naturalistic or are complex and contain a non-naturalistic constituent, then the concepts of them must be wholly or partly *a priori*. On the same hypothesis I should be prepared to argue that such judgments as 'Any act of promise-keeping tends as such to be right' must be synthetic and *a priori*. Now it is a well-known and plausible epistemological theory that there are no *a priori* concepts and no synthetic *a priori* judgments. If I am right, anyone who feels no doubt about this epistemological theory can safely reject the analysis of moral judgments which makes them contain non-naturalistic constituents. On the other hand, anyone who feels bound to accept that analysis of moral judgments will have to reject this epistemological theory.

In the discussion which follows I shall confine myself to the concepts *right* and *wrong*, in the specifically moral sense, and to judgments in which they occur as predicates. I think that most of what I say could be transferred *mutatis mutandis* to the concepts *morally good* and *evil* and to judgments in which they occur.

As Price points out, the words 'right' and 'wrong' are used in at least two different senses. This is made obvious by the fact that the sentence 'It is always right for a person to do what he honestly believes to be right, and wrong for him to do what he honestly believes to be wrong', is intelligible and would generally be admitted to be in some sense true. The two senses in which 'right' and 'wrong' occur in this sentence may be described as the 'subjective' and the 'material'. An act is subjectively right if the consequences which the agent *expects* it to have are such as he *thinks* would be materially right in the situation as he *believes* it to be. We shall be concerned here only with material rightness and wrongness. Let us call sentences in which the words 'right' or 'wrong', used in the material sense, occur as predicates 'deontic sentences'. An example would be 'Any act of promise-breaking tends as such to be wrong'.

I shall first distinguish certain alternative analyses which have been proposed for the situations expressed by deontic sentences, and then I shall consider certain alternative theories which might be held concerning deontic knowledge or belief. In the course of the discussion I shall try to bring out the relations between the two sets of theories.

(1) *Alternative Analyses of Deontic Sentences*

When a person utters such a sentence as 'That act is right' he seems *prima facie* to be expressing a judgment, and in that judgment he seems *prima facie* to be ascribing to a subject a predicate which has no reference to his own or other men's sensations, emotions, desires, or opinions. But we know that such appearances may be misleading. Such sentences as 'This food is nice' and 'That thing is yellow' are of the same grammatical form as 'That act is right'. Yet everyone would hold that the predicate of the first refers to the speaker's sensations of taste, and many people would hold that the predicate of the second refers to the visual sensations of human beings. So the first question to be asked is this. Do sentences like 'That act is right' express judgments at all? If not, what do they express?

As is well known, there is a theory that such sentences do not really express judgments at all. It has been held that they express only certain emotions felt by the speaker, or certain desires of his, or certain commands. I shall call this the 'interjectional theory'. Price does not consider this extreme view. If it had been put to him, he would probably have regarded it as too fantastically absurd to be taken seriously. It is, indeed, a kind of theory which can be swallowed only after one has undergone a long and elaborate process of 'conditioning' which was not available in the eighteenth century.

Suppose that the interjectional theory is rejected. Suppose we hold that deontic sentences do express judgments of *some* kind, and that at any rate the fact that they are in the indicative mood is not misleading. The next suggestion is that the judgments which they express are really about certain human experiences, certain sensations or emotions or desires. I shall call this the 'subjective theory'. I shall now point out that it may take a great number of different forms, and shall try to classify them.

The factor common to all forms of the subjective theory is that there is a peculiar kind of experience which human beings are liable to have when they contemplate certain acts, e.g. acts of promise-keeping or of treachery, just as there is a peculiar kind of experience which they have when they look at certain objects, e.g. at snow or at soot. I propose to call this at present by the intentionally vague name 'moral feeling'. I use this term because it covers both sensation and emotion. Since deontic judgments take the two opposite forms 'That is right' and 'That is wrong', it must be assumed that moral feeling takes two opposite forms. There are analogies to this both in sensation and emotion. There are the opposed temperature-sensations of hotness and coldness, and there are the opposed non-moral emotions of love and hate. I shall speak of the 'pro-form' and the 'anti-form' of moral feeling, and will assume that the former is associated with judgments of rightness and the latter with those of wrongness. The first division of subjective theories is into *sensational* and *emotional*, according to whether moral feeling is held to be analogous to sensation and moral judgment to be analogous judgments of sense-perception, or whether the feeling is held to be a form of emotion and the judgments to be concerned with that emotion.

The next division of subjective theories is into what I will call the 'intra-subjective' and the 'trans-subjective' varieties. According to the first of these a person who judges that so-and-so is right is asserting something about *his own* moral pro-feelings only. He is not saying anything about the moral feelings of other men. According to the second variety such a person is asserting something about all men, or most men, or a certain restricted class of men and not only about himself.

Lastly, each of these two varieties of the subjective theory can be subdivided into what I call an 'occurrent' and a 'dispositional' form. On the occurrent form of the intra-subjective variety of the subjective theory a person who says that so-and-so is right asserting only that at this moment he is having a moral pro-emotion towards so-and-so. On the occurrent form of the trans-subjective variety of the theory he is asserting that all or most members of a certain class of men, e.g. most members of the *Athenæum*, are at present having a moral pro-emotion towards so-and-so. On the dispositional form of the intra-subjective variety of the theory he is asserting that he has a disposition to feel a moral pro-emotion whenever he contemplates so-and-so or other acts like it. He may not be feeling such an emotion at the moment when he is saying that so-and-so is right. He might not be actually witnessing or thinking of such an act at the time; or, if he were, he might be in some special occurrent state, such as anger or jealousy, which is inhibiting or reversing his disposition to feel moral pro-emotion. On the dispositional form of the trans-subjective variety of the theory he is asserting that all or most men or all or most members of a certain class of men have a disposition to feel moral pro-emotion when they contemplate so-and-so or other acts like it. He might have strong reason to believe this even if he lacked that disposition himself. I have, e.g., strong reason to believe that most men have a disposition to like the taste and smell of apples, though I personally loathe them.

It appears then that there are at least eight possible species of the subjective theory, according as it is (i) sensation or emotional, (ii) intra-subjective or trans-subjective, or (iii) occurrent or dispositional. There are two remarks that I would make at this point.

(i) Even on the occurrent intra-subjective form of the theory such a statement as 'That act is wrong' could be questioned without accusing the speaker of lying about his own feelings at the time. But this could happen only in one way. The speaker might be mistaken about the kind of feeling which he is having when contemplating this act. He might think that he is having a moral anti-feeling when really he is having what Sidgwick calls a 'feeling of quasi-moral repugnance'. I have no doubt that such mistakes are often made by people, e.g., about their own feelings towards abnormal sexual desires and practices. (ii) I am inclined to think that the only form of the theory that is worth serious consideration is the trans-subjective dispositional form of it. But I should admit that it is not unplausible to hold that *sometimes* when a person says that so-and-so is right or that it is wrong he may be talking only of his own disposition to have a moral pro-feeling or anti-feeling when he contemplates such acts.

So far I have spoken only of singular deontic judgments, i.e. those of the form 'That act is right (or is wrong)'. But there are also universal deontic judgments, such as 'Any act of promise-keeping tends as such to be right' or 'Any act of deliberate deception tends as such to be wrong'. How would the subjective theory deal with the latter? Let us take, e.g., the trans-subjective dispositional form of the subjective theory and consider how it would deal with 'Any act of promise-keeping tends as such to be right'. It would say that this is equivalent to 'Any person contemplating an act which he believed to be one of promise-keeping would tend to have a moral pro-feeling in so far as he confined his attention to that aspect of the act.' No doubt this might require various qualifications, e.g., we might have to substitute 'any *normal* person' for 'any person' in order to allow for moral lunatics, and we might have to add 'provided he were in a normal state at the time' in order to allow for the possibility of his disposition to have a moral pro-feeling being inhibited or reversed if he were in a state of rage or of jealousy. But the general principle is clear enough.

Next let us suppose that all forms of the subjective theory are dismissed. We should then have to accept some form of what I will call the 'objective theory'. According to this a deontic judgment ascribes to an act a certain quality or relation or relational property which has no reference to the feelings or desires or opinions of the speaker or of anyone else concerning that act. Such judgments would be significant and might be true even if no human being had ever had moral feelings of any kind.

No doubt the objective theory might take many different forms. But for our purpose the most important principle of division is the following. Let us describe an 'ethical sentence' by enumeration as any sentence in which the words 'right' or 'wrong', 'ought' or 'ought not', 'morally good' or 'morally evil' or mere dictionary equivalents of them occur. Now, if the words 'right' and 'wrong' denote opposite forms of a certain objective characteristic, the following possibilities are open about that characteristic. (i) It may be simple and therefore indefinable, as, e.g., the quality of sensible yellowness and the relation of temporal precedence are. (ii) It may be complex and therefore definable. If so, it may be definable (*a*) only by means of ethical sentences or (*b*) without the use of such sentences. The following alleged definitions of 'right' would illustrate these two possibilities. The first would be exemplified if 'right' could be defined only as 'what it is *fitting* to approve' or only as 'what is conducive to *morally good* experiences'. The second would be exemplified if 'right' were definable as 'conducive to social stability' or as 'productive of a balance of *pleasant* experiences'. I propose to give the name 'naturalistic to (i) all forms of the subjective theory, and (ii) any form of the objective theory which holds that 'right' and 'wrong' are definable without the use of ethical sentences. I shall give the name 'non-naturalistic' to any form of the objective theory which holds that 'right' and 'wrong' are either indefinable or definable only by means of ethical sentences. For the present purpose it is not important to consider whether this use of 'naturalistic' and 'non-naturalistic' agrees exactly either in extension or in intension with Professor Moore's usage.

Before leaving this topic there is one further remark to be made. I think it is fair to say that most competent persons who have reflected on this subject in recent years would agree that the only alternatives worth serious consideration are some form of either (*a*) the interjectional theory, or (*b*) the dispositional variety of the subjective theory, or (*c*) the non-naturalistic variety of the objective theory. Perhaps I should add that under the head of 'competent persons' in this connection I do not include the eminent natural scientists who from time to time take a holiday from their professional labours in order to instruct us in ethical theory.

(2) *Alternative Epistemological Theories of Deontic Cognition*

I shall begin by considering singular deontic judgments, i.e. ones of the form 'That act is right (or is wrong)'. Presumably those moralists who hold a moral sense theory intend at least to assert that these judgments are analogous in certain important respects to judgments of sense perception, such as 'That thing is yellow'.

Now the first thing to notice is that two very different accounts may be given of such judgments as 'That thing is yellow'. These may be described as the naively realistic account and the dispositional account. I will now explain these terms.

(i) I think that the plain man in his plainer moments uncritically takes for granted that the very same sensible quality of yellowness which is presented to him when he looks at a bit of gold in white light literally pervades the surface of that bit of gold, not only when he is looking at it in white light, but also and in precisely the same sense when no one is looking at it and when it is in the dark. He believes that looking at the thing and its being illuminated by white light serve only to *reveal* to him the yellowness which has been there all the time in precisely the form in which it is now presented to him. This is what I call the 'naïvely realistic interpretation'. Price seems to have thought that this, or something like it, is what plain men believe. He also thought that this belief is not only mistaken, but can be seen to be internally inconsistent by anyone who reflects carefully on the natures of sensible yellowness and of material objects. I must confess that I cannot see this myself.

(ii) A person who makes the judgment 'That thing is yellow' may be expressing *only* his belief that it would present a yellow appearance to any normal human being who might at any time view it in white light. No doubt a person who accepts the naïvely realistic interpretation also believes this conditional proposition. But this belief is certainly not the whole of what he expresses by saying 'That thing is yellow', and it might not even be a part of it. It might be for him only a very obvious and immediate consequence of what he expresses by that statement. I give the name 'dispositional account' to the view that the whole meaning of such judgments as 'That thing is yellow' is a conditional proposition of the kind which I have just enunciated.

The next point to notice is this. If a person believes that a certain thing would present a yellow appearance to any normal human being who should at any time view it in white light, he does not generally accept this conditional proposition as an ultimate fact. He generally amplifies it as follows. He ascribes to the thing a certain intrinsic property, and he ascribes to each human being a certain other intrinsic property correlated with the former. Let us call these respectively the 'objective' and the 'subjective correlate' in the perception of yellowness. It is held that when and only when a certain relationship is set up between a human being and this thing the subjective correlate in the person and the objective correlate in the thing together cause the thing to present a yellow appearance to the person.

This is common ground to the holders of the naïvely realistic and of the dispositional account. But there is a profound difference between them in point of detail. On the naïvely realistic interpretation the objective correlate just is that quality of sensible yellowness which, according to that theory, is spread out over the surface of the thing ready to be presented whenever the appropriate revelatory conditions are fulfilled. The subjective correlate just is the power of prehending the yellowness of yellow things when such conditions are fufilled. That power is activated whenever a person who possesses it stands in a certain bodily and mental relation to a thing which possesses yellowness.

On the dispositional interpretation the objective correlate is generally held to be a certain kind of minute structure and internal agitation in a thing which is not itself literally and non-dispositionally coloured. Again, the subjective correlate is not now the power of prehending the objective correlate. We have no such power. It is the capacity to have sensations of a certain kind, called 'sensations of yellowness'; and these are not prehensions of a quality of yellowness inherent in the thing perceived. There is no such quality. That power is activated whenever a person who possesses it stands in a certain bodily and mental relation to a thing which has this peculiar kind of minute structure and internal agitation.

I do not think that anyone who accepted the dispositional interpretation would give the name 'yellowness' to that minute structure and internal cogitation of a colourless object which, according to him, is the objective correlate of sensations of yellow. He would confine the name 'yellow' to (*a*) the peculiar sensible quality of certain sensations, e.g., those which he has when he looks at the yolk of an egg in white light, and (*b*) the dispositional property which certain things have of giving rise to such sensations in a normal human observer when he views them in white light. If he were wise, he would distinguish these two usages of the word as 'sensible' and 'physical' yellowness; or he might prefer the more general phrases 'occurrent' and 'dispositional' yellowness. To the minute structure and internal agitation which are the objective correlate of the perception of things as yellow we might give the name 'physical correlate of yellowness'.

We can now see that the moral sense theory of singular deontic judgments might take two entirely different forms, viz. a naïvely realistic one and a dispositional one. Both would start from the common ground that there is a peculiar kind of experience which human beings are liable to have when they contemplate certain acts, and that this can take either of two opposite forms, viz. a pro-form and an anti-form. Both would hold that this experience is of the nature of feeling, where 'feeling' is used to include both sensation and emotion as distinguished from thought. From this common basis they diverge as follows:

The naïvely realistic form of the moral sense theory would take moral feeling to be like what visual sensation is supposed to be on the naïvely realistic view of visual perception. When a person contemplates a certain act and has a moral pro-feeling in doing so that feeling either is or involves a prehension by him of a certain characteristic, viz. rightness, in the act; and that characteristic belongs literally and non-dispositionally to the act quite independently of whether anyone happens to contemplate it or to have a moral pro-feeling when doing so. (I have used the alternative phrase 'is or involves a prehension' rather than the simpler phrase 'is a prehension' because it might well be held that a moral feeling is never *just* a prehension of the objective rightness or wrongness of a contemplated act, but is always such a prehension qualified by a certain kind of emotional tone.)

I am fairly certain that the adherents of the moral sense theory did not interpret it in this way; for they did not, I think, put a naïvely realistic interpretation on visual sense-perception. But some of them may quite likely have thought that plain men mistakenly put this interpretation both on such judgments as 'That act is right' and on such judgments as 'That thing is yellow'. On the other hand, I suspect that Professor Moore, when he compared intrinsic goodness with yellowness in *Principia Ethica*, was tacitly assuming something like the naïvely realistic interpretation of both such judgments.

The dispositional form of the moral sense theory would take moral feeling to be either (*a*) a special kind of emotion or (*b*) a sensation analogous to those of taste or smell and not to those of sight. I suppose that hardly anyone would put a naïvely realistic interpretation on such perceptual judgments as 'That is bitter' even if he were inclined to put such an interpretation on judgments like 'That is yellow'.

Starting from this basis the theory might take the dispositional form in one or other of its main varieties. The feature common to all of them would be that the moral feeling which a person has when he contemplates an act neither is nor involves a prehension by him of an independent non-dispositional characteristic of rightness inherent in that act. On the trans-subjective variety of this theory a person who says that an act is right means, roughly speaking, no more than that any normal person who should contemplate this act when he was in a normal condition would have a moral pro-feeling. On the intra-subjective variety of the theory the speaker would mean the same kind of thing with 'he himself' substituted for 'any normal person'. I have little doubt that most upholders of the moral sense theory meant to assert the trans-subjective variety of the dispositional form of it. But they did not always make this clear to their readers, and perhaps they were not always clear about it themselves.

It is perhaps worth remarking that the moral sense theory might conceivably take the occurrent intra-subjective form. It might allege that, when a person calls an act right, all that he means is that his present contemplation of it is accompanied by a moral pro-feeling. I think that this form of the theory is so obviously inadequate that supporters of the moral sense doctrine can hardly have meant to assert it. But some of them may have incautiously made statements which would suggest that this is what they meant, and their opponents may sometimes have found it convenient to seize upon these as readily assailable Aunt Sallies. It seems to me that the only two forms of the moral sense theory that are worth serious consideration are the naïvely realistic form and the trans-subjective variety of the dispositional form. I shall now consider them in turn.

(2.1) *Naïvely Realistic Form of the Moral Sense Theory.* The only kinds of sense-perception which can with any plausibility be interpreted in a naïvely realistic way are visual and tactual perception. Therefore the naïvely realistic form of the moral sense theory will have very little to recommend it if singular deontic judgments differ from judgments of visual and tactual perception in just those respects which make a naïvely realistic interpretation of the latter plausible. It seems to me that the relevant differences are profound and that the analogies are superficial.

(i) In stating the moral sense theory I have so far used the intentionally vague phrase 'having a moral pro-feeling or anti-feeling when one *contemplates* an action'. If singular deontic judgments are to be analogous to judgments of visual or tactual sense-perception, this must be held to be analogous to having a sensation of yellowness when one *looks at* the yolk of an egg or having a sensation of coldness and hardness when one *touches* a block of ice. Is there any such analogy?

We must begin by distinguishing two cases, viz. (*a*) where one person makes a deontic judgment about an act done by another, and (*b*) where he makes such a judgment about an act done by himself.

(*a*) One person never can perceive the act of another, if by 'act' we mean something to which moral predicates can be applied. He can perceive only some bit of overt behaviour on the part of another, e.g., writing a cheque and handing it over to a third person. That bit of overt behaviour may be an act of forgery or of paying a debt or of subscribing to a charity or of bribing an official. As a subject of moral predicates it is a different act according to the different intentions with which it is done. Now one person can contemplate another's intentions only in the sense of making them objects of *thought* and never in that of *perceiving* them.

I think that this suffices to wreck the moral sense theory in its naïvely realistic form as applied to singular deontic judgments made by one person about the acts of another. Even if a naïvely realistic account of such judgments as 'That thing is yellow' were acceptable, there would be no analogy between them and such judgments as 'That act is right' when the judger and the agent are different. For 'that thing', e.g., a certain bit of gold, is perceived by the person who makes the judgment that it is yellow. The thing is *perceived*; it is perceived *as yellow*; and the sensation of yellowness is an *essential constituent* of the perception of the thing. The naïvely realistic account of the situation is that the percipient is acquainted with the surface of the thing, and that the latter reveals to the percipient through his sensation of yellow that objective non-dispositional quality of yellowness which it possesses independently of human observers and their sensations. This account is here *prima facie* highly plausible. But 'that act', if done by another, is not perceived except as a bit of overt behaviour. In respect of those characteristics which make it a possible subject for moral predicates it can only be *conceived.* The moral feeling, even if it be a sensation and not an emotion only, is not an essential constituent of the perception of the act as a bit of overt behaviour; only visual sensations are essential constituents of that perception. And finally the relation of the moral pro-feeling or anti-feeling to the *conception* of the act as, e.g., one of debt-paying or one of bribery cannot possibly be like the relation of a sensation to a perception of which it is a constituent, e.g., the relation of a sensation of yellowness to the visual perception of a thing as yellow.

(*b*) When a deontic judgment is passed by a person on one of his own acts the above criticism does not hold. In performing an act a person is or may be directly aware of his own intentions.

He knows it directly as an act of intended bribery or forgery or debt-paying or whatever it may be, and not merely as a bit of overt behaviour of a certain kind. Similarly, in retrospection a person generally knows by personal memory what were his intentions in his own past acts. No doubt introspective self-perception and personal memory are very different in important respects from sense-perceptions. But they agree with it, and differ from one's awareness of the experiences of another person in being ostensibly instances of direct acquaintance with particulars. It seems to me then that, if the Moral Sense Theory in its naïvely realistic form is to be defended, it must be confined in the first instance to deontic judgments made by a person about his own acts. We might suppose that he derives his notions of rightness and wrongness from perceiving those characteristics in certain of his own acts by means of moral sensations. Once he has acquired the notions in this way he can proceed to apply them to the acts of other persons; although he cannot perceive these and therefore cannot perceive their rightness or wrongness, but can have only conceptual cognition about them.

Now I think that there is a very serious objection to this view. It is certain that I have moral pro-feelings and anti-feelings *both* when I introspect or remember certain acts of my own and when I conceptually cognize the similar acts of other persons. Now I cannot detect any relevant difference between my moral feelings in the two cases. But, as we have seen, it is impossible in the latter case to hold that there is any analogy to visual sense-perception as interpreted by the naïvely realistic theory. It is impossible to hold here that the moral feeling is a state of acquaintance with an objective characteristic of rightness or wrongness in the cognized act. Therefore it seems unreasonable to suppose that the precisely similar moral feelings which one has when introspectively perceiving or remembering one's own acts is susceptible of a naïvely realistic interpretation.

I pass now to another profound *prima facie* difference between singular deontic judgments and judgments of visual or tactual perception. If I judge that a certain act is right or that it is wrong, it is always sensible for anyone to raise the question 'What *makes* it right or *makes* it wrong?' The answer that we expect to such a question is the mention of some non-ethical characteristic of the act, e.g., that it is an act of promise-keeping, of giving a false answer to a question, and so on. Let us call these 'right-inclining' and 'wrong-inclining' characteristics. Now the connection between the presence of any of these non-ethical characteristics and the tendency of an act to be right or to be wrong seems to be necessary and self-evident, not causal and contingent. (I say the '*tendency* to be right or to be wrong' and not just 'rightness' or 'wrongness' for a reason which will be familiar to all readers of Ross's ethical writings. One and the same act may be, e.g., an act of truth-telling and one of betrayal. It is not self-evident that such an act is resultantly right or resultantly wrong. But it might well be held to be self-evident that it tends to be right in respect of being an act of truth-telling and to be wrong in respect of being one of betrayal, and that it would be right if it had no wrong-inclining characteristic and would be wrong if it had no right-inclining characteristic. These points were made clearly enough by Price, but have since been made much more clearly by Ross.)

Now the fact which I have just mentioned is relevant to both forms of the moral sense theory, but for the present we are concerned only with the naïvely realistic form of it. If I look at a thing and judge it to be yellow, it is not particularly sensible to ask 'What makes it yellow?' The question is sensible only if it is interpreted causally, e.g., in some cases the answer might be that it contains saffron. And a more ultimate answer would be that it has such and such a minute structure and internal agitation. Now on the naïvely realistic theory the thing is pervaded literally and non-dispositionally by an inherent quality of yellowness; and there is no self-evident necessity for all things which have a certain kind of minute structure and internal agitation and only such things to be pervaded by yellowness. It is simply a contingent general connection between two sets of properties of a material thing, viz. certain geometrical and kinematic properties, on the one hand, and a certain objective colour, on the other. The connection between being an act of promise-breaking and tending to be wrong does not seem to be in the least like this.

It is worth while to remark before leaving this topic that, even if our cognition of the rightness or wrongness of acts were analogous to visual or tactual perception interpreted in the naïvely realistic way, it is quite certain that our cognition of right-inclining and wrong-inclining characteristics is not. Such characteristics as being an intentional breach of promise, an intentional return of a borrowed article, and so on, are highly complex relational properties. They can be cognized only *conceptually*; it is non-sensical to suggest that they could be cognized by anything analogous to sense-perception or to introspective self-perception.

On the other hand, the fact, if it be a fact, that the connection between certain non-ethical characteristics and the tendency to be right is necessary and self-evident is not in itself a reason for denying that rightness and wrongness are cognized by something analogous to sensation interpreted in a naïvely realistic way. For the connection between having shape and having size is necessary and self-evident, and yet both these characteristics are cognized by visual sense-perception.

I think that the upshot of this discussion is that there is little to be said for and much to be said against the moral sense theory in its naïvely realistic form as applied to deontic judgments. We can therefore pass to the dispositional form of the theory.

(2.2) *Dispositional Form of the Moral Sense Theory.* I do not think that we shall be unfair to the theory if we confine our attention to the trans-subjective variety of it and if we assume that moral feeling is of the nature of emotion rather than sensation.

I shall begin with some general remarks about emotion. (i) An emotion, e.g., an experience of fearing or hating, as distinct from an emotional mood, such as a state of apprehension or of crossness, is always directed to a cognized object. This may be real or hallucinatory, e.g. one may be afraid of a real man who is pointing a revolver at one or of an hallucinatory appearance of such a man in a dream. Again, if the object be real, it may be correctly or more or less incorrectly cognized, e.g. one may be afraid of a real physical object which one sees when crossing a field in twilight and takes to be a man pointing a revolver at one, and this object may really be a harmless scarecrow.

(ii) We must distinguish between what I will call 'mediated' and 'unmediated' emotions. Sometimes when a person feels a certain emotion towards a certain object he has an experience which may be described as feeling that emotion towards that object *in respect of* certain characteristics which he believes (rightly or wrongly) that it possesses. In that case I shall say that his emotion is *mediated* by this belief about the characteristics of the object, and I shall call these characteristics the 'mediating characteristics' of the emotion. Often, however, the emotion is not felt in respect of any characteristic which the experient believes the object to have. In that case I shall say that the emotion is *unmediated*. If I am angry with a person, e.g., I may feel this anger in respect of some fault which I believe (rightly or wrongly) that he has committed. But I may feel angry with a person, and still more obviously I may dislike him, just directly and, as we say, 'for no assignable reason'. This is an example of an *unmediated* emotion.

(iii) Presumably every occurrence of any emotion, whether mediated or unmediated, has a *total cause*. In many cases, no doubt, an essential factor in that cause is the presence of certain characteristics in the object. I will call these 'evoking characteristics'. In the case of a mediated emotion the evoking and the mediating characteristics may be, and no doubt often are, wholly or partly the same. But very often they must be different; for the object often does not really have the characteristics which the experient believes it to have and in respect of which he feels his emotion towards it.

(iv) It is commonly held that certain kinds of emotion are in some sense 'appropriate to' objects which have certain characteristics, and that they are 'inappropriate to' objects which lack these or which have certain others, e.g., fear is held to be appropriate only to objects which are dangerous. Again, it is held for a given degree of dangerousness there is, within fairly narrow limits, a fitting degree of fear. To fear objects which are not really dangerous is described as 'irrational'; and to fear intensely objects which are only slightly dangerous is described as 'inordinate'.

It is a well-known fact that if a person begins by feeling an unmediated emotion towards an object he is very liable to go on to ascribe to that object such characteristics as would make the emotion appropriate and to ascribe to those characteristics such a degree as would make his emotion ordinate. A very familiar example of this is provided by persons who are jealous of others. Lastly, if a person feels a mediated emotion towards an object in respect of a characteristic to which that emotion is inappropriate, he is very liable to divert his attention from this fact and to ascribe to the object another characteristic in respect of which the emotion would be appropriate. These tendencies, which have been perfectly familiar to playwrights, preachers and plain men throughout the ages, have been hailed as great discoveries of modern psychology under the name of 'rationalization'.

We are now in a position to consider the trans-subjective dispositional form of the moral sense theory. In essence the theory is that such judgments as 'That act is right (or is wrong)' are analogous to such judgments as 'That food is nice (or is nasty)'. The correct analysis of them is some variant on the formula 'That act would evoke a moral pro-emotion (or anti-emotion) in any human being who might at any time contemplate it'. There might have to be qualifications about the individual being 'normal' and being 'in a normal state', but we need not trouble about them at present.

Now this form of the theory does avoid the first objection which I made against the naïvely realistic form of it. It does not have to assume that one person literally has knowledge by acquaintance of the intentions of another. It does not have to assume that the experience of having a moral feeling when contemplating an act of one's own is fundamentally different in kind from that of having a moral feeling when contemplating a similar act of another person. For we can and do have emotions towards objects which are cognized only conceptually, and we can and do feel such emotions in respect of characteristics whose presence is only conceived and not perceived.

It seems to me that the main difficulties of the theory can be summed up in the following three questions: (i) Can it deal with the fact that judgments like 'That act is right' seem always to be grounded upon the supposed presence in the act of some non-ethical right-inclining characteristics, such as being the fulfilment of a promise? (ii) If so, can it deal with the further fact that the connection between a right-inclining characteristic and the rightness which it tends to convey seems to be necessary and synthetic? And (iii) can it deal with the fact that it seems not only intelligible but also true to say that moral pro-emotion is felt towards an act in respect of the characteristic of *rightness* and moral anti-emotion in respect of the characteristic *wrongness?* I shall take these three questions in turn.

(i) I think that a fairly plausible answer, so far as it goes, can be made to the first question. We shall have to say that the right-inclining characteristic which is the ground of the judgment 'That act is right' just is the mediating characteristic of the moral pro-emotion which is felt towards such acts. To say that every moral judgment is founded upon some non-ethical characteristic of the act which is its subject will be equivalent to saying that every moral emotion is a mediated emotion. Such characteristics as being an act of promise-keeping will be mediating characteristics for moral pro-emotion; such characteristics as being an act of lying or of deliberate cruelty will be mediating characteristics of moral anti-emotion.

It should be noticed that the theory can account quite plausibly for the facts which Ross describes under the head of his distinction between '*prima facie* duties' and 'a duty proper'. (I prefer to use the phrases 'components of obligation' and 'resultant obligation'.) An act is known or believed to have various characteristics, e.g. to be an act of truth-telling, a breach of confidence, and an optimific act. The first and the third of these features give rise to components of obligation of various degrees of urgency towards doing it; the second gives rise to a component of a certain degree of urgency against doing it. According to circumstances the resultant obligation may be to do it or to avoid doing it. Now it is a perfectly familiar fact that an object may have several characteristics, and that it may call forth an emotion of one kind in respect of some of them and an emotion of the opposite kind in respect of others; so that the emotion towards the object as a whole may be predominantly of the opposite kind. The present theory would say that we tend to feel a moral pro-emotion of a certain strength towards the act in respect of its being one of truth-telling and in respect of its being optimific; that we tend to feel a moral anti-emotion of a certain strength towards it as being a breach of confidence; and that our moral emotion towards it as a whole is the resultant of these two tendencies, and may be either predominantly *pro* or predominantly *anti* according to circumstances.

(ii) The second question is much harder. It is alleged, e.g., that the proposition 'Any act of promise-keeping tends as such to be right, and any act of promise-breaking tends as such to be wrong' is necessary, self-evident, and synthetic. On the present theory of deontic judgments this would be equivalent to something like the following proposition: 'It is necessary, self-evident and synthetic that any human being who should contemplate an act which he believed to be one of promise-keeping would tend to feel a moral pro-emotion towards it, and that he would tend to feel a moral anti-emotion towards any act which he believed to be one of promise-breaking'.

Now it might be objected that the latter statement is certainly false. It is a purely contingent fact that human beings have a disposition to feel moral emotions at all. They might have been as devoid of them as they are of a disposition to have special sensations in presence of magnets. Moreover, granted that they do have such an emotional disposition, it is a purely contingent fact that moral emotions are mediated in the particular ways in which they are. It is quite conceivable that the belief that an act is one of promise-keeping should have mediated a moral *anti*-emotion, and that the belief that it is one of promise-breaking should have mediated a moral *pro*-emotion; just as it is conceivable that men should have liked the taste of castor oil and disliked that of sugar. In that case, on the present theory, promise-breaking would have tended to be right and promise-keeping to be wrong; just as castor oil would have been nice and sugar nasty.

So the objection comes to this. If the present form of the moral sense theory were true, certain propositions which are in fact necessary and knowable *a priori* would have been contingent and knowable only empirically. Therefore the theory is false. I am sure that this is the most important of Price's objections to the moral sense theory, though I have developed it in my own way. What are we to say about it?

It is plain that there are only two lines of defence open to the present form of the moral sense theory. (*a*) One is to argue that propositions like 'Any act of promise-keeping tends as such to be right' are *not* necessary. (*b*) The other is to argue that propositions like 'Any human being who should contemplate an act which he believed to be one of promise-keeping would tend to feel a moral pro-emotion towards it' are *not* contingent. Let us consider the two alternatives in turn:

(*a*) I think that this line of argument would divide into two parts, which might be called the 'offensive' and the 'defensive'. The offensive part would take the opposite view as a hypothesis and try to show that it is untenable. The defensive part would try to explain why certain propositions which are in fact empirical and contingent appear to many people to be *a priori* and necessary.

(*a, a*) The offensive part may be put as follows: What precisely do our opponents maintain? If we may take Price as their ablest representative, they seem to assert something like the following doctrine. Suppose that a person reflects, e.g., on the situation of being asked a question and on the notions of responding to it by a true answer and responding to it by a false answer. Then he will find it self-evident that the former kind of response has a certain relation of 'moral fittingness' and that the latter has an opposite relation of 'moral unfittingness' to such a situation. This relation of moral fittingness or unfittingness is held to be unique and unanalysable. And the process of recognizing that it necessarily holds between certain kinds of response and certain kinds of situation is held to be analogous to that of recognizing that certain mathematical terms, e.g. stand in certain mathematical relations.

Now the objection which will be made by supporters of the moral sense theory is twofold. It will be said that the doctrine just enunciated involves *a priori* concepts and synthetic *a priori* judgments, and that neither of these is admissible. We will take these two points in order.

If there is a simple unanalysable relation of moral fittingness or unfittingness, it is certainly not manifested to us by any of our senses. We literally *see* that one coloured patch is surrounded by another; we literally *hear* that two notes, sounded together or in very close succession, concord or discord with each other; and so on. In such cases we presumably derive our ideas of the relation of *surrounding* and the relation of *concording or discording* by comparison and abstraction from such sensibly presented instances of terms standing in these relations. It is plain that we do not acquire the idea of moral fittingness or unfittingness in this way. Nor do we derive the idea from instances of terms presented to us by introspection as standing in that relationship. Introspection presents us with certain of our own experiences as standing in certain temporal relations, e.g., as being in the same specious present and partly overlapping in time, and so on. Again, since the relation of moral fittingness or unfittingness is held to be simple and unanalysable, the idea of it cannot be one which we have constructed in thought from elements presented separately or in different contexts by sensation or introspection or both. (The idea of the complex relationship of a colonel to the subordinate officers of his regiment, e.g., is no doubt reached in some such way as this.) But it is held by many philosophers to be a fundamental epistemological principle that every idea is either derived by abstraction from instances presented in sensation or introspection or is an intellectual construction from elements so derived. If this principle be admitted, it is impossible that we should have any conception of the relations of moral fittingness and unfittingness as described by such moralists as Price.

For my part I attach very little weight to this argument. I can see nothing self-evident in what I will call for short 'Hume's epistemological principle', and I am not aware that any conclusive empirical evidence has been adduced for it. It seems to me to be simply a useful goad to disturb our dogmatic slumbers, and a useful guide to follow until it begins to tempt us to ignore some facts and to distort others. I am inclined to think that the concepts of cause and of substance are *a priori* or contain *a priori* elements; at any rate I have never seen any satisfactory account of them in accordance with Hume's principle.

The second point in the offensive part of the argument is this: Suppose, if possible, that 'right' and 'wrong' are simple unanalysable notions, as Price, e.g., held them to be. Then any proposition which asserts a connection between some non-ethical characteristic, such as promise-keeping, and tendency to be right must be synthetic. Now a proposition may be synthetic and contingent or analytic and necessary, but it is an admitted general principle that no proposition can be both synthetic and necessary. Therefore the combined doctrine that 'right' and 'wrong' are unique unanalysable notions and that such propositions as 'Any act of promise-keeping tends as such to be right' are necessary must be false.

Such an argument would have different effects on different persons. Suppose that A and B are both quite convinced up to a certain moment of the truth of a certain general principle, and suppose that at that moment C brings to their notice an apparent counter-instance. If each is to be self-consistent, *something* will have to give way in each of them. But it need not be the same something. A may remain completely certain of the general principle; he will then have to maintain that the instance is only apparently contrary to it and explain why it seems to be so. B may find it impossible to doubt that the instance is contrary; he will then be forced to give up the general principle and explain why it seemed evident. These are the two extreme possibilities. Between them are numberless possible intermediate alternatives, where the person concerned is led to feel *some* doubt of the unqualified truth of the principle and *some* doubt whether the apparent counter-instance really conflicts with it. Speaking for myself, I occupy one of these intermediate positions. As for Price, he would have been completely unmoved by this kind of argument. For he held, in full knowledge of Hume's doctrine and in conscious opposition to it, that there are plenty of synthetic necessary facts in other departments beside that of morals. For these reasons I think that it is rather futile to rely on a general argument of this kind.

(α, β) The defensive part of the argument might take the following line. Civilized men throughout human history have been assiduously conditioned in infancy and youth by parents, nurses, schoolmasters, etc., to feel moral pro-emotions towards acts of certain kinds and to feel moral anti-emotions towards acts of certain kinds. Moreover, if we consider what kinds of acts are the objects of moral pro-emotions and what kinds are the objects of moral anti-emotions we notice the following facts about them. The former are acts whose performance by most people on most occasions when they are relevant is essential to the stability and efficient working of any society. The latter are acts which, if done on many occasions and by many people, would be utterly destructive to any society. On the other hand, the former are acts which an individual is often strongly tempted to omit, and the latter are acts which he is often strongly tempted to commit. This is either because we have strong natural impulses moving us to omit the former and to commit the latter, or because the attractive consequences of the former and the repellent consequences of the latter are often remote, collateral, and secondary. It follows that any group of men in which, from no matter what cause, a strong pro-emotion had become associated with acts of the first kind and a strong anti-emotion with acts of the second kind would be likely to win in the struggle for existence with other groups in which no such emotions existed or in which they were differently directed. Therefore it is likely that most of the members of all societies which now exist would be descendants of persons in whom strong moral pro-emotions had become attached to acts of the first kind and strong anti-emotions to acts of the second kind. And most existing societies will be historically and culturally continuous with societies in which such emotions had become attached to such acts. These causes, it might be argued, conspire to produce so strong an association between such emotions and such acts in most members of every existing society that the connection between the emotion and the act seems to each individual to be necessary.

No doubt this line of argument will produce different effects on different persons. For my own part I am inclined to attach a good deal of weight to it.

(*b*) I pass now to the second kind of defence which might be made for the dispositional form of the moral sense theory. This is to contend that the proposition about human emotional dispositions which, according to the theory, is equivalent to 'Any act of promise-keeping tends as such to be right' *is* necessary. It might be thought that this contention is so palpably absurd as not to be worth putting forward. But I believe that a case can be made for it, and I propose to make it.

We must begin by noting that the proposition which is equivalent to 'Any act of promise-keeping tends as such to be right' could not with any plausibility be taken to be the crude unqualified proposition 'Any human being has a disposition to feel a moral pro-emotion whenever he contemplates an act which he believes to be one of promise-keeping'. So far from being necessary the latter proposition is not even true. To make it true it will have to be qualified somewhat as follows. We must substitute for it the proposition 'Any *normal* human being has a disposition to feel a moral pro-emotion towards any act which he believes to be one of promise-keeping if he contemplates it when he is in a *normal* state'.

Now it might be argued that, when the proposition is thus qualified, it *is* necessary. For, it might be said, it has then become *analytic*. It is part of the definition of a 'normal' human being that he has a disposition to feel moral emotion, and that he will feel that emotion in its pro-form towards acts which he believes to be ones of promise-keeping, of truth-telling, or beneficence, and so on. And it is part of the definition of 'being in a normal state' that when one is in such a state this moral-emotional disposition will not be inhibited altogether or excited in abnormal ways.

No doubt the immediate answer which an opponent of the moral sense theory would make to this contention is the following: He would say that such propositions as 'Any act of promise-keeping tends as such to be right' are not only necessary but *synthetic*. The defender of the dispositional form of the moral sense theory has shown that, on his analysis, they would be necessary only at the cost of showing that they would be *analytic*. This answer is correct so far as it goes, but I think that the defender of the moral sense theory could rebut it as follows.

The fact is that it is often by no means easy to say whether a proposition is analytic or not. The analytic propositions of real life are not like the trivial examples in logic-books, such as 'All Negroes are black' or 'All right angles are angles'. The following are much better worth considering, e.g. 'The sun rises in the east'. 'A freely suspended magnet sets itself with its axis pointing north and south', and 'Pure water boils at 100° C under a pressure of 76 centimetres of mercury'. The first of these is analytic if 'east' and 'west' are defined by means of the sun, and synthetic if they are defined by means of the magnetic or the gyroscopic compass. The second is analytic if 'north' and 'south' are defined by means of the magnetic compass, and synthetic if they are defined by means of the sun or the gyroscopic compass. The third might be taken as a definition of '100° C'. But if that term were defined in some other way, e.g., thermo-dynamically, as on Lord Kelvin's absolute scale, it might be regarded as an analytic proposition about *pure water*. For an important element in the definition of 'pure water' is that it has a certain boiling point under certain standard conditions.

Two important points emerge from these examples. The first is that the same type-sentence may express both an analytic and a synthetic proposition, and that a person who uses several tokens of this type even in a single discourse may sometimes be expressing the analytical and sometimes the synthetic proposition. The former is necessary and the latter is contingent. It would not be surprising if a person should sometimes become confused in such cases and think that every token of this type expresses *one and the same proposition* which is *both* synthetic and necessary.

The second point is this. Such an analytic proposition as 'Pure water boils at 100° C under a pressure of 76 centimetres of mercury' has at the back of it a whole system of interconnected empirical generalizations, apart from which it would never have been worth anyone's while to formulate it. It would take me far too long even to begin to state a few of these empirical generalizations. It will suffice to say that they are all represented in the various qualifications which make the proposition 'Pure water boils at 100° C under a pressure of 76 centimetres of mercury' analytic.

Now it might be suggested that facts like these throw some light on the alleged synthetic necessity of such propositions as 'Any act of promise-keeping tends as such to be right', and on the claim of defenders of the dispositional form of the moral sense theory that the equivalent propositions about human emotional dispositions are necessary because analytic.

The proposition 'Any act of promise-keeping would tend to call forth a moral pro-emotion in any *normal* human being who might contemplate it when in a *normal* state' is obviously rather like the proposition 'Any sample of *pure* water boils at 100° C under the *normal* atmospheric pressure, i.e. 76 centimetres of mercury'. Just as the latter is analytic, but is founded on a whole mass of interconnected empirical generalizations, so is the former. I will now try to justify this statement.

It is an empirical fact that the vast majority of men have a disposition to feel moral emotions, and that the minority who lack it differ in many other ways from the majority of their fellows. It is an empirical fact that there is very substantial agreement among men in the kinds of act which call forth moral pro-emotion and in the kinds which call forth moral anti-emotion. The small minority of men who habitually feel moral pro-emotion where most of their fellows feel moral anti-emotion, or *vice versa*, are generally found to be odd and abnormal in many other ways. There is, in fact, so high a degree of positive association between moral and non-moral normality that it would make very little difference in practice whether we defined a 'normal' man solely by reference to his moral dispositions or solely by reference to his non-moral dispositions, or by reference to a mixture of both. But the proposition that any normal human being would tend to feel a moral pro-emotion towards any act which he believed to be one of promise-keeping would be synthetic if one defined 'normality' solely by reference to non-moral dispositions, whilst it might well be analytic if one defined it wholly or partly in terms of moral dispositions.

Again, there is a very high degree of positive association between the tendencies to feel moral pro-emotion towards acts of promise-keeping, of truth-telling, of beneficence, etc.; and there is perhaps an even stronger degree of positive association between the tendencies to feel moral anti-emotion towards acts of treachery, of unfairness, of cruelty, etc. Therefore it would make little practical difference which of these mediating characteristics was included and which was omitted from the definition of 'normality'. Now, if the tendency to feel moral pro-emotion towards any act which is believed to be one of promise-keeping were included in the definition of 'normality', the proposition that any normal man would tend to feel such an emotion towards such acts would be analytic; whilst, if this were omitted and 'normality' were defined by reference to some of the other mediating characteristics of moral emotion, this proposition would be synthetic.

It therefore seems likely that, if the analysis which the dispositional form of the moral sense theory offers for such propositions as 'Any act of promise-keeping tends as such to be right' were correct, a sentence of this type might often express a proposition which is analytic and necessary and might as often express one that is synthetic and contingent. If so, it is not unlikely that a confusion should arise and that it should be thought that *every* such sentence expresses one and the same proposition which is *both* necessary and synthetic.

It remains to say something of the qualification 'when in a normal state', which has to be added to make the statement universally true, and which at the same time makes it more nearly analytic. It may be compared to the qualifications about the water being pure and the barometric pressure being normal in my example about boiling-point.

At the back of this qualification lie certain negative and certain positive empirical facts. It is found that a person who generally does feel moral pro-emotions towards acts of certain kinds and moral anti-emotions towards acts of certain other kinds will on some occasions not do so. He may feel no moral emotion; or perhaps on very exceptional occasions the normal form of his moral emotion may be reversed. These are the negative facts. The positive facts are certain empirical generalizations about the kinds of occurrent conditions under which such inhibitions or reversals of moral emotion tend to take place. 'Being in a normal state' is then defined in terms of the absence of such conditions, e.g. not being angry with or jealous of or frightened by the agent whose act is being contemplated. Now, although one has at the back of one's mind a fairly adequate but rather confused idea of these negative conditions, only one or two of them will be explicitly before one's mind on any particular occasion when one uses the expression 'in a normal state'. According as one or another is in the foreground on a given occasion the same sentence may express an analytic or a synthetic proposition.

I suggest, then, that defenders of the dispositional form of the moral sense theory might attempt in some such ways as these to rebut the objection that, whilst propositions like 'Any act of promise-keeping tends as such to be right' are *necessary and synthetic*, the propositions which it asserts to be their equivalents are either *contengent or analytic*.

(iii) The third difficulty which the moral sense theory, in the form of it which we are considering, has to meet is this. It might be alleged that the mediating characteristics in respect of which a person feels moral pro-emotion or anti-emotion towards an act which he contemplates are the supposed *rightness* or *wrongness* of the act. Suppose, e.g., that a person feels a moral anti-emotion when he contemplates an act which he believes to be one of promise-breaking. Then, it might be said, he does so only in so far as he believes promise-breaking to be wrong. Suppose that he believed the act to be one of promise-breaking but did not believe that such acts tend to be wrong. Then, it might be alleged, there is no reason to think that he would feel a moral anti-emotion towards it.

Let us begin by considering what view a Rationalist, like Price, would take on this question of the mediating characteristics of moral emotion. I think that the following is fair statement of his position. It is a necessary proposition that any rational being who contemplated an act which he believed to be one of promise-breaking would tend to feel towards it a moral anti-emotion. But, though true and necessary, it is not self-evident. It is a logical consequence of two more fundamental propositions, each of which is self-evident. They are these: (*a*) It is self-evident to any rational being that any act of promise-breaking tends as such to be wrong. (*b*) It is self-evident that any rational being who contemplated an act which he believed to be wrong would feel towards it a moral anti-emotion.

We have already considered what the supporters of the moral sense theory might say about the first of these propositions. What are we to say about the second? It seems to me that everything depends here on how much we put into the connotation of the phrase 'rational being'. On a narrower interpretation of that phrase proposition (*b*) is synthetic but contingent, on a certain wider interpretation that proposition becomes necessary but analytic. Sometimes the one interpretation and sometimes the other is at the back of one's mind without one realizing the fluctuation, and so one is inclined to think that proposition (*b*) is both necessary and synthetic.

A 'rational being', on the narrowest interpretation, means roughly one who is capable of comparing, abstracting, and forming general notions; who is capable of seeing necessary connections and disconnections between terms and between propositions; and who has the power of making inferences, both deductive and inductive. I call this the 'narrowest' interpretation, because it takes account only of cognitive characteristics and leaves out emotional and conative ones. The next stage in widening it would be to include in the definition of a 'rational being' what I will call 'purely intellectual' emotions and conations, e.g. intellectual curiosity, taking pleasure in neat arguments and displeasure in clumsy ones, desire for consistency in one's beliefs, and desire to apportion the strength of one's beliefs to the weight of the evidence.

Let us say that a person who had the cognitive, conative and emotional dispositions which I have just enumerated would be rational 'in the ethically neutral sense'. Suppose that Price were correct in thinking that moral fittingness and unfittingness are relations which hold of necessity between certain types of response and certain types of situation. Then a person who was rational in the ethically neutral sense would in principle be capable of having ideas of right and wrong and of making moral judgments. (I say 'in principle' because (*a*) he would, by definition, have the *general* capacity to see necessary connections between terms and between propositions, whilst (*b*) it might happen that his insight in this particular department was lacking, as that of some rational beings is in the department of mathematical relations.) But, so far as I can see, there would not be the slightest inconsistency in supposing that a being who was rational in the ethically neutral sense, and did in fact have the ideas of right and wrong and make moral judgments, was completely devoid of specifically moral emotion and conation. The fact that he knew or believed *a* to be right and *b* to be wrong might arouse in him neither moral pro-emotion towards the former nor moral anti-emotion towards the latter, and it might not evoke in him the slightest desire to do *a* or to avoid doing *b* or *vice versa*. I cannot see any *logical* impossibility in the existence of such a being; whether it would involve a conflict with some of the *de facto* laws of psychology I do not know.

Now the vast majority of the beings whom we know to be rational in the ethically neutral sense do in fact feel moral pro-emotion towards acts which they believe to be right and moral anti-emotion towards those which they believe to be wrong, and they are in fact to some extent attracted towards doing the former and repelled from doing the latter. Moreover, it is *logically* impossible that these specifically moral emotions and desires should exist in a being who was not rational in the ethically neutral sense; for their characteristic objects can be presented only by a process of reflective thinking. The wider interpretation of the phrase 'rational being' includes these specifically moral conative and emotional characteristics in addition to those which constitute the definition of 'rational' in the ethically neutral sense. It is, of course, logically impossible that a person who is rational in this widest sense should fail to feel moral pro-emotion towards what he believes to be right and moral anti-emotion towards what he believes to be wrong. But this is a merely analytical proposition. It is synthetic and contingent that a person who is rational in the ethically neutral sense should be so in the wider ethical sense also. But the fact that rationality in the ethically neutral sense is almost invariably accompanied in our experience by the additional features which convert it into ethical rationality and the fact that the latter logically entail the former produce a confusion in our minds. We are thus led to think that the proposition that any rational being would feel a moral pro-emotion towards any act which he believed to be right and a moral anti-emotion towards any that he believed to be wrong is both necessary and synthetic.

So much for the Rationalist account of moral emotion and its mediation by the characteristics of rightness and wrongness. What can the moral sense theory, in its trans-subjective dispositional form, make of the alleged facts?

On the face of it this theory is presented with the following difficulty. Suppose that we try to combine the alleged fact that rightness and wrongness are the mediating characteristics for moral emotion with the analysis of moral judgments given by the theory in question. Then we seem to be committed to the following proposition: 'A person will tend to feel a moral anti-emotion towards an act which he believes to be one of promise-breaking so far and only so far as he believes that most persons when in a normal condition would feel such an emotion in contemplating such an act'. Now this has a *prima facie* appearance of circularity; and, even if it be neither logically nor causally circular, it certainly does not seem very plausible.

The first remark that I have to make is that the objection just stated rests on a premise which is plausible but false. It tacitly assumes that, if the correct analysis of the proposition '*S* is *P*' is '*S* is p_1-andp_2', then anyone who is believing the former proposition is *ipso facto* believing the latter. Now there may be some sense of 'believe' in which this is true; but there certainly is an important sense in which it is false. It is quite obvious that a number of persons who accept different and incompatible analyses of a proposition may all believe it; and therefore there must be a sense in which some at least of them believe it without *ipso facto* believing the proposition which is its correct analysis. This is particularly obvious in the present case. Nearly everyone believes that acts of promise-breaking tend as such to be wrong; but some of these persons think that wrongness is a simple characteristic, others think that it can be analysed in one way, and others think that it can be analysed in various other ways. So, even if the correct analysis of '*x* is wrong' is 'Any normal person who should contemplate such an act as *x* when in a normal state would feel a moral anti-emotion towards it', it does not follow that the correct analysis of 'A believes that *x* is wrong' is 'A believes that any normal person who should contemplate such an act as *x* when in a normal state would feel a moral anti-emotion towards it'. So it is not fair to say that the moral sense theory must hold that anyone who feels a moral anti-emotion towards an act in respect of his belief that it is wrong is *ipso facto* feeling that emotion in respect of his belief that any normal person who would feel such an emotion if he were to contemplate such an act while in a normal state.

I suppose that this argument would be generally admitted as applied to the case of a person who did not accept, or did positively reject, the analysis of moral judgments proposed by the moral sense theory. But it might be said that it will not apply to the case of a person who accepts that analysis. I think, however, that even this could be questioned. A person may have assented to a certain analysis of a proposition when the question of its analysis and the arguments *pro* and *con* were before his mind. He may continue to accept it, in the *dispositional* sense that he *would* assent to it again at any time when the question was raised for him. But during the intervals he may often have the experience of believing the proposition without thinking of the analysis of it which he has accepted. Therefore it seems to me that even an adherent of the moral sense theory might often feel a moral anti-emotion towards an act in respect of his belief that it is wrong without *ipso facto* feeling that emotion in respect of the belief that it has those characteristics which he holds to be the correct analysis of 'being wrong'.

So much for the dialectics of the matter. But what is really happening when a person is said to feel a moral pro-emotion or anti-emotion towards an act in respect of his belief that it is right or that it is wrong? We must begin by distinguishing what I will call 'first-hand' and 'second-hand' emotion. Suppose that a certain word has been very often used in connection with objects towards which a certain kind of emotion has been felt and that it has seldom or never been used except on such occasions. Then this word may come to act as a stimulus calling forth this kind of emotion. When the emotion is evoked in this way I call it 'second-hand'.

Now there is no doubt that a great deal of moral emotion is, in this sense, second-hand. And there is no doubt that the words which have come by association to act as evokers of second-hand moral emotion are the words 'right' and 'wrong'. When a person is said to feel a moral emotion towards an act in respect of his belief that it is right or that it is wrong what is really happening is very often the following. He knows or believes that acts of this kind are commonly *called* 'right' or called 'wrong'. He repeats these words *sotto voce* to himself or has auditory images of them when he thinks of the act in question; and by association they evoke a second-hand moral pro-emotion or anti-emotion towards the act. Plainly there is nothing in this to cause difficulty to the supporters of the moral sense theory.

But of course this does not cover the whole field. There *is* first-hand moral emotion; indeed, if no one had ever felt a first-hand emotion of a given kind, it is difficult to believe that anyone could now feel a second-hand emotion of that kind. What is happening when a person is said to be feeling a *first-hand* moral emotion towards an act in respect of his belief that it is right or that it is wrong? I can give only a very tentative answer to this question, based on my own imperfect introspection of a kind of situation with which I am not very familiar.

It *seems* to me that in such cases I do not first recognize or think that I recognize a quality or relation of rightness or wrongness in the act, and *then* begin to feel a moral pro-emotion or anti-emotion towards it in respect of this knowledge or belief. What I seem to do is to consider the act and its probable consequences under various familiar headings. 'Would it do more harm that good? Would it be deceitful? Should I be showing ingratitude to a benefactor if I were to do it? Should I be shifting on to another person's shoulders a burden or a responsibility which I do not care to bear for myself?' In respect of each of these aspects of the act and its consequences I have a tendency to feel towards the act a certain kind of moral emotion of a certain degree of intensity. These emotional dispositions were largely built up in me by my parents, schoolmasters, friends and colleagues; and I know that in the main they correspond with those of other persons of my own nation and class. It seems to me that I call the act 'right' or 'wrong' in accordance with my final moral-emotional reaction to it, after viewing it under all these various aspects, and after trying to allow for any permanent or temporary emotional peculiarities in myself which may make my emotional reaction eccentric or unbalanced. By the time that this has happened the features which I had distinguished and had viewed and reacted to separately have fallen into the background and are again fused. They are the real mediating characteristics of my moral pro-emotion or anti-emotion; but I now use the omnibus words 'right' or 'wrong' to cover them all, and say that I feel that emotion towards the act in respect of my belief that it is right or that it is wrong.

X

SOME OF THE MAIN PROBLEMS OF ETHICS (1946)[1]

Ethics, in the sense in which that word is used by philosophers, may be described as the theoretical treatment of moral phenomena. I use the phrase 'moral phenomena' to cover all those facts and only those in describing which we have to use such words as 'ought', 'right and wrong', 'good and evil', or any others which are merely verbal translations of these.

Moral phenomena fall into three distinct, though closely interconnected groups, viz. moral judgment, moral emotion, and moral volition. Suppose that I know or believe that I *ought* to keep a promise, though it might be more convenient to break it; that it is *wrong* to inflict useless pain on an innocent person, though it might be pleasant to score off him in public; that love is a *good* emotion and jealousy an *evil* one; and so on. These bits of knowledge or belief are instances of moral judgments. Suppose that I believe myself to have behaved wrongly on a certain occasion and that I feel *remorse* or *self-disapproval*, as distinct from mere fear of punishment or embarrassment at being found out, on that account. These feelings will be instances of moral emotion. Suppose, finally, that I have to decide between two alternative courses of action, one of which I believe to be *right*, and the other of which is pleasanter in itself or more attractive in its probable consequences. In so far as I am influenced in my decision by the thought that one of them is *right* and that the other would be wrong, and by the desire to do what is right as such, this is an instance of moral volition.

Analysis of Moral Judgments

The first and most fundamental problem of Ethics is about the

[1] Reprinted from *Philosophy*, Volume XXI, July 1946, by courtesy of the editors.

nature of moral judgments and the concepts 'ought', 'right', 'good', etc., which are the most characteristic elements in them. Suppose I assert, deliberately and reflectively and not merely talking like a parrot, that A on a certain occasion ought not to have broken a promise which he had made to B. Then, *prima facie*, the following things seem to be true: (1) That in uttering this sentence, which I will call a 'moral sentence in the indicative mood', I am asserting an *opinion* (correct or incorrect) which I hold, and am not merely expressing an emotion which I feel. (2) That the opinion which I am asserting is not merely about my own feelings or wishes or beliefs. In saying that A ought to have kept his promise to B, I seem to be asserting about A and B and their relationship something which is no more about me and my attitude towards them than if I had asserted that A is B's second cousin. (3) That what I assert about A's breach of his promise to B, viz. that it was *wrong* and *ought not* to have happened, is something unique and peculiar, though perfectly familiar and intelligible to everyone. It cannot be expressed by any form of words which does not contain the words 'right' or 'ought' or some others which are obviously mere verbal translations of them.

Now all these *prima facie* appearances have been questioned on more or less plausible grounds by competent moral philosophers, and this has led to some of the most fundamental discussions in ethics. I will now say something of the various alternative views which have been held on these points.

1. *The Interjectional Analysis*. The most radically sceptical view is that what appear to be moral judgments are not really *judgments*, i.e. assertions of knowledge or opinion, at all; but are merely expressions of a certain kind of *emotion*. It is alleged that, when a person utters such a sentence as, 'This is wrong' or 'That is evil', he is really only expressing a certain kind of anti-emotion towards this or that. It is true that he uses a form of sentence which inevitably suggests that he is asserting an opinion and not merely expressing an emotion. For the sentence is of the same grammatical form as if he had said 'This is triangular', which is certainly an assertion of opinion. But, it is alleged, the gram-

matical form is misleading in the case of moral sentences in the indicative.

I propose to call this theory the *interjectional analysis*. On this view there are no moral judgments; there are only what might be called 'ostensible moral judgments'. Moral sentences in the indicative mood are really interjections, like 'Hurray!' or 'Blast!', masquerading as assertions of opinion.

2. *The Autobiographical Analysis*. Suppose we reject the interjectional analysis. Suppose we hold that, when a person utters a moral sentence in the indicative, he really is making a moral judgment. Then the next most sceptical view is that what he is asserting is simply that he feels a certain kind of emotion, *pro* or *anti*, towards the subject which he pronounces to be right or wrong, good or evil. I shall call this the *autobiographical analysis*.

It must be noticed that it could take two different forms. (*a*) It might be held that, when I judge that so-and-so is right, what I am asserting is simply that I here and now am feeling towards so-and-so a certain kind of pro-emotion. If so, my judgment is analogous to 'This butter tastes nice' uttered by a person while eating that butter. (*b*) It might be held that what I am asserting is that I have a *disposition* to feel this kind of pro-emotion towards such persons or acts or situations as so-and-so. If so, my judgment is analogous to 'I like butter'. A person might truly say that he likes butter even if, on the occasion when he said so, he found the taste of butter repulsive because, e.g., he was feeling bilious. I shall call these two forms of the autobiographical analysis respectively the *occurrent* and the *dispositional* form.

It might be thought that there is no difference between the interjectional analysis and the occurrent form of the autobiographical analysis. This would be a mistake. There is a difference between merely expressing an emotion by means of an exclamation, e.g., ejaculating 'Damn!' when one is annoyed at losing one's collar-stud, and asserting that one is feeling such and such an emotion towards such and such an object, e.g., saying, 'I am annoyed at finding that I have lost my collar-stud'. An animal, e.g., can express an emotion of anger by snarling, but it cannot make the judgment which a man would express by saying, 'I am angry with so-and-so'. On the interjectional analysis to utter a moral sentence in the indicative is like expressing a feeling of annoyance with so-and-so by exclaiming, 'Damn you!'; on the occurrent form of the autobiographical analysis it is like stating that one is feeling annoyed with so-and-so.

3. *The Statistical Analysis*. Suppose next that both forms of the autobiographical analysis are rejected also. It is still possible to suggest an analysis in terms of pro-emotion and anti-emotion. The suggestion would be that, when I judge that so-and-so is right, what I am asserting is that all or most men, or all or most members of some more restricted class, e.g. Englishmen or Etonians, have a disposition to feel a certain kind of pro-emotion towards persons or acts or situations like so-and-so. On this view moral judgments may be compared to such a judgment as 'Jazz music is popular'. This might be truly asserted by a person even if he were himself indifferent to jazz music or heartily disliked it. I shall call this the *statistical analysis*.

Before going further I want to make two remarks about the three alternative kinds of analysis which I have been describing. (*a*) All three of them are stated in terms of certain emotions which a person may feel towards himself or towards another person or towards an action or a relationship. They may therefore all be described as *emotional-reaction theories*. (*b*) The interjectional analysis and the two forms of autobiographical analysis agree with each other and differ from the statistical analysis in the following respect. The former may be described as *intra-subjective*. For, according to them, when a person utters a moral sentence in the indicative, what he is doing is either to express an emotion which *he* is feeling or to make an assertion to the effect that *he* is feeling a certain emotion or has a disposition to feel it. The statistical analysis, on the other hand, may be described as *trans-subjective*. For, according to it, when a person utters such a sentence he is asserting something about a whole class of persons which may or may not happen to include himself.

4. *The Objective Analysis*. Finally, let us suppose that all forms

of emotional reaction theory are rejected. Then we must hold that a person who makes a moral judgment is ascribing to its subject a certain property which would belong to it even if no one had ever contemplated it or felt any kind of emotion towards it. On this view A's judgment that B's act of telling a lie on a certain occasion was wrong is comparable, in this respect at any rate, to a person's judgment that the weather in Cambridge on a certain day was rainy. He may indeed have been *influenced* by his emotions to make this assertion; but what he asserts is not *about* the emotions of himself or anyone else towards the weather in Cambridge on that day. Let us call this the *Objective Analysis* of moral judgments.

Naturalistic v. Non-naturalistic Theories

The question of analysis brings us to another question which is closely connected with it. Are moral predicates, such as *right*, *ought* and *good*, unique and peculiar; or can they be completely analysed and defined in terms of non-moral predicates? Theories which answer this question in the affirmative are called *naturalistic*; those which answer it in the negative are called *non-naturalistic*. The following would be typical examples of naturalistic theories. '*Better* conduct means conduct that comes later in the course of evolution and is more complex and unified than earlier conduct of the same kind'. '*Right* action means action which tends to promote the stability and increase the complexity of society'. 'To say that a person *ought* to do so-and-so means that, if he does not, he will be punished either in this life by his fellow-men or in the next by God'.

It should be noticed that, if any form of the emotional reaction analysis be true, the question is answered automatically in favour of naturalism. Ethics becomes a branch of psychology. Nevertheless, there would remain a somewhat similar question even for those theories. It would take the following form. 'Is the emotion which we express, or assert ourselves to feel or to have a disposition to feel, or which we assert that most members of a certain class have a disposition to feel, when we utter a moral sentence in the indicative an emotion of a quite unique kind?

Or is it just a combination of emotions, e.g. fear, love, hope, etc., each of which can occur in non-moral contexts?'

If the objective analysis be correct, the question of Naturalism *v.* Non-naturalism remains quite open, and special arguments are needed to answer it.

The importance of the question is this. If Non-naturalism be true, Ethics is an autonomous science with an irreducibly peculiar subject-matter, though it will still have very intimate connections with certain other sciences, such as psychology, sociology, etc. But, if Naturalism be true, Ethics is not an autonomous science; it is a department or an application of one or more of the natural or the historical sciences. Now the reduction of a plurality to a unity is a source of intellectual satisfaction, and therefore philosophers have a strong motive for trying to produce a workable naturalistic theory.

Right-making and Good-making Characteristics

We pass now to another very important problem. It may be introduced as follows. If a person says of anything that it is right or that it is wrong, it is always sensible to ask, 'Why? What *makes* it right or *makes* it wrong, as the case may be?' The sort of answers that one expects to such questions are: 'Because it will relieve pain', 'Because it is a breach of promise', and so on. Similar remarks apply, *mutatis mutandis*, to good and evil. If anything is said to be good or to be evil, it is always sensible to ask what makes it so. The sort of answers which one expects to get are: 'Because it is an act of courage', 'Because it is a feeling of pleasure at another man's misfortune', and so on.

We may generalize this as follows. Moral characteristics are always dependent upon certain other characteristics which can be described in purely neutral non-moral terms. Let us call those non-moral characteristics whose presence in anything confers rightness or wrongness on it *right-making* and *wrong-making* characteristics. And let us define *good-making* and *bad-making* characteristics in a similar way.

We will begin with right-making and wrong-making characteristics. On the face of it there is a whole mass of these. E.g.

being a breach of promise, being a deliberately misleading answer to a question, being an intentional infliction of needless pain, and dozens more, are characteristics which may plausibly be said to make an act wrong.

Now an extremely important question is whether we can discover any kind of systematic unity among all these various right-making and wrong-making characteristics. Can we reduce them to a few fundamental ones? Can we perhaps reduce them all to a single fundamental one? Moral philosophers have naturally tried their hardest to do this, since it would plainly be tidier and more satisfactory to the intellect if it could be done.

When we reflect on this problem we notice the following fact. At first one is inclined to say that *every* lie is as such wrong, that *every* breach of promise is as such wrong, and so on. But one soon finds that there are cases where this is not plausible; e.g. is it certain that a lie told to an invalid or a breach of promise to a child is wrong when the results of telling the truth or keeping the promise would be extremely bad for him? Again, there are cases where any possible action will, e.g., be either a lie or a breach of promise. Suppose, e.g., that A has told me a secret on my promise not to reveal it, and that B afterwards asks me a question which I can neither answer truly nor refuse to answer at all without revealing the secret. Then whatever I may do in response to B's question will be either a breach of my promise to A or a lie told to B. But we are not prepared to say that whatever I do in such a situation will be wrong. On the contrary, we should hold that in some cases it would be my duty to tell the truth to B and thus break my promise to A whilst in others it would be my duty to keep my promise to A and thus deceive B.

For such reasons it is necessary to modify our notion of right-*making* and wrong-*making* characteristics and to talk instead of right-*tending* and wrong-*tending* characteristics. An intentionally deceptive answer to a question *tends* as such to be wrong, and so too does a breach of promise. If an act were nothing but an answer to a question, it would be right if true and wrong if false. If an act were nothing but the keeping or the breaking of a promise, it would be right if it were the former and wrong if it were the latter. But, if an act is *both* a true answer to a question and a breach of a promise, we can say only that it *tends* to be right in the former respect and *tends* to be wrong in the latter. The right act in such circumstances will be the one that makes the best compromise between the various moral claims on the agent, after allowing due weight to the relative urgency of each claim. We might compare the claims which arise from various right-tending and wrong-tending characteristics to forces of various magnitudes and directions acting on a body at the same time. And we might compare what I will call the *resultantly right course of action* to the course which a body would pursue under the joint action of such forces. Looking at the situation from the point of view of the agent, we can say that each right-tending and wrong-tending characteristic imposes on him a *component obligation* of a certain degree of urgency; and that his *resultant obligation* is to make the best compromise that he can between his various component obligations.

When we consider the various right-tending and wrong-tending characteristics we find that they can be divided into two great groups, which I will call *teleological* and ostensibly *non-teleological*.

1. One characteristic which tends to make an act right is that it will produce at least as good consequences as any alternative open to the agent in the circumstances. And one which tends to make it wrong is that it will produce less good or more evil consequences than some other act open to the agent. We can sum this up by saying that the property of being *optimific* is a very important right-tending characteristic. I call it *teleological* because it refers to the goodness of the ends or consequences which the act brings about.

2. Now there are also many characteristics which are certainly right-tending or wrong-tending but are not *prima facie* reducible to the property of being optimific. No doubt truth-telling and promise-keeping do in the end and on the whole lead to better consequences than lying and breach of promise. But most people do not feel that this is the reason why truth-telling and promise-keeping tend to be right. They feel that the mere fact of being

asked a question or having made a promise imposes on one an urgent component obligation to answer truly or to perform what one has promised, quite independently of whether the consequences will be good or bad. I therefore call these right-tending and wrong-tending characteristics *ostensibly non-teleological.*

We have already seen that various ostensibly non-teleological right-making characteristics may lead to conflicting component obligations. It is also true that the ostensibly non-teleological obligation to tell the truth, e.g., may conflict with the teleological obligation to produce as much good and as little evil as possible. Consider, e.g., the following as a case. A commanding officer knows that one of his subordinates, who has been killed, has displayed disgraceful cowardice. No one else knows this or will ever do so unless the officer divulges it. The dead man's mother asks the officer leading questions about the circumstances of her son's death. If he tells the truth the mother will be made miserable for life and no one will be a penny the better. If he tells a suitable lie the mother will retain her ideals and be made happy and no one will be a penny the worse. Here there seems to be a plain conflict between the teleological obligation to produce as much good and as little evil as possible and the ostensibly non-teleological obligation to answer questions truly.

Ostensibly non-teleological obligations can be subdivided into two groups, which I will call *non-distributive* and *distributive.* Truth-telling is an example of the former. Distributive obligations are concerned with the right distribution of benefits and disadvantages. Suppose that I am the sole executor and trustee under the will of a certain rich man. He has made two wills. In the first he has distributed his property more or less equally among a number of needy and deserving persons and institutions. In the second he has left the whole of it to a worthless rich relative. I am the only person now alive who knows that the second will has been made, and I could safely destroy it and carry out the provisions of the first. It is obvious that by doing this I should produce more good and less evil than by divulging the second will. Nevertheless I am under an extremely urgent ostensibly non-teleological obligation to distribute the property in accordance with the testator's second will, whilst my purely teleological obligation would be to distribute it in accordance with the first.

Now much the most important attempt which has been made to reduce all the many and various right-tending characteristics to a single one is the theory called *Utilitarianism*. According to this one's only ultimate obligation is teleological; the only ultimate reason why an act is right is that it is optimific, and the only ultimate reason why any act is wrong is that it would produce less good or more evil consequences than some other act open to the agent in the circumstances. All ostensibly non-teleological obligations, whether distributive or non-distributive, are secondary and derivative from the one teleological obligation to act optimifically. The only reason why there is a component obligation to keep promises, to answer questions truly, and so on, is that on the whole such action will secure the best consequences in frequently recurring kinds of situation, such as having made a promise, being asked a question, etc. Suppose that a situation should occur in which, when all the remote, secondary, and collateral consequences as well as the immediate ones have been taken into account, the result of telling a lie or breaking a promise would be better than that of telling the truth or keeping the promise. Then it will be right to lie or to break one's promise, and wrong to tell the truth or keep faith.

It is plain that, if Utilitarianism can be made to cover the facts without distorting them, it has several advantages. (1) It gives us the intellectual satisfaction of reducing a litter of disconnected grounds of obligation to a single one. (2) To many people it does seem difficult to believe on reflection that it can *ever* be right to do what will have worse consequences when one could have done something else which would have better consequences. (3) Utilitarianism gives a plausible explanation for the various degrees of urgency of the various ostensibly non-teleological component obligations; and it provides, in theory at any rate, a rule for compounding such obligations when several of them co-exist and conflict with each other.

I will now say something about *good*-tending and *bad*-tending characteristics. The general principles are the same as in the case of right-tending and wrong-tending ones. It is plain that *prima facie* there are a number of different characteristics which tend to make a person or an experience or an action good, and a number which tend to make it bad. Now several of these may be present together in a single subject; and the question whether it is resultantly good or resultantly bad, and, if so, to what degree, will depend on the nature and the proportion of its various good-tending and bad-tending characteristics.

Here again there is naturally a strong desire among philosophers to try to reduce the litter of various good-tending characteristics to a single good-making one. The best known effort in this direction is the theory known as *Ethical Hedonism.* This theory involves the following propositions. (1) Nothing is either good or bad in the primary sense except actual experiences. (2) The only characteristic of an experience which makes it good is its pleasantness, and the only one which makes it bad is its unpleasantness. (3) The degree of goodness of a pleasant experience depends jointly on its duration and on the degree of its pleasantness. According to this theory anything other than an experience which is called 'good' is so called in a secondary and derivative sense, viz. in so far as it contributes or tends to contribute to the occurrences of pleasant experiences and the non-occurrence of unpleasant ones.

If both Utiltarianism and Ethical Hedonism could be accepted, we should have introduced the greatest possible unity into the region of moral phenomena. Unfortunately each of them seems to be too simple to cover the facts without distorting them.

Before leaving this part of the subject I will make two remarks connecting it with the topic of analysis which I discussed earlier.

1. Suppose that a person has persuaded himself that there is one and only one right-making characteristic, e.g. that of being optimific, or one and only one good-making characteristic, e.g. pleasantness. Then he is very liable to make the following mistake. He is apt to think that he has proved that 'right' *means* optimific or that 'good' *means* pleasant, i.e. that he has provided an analysis of rightness or of goodness, as the case may be. All that he has really shown in the first case, e.g. is that, if the words 'right'

and 'optimific' are names of two different characteristics, then these two mutually involve each other. That is quite different from showing that the two words are really names for the same characteristic, and that what is meant by 'optimific' is the analysis of what is meant by 'right'. The distinction can be made quite clear by a simple non-ethical example. To be an equilateral triangle means to be a plane figure bounded by three equal straight lines. To be an equiangular triangle means to be a plane figure with three angles, all of which are equal. Evidently these are two different characteristics. But they mutually involve each other; for any figure which has either property necessarily has both. It seems not unlikely that many people who have thought they have given a naturalistic analysis of moral judgments have made this mistake; and that really they have done no more than to produce reasons for thinking that there is one and only one right-making or good-making characteristic, and have then proceeded to identify rightness or goodness with this.

2. In discussing right-tending and good-tending characteristics I have spoken in terms of the objective analysis of moral judgments. It is important to notice that the same problem exists in a slightly modified form if we accept the emotional-reaction analysis. In that case what we have called a 'right-tending' or a 'good-tending' characteristic will be one which tends to call forth the peculiar emotion in its *pro*-form. What we have called 'conflicts of component obligations' will depend on the fact that the same act may have features which call forth the *pro*-emotion and others which call forth the *anti*-emotion. What we have called 'resultant obligation' will be connected with one's total emotional reaction to an object which has some features that tend to call forth the *pro*-emotion and others which tend to call forth the *anti*-emotion.

Intention and Rightness

When a person performs a deliberate action he does so in view of his knowledge and beliefs about the present situation and with certain expectations about the consequences which will ensue. These two factors are closely connected; for his expectations about the consequences are in part determined by his knowledge or beliefs about the present situation. I shall say that an act is *intentional* in respect of (1) all those features and only those which the agent knows or believes to be present in the initial situation, and (2) all those consequences and only those which he expects to follow. Now a person's information on both these matters will always be incomplete and it may be in part mistaken. No man can foresee the very remote consequences of an action; and anyone may be mistaken about some of its immediate consequences, either through miscalculation or through inadequate or inaccurate information about present circumstances. Suppose, e.g., that a person receives a letter purporting to come from his old nurse and that he is moved to send her a postal money-order in the belief that she is in want and with the expectation that it will enable her to buy comforts. It may be that in fact the nurse has died, that the letter has been written in her name by a dishonest relative, and that the money will be spent by him on drink. What this man intended to do was to bring relief to his old nurse; what he in fact did was to enable a dishonest stranger to get drunk.

Now, if we consider the agent's intention in this example, we are inclined to say that he acted rightly. But, if we consider the actual facts of the situation and the consequences, we are inclined to say that he acted wrongly and that the right action would have been to refuse to send money and to have reported the matter to the police. Thus we are faced with the problem of the relation between intention and rightness or wrongness.

This question may be approached in the following way. Any act which can be called 'right' or 'wrong' can be viewed from two standpoints, viz. that of the agent who does it and that of the patient who is affected by it. In general these will be different persons, though there are special cases in which the agent and the patient are the same person at an earlier and a later stage of his life. Now in considering whether an act is right or wrong we must view it, so to speak, from both ends, i.e. in relation to the patient and in relation to the agent. In relation to the patient an act is right if and only if it fulfils his claims on the agent, or, as we say, 'gives the patient his rights in the matter concerned'. From this standpoint the agent's intention is irrelevant. In relation to the agent an act is right if and only if it is done with the intention of fulfilling the patient's claim and giving him his rights in the matter. From this standpoint anything in the actual consequences which is outside or contrary to the agent's intention is irrelevant.

I propose to call any act which in fact fulfils the claims of the patient upon the agent *materially right*, regardless of whether the agent intended it to have this consequence or not. I propose to call any act which was intended by the agent to bring about the fulfilment of the patient's claims *formally right*, regardless of whether it does in fact have that result or not. A *perfectly right* act in a given situation would be one that was both formally and materially right. It would be an act which was intended by the agent to give to the patient his rights and which did in fact do so. Owing to incomplete or incorrect information on the part of the agent, or to defects in his powers of inference, it may happen that an act which is formally right is materially wrong, or that one which is formally indifferent or wrong is materially right. It should be noticed that the notion of material rightness is, in a certain sense, more fundamental than that of formal rightness. For what is formally right for the agent to do is to try to secure to the patient what is materially right for him to have done to him.

There remains, however, a further serious complication to be considered. So far I have supposed that the agent makes no *ethical* mistakes. I have supposed only that he may have incomplete or inaccurate information about *matters of fact* and may make mistaken inferences on such matters from his information. I have assumed that he knows what ought to happen to the patient if his factual information were adequate and accurate. But of course the agent *may* be ignorant or mistaken about *ethical* matters too.

Suppose, e.g., that a person is brought up in a community in which it is held to be a duty to carry on a family vendetta, and that he accepts that opinion. Let us assume, for the sake of argument, that it is mistaken, and that it is wrong to kill a member of another family simply because one of his ancestors killed one of one's own family. Suppose that this person is in a situation in which he can either kill a certain member of the family or let him escape. Whichever alternative he chooses we are inclined to say that he acts wrongly. If he kills the patient, he intentionally does to him what he believes ought to be done to him, but this is in fact what ought not to be done to him. If he lets the patient escape, he intentionally does to him what he believes ought not to be done to him, but this is in fact what ought to be done to him.

It is plain that we are here concerned with yet another sense of 'right' and 'wrong'. I propose to call it *subjective* rightness and wrongness. An act is subjectively right if and only if the effects which the agent expected it to have on the patient are those which he believed that the patient is entitled to have produced in him.

The relations between the various senses of 'right' which I have distinguished may be summarized as follows. (1) A person could be sure of doing a *perfectly right* act only if both his relevant factual and his relevant ethical beliefs were complete and correct and if he had made no mistakes in his inferences. It is therefore plain that, if a person ever does a perfectly right act, it is largely a matter of luck that he does so. (2) A person could be sure of doing a *formally right* act, even if his factual information were incomplete or inaccurate and he made mistakes in his inferences, provided that the effects which he *thinks* his act would have upon the patient are such as the latter *really would* be entitled to if his nature and situation were as the agent *believes* them to be. Therefore when an agent's relevant ethical information is incomplete or incorrect it is a matter of luck if he performs a formally right act. (3) A person could be sure of doing a *subjectively right* act, no matter how inadequate or inaccurate his factual and his ethical beliefs might be or how mistaken he may be in his inferences provided only that the effects which he *thinks* his act will have on the patient are such as he *thinks* that the latter would be entitled to if his nature and situation were as the agent *believes* them to be. It is therefore plain that a person who is ignorant, stupid, and misinformed about facts, who is incapable of drawing reasonable inferences, and who is insensitive or crazy in his opinions about what is materially right and wrong, may perform acts that are subjectively right. So it is not surprising that such acts may inflict the most terrible wrongs on those whom they effect.

The problems which we have been discussing arise because we fail to distinguish these three senses of 'right' and 'wrong', and use these words in a vague way to include them all, sometimes having one meaning predominantly before our minds and sometimes another.

Motives and their Ethical Function

Among the characteristics which an agent believes an action to have, and among the consequences which he expects to follow from it, some will attract him towards doing it, some will repel him from doing it, and others will leave him indifferent. Suppose, e.g., that a person contemplates throwing a bomb at a ruler in a public procession. He may expect that the effects will include the death of the ruler, the death or injury of a number of innocent bystanders, and the breakage of a number of windows in the neighbourhood. The first part of the expected consequences may attract him, the second may repel him, and the third may leave him indifferent. A person's total motive *in* doing a certain action consists of all that he believes about the action itself and all that he expects about its consequences, which either attracts him towards or repels him from doing it. The former constitutes his total motive *for* doing it, and the latter his total motive *against* doing it. If, in fact, he does it, he does it *because* of his motives for doing it and *in spite of* his motives against doing it. Suppose, e.g., that the anarchist in my example is in general a humane man and that he decides to throw the bomb at the ruler. Then his motive for doing so is the attractive belief that it will kill the ruler; his motive against doing so is the repellent belief that it will kill or injure innocent bystanders; and he acts because of the former and in spite of the latter motive.

It is plain that there are two aspects to any motive, viz. a cognitive and a conative-emotional aspect. The cognitive aspect of a motive is the fact that it is a *belief* about the nature of the action or an *expectation* about its consequences. The conative aspect is the fact that the agent has a certain disposition to be *attracted or repelled* which is excited by this belief.

When we know what was a person's intention in doing an action and what consequences in fact followed from it, we are in a position to judge whether it was subjectively right, or formally right, or perfectly right, without needing to know anything about his motives in doing the action. But it is quite obvious that a man's motives in doing an action have a very important bearing on *some* kind of moral judgment which we make either on the agent or on the action. This fact is indicated in ordinary speech by such phrases as 'He did the right thing from the wrong motive'.

Suppose, e.g., that a man performs an act which is intended to secure the just punishment of a criminal. He will forsee that the criminal will suffer directly and his family and friends indirectly, so this must be included as part of his intention. Now it may be that the belief that the law will be vindicated, that other men will be deterred from committing similar crimes, and that the criminal may be reformed, is an attracting one; that the belief that the criminal and his family will suffer is a repelling one; and that the agent acts because of the former and in spite of the latter. If so, we should be inclined to say, not only that his action was right, but also that his motives in doing it were good. But it may be that the belief that the law would be vindicated, other men deterred, and the criminal perhaps reformed, exercised no attraction on the agent. He had, perhaps, had a quarrel with the criminal or was jealous of him; and what attracted him was his belief that the criminal and his family would suffer. If so, the action would still be right in any of the senses which we have considered, but we should certainly say that the agent's motive in doing it was bad.

I have no doubt that the words 'right' and 'wrong' have, in addition to the ambiguities which we have already cleared up, the further ambiguity that they are sometimes used to include a reference to this agent's motives and sometimes used without such a reference. I think that it is on the whole more convenient explicitly to exclude reference to motives from our description of right and wrong action. One important reason for drawing the line at this point is the following. A person can choose which of several alternative possible actions he will do. But he cannot, in the same sense, choose which of several alternative motives shall attract him towards or repel him from doing a certain action. Now the predicates 'right' and 'wrong' are commonly understood to be confined to that which is directly dependent on a person's volition, in the sense in which his actions are so and his motives in acting are not.

Specifically Moral Motivation and Emotion

It seems, *prima facie*, that human beings have a great many different desires, and that these cannot all be reduced to a single head. Naturally attempts have been made to do this. The most celebrated of them is the theory called *Psychological Hedonism*. This asserts that the only ultimate objects of desire for any person are to get and to prolong pleasant experiences and to avoid and cut short unpleasant ones. It is now generally admitted by competent authorities that this theory cannot be maintained, and that such plausibility as it has depends upon certain verbal ambiguities.

Now, *prima facie*, there appears to be among our other desires and aversions one which is specifically moral. It seems that, if one believes that a certain course of action would be *right*, that belief stirs a certain conative disposition in one and is a motive for doing it. If, on the other hand, one believes that an action would be *wrong*, that belief stirs the same conative diposition and is a motive against doing it. These desires and aversions are often opposed to very strong non-moral desires and aversions, and they feel very peculiar in comparison with the latter whether they happen to oppose them or to reinforce them. For this reason they are commonly marked out by the name *feelings of obligation*, and some philosophers have thought it inappropriate to classify them as desires and aversions. For my part I see no objection to classifying them in this way, provided that one does not lose sight of their peculiarities. Therefore I propose to describe this peculiar kind of desire and aversion as the *desire to do what is right as such.*

Now the following questions arise at this point. (1) Is there really a desire to do what is right as such, or is the opinion that there is mistaken? Is it the case that, whenever a person thinks that he is attracted towards a course of action by the belief that it would be right or repelled from it by the belief that it would be wrong, he is really being attracted or repelled, *not* by these beliefs, but by beliefs about certain *non-moral* features of the act or of its consequences? (2) Supposing that there is a desire to do what is right as such, is it ever *sufficient* to determine one's actions, or does it always need to be supported by some non-moral motive, such as desire for praise or fear of punishment? (3) Supposing that this desire exists and is sufficient to determine one man's action *in the absence* of opposing motives, is it ever sufficient by itself to *overcome* opposing motives when they are present? Or must it in such cases always be reinforced by some non-moral motive? (4) Supposing that Question 3 is answered in the affirmative, is there any sense, and if so what, in which we can say that the desire to do what is right as such *always could have* overcome *all* opposing motives, even when it did not in fact do so? (5) Is it essential for the validity of moral judgments that Question 4 should be answered in the affirmative? And, if an affirmative answer is relevant to the validity of some but not all moral judgments, which are those to which it is relevant?

It will be seen that Questions 4 and 5 bring us to the problem of Free-Will *v.* Determinism and its bearing on morality.

As regards Question 1 it is important to notice and to avoid the following very common fallacy. Suppose it could be shown that what we take to be the desire to do what is right as such has developed, either in the history of each individual or in that of the human race, on regular principles out of desires which were all purely non-moral. (More or less plausible attempts to show this have been made, e.g., by certain psychoanalysts, on the one hand, and by certain sociologists, on the other.) It would be a fallacy to conclude that what we take to be the desire to do what is right as such is not what it appears to be, but is really just one or a combination of purely non-moral desires. An account of the stages out of which something developed in a regular way is one thing, and an analysis of it as it is when fully developed is another. But it is very common to confuse the two and to imagine that one has shown that the end-term of such a process just consists of the earlier terms in a disguised form.

This fallacy is often made plausible by the use of question-begging epithets for describing the earlier phases in such a process of development. Thus, e.g., some psychoanalysts describe an emotion which is supposed to occur in babies at the pre-moral stage by the name 'feeling of *guilt*'. Now the phrase 'feeling of guilt', if taken literally, means an emotion which a person feels towards himself in respect of his belief that he has done something *morally wrong*. It is therefore quite meaningless to suggest that anyone who has not already got the notion of right and wrong can literally have a feeling of guilt. The phrase 'feeling of guilt' must therefore be used in some unexplained metaphorical sense. But the use of it to describe the pre-moral stages illegitimately helps the suggestion that the end-term contains nothing that was not present in the earlier phases.

This brings us to the general notion of specifically moral emotion. By this I mean emotions which appear *prima facie* to be felt towards persons or actions in respect of certain *moral* characteristics which they are believed to have. Such emotions may be either reflexive or non-reflexive. The former are felt by a person towards himself or his own actions, e.g. feelings of guilt, of remorse, of self-approval, etc. The latter are felt towards another person or his actions, e.g. feelings of moral approval or disapproval felt by one person for the acts of another.

The only remark that I wish to make here about them is that their apparent existence presents a considerable difficulty to any form of the emotional attitude analysis of moral judgments. According to such analyses, to be right or to be wrong consists in being the object of moral approval or disapproval, as the case may be, to some person or class of persons. But, *prima facie*, an action becomes the object of a feeling of moral approval or disapproval to a person only in so far as he already believes it to be right or to be wrong, as the case may be. There is certainly the appearance of a vicious circle here, and it remains to be seen whether supporters of the emotional attitude type of analysis can show that this appearance of circularity is delusive.

Epistemological Questions

The last set of problems which I wish to mention can be stated as follows. How do we come to have ideas of specifically moral terms, such as *right*, *ought*, *morally good*, and so on? And how do we come to know or believe propositions connecting non-moral characteristics, such as truth-telling or promise-breaking with moral characteristics such as rightness or wrongness? These may be described as epistemological questions. It is plain that the answers to them will be closely bound up with the answers to the questions how moral judgments should be analysed.

Suppose, e.g., that the interjectional analysis were correct. Then there are no moral judgments and therefore no moral predicates. The first question would then have to be transformed into the following. How do we come to make the mistake of thinking that we are ascribing to subjects predicates of a peculiar kind when in fact we are merely expressing certain emotions towards objects? The second question would have to be transformed somewhat as follows. Is it just an ultimate fact about human nature that most people tend to feel a certain kind of emotion when they contemplate, e.g., an act of promise-breaking; or is this explicable by general psychological principles and the particular influences to which most people are subjected in early childhood?

Suppose, next, that the interjectional analysis is false, but that it were true that moral concepts, such as *right* and *ought*, are definable in terms of certain kinds of pro-emotion and anti-emotion. Then the origin of such concepts would presumably be like that of our concepts of other psychological terms. We should feel these pro-emotions and anti-emotions on certain occasions, we should introspect them and compare and contrast them with other experiences which we have and introspect, and then by a process of abstraction, we should form the idea of their characteristic emotional quality. Then, finally, we should define 'right' and 'ought' in terms of emotions which have this quality. Moral concepts would in fact be empirical in origin.

Now, if this kind of analysis of moral judgments were correct, what we have called 'right-tending' and 'wrong-tending' characteristics would be those characteristics which tend to evoke pro-emotions or anti-emotions of a certain specific kind towards persons or actions which are believed to possess them. So the second question would reduce to the following. How do we come to know or to believe that such and such non-moral characteristics of persons or actions tend to evoke in those who believe them to be present such a pro-emotion or anti-emotion? Presumably the answer would be that we derive such beliefs by generalizing from our experience. We observe that a belief that an act has a certain non-moral characteristic, e.g., that it is an intentionally misleading answer to a question, is regularly accompanied by an anti-emotion of a specific kind towards the act in question. And we base upon this an inductive generalization. Such beliefs would in fact be empirical and inductive in origin.

Even if all forms of the emotional attitude analysis were rejected and some form of the objective analysis were accepted, it would still be reasonable to hold that both moral concepts and moral judgments are of empirical origin, provided only that a *naturalistic* form of the objective analysis is adopted. But, if we feel obliged to accept a *non-naturalistic* theory of moral judgments and concepts, the case is altered.

Let us define an 'empirical concept' as the concept of a characteristic which is either (*a*) manifested to us in sensation or introspection, or (*b*) is definable in terms of such characteristics together with the notions of cause or substance or both. (The concepts of sensible redness and of anger, e.g., come under the first heading; those of physical redness and irascibility, e.g., come under the second.) If we adopt this definition, it seems certain that the concepts of moral characteristics, such as *right, ought, and morally good*, cannot be empirical unless those characteristics are naturalistic. Therefore anyone who accepts a non-naturalistic account of moral characteristics is almost certainly committed to the proposition that moral concepts are non-empirical. Now many philosophers accept, either as self-evident or as a postulate, the principle that all concepts are empirical. If one is quite sure of this epistemological principle, one will have to reject the non-naturalistic account of moral characteristics, no matter how plausible it may seem on other grounds. If one is quite sure of the non-naturalistic account of moral characteristics, one will have to reject this epistemological principle, no matter how self-evident it may seem or how useful it may be as a postulate. If, on the other hand, one is not quite sure of either, the conflict will tend to diminish one's confidence in both.

Again, it seems plain that, if *right* and *good* are non-naturalistic characteristics, the propositions connecting them with right-tending or good-tending non-moral characteristics, such as promise-keeping or tendency to promote happiness must be *synthetic*. Now to many people it seems that such propositions as 'Any act of promise-keeping tends as such to be right' are *necessary* and *self-evident* like the axioms of pure mathematics. But it is also a very widely accepted epistemological principle that there can be no synthetic necessary propositions. There are, according to this principle, synthetic propositions and there are necessary propositions; but the former are all contingent and empirical, and the latter are all analytic. Now a person who holds that moral characteristics are non-naturalistic seems committed to holding that such propositions as 'Any act of promise-keeping tends as such to be right' are either (*a*) contingent empirical generalizations, or (*b*) synthetic necessary propositions. The former alternative conflicts with the *prima facie* appearance that these propositions are self-evident and necessary; the latter conflicts with the epistemological principle that all necessary propositions are analytic. Thus he must either reject the principle or try to show how it is that such propositions appear to be necessary and self-evident although they are in fact contingent and empirical.

I have now completed my account of what seems to me to be the main problems of Ethics. I have confined myself to stating alternatives and indicating the connections and disconnections between them. This is not very exciting, but I think it is a necessary preliminary to anything more positive.

XI

EGOISM AS A THEORY OF HUMAN MOTIVES (1950)[1]

There seem *prima facie* to be a number of different kinds of ultimate desire which all or most men have. Plausible examples would be the desire to get pleasant experiences and to avoid unpleasant ones, the desire to get and exercise power over others, and the desire to do what is right and to avoid doing what is wrong. Very naturally philosophers have tried to reduce this plurality. They have tried to show that there is one and only one kind of ultimate desire, and that all other desires which seem at first sight to be ultimate are really subordinate to this. I shall call the view that there really are several different kinds of ultimate desire *Pluralism of ultimate desires*, and I shall call the view that there is really only one kind of ultimate desire *Monism of ultimate desires*. Even if a person were a Pluralist about ultimate desires, he might hold that there are certain important features common to all different kinds of ultimate desire.

Now much the most important theory on this subject is that all kinds of ultimate desire are *egoistic*. This is not in itself necessarily a monistic theory. For there might be several irreducibly different kinds of ultimate desire, even if they were all egoistic. Moreover, there might be several irreducibly different, though not necessarily unrelated, senses of the word 'egoistic'; and some desires might be egoistic in one sense and some in another, even if all were egoistic in some sense. But the theory often takes the special form that the only kind of ultimate desire is the desire to get or to prolong pleasant experiences, and to avoid or to cut short unpleasant experiences, for oneself. That *is* a monistic theory. I shall call the wider theory *Psychological Egoism*, and

[1] Reprinted from the *Hibbert Journal*, Volume XLVIII, January 1950, by courtesy of the trustees of the Hibbert Trust.

this special form of it *Psychological Hedonism*. Psychological Egoism might be true, even though Psychological Hedonism were false; but, if Psychological Egoism be false, Psychological Hedonism cannot be true.

I shall now discuss Psychological Egoism. I think it is best to begin by enumerating all the kinds of desire that I can think of which might reasonably be called 'egoistic' in one sense or another.

(1) Everyone has a special desire for the continued existence of himself in his present bodily life, and a special dread of his own death. This may be called *desire for self-preservation*. (2) Everyone desires to get and to prolong experiences of certain kinds, and to avoid and to cut short experiences of certain other kinds, because the former are pleasant to him and the latter unpleasant. This may be called *desire for one's own happiness*. (3) Everybody desires to acquire, keep, and develop certain mental and bodily powers and dispositions, and to avoid, get rid of or check certain others. In general he wants to be or to become a person of a certain kind, and wants not to be or to become a person of certain other kinds. This may be called *desire to be a self of a certain kind*. (4) Everyone desires to feel certain kinds of emotion towards himself and his own powers and dispositions, and not to feel certain other kinds of reflexive emotion. This may be called *desire for self-respect*. (5) Everyone desires to get and to keep for himself the exclusive possession of certain material objects or the means of buying and keeping such objects. This may be called *desire to get and keep property*. (6) Everyone desires to get and to exercise power over certain other persons, so as to make them do what he wishes, regardless of whether they wish it or not. This may be called the *desire for self-assertion*. (7) Everyone desires that other persons shall believe certain things about him and feel certain kinds of emotion towards him. He wants to be noticed, to be respected by some, to be loved by some, to be feared by some, and so on. Under this head come the *desire for self-display*, for *affection*, and so on.

Lastly, it must be noted that some desires, which are concerned primarily with other things or persons, either would not exist at all or would be very much weaker or would take a different form if it were not for the fact that those things or persons already stand in certain relations to oneself. I shall call such relations *egoistic motive-stimulants*. The following are among the most important of these. (i) The relation of ownership. If a person owns a house or a wife, e.g. he feels a much stronger desire to improve the house or to make the woman happy than if the house belongs to another or the woman is married to someone else. (ii) Blood-relationship. A person desires, e.g., the well-being of his own children much more strongly than that of other children. (iii) Relations of love and friendship. A person desires strongly, e.g. to be loved and respected by those whom he loves. He may desire only to be feared by those whom he hates. And he may desire only very mildly, if at all, to be loved and respected by those to whom he feels indifferent. (iv) The relationship of being fellow-members of an institution to which one feels loyalty and affection. Thus, e.g., an Englishman will be inclined to do services to another Englishman which he would not do for a foreigner, and an Old Etonian will be inclined to do services to another Old Etonian which he would not do for an Old Harrovian.

I think that I have now given a reasonably adequate list of motives and motive-stimulants which could fairly be called 'egoistic' in some sense or other. Our next business is to try to classify them and to consider their inter-relations.

(1) Let us begin by asking ourselves the following question. Which of these motives could act on a person if he had been the only person or thing that had ever existed? The answer is that he could still have had desires for *self-preservation*, for *his own happiness*, to be a *self of a certain kind*, and for *self-respect*. But he could not, unless he were under the delusion that there were other persons or other things, have desires for *property*, for *self-assertion*, or for *self-display*. Nor could he have any of those desires which are stimulated by family or other alio-relative relationships. I shall call those desires, and only those, which could be felt by a person who knew or believed himself to be the only existent in the universe, *self-confined*.

(2) Any desire which is not self-confined may be described as

extra-verted; for the person who has such a desire is necessarily considering, not only himself and his own qualities, dispositions, and states, but also some other thing or person. If the desire is egoistic, it will also be *intro-verted*; for the person who has such a desire will also be considering himself and his relations to that other person or thing, and this will be an essential factor conditioning his experience. Thus a self-confined desire is purely intro-verted, whilst a desire which is egoistic but not self-confined is both intro-verted and extra-verted. Now we may subdivide desires of the latter kind into two classes, according as the primary emphasis is on the former or the latter aspect. Suppose that the person is concerned primarily with himself and his own acts and experiences, and that he is concerned with the other thing or person only or mainly as an object of these acts or experiences or as the other term in a relationship to himself. Then shall I call the desire *self-centred*. I shall use the term *self-regarding* to include both desires which are self-centred and those which are self-confined. Under the head of self-centred desires come the desire for *property*, for *self-assertion*, for *self-display*, and for *affection*.

(3) Lastly, we come to desires which are both intro-verted and extra-verted, but where the primary emphasis is on the other person or thing and its states. Here the relationship of the other person or thing to oneself acts as a strong egoistic motive-stimulant, but one's primary desire is that the other person or thing shall be in a certain state. I will call such desires *other-regarding*. A desire which is other-regarding, but involves an egoistic motive-stimulant, may be described as *self-referential*. The desire of a mother to render services to her own children which she would not be willing to render to other children is an instance of a desire which is other-regarding but self-referential. So, too, is the desire of a man to inflict suffering on one who has injured him or whom he envies.

Having thus classified the various kinds of egoistic desire, I will now say something about their inter-relations.

(1) It is obvious that self-preservation may be desired as a necessary condition of one's own happiness; since one cannot

acquire or prolong pleasant experiences unless one continues to exist. So the desire for self-preservation *may* be subordinate to the desire for one's own happiness. But it seems pretty clear that a person often desires to go on living even when there is no prospect that the remainder of his life will contain a balance of pleasant over unpleasant experiences. This attitude is expressed very strongly in the loathesome lines of Maecenas which Seneca has handed down to posterity:

> *Debilem facito manu, debilem pede coxo*
> *tuber adstrue gibberum, lubricos quate dentes;*
> *vita dum superest, bene est; hanc mihi, vel acuta*
> *si sedeam cruce, sustine.*

(2) It is also obvious that property and power over others may be desired as a means to self-preservation or to happiness. So the desire to get and keep property, and the desire to get and exert power over others, *may* be subordinate to the desire for self-preservation or for one's own happiness. But it seems fairly certain that the former desires are sometimes independent of the latter. Even if a person begins by desiring property or power only as a means—and it is very doubtful whether we always do begin in that way—it seems plain that he often comes to desire them for themselves, and to sacrifice happiness, security, and even life for them. Any miser, and almost any keen politician, provides an instance of this.

It is no answer to this to say that a person who desires power or property enjoys the experiences of getting and exercising power or of amassing and owning property, and then to argue that therefore his ultimate desire is to give himself those pleasant experiences. The premise here is true, but the argument is self-stultifying. The experiences in question are pleasant to a person only in so far as he desires power or property. This kind of pleasant experience presupposes desires for something other than pleasant experiences, and therefore the latter desires cannot be derived from desire for that kind of pleasant experience.

Similar remarks apply to the desire for self-respect and the desire for self-display. If one already desires to feel certain emotions towards oneself, or to be the object of certain emotions in others, the experience of feeling those emotions or of knowing that others feel them towards you will be pleasant, because it will be the fulfilment of a pre-existing desire. But this kind of pleasure presupposes the existence of these desires, and therefore they cannot be derived from the desire for that kind of pleasure.

(3) Although the various kinds of egoistic desire cannot be reduced to a single ultimate egoistic desire, e.g. the desire for one's own happiness, they are often very much mixed up with each other. Take e.g., the special desire which a mother feels for the health, happiness, and prosperity of her children. This is predominantly other-regarding, though it is self-referential. The mother is directly attracted by the thought of her child as surviving, as having good dispositions and pleasant experiences, and as being the object of love and respect to other persons. She is directly repelled by the thought of his dying, or having bad dispositions or unpleasant experiences, or being the object of hatred or contempt to other persons. The desire is therefore other-regarding. It is self-referential, because the fact that it is *her* child and not another's acts as a powerful motive-stimulant. She would not be prepared to make the same sacrifices for the survival or the welfare of a child which was not her own. But this self-referential other-regarding motive is almost always mingled with other motives which are self-regarding. One motive which a woman has for wanting her child to be happy, healthy and popular is the desire that other women shall envy her as the mother of a happy, healthy and popular child. This motive is subordinate to the self-centred desire for self-display. Another motive, which may be present, is the desire not to be burdened with an ailing, unhappy, and unpopular child. This motive is subordinate to the self-contained desire for one's own happiness. But, although the self-referential other-regarding motive is nearly always mixed with the motives which are self-centred or self-confined, we cannot plausibly explain the behaviour of many mothers on many occasions towards their children without postulating the other-regarding motive.

We can now consider the various forms which Psychological Egoism might take. The most rigid form is that all human motives are ultimately egoistic, and that all egoistic motives are ultimately of one kind. That one kind has generally been supposed to be the desire for one's own happiness, and so this form of psychological Egoism may in practice be identified with Psychological Hedonism. This theory amounts to saying that the only ultimate motives are *self-confined*, and that the only ultimate self-confined motive is *desire for one's own happiness*.

I have already tried to show by examples that this is false. Among self-confined motives, e.g., is the desire for self-preservation, and this cannot be reduced to desire for one's own happiness. Then, again, there are self-regarding motives which are self-centred but not self-confined, such as the desire for affection, for gratitude, for power over others, and so on. And, finally, there are motives which are self-referential but predominantly other-regarding, such as a mother's desire for her children's welfare or a man's desire to injure one whom he hates.

It follows that the only form of Psychological Egoism that is worth discussing is the following. It might be alleged that all ultimate motives are *either* self-confined *or* self-centred *or* other-regarding but self-referential, some being of one kind and some of another. This is a much more modest theory than, e.g. Psychological Hedonism. I think that it covers satisfactorily an immensely wide field of human motivation, but I am not sure that it is true without exception. I shall now discuss it in the light of some examples.

Case A.

Take first the case of a man who does not expect to survive the death of his present body, and who makes a will, the contents of which will be known to no one during his lifetime.

(1) The motive of such a testator cannot possibly be the expectation of any experiences which he will enjoy after death through the provisions of his will being carried out; for he believes that he will have no more experiences after the death of his body. The only way in which this motive could be ascribed

to such a man is by supposing that, although he is intellectually convinced of his future extinction, yet in practice he cannot help imagining himself as surviving and witnessing events which will happen after his death. I think that this kind of mental confusion is possible, and perhaps not uncommon; but I should doubt whether it is a plausible account of such a man's motives to say that they all involve this mistake.

(2) Can we say that his motive is the desire to enjoy during his life the pleasant experience of imagining the gratitude which the beneficiaries will feel towards him after his death? The answer is that this may well be *one* of his motives, but it cannot be primary, and therefore cannot be the only one. Unless he desired to be thought about in one way rather than another after his death, the present experience of imagining himself as becoming the object of certain retrospective thoughts and emotions on the part of the beneficiaries would be neither attractive nor repulsive to him.

(3) I think it is plain, then, that the ultimate motive of such a man cannot be desire for his own happiness. But it might be desire for power over others. For he may be said to be exercising this power when he makes his will, even though the effects will not begin until after his death.

(4) Can we say that his motive in making the will is simply to ensure that certain persons will think about him and feel towards him in certain ways after his death? In that case his motive would come under the head of self-display. (This must, of course, be distinguished from the question, already discussed, whether his motive might be to give himself the pleasant experience of imagining their future feelings of gratitude towards him.) The answer is that self-display, in a wide sense, may be a motive, and a very strong one, in making a will; but it could hardly be the sole motive. A testator generally considers the relative needs of various possible beneficiaries, the question whether a certain person would appreciate and take care of a certain picture or house or book, the question whether a certain institution is doing work which he thinks important, and so on. In so far as he is influenced by these considerations, his motives are other-

regarding. But they may be all self-referential. In making his will he may desire to benefit persons only in so far as they are *his* relatives or friends. He may desire to benefit institutions only in so far as *he* is or has been a member of them. And so on. I think that it would be quite plausible to hold that the motives of such a testator are all either self-regarding or self-referential, but that it would not be in the least plausible to say that they are all self-confined or that none of them are other-regarding.

Case B.

Let us next consider the case of a man who subscribes anonymously to a certain charity. His motive cannot possibly be that of self-display. Can we say that his motive is to enjoy the pleasant experience of self-approval and of seeing an institution in which he is interested flourishing? The answer is, again, that these motives may exist and may be strong, but they cannot be primary and therefore cannot be his only motives. Unless he wants the institution to flourish, there will be nothing to attract him in the experience of seeing it flourish. And, unless he subscribes from some other motive than the desire to enjoy a feeling of self-approval, he will not obtain a feeling of self-approval. So here, again, it seems to me that some of his motives must be other-regarding. But it is quite possible that his other-regarding motives may all be self-referential. An essential factor in making him want to benefit this institution may be that it is *his* old college or that a great friend of *his* is at the head of it.

The question, then, that remains is this. Are there any cases in which it is reasonable to think that a person's motive is not egoistic in any of the senses mentioned? In practice, as we now see, this comes down to the question whether there are any cases in which an other-regarding motive is not stimulated by an egoistic motive-stimulus, i.e. whether there is any other-regarding motive which is not also and essentially self-referential.

Case C.

Let us consider the case of a person who deliberately chooses to devote his life to working among lepers, in the full knowledge that he will almost certainly contract leprosy and die in a particularly loathesome way. This is not an imaginary case. To give the Psychological Egoist the longest possible run for his money I will suppose that a person is a Roman Catholic priest, who believes that his action may secure for him a place in heaven in the next world and a reputation for sanctity and heroism in this, that it may be rewarded posthumously with canonization, and that it will redound to the credit of the church of which he is an ordained member.

It is difficult to see what self-regarding or self-referential motives there could be *for* the action beside desire for happiness in heaven, desire to gain a reputation for sanctity and heroism and perhaps to be canonized after death, and desire to glorify the church of which one is a priest. Obviously there are extremely strong self-confined and self-centred motives *against* choosing this kind of life. And in many cases there must have been very strong self-referential other-regarding motives *against* it. For the person who made such a choice must sometimes have been a young man of good family and brilliant prospects, whose parents were heart-broken at his decision, and whose friends thought him an obstinate fool for making it.

Now there is no doubt at all that there was an other-regarding motive, viz. a direct desire to alleviate the sufferings of the lepers. No one who was not dying in the last ditch for an over-simple theory of human nature would deny this. The only questions that are worth raising about it are these. (1) Is this other-regarding motive stimulated by an egoistic motive-stimulus and thus rendered self-referential? (2) Suppose that this motive had not been supported by the various self-regarding and self-referential motives *for* deciding to go and work among the lepers, would it have sufficed, in presence of the motives *against* doing so, to ensure the choice that was actually made?

As regards the first question, I cannot see that there was any special pre-existing relationship between a young priest in Europe and a number of unknown lepers in Asia which might plausibly be held to act as an egoistic motive-stimulus. The lepers are neither his relatives nor his friends nor his benefactors nor members of any community or institution to which he belongs.

As regards the sufficiency of the other-regarding motive, whether stimulated egoistically or not, in the absence of all self-regarding motives tending in the same direction, no conclusive answer can be given. I cannot prove that a single person in the whole course of history *would* have decided to work among lepers, if all the motives against doing so had been present, whilst the hope of heaven, the desire to gain a reputation for sanctity and heroism, and the desire to glorify and extend one's church had been wholly absent. Nor can the Psychological Egoist prove that *no* single person would have so decided under these hypothetical conditions. Factors which cannot be eliminated cannot be shown to be necessary and cannot be shown to be superfluous; and there we must leave the matter.

I suspect that a Psychological Egoist might be tempted to say that the intending medical missionary found the experience of imagining the sufferings of the lepers intensely unpleasant, and that his primary motive for deciding to spend his life working among them was to get rid of this unpleasant experience. This, I think, is what Locke, e.g., would have had to say in accordance with his theory of motivation. About this suggestion there are two remarks to be made.

(1) This motive cannot have been primary, and therefore cannot have been the only motive. Unless this person desired that the lepers should have their sufferings alleviated, there is no reason why the thought of their sufferings should be an unpleasant experience to him. A malicious man, e.g., finds the thought of the sufferings of an enemy a very pleasant experience. This kind of pleasure presupposes a desire for the well-being or the ill-being of others.

(2) If his primary motive were to rid himself of the unpleasant experience of imagining the sufferings of the lepers, he could hardly choose a less effective means than to go and work among them. For the imagination would then be replaced by actual sense-perception; whilst, if he stayed at home and devoted him-

self to other activities, he would have a reasonably good chance of diverting his attention from the sufferings of the lepers. In point of fact one knows that such a person would reproach himself in so far as he managed to forget about the lepers. He would *wish* to keep them and their sufferings constantly in mind, as an additional stimulus to doing what he believes he ought to do, viz. to take active steps to help and relieve them.

In this connection it is important to notice the following facts. For most people the best way to realize the sufferings of strangers is to imagine oneself or one's parents or children or some intimate and beloved friend in the situation in which the stranger is placed. This, as we say, 'brings home to one' his sufferings. A large proportion of the cruelty which decent people applaud or tolerate is applauded or tolerated by them only because they are either too stupid to put themselves imaginatively into the position of the victims or because they deliberately refrain from doing so. One important cause of their deliberately refraining is the notion of retributive justice, i.e. the belief that these persons, or a group taken as a collective whole to which they belong, have *deserved* suffering by wrongdoing, and the desire that they shall get their deserts. Another important cause of this deliberate refrainment is the knowledge that one is utterly powerless to help the victims. However this may be, the fact that imagining oneself in their position is often a necessary condition of desiring to relieve the sufferings of strangers does not make that desire self-referential. Imagining oneself in their place is merely a condition for becomimg vividly *aware of* their sufferings. Whether one will then desire to relieve them or to prolong them or will remain indifferent to them, depends on motives which are not primarily self-regarding or self-referential.

I will now summarize the results of this discussion.

(1) If Psychological Egoism asserts that all ultimate motives are self-confined; or that they are all either self-confined or self-centred, some being of one kind and some of the other; or that all self-confined motives can be reduced to the desire for one's own happiness; it is certainly false. It is not even a close approximation of the truth.

(2) If it asserts that all ultimate motives are either self-regarding or self-referential, some being of one kind and some of the other; and that all other-regarding motives require a self-referential stimulus, it is a close approximation to the truth. It is true, I think, that in most people and at most times other-regarding motives are very weak unless stimulated by a self-referential stimulus. As England's wisest and wittiest statesman put it in his inimitable way: 'Temporal things will have their weight in the world, and, though zeal may prevail for a time and get the better in a skirmish, yet the war endeth generally on the side of flesh and blood, and will do so until mankind is another thing than it is at present.'[1]

(3) Nevertheless, Psychological Egoism, even in its most diluted form, is very doubtful if taken as a universal proposition. Some persons at some times are strongly influenced by other-regarding motives which cannot plausibly be held to be stimulated by a self-referential stimulus. It seems reasonable to hold that the presence of these other-regarding motives is *necessary* to account for their choice of alternatives which they do choose, and for their persistence in the course which they have adopted, though this can never be conclusively established in any particular case. Whether it is also *sufficient* cannot be decided with certainty, for self-regarding and self-referential components are always present in one's total motive for choosing such an action.

I think that the summary which I have just given fairly represents the results of introspection and reflection on one's own and other men's voluntary action. Yet Psychological Egoism in general and Psychological Hedonism in particular have seemed almost self-evident to many highly intelligent thinkers, and they do still seem highly plausible to nearly everyone when he first begins to speculate on human motivation. I believe that this depends, not on empirical facts, but on certain verbal ambiguities and misunderstandings. As so often happens in philosophy, clever people accept a false general principle on *a priori* grounds and then devote endless labour and ingenuity to explaining away plain facts which obviously conflict with it. A

[1] Halifax: *The Character of a Trimmer.*

full discussion of the subject would require an analysis of the confusions which have made these theories seem so plausible; but this must be omitted here.

I must content myself with the following remarks in conclusion. I have tried to show that Psychological Egoism, in the only form in which it could possibly fit the facts of human life, is not a monistic theory motives. On this extended interpretation of the theory of the only feature common to all motives is that every motive which can *act on* a person has one or another of a large number of different kinds of special *reference to* that person. I have tried to show that this certainly covers a wide very field, but that it is by no means certain that there is even this amount of unity among *all* human motives. I think that Psychological Egoism is much the most plausible attempt to reduce the *prima facie* plurality of ultimate kinds of desire to a unity. If it fails, I think it is most unlikely that any alternative attempt on a different basis will succeed.

For my part I am inclined to accept an irreducibly pluralistic view of human motives. This does not, of course, entail that the present irreducible plurality of ultimate motives may not have evolved, in some sense of that highly ambiguous word, out of fewer, either in the history of each individual or in that of the human race. About that I express no opinion here and now.

Now, if Psychological Hedonism had been true, all conflict of motives would have been between motives of the *same kind*. It would always be of the form 'Shall I go to the dentist and certainly be hurt now but probably avoid thereby frequent and prolonged toothache in future? Or shall I take the risk in order to avoid the certainty of being hurt by the dentist now?' On any pluralistic view there is also conflict between motives of irreducibly *different kinds*, e.g. between aversion to painful experience and desire to be thought manly, or between a desire to shine in conversation and aversion to hurting a sensitive person's feelings by a witty but wounding remark.

It seems to me plain that, in our ordinary moral judgments about ourselves and about others, we always unhestitatingly assume that there can be and often is conflict between motives of radically different kinds. Now I do not myself share that superstitious reverence for the beliefs of common sense which many contemporary philosophers profess. But I think that we must start from them, and that we ought to depart from them only when we find good reason to do so. If Psychological Hedonism, or any other monistic theory of motives had been true, we should have had to begin the study of ethics by recognizing that most moral judgments which we pass on ourselves or on others are made under a profound misapprehension of the psychological facts and are largely vitiated thereby. If Psychological Hedonism, e.g., had been true, the only ethical theory worth discussing would have been an egoistic form of ethical Hedonism. For one cannot be under an obligation to attempt to do what is psychologically impossible. And, on the hypothesis of Psychological Hedonism, it is psychologically impossible for anyone ultimately to desire anything except to prolong or acquire experiences which he knows or expects to be pleasant and to cut short or avoid experiences which he knows or expects to be unpleasant. If it were still possible to talk of having duties at all, each person's duties would be confined within the limits which that psychological impossibility marks out. And it would clearly be impossible to suppose that any part of anyone's ultimate motive for doing any act is his belief that it would be right in the circumstances together with his desire to do what is right as such. For, if Psychological Hedonism were true, a desire to do what is right could not be ultimate, it must be subordinate to the desire to get or prolong pleasant experiences and to avoid or cut short unpleasant ones.

Now it is plain that such consequences as these conflict sharply with common-sense notions of morality. If we had been obliged to accept Psychological Egoism, in any of its narrower forms, on its merits, we should have had to say: 'So much the worse for the common-sense notions of morality!' But, if I am right, the morality of common sense, with all its difficulties and incoherences, is immune at least to attacks from the basis of Psychological Egoism.

XII

SELF AND OTHERS[1] (1953)

It seems fitting that the subject of a Herbert Spencer Lecture should be one that looks slightly old-fashioned, and it is desirable that it should not in fact be quite obsolete. I have therefore decided to discuss certain ethical questions which interested Spencer and his contemporaries, such as Sidgwick; which are of perennial interest; but which have now for many years been out of the limelight. I have lumped these questions together under the head of 'Self and Others', which was as adequate a short title as I could think of.

It will be convenient to start by considering two closely connected principles, formulated by Sidgwick, which lead, as we shall see, to what I am going to call 'Ethical Neutralism'. One of them is about good and evil, and the other about obligation. I will state them in Sidgwick's own words. (1) 'The good of any individual is of no more importance, from the point of view of the universe, than the good of any other'. (2) 'It is my duty to aim at good generally, so far as I can bring it about, and not merely at any particular part of it'. Sidgwick claimed that these principles are self-evident, and compared them to mathematical axioms.

It cannot be said that, as stated, they are as clear and unambiguous as one could wish. Let us us begin with the phrase 'the good of an individual'. It seems clear that we must distinguish between being a valuable or disvaluable *person*, on the one hand, and having a valuable or disvaluable *life-history*, on the other. The value or disvalue of a person depends primarily on the nature, the relative strength, and the organization or disorganization of his cognitive, conative, and emotional dispositions. The value or disvalue of his life history depends primarily on the nature, order, and interrelations of his experiences and actions, simultaneous and succes-

[1] Published by courtesy of the directors of the Herbert Spencer Lectures, Oxford University.

sive. No doubt the two are intimately inter-connected, but they remain fundamentally different. Cases might arise where one would have to choose between making a person better at the cost of making his life-history worse, or conversely. So 'the good of an individual' must be taken to cover both the value which resides in his personality and that which resides in his life-history.

Let us next consider the phrase 'from the point of view of the universe'. Sidgwick certainly did not believe that the universe literally has a point of view. And, *if* he had, one might well ask why it should be proper for any of us to adopt it. I think that the meaning of the principle can be expressed without using this phrase. Suppose that A and B are two individuals. They will always be unlike in many respects. They will have started with more or less dissimilar innate dispositions; they will have had more or less dissimilar experiences, and will thus have acquired dissimilar dispositional modifications; and they will stand in dissimiliar relationships to other persons and things. In consequence of these qualitative and relational unlikenesses, the balance of good and evil in the world might be changed to a very different extent according to whether an experience of the same perfectly determinate kind were now to be produced in A and not in B, or in B and not in A. Sidgwick certainly did not wish to deny this perfectly obvious fact. I suggest that what he wanted to assert is this. Suppose that the balance of good and evil in the world *would* be changed to a different extent according to whether a precisely similar experience were to be produced in A and not in B or in B and not in A. Then this difference in value could not be due to the mere *numerical otherness* of A and B. It must always depend on some specific unlikeness in their qualities or dispositions or in their past history or present relationships. This is the only interpretation which I can suggest which makes the principle intelligible and obviously true. And, on that interpretation, it seems to me completely trivial.

Let us now consider the second principle. This alleges that 'it is my duty to aim at good generally, so far as I can bring it about, and not merely at any particular part of it'.

We must begin by calling to mind that Sidgwick was a

Utilitarian about right and wrong and an Ethical Hedonist about good and evil. It seems to me, however, that we can deal with this principle without presupposing either of these two doctrines. For, on any view, *one* important *prima facie* duty is to produce and conserve good and to avert and diminish evil. And, on any view, we must distinguish between making a *person* better or worse and making his *life-history* better or worse, and we must include both under the head of doing good to him or harm to him. For the present purpose it does not matter whether we do or do not believe that the value or disvalue of a person can be defined in terms of that of his experiences, and it does not matter whether the value or disvalue of an experience does or does not depend solely on its pleasantness or unpleasantness respectively. We can take the principle to be concerned with the way in which an agent is obliged or permitted or forbidden to distribute his beneficent activities as between the various persons whose characters or life-histories he can effect for good or for ill.

On this understanding Sidgwick's second principle can be formulated as follows. The *only* legitimate ground for devoting more of one's beneficent activities to one person or group of persons rather than to another, among those whose characters or life-histories one can effect, is that by so doing one will produce more good or avert more evil *on the whole* than by making no selection or a different selection among one's possible beneficiaries.

What it comes to is this. A person may be, and in fact generally is, justified in limiting the range of his beneficent efforts, and in distributing them unequally within that limited range. But such limitation in range, and such inequality of distribution, *always* need justification, and they can be justified *only* on the following ground. It must be able to be shown that, owing to the agent's limited powers and resources, to the limitations of his knowledge and his natural sympathies, to the natural affection which only certain persons feel for him, and so on, he can produce most good or avert most evil *on the whole* by confining his beneficent activities to *a certain restricted part*.

Now this principle is by no means trivial, for I suppose that most people would be inclined *prima facie* to reject it as soon as they realised its implications, even if they were inclined to accept it as self-evident when they contemplated it in abstraction. For the common opinion certainly is that a person has a more urgent duty to benefit those who stand in certain relations to him, e.g. his children or his parents, than to benefit others who do not; and that this special urgency depends *directly* on those special relationships.

Whether Sidgwick's second principle be true or false, it has an important corollary, which we must now consider. Among those whose lives or personalities a man can effect for good or for ill is *himself*. Obviously each of us stands in a unique relation to himself, viz. that of personal identity. It is equally obvious that each of us stands to all other persons in a unique relation of an opposite kind, viz. personal diversity. Now it might be thought that either or both of these relationships impose special claims or special limitations on a person's beneficence.

The doctrine that each of us has a special obligation to benefit *himself*, as such, may be called *Ethical Egoism;* and the doctrine that each of us has a special obligation to benefit *others*, as such, may be called *Ethical Altruism*.

Now a plain consequence of Sidgwick's second principle is that both these doctrines are false, and that what may be called *Ethical Neutralism* is true. Suppose that, on a certain occasion, a person would increase the balance of good over evil in the world more by benefiting another, at the cost of foregoing a benefit or inflicting an injury on himself, than by any other action then open to him. Then it would be his duty to do this. Suppose that, on a certain other occasion, a person could increase that balance more by benefiting himself, at the cost of withholding a benefit from another or inflicting an injury on him, than by any other action then open to him. Then it would be his duty to do that.

I will now consider in some detail these three alternative doctrines about self and others. The first point which I will make is that neither Ethical Egoism nor Ethical Altruism can be rejected *in limine* as involving an internal inconsistency. Each of these doctrines might be held in milder or more extreme forms. It will suffice if I take the most extreme form of each, and show that it is internally coherent.

The extreme form of Ethical Egoism might be stated as follows. Each person is under a direct obligation to benefit him self as such. He is under no *direct* obligation to benefit any other person, though he will be under an indirect obligation to do this so far and only so far as that is the most efficient means available to him for benefiting himself. He is forbidden to benefit another person, if doing so will in in the long run be detrimental to himself.

Now suppose that A is an Ethical Egoist of this extreme kind. He can admit that, if a certain experience or a certain disposition of *his own* would be intrinsically good, a precisely similar experience or disposition of B's would *caeteris paribus* be also and equally good, i.e. he can admit Sidgwick's first principle. But he will assert that his duty is not to produce good experiences and good dispositions as such, without regard to the question of who will have them. A has an obligation to produce good experiences and good dispositions in A, and no direct obligation to produce them in B or in anyone else. Similarly, B has an obligation to produce good experiences and good dispositions in B, and no direct obligation to produce then in A or anyone else. A can admit this about B, and B can admit it about A. Plainly there is no *internal inconsistency* in this doctrine. What it is inconsistent with is Sidgwick's principle that each of us has an unqualified obligation to maximize the balance of good over evil in the lives and personalities of all whom he can affect, and to pay no regard to the question which particular individuals or classes of individuals these goods and evils will occur in, except in so far as that may affect the balance.

In a similar way it could be shown that there is no internal inconsistency in Ethical Altruism, even in its most extreme form. It would be waste of time to give the argument in detail. But it will be worth while to state in passing what would be the extreme form of Ethical Altruism. It would come to this. Each person is under a direct obligation to benefit others as such. He is under no direct obligation to benefit himself as such, though he is under an indirect obligation to do this so far and only so far as that may be the most efficient means available to him for benefiting others. He is forbidden to benefit himself, if so doing will in the long run be detrimental to others.

A useful way of putting the difference between Neutralism, on the one hand, and the two rival doctrines, on the other, is this. Neutralism assumes that there is a certain *one* state of affairs, viz. the maximum balance of good over evil in the lives and personalities of the contemporary and future inhabitants of the world, at which *everyone* ought to aim as his *ultimate* end. Differences in the proximate ends of different persons are justified only in so far as the realization of the one ultimate end is best secured in practice by each person aiming, not directly at it, but at a proximate end of a more limited kind. The other two doctrines, at any rate in their extreme forms, deny that there is any *one* state of affairs at which *everyone* ought to aim as his ultimate end. There are, in fact, as many different ultimate ends as there are agents. On the egoistic theory, the ultimate end at which A should aim is the maximum balance of good over evil in A's life and personality. The same holds *mutatis mutandis* for B, C, etc. On the altruistic theory the ultimate end at which A should aim is the maximum balance of good over evil in the lives and personalities of all *others-than*-A. The same holds *mutatis mutandis* for B, C, etc. From this point of view the main difference between Egoism and Altruism is the following. For Egoism the various ultimate ends are mutually exclusive, whilst for Altruism the ultimate ends of any two persons have a very large field in common.

Before leaving this topic I would call attention to the following point. Suppose that an act will affect a certain person B and him alone. Then there will be a characteristic dissimilarity in the act according to whether it is done by B himself or by any other person. If it is done by B, it will be a *self-affecting act*; if it is done by any other person, it will be an *other-affecting act*. Now this kind of dissimilarity between acts, though it depends merely on the numerical identity or the numerical otherness of the agent-self and the patient-self, may be ethically relevant. If the agent-self and the patient-self be the same, the act may be right; if they are different, it may be indifferent or positively wrong. And the converse may be equally true. It is misleading to compare an act which is only self-affecting with one which would be other-affecting, however alike they may be in their consequences and in all other respects. For this dissimilarity may be ethically relevant. Undoubtedly common sense thinks that it is often highly relevant. To give to oneself an innocent pleasure is generally regarded as morally indifferent. To give to another a similar pleasure may be regarded as praiseworthy or even as obligatory. When we bear these facts in mind we see that Ethical Egoism and Ethical Altruism, even in their extreme form, are not merely free from internal inconsistency. They are also completely general and symmetrical as regards all individuals. It cannot be fairly objected to either of them that it gives an irrational preference to any individual, as such, over any other.

Let us now consider the three rival principles on their merits. I will begin with Ethical Neutralism. The first thing to be said about it is this. Suppose we define the phrase 'optimific act' as follows. An act is *optimific* if and only if its consequences in the long run would be *no worse* on balance than those of any other act open to the agent at the time. Then Neutralism is the only one of the three principles which could be combined with the doctrine that the right act in any situation *necessarily* coincides with an act which is optimific in that situation. Now many persons have found the latter doctrine, viz. Utilitarianism, self-evident. Anyone who does so is committed to Neutralism, whether he finds the the latter self-evident on inspection or not. But such logical entailments always cut both ways. Anyone who feels doubts about Neutralism ought, to that extent, to feel doubts about Utilitarianism, even if on other grounds he were inclined to accept it.

The second comment to be made is this. The implications of Neutralism certainly do not commend themselves *prima facie* to common sense. It seems to be in some directions immorally selfish and in others immorally indiscriminate. It seems to ignore altogether the ethical relevance of the distinction between acts which are only self-affecting and those which are other-affecting. And among acts which are primarily other-affecting it denies any *direct* ethical relevance to the difference between more and less intimate relationships between an agent and his possible beneficiaries. Yet *prima facie* the special urgency of the claims of certain others upon one's beneficence seems to be founded *directly* on certain special relationships of those others to oneself. I shall return to this point at the end of the lecture; in the meanwhile I will consider Ethical Egoism and Ethical Altruism on their respective merits.

Ethical Egoism, unlike Neutralism, could take many forms. In its extreme form I think it may be rejected at once. I doubt whether anyone would seriously consider it unless, like Spinoza, he had already accepted *Psychological* Egoism. If a person is persuaded that it is psychologically impossible for anyone to act non-egoistically, he will have to hold that each man's duties are confined within the sphere which that psychological impossibility marks out. But, it seems to me, there is no valid reason for accepting psychological egoism. I propose, therefore, to consider a milder form of Ethical Egoism, viz. that which Bishop Butler enunciated in the following famous sentence: 'Though virtue . . . does indeed consist in affection to and pursuit of what is right and good as such, yet . . . when we sit down in a cool hour we can neither justify to ourselves this or any other pursuit till we are satisfied that it will be for our happiness or at least not contrary to it.'

Before considering this dictum critically I will make two historical remarks about it. The first is that Butler states it as a concession which he is willing to make for the sake of argument, and does not explicitly commit himself to it. The second is that Sidgwick, who was an exceptionally clear-headed and honest thinker, found *both* this principle *and* Neutralism self-evident when he contemplated each separately, and saw that they are incompatible with each other.

I find Butler's principle far from easy to interpret. The main difficulty is in the phrase 'justify to ourselves'. I think we may fairly assume that Butler held it to be *psychologically possible* for a person to undertake a course of action simply because he believes it to be right in the circumstances. For, otherwise, 'virtue' as defined by him would be a psychological impossibility. It is surely incredible that he should have held that. So what he must be saying would seem to be this. Although a person *can* undertake a certain course of action simply because he believes it to be right, and although he is acting *virtuously* only if he does so from that motive, his action still in some sense needs justification. It will not be justified in this sense, whatever that may be, unless it will be for the agent's happiness or at least not contrary to it.

Now does 'justification' here mean *moral* justification, or justification in some other sense which is not specifically moral? To justify an act *morally* it is surely necessary and sufficient to show that it is *morally right* for the agent to undertake it in the actual circumstances. I suspect that Butler must have had some kind of not specifically moral justification in mind. I suspect that he must have had the feeling that, however *right* an act may be, it must be condemned in a certain non-moral sense, e.g. as 'silly' or 'quixotic', unless it will confer some advantage on the agent personally or at least not be to his detriment. If so, it is difficult to see how specifically moral justification and this kind of non-moral *desideratum* can be weighed against each other, and why the latter should apparently be held to be in the last resort preponderant.

Let us, therefore, try to interpret 'justifiable' as meaning *morally* justifiable, and let us discuss the principle for ourselves on that interpretation, without regard to what Butler may have meant by it. On that view the principle would come to this. A person may believe a certain action to be right without considering whether it will make for his happiness or not. And he may undertake it simply because he believes it to be right and desires to do what is right as such. But, unless it makes for his happiness or is at least not contrary to it, it will not in fact *be* right.

In order to see what this comes to let us contrast it with ordinary Hedonistic Utilitarianism and with the Neutralism which is the corollary of the latter. Let us imagine a person who started as an ordinary hedonistic Utilitarian, and then came to accept this principle. What is the minimum change that he would have to make in his original position?

Even when he was an ordinary Hedonistic Utilitarian he would have had to consider *inter alia* the effects on his own happiness of each alternative possible course of action. But at that stage he would not attach either more or less weight to its effects on his own happiness as such than to its effects on the happiness of any other person. But, when he came to accept the Butler principle, he would have to reject as wrong, without regard to its effects on the welfare or illfare of others, every alternative which would not make for his own happiness or at any rate every alternative which would be contrary to his own happiness. It is only to the alternatives which remain after this preliminary process of elimination that he would apply the principles of ordinary Hedonistic Utilitarianism.

So far I have left unanalysed Butler's phrase 'being for one's own happiness or at least not contrary to it'. It remains to consider this. Let us suppose that the agent has open to him some alternatives which would *worsen* his hedonic state, some which would *leave it unchanged* on balance, and some which would *improve* it to various degrees. It seems clear that the principle would require him, under these circumstances, to reject any alternative which would *worsen* his hedonic state. But it is not clear that it would require him to reject *in limine* an alternative which would leave his hedonic state unchanged, in favour of one which would positively improve it. Nor is it clear that it would require him to reject, among those alternatives which would positively improve his hedonic state, any alternative which would improve it *less than* some other. What force is to be attached to the concessive phrase 'or at least not contrary to it'? Is egoistic honour satisfied by the minimal interpretation, or does it demand the maximal interpretation in the circumstances supposed?

In order to give the principle every chance I will put the *minimal* interpretation on it. On that interpretation it comes to this. Suppose that a person has alternatives open to him, some of which would worsen his hedonic state, some of which would leave it unchanged, and some of which would improve it to various degrees. Then, *before* considering the effects of these alternatives on the welfare or illfare of others, he must reject as wrong all alternatives which would *worsen* his hedonic state. But among the alternatives which are then left he need not reject as wrong those which would leave his hedonic state unchanged, in favour of those which would improve it. Among the latter he need not reject as wrong those which would improve it less than some others would do.

Now I do not find the least trace of self-evidence in the principle, even when thus minimally interpreted. Moreover, it is plainly in conflict with many of the moral judgments of common sense, for what that may be worth. It is often, e.g., held to be highly praiseworthy to choose an alternative which will positively worsen one's own hedonic state, if this is the only or the best means of securing some end which is valuable in itself, or if it is done for the sake of persons to whom the agent stands in certain special relationships. Even when we are not prepared to say that such an act of self-sacrifice is a duty, this is often not because we think it wrong, but because we think that the agent is doing something which is highly creditable to him but is more than the minimum which duty demands. But there are many cases in which we should be inclined to say that such an act is neither more nor less than a duty. This might be said, e.g., of certain acts of this kind done by a mother for her child, or by a son or daughter for an aged and infirm parent.

The principle would be more plausible if it were stated, not in terms of the agent's happiness or even of other forms of valuable experience, but in terms of improvement or injury to his personality. Let us then restate the principle as follows: Before an agent considers the effects of the various alternatives open to him on the welfare or illfare of others, he must reject as wrong any alternative which will *worsen his own personality*. There are two remarks to be made about this.

In the first place, it is commonly held to be permissible or even obligatory for a person who stands in certain relations to others deliberately to sacrifice his *life*, if certain very valuable results can be secured for them in that way and in no other. One example is that of an officer deciding to blow up a certain bridge, where he will undoubtedly perish in the explosion but may save his country from invasion. Another is that of the captain of a sinking ship deliberately remaining on board in order that the passengers may have the best chance of being saved. Such cases might perhaps be covered by restating the principle in the following more restricted form: Among the alternatives which are *compatible with his own survival* an agent must reject as wrong any which will worsen his own character and personality.

The second point to note is an ambiguity in the phrase 'to improve or to worsen a man's personality'. This may be used in a specifically moral sense, or in a wider sense which may refer to other than specifically moral excellences and defects. In this wider sense one's personality is improved if one's table-manners or one's golf-handicap or one's powers of appreciating classical music are bettered. Now I do not think that anyone would find the amended principle plausible if 'worsening the agent's personality' were taken to include producing ill-effects on his *non-moral* powers and dispositions. We regard it as always regrettable, but often permissible and sometimes obligatory, for an agent to do an act which involves cramping his personality and foregoing many possible and desirable developments of it. Any intelligent and sensitive person who decides to devote his or her life to working among the sick or the insane inevitably does this, and we do not regard all such decisions as *ipso facto* morally wrong.

The case for the principle is at its strongest if it is put in the following highly restricted form: Among the alternatives open to him, which involve his own survival, an agent must reject as wrong any which will worsen his *moral* character. I think that common sense *would* feel rather uncomforable in enjoining any such act on a person as a *duty*. But I doubt whether it would be prepared to say that every such act is *ipso facto* wrong. A daughter who gives up her life to tending a peevish invalid mother, instead of marrying and having children, certainly foregoes many possibilities of *moral* development and is likely to develop certain *moral* defects. Possibly her moral character may be improved in some directions, but it seems very doubtful whether the moral gain generally outweighs the moral loss and damage. Yet common sense hesitates to say that such a course of action is wrong. It just feels uncomfortable, and turns its attention as quickly as possible to more cheerful subjects.

The upshot of the discussion is that I am unable to suggest any form of Ethical Egoism, however qualified and attenuated, which appears to be self-evident and which is not plainly at variance with the moral judgments which ordinary people would make in certain particular cases. I pass therefore to the claims of Ethical Altruism.

This, like Ethical Egoism, can take many different forms. Unlike Ethical Egoism, even the most extreme form of it would hardly be rejected off-hand as plainly immoral, at any rate in countries where there is a Christian tradition. It might be described as quixotic or impracticable, but hardly as immoral. No doubt there is a sound practical motive for this more favourable attitude. We realize that most people are far more liable to err on the egoistic than on the altruistic side, and that in a world where so many people are too egoistic it would be unwise to do or say anything to discourage altruism. We also feel that there is something morally admirable in the will and the power to sacrifice one's own well-being—even one's own *moral* development—for the good of others. We therefore hesitate to condemn publicly even those instances of altruistic behaviour which we privately regard as excessive; and we console ourselves with the thought that there is no great risk of their becoming unduly frequent.

But, when this has been said, it must be admitted that there is no trace of self-evidence in the extreme forms of Ethical Altruism, and that they conflict in particular cases with the moral judgments of common sense. It is true that we might hesitate to say that a person has a direct *prima facie* obligation to seek his own happiness. But we certainly condemn morally a person who acts highly imprudently, i.e. one who unreasonably discounts his own probably future pleasures and unpleasures in comparison with those which are immediately within his reach. It seems plausible to hold that such condemnation is at least in part *direct*, and that it is not wholly based on one's awareness of the fact that such a person is likely to become a burden to others. And when we turn from the good and bad experiences which a person may have in the course of his life to the goodness or badness which resides in his personality, we notice the following fact. Common sense appears to hold that each of us is under a fairly strong obligation to develop his own physical and intellectual powers, to organize his character into a coherent system, and not to allow himself to rust or to run to seed. No doubt one important ground for regarding self-culture and self-development as a duty is that they are necessary conditions for being *useful to others*. But I do not think it is plausible to hold that this is *merely* an indirect obligation, wholly subordinate to the direct obligation to be useful to others.

Let us, then, ignore the extremer forms of Ethical Altruism, and consider for a moment a principle which might be regarded as an altruistic counterpart to Butler's egoistic principle. This is Kant's famous maxim that it is always wrong to treat a person as a mere means, and a duty to treat him as an end. It is true that Kant held that this maxim should govern a person's dealings with himself as well as his dealings with others. But, if we confine our attention to the latter application of it, we might regard Kant's principle as setting a limit to the sacrifices which a person may legitimately impose on others, just as Butler's principle sets a limit to those which he may legitimately impose on himself.

I think that the terminology of 'means' and 'end' is unfortunate here, and that the word 'end' fails to express what Kant may have had in mind. The word 'end', when used in its ordinary sense, signifies primarily a possible state of affairs which someone desires to be realized, and towards the realization of which he can contribute by appropriate action. Now this possible state of affairs may be the future existence of an object of a certain kind, which does not at present exist, e.g. of a certain building which a person has planned and desires to have built. In that case this proposed object itself may be called an 'end' in a derivative sense in relation to that person. I believe that these two inter-related senses are the only ones in which the word 'end' is commonly used, and the only ones in which it is correlative to the word 'means'. A 'means' is any object which a person uses as an instrument in carrying out a course of action undertaken in order to realize a possible state of affairs which is an end to him.

Now it is obvious enough that a person can be and often is treated as a *means*. A miner is so treated in so far as he is used for hewing coal, and a criminal is so treated when he is publicly punished in order to deter himself or others from similar criminal actions in future. But it is not at all clear that a person can be treated as an *end*, in the ordinary sense in which the terms 'end' and 'means' are correlatives. It is plain that a person *cannot* be an end in the first sense which I have mentioned. For a person is not a possible state of affairs. A person might be an end in the second sense, viz. an object whose existence someone desired to be realized and which will come into being through the deliberate action of that someone. In this sense a person might be an end to a eugenist or to an educator who had deliberately had him generated or subsequently moulded in accordance with his plans. In this sense a person may even be an end to himself, in perfectly intelligible phraseology. A man may, e.g., in early life form the desire to become a yogi, and by a long course of appropriate training and self-discipline he may eventually effect the transformation in his character and powers which he has sought. Such a person, in his later state, is an end in relation to himself as he was in his earlier states. Moreover, in such a case he has also continually used himself, in respect of certain of his powers and dispositions, as the means or instrument whereby he has eventually realized himself as an end.

When Kant talked of treating a person as a *means* I see no reason to doubt that he was using the word in its ordinary familiar sense. But when he talked of treating a person as an *end* I very much doubt whether he was using that word in any sense which is familiar and correlative to *means*. From the context I should judge that he meant treating a person as an entity which can significantly be said to have legal and moral *rights*, to be morally *responsible* for its actions, to *deserve* pleasure as a reward and pain as a punishment for certain of his actions, and so on. To treat a person as a mere instrument is certainly to ignore such facts about him. But on the other hand, to treat him as a bearer of rights and duties, merits and demerits, is not appropriately described as treating him as an end.

The minimal interpretation which we might put on Kant's principal is this. It is always wrong to treat a *person* as if he were a mere animal, and still more wrong to treat him as if he were a mere inanimate object. For a person is a being who not only has sensations which may be painful and desires which may be thwarted, like an animal. He has also the power of rational and of reflective cognition; ideas of right and wrong, good and evil; and all those conative and emotional peculiarities, such as a sense of duty, feelings of remorse, etc., which depend on the former properties. In considering how to treat a person it can never be right simply to ignore those features which distinguish him from a mere animal and still more from an inanimate object.

When thus interpreted the principle is no doubt true and highly important. But it does not follow that, when one *has* taken account of the features which distinguish a person from a brute or an inanimate thing, and *has* endeavoured to give due weight to them, it is never right to treat him in certain respects as if he were the one or the other. It is not clear, e.g., that it is never right to compel a person to do what he believes to be wrong, e.g., to have his children vaccinated; or to restrain him from doing what he believes to be his duty, e.g., from sacrificing his first-born to Moloch. For, although he is a person, he is not the only one; and there may be situations in which, unless you treat a certain person as if he were a dangerous animal, he will infringe the rights and liberties and consciences of many other persons.

The sentiments of common sense at the present time in Western countries on such issues are highly complex and very mixed. The following remarks will serve to illustrate this.

(1) It is generally held to be permissible for an individual or

a community to take the *life* of a person under certain circumstances. Any individual may do this if he is attacked and has serious reason to believe that he cannot save himself or those dependent on him from death or serious injury at any less cost. When a country is at war those of its citizens who are members of its armed forces, not only *may* do this, but are under an *obligation* to do it to a member of an opposing force who refuses to surrender. A community may do it, through its authorized agent, to a citizen who has been convicted of murder and sentenced to death by due process of law; and it is the duty of the executioner to carry out the sentence. All this would have been accepted by Kant. Yet it is surely difficult to hold, without a great deal of palpable sophistication, that the attacker, the enemy soldier, and the condemned murderer are being treated as *ends* in any ordinarily accepted sense of that word. I think it is true that the attacker and the enemy soldier are also not being treated as *mere means*. The murder *is* being treated as a means in so far as the execution is intended to deter or to reform others.

(2) It is commonly held that there are circumstances in which it is right for A to take B's life, but it would be wrong for B to take his own life. Thus it is right and dutiful for the executioner to take the life of the condemned murderer, but wrong for the latter to anticipate him by committing suicide. (This furnishes a good example of the ethical relevance which common sense ascribes to the distinction between self-affecting and other-affecting acts.)

(3) On the other hand, common-sense holds that it may be right and praiseworthy for a person voluntarily to make sacrifices which it would be wrong for anyone else to impose on him. Thus, e.g., a medical research worker with no one dependent on him would be admired if he were to subject himself voluntarily to some process of treatment which might injure him permanently or kill him but which might lead to a valuable discovery. But it would be thought monstrously wrong to subject anyone against his will to such a process of treatment, or even, I think, to try to persuade him to subject himself to it.

(4) Common sense in contemporary Western societies holds very strongly that it is unconditionally wrong to subject an *innocent* person to loss or suffering in respect of a crime committed by another, even where there is good reason to believe that this would be more effective as a deterrent than any punishment that could be inflicted on the criminal himself. There is perhaps no other point at which pure Utilitarianism is in such complete and obvious conflict with common-sense morality as here. Even if a convincing case could be made out on Utilitarian grounds for the principle that only the guilty should suffer in respect of a crime—and it is very doubtful whether this could be done—common sense would feel that this line of argument is wholly irrelevant.

In view of such facts as I have stated above, it would be extremely hard to formulate any unconditional general principle about the limitation of the sacrifices which can be legitimately imposed on others. I suspect that any such formulation would have to contain so many qualifications that it could make no claim to embody a self-evident principle.

In considering Neutralism, Ethical Egoism, and Ethical Altruism I have in each case indicated some important points in which the doctrine seems to conflict with the morality of common sense. I will now consider briefly what seems to be the attitude of common sense towards the issue of self and others. I think that this position may be best described as *Self-referential Altruism*.

Common sense considers that the question whether an act is only self-affecting or is also other-affecting is often highly relevant to whether it is permissible or omissible, morally admirable or morally indifferent or morally culpable.

Its attitude is *altruistic* in the following respects. It considers that each of us is often under an obligation to sacrifice his own happiness, and sometimes to sacrifice the development of his own personality and even to give up his life, for the benefit of certain other persons and institutions, when it is quite uncertain whether on the whole more good will be produced or more evil averted by so doing than by acting otherwise. It tends to admire such acts, even when it regrets the necessity for them, and even when it thinks that on the whole they had better not have been done. It has no admiration, as such, for acts directed towards making one's own life happy, even when they do no harm to others. It does indeed admire acts directed to the development and improvement of the agent's own personality, whether in moral or in non-moral respects. But I think that its admiration is not very strong unless they are done against exceptionally great external obstacles (e.g. poverty or a criminal environment) or exceptionally great internal handicaps (e.g. ill-health or disablement or unusually violent passions).

On the other hand, the altruism which common sense approves is always *limited in scope*. It holds that each of us has specially urgent obligations to benefit certain individuals and groups which stand in certain special relations to *himself*, e.g. his parents, his children, his follow-countrymen, etc. And it holds that these special relationships are the ultimate and sufficient ground for these specially urgent claims on one's beneficence.

The above paragraphs express what I mean by saying that the altruism which common sense accepts is self-referential. In conclusion I wish to raise this question. Could this common-sense position be circumvented by a person who found Neutralism self-evident, or by one who found the Utilitarian principle self-evident and was thus committed to Neutralism at the next move?

Such a person would, I think, have to do the following two things:

(1) He would have to show that all those special obligations which common-sense takes to be founded *directly* upon special relations of others to the agent, are *derivable* (so far as they are valid at all) from the one fundamental obligation to maximize the balance of good over evil in the lives and personalities of all contemporary and subsequent inhabitants of the world, taken as a whole. He would try to do this by reference to the obvious facts that each of us is limited in his powers and resources, in his knowledge of the needs of others, and in the range of his natural sympathies; and that each of us is an object of interest,

affection, and natural expectation only to a limited class of his fellow-men. The best that the Neutralist could hope to achieve on these lines would be to reach a system of *derived* obligations, which agreed roughly in scope and in relative urgency with that set of obligations which common sense (mistakenly, on his view) takes to be founded *directly* upon various special relationships. In so far as this result was reached, the Neutralist might claim to accept in outline the same set of obligations which common sense does; to correct common-sense morality in matters of detail; and to substitute a single coherent system of obligations, deduced from a single self-evident moral principle and a number of admitted psychological facts, for a mere heap of unrelated and separately grounded obligations. To have tried to carry this out in great detail and with much plausibility is one of the solid achievements of Sidgwick in his *Methods of Ethics*.

(2) To complete his case, the Neutralist would have to try to explain how common sense comes to make the fundamental mistake which, according to him, it does make. It seems to me that he might attempt this with some plausibility on the following lines. And here we make that concluding bow to the theory of evolution, without which a Herbert Spencer Lecture would surely be incomplete.

(i) Any society in which each member was prepared to make sacrifices for the benefit of the group as a whole and of certain smaller groups within it would be more likely to flourish and persist than one whose members were not prepared to make such sacrifices. Now egoistic and anti-social motives are extremely strong in everyone. Suppose, then, that there had been a society in which, no matter how, there had arisen a strong additional motive (no matter how absurd or superstitious) in support of self-sacrifice, on appropriate occasions, by a member of the group for the sake of the group as a whole or for that of certain smaller groups within it. Suppose that this motive was thereafter conveyed from one generation to another by example and by precept, and that it was supported by the sanctions of social praise and blame. Such a society would be likely to flourish, and to overcome other societies in which no such additional motive for limited self-sacrifice had arisen and been propagated. So its ways of thinking in these matters, and its sentiments of approval and disapproval concerning them, would tend to spread. They would spread directly through conquest, and indirectly by the prestige which the success of this society would give to it in the eyes of others.

(ii) Suppose, next, that there had been a society in which, no matter how, a strong additional motive for *unlimited* self-sacrifice had arisen and had been propagated from one generation to another. A society in which each member was as ready to sacrifice himself for other societies and their members as for his own society and its members, would be most unlikely to persist and flourish. Therefore such a society would be very likely to succumb in conflict with one of the former kind.

(iii) Now suppose a long period of conflict between societies of the various types which I have imagined. It seems likely that the societies which would still be existing and would be predominant at the latter part of such a period would be those in which there had somehow arisen in the remote past a strong pro-emotion towards self-sacrifice confined within the society, and a strong anti-emotion towards extending it beyond those limits. Now these are exactly the kinds of society which we do find existing and flourishing in historical times.

The Neutralist might therefore argue as follows. Even if Neutralism be true, and even if it be self-evident to a philosopher who contemplates it in a cool hour in his study, there are powerful historical causes which would tend to make certain forms of restricted Altruism or qualified Egoism *seem* to be true to most unreflective persons at all times and even to many reflective ones at most times. Therefore the fact that common-sense rejects Neutralism, and tends to accept this other type of doctrine, is not a conclusive objection to the *truth*, or even to the *necessary* truth, of Neutralism.

XIII

EMOTION AND SENTIMENT (1954)[1]

Emotions, as I shall maintain, are *cognitions* with a certain kind of psychical quality. Cognitions are a subclass of *experiences*. I shall therefore begin by classifying experiences in general and cognitions in particular. It is only after that has been done that one can profitably discuss emotions and sentiments.

CLASSIFICATION OF EXPERIENCES

Experiences may be divided into those which *do not* and those which *do* have an epistemological object. The former may be called *pure feelings*. The natural question to ask with regard to a feeling is: '*How* are you feeling?' And the natural answer is to utter some adjective (or, more properly, adverb), such as 'Hot', or 'Tired', or 'Cross'. To feel tired is to be feeling *in a certain way*; it is not to be *aware of a certain object*, real or fictitious. On the other hand, there are many experiences about which it is natural to ask: 'What is the *object* of your experience?' or 'What is it *about*?' If a person says that he is seeing or hearing or thinking, it is natural to ask: '*What* are you seeing?' or '*What* are you hearing?' or '*What* are you thinking about?'. And the answer that one expects is the utterance of some substantive or phrase equivalent to a substantive, e.g., 'A red flash', 'A squeaky noise', 'The square-root of minus 1'. I shall say that experiences of the latter kind 'have an epistemological object' or are 'epistemologically intentional'. All such experiences may be called *cognitions*.

It is important to notice that an experience may be epistemologically intentional, even if it be a *delusive quasi-perception* or a

[1] Reprinted from the *Journal of Aesthetics and Art Criticism*, Volume XIII. December 1954, by courtesy of the editors.

thought of something which does not and perhaps could not exist. A person who in a dream ostensibly sees a man pointing a revolver at him is having an epistemologically intentional experience, although there is no *ontological object* (i.e. no actual man, pointing an actual revolver at him at the time) corresponding to it. Similarly, a person who is thinking of a phoenix is having an epistemologically intentional experience. He is certainly thinking of *something* and he could describe what he is thinking of. If he were thinking of a dragon, instead of a phoenix, he would be thinking of something *different* and would give a *different* description. And that, in spite of the fact that there never have been, and perhaps could not be, in nature either phoenixes or dragons.

So we begin by dividing experiences into *pure feelings* and *cognitions*. The former are those which have only psychical qualities and do not have epistemological objects. The latter are those which have epistemological objects. Cognitions may have psychical qualities as well as epistemological objects; some of them certainly do, and perhaps all of them do. A pure feeling cannot significantly be described either as veridical or as delusive. These alternatives can be significantly predicated only of cognitions. A cognition is *veridical* if there is an ontological object answering to the description which the experient would naturally give of its epistemological object, i.e. the description which he would offer in answer to the question: 'What are you cognizing?'. It is *totally delusive*, if there is no ontological object answering even remotely to this. It is *more or less delusive*, if there is an ontological object which answers in certain respects more or less closely to the description which the experient would naturally give of its epistemological object, but which fails in other respects to do so.

CLASSIFICATION OF COGNITIONS

For our purpose cognitions may be sub-divided into *intuitive*, *perceptual*, and *conceptual*. *Intuitive cognition* is direct prehension of particular existents. These always present themselves to the person who prehends them as having certain qualities, e.g. redness, squeakiness, etc., or as standing in certain mutual relations, e.g. spatial adjunction or separation, temporal overlapping or complete sequence, and so on. So far as we know, a human being is capable of prehending particulars of three and only three kinds, viz. *sensibilia* (i.e. colour expanses, sounds, smells, etc.), *his own mental images*, and *his own experiences*.

Perceptual cognition may be described as cognition of particular existents which seem *prima facie* to be purely intuitive, but which is found on careful consideration to be not wholly so. It always involves prehension of particulars, but it also involves non-inferential beliefs or *quasi*-beliefs, which are psychologically based on that prehension, but go beyond the information which it by itself supplies. The three most important kinds of perceptual cognition (when thus defined) are *sense-perception*, *reminiscence*, and *self-perception*. The intuitive bases of these are respectively the sensing of sensibilia, the imaging of mental images, and reflexive acquaintance with one's own experiences. In each case the presence of intuitive cognition, and the absence of explicit inference or even of a noticeable process of associative transition, is likely to make it seem that the cognition is *wholly* intuitive.

Under the head of *conceptual cognition* I include all those processes which operate with general ideas or abstract concepts. By means of it an individual can think of things and persons and events and situations which he is not prehending and is not perceiving or remembering. He does this by thinking of a certain combination of characteristics, which together constitute a description of a certain possible thing or person or event or situation. He then thinks of the object as '*a* so-and-so' or as '*the* so-and-so' which answers to this description. We can of course *imagine* or *suppose* that there is something answering to a certain description without actually *believing* that there is. We can do so when we positively know that there is not. This happens, e.g. in either composing or understanding an admittedly fictitious narrative. A great deal of cognition, which seems *prima facie* to be purely perceptual, turns out on closer inspection to be partly conceptual. It seems likely that all one's cognitions of other persons' minds and of their experiences consists of conceptual cognition based on one's perception of their bodies, their gestures, their speech, and so on.

EMOTIONS AND EMOTIONAL MOODS

We are now in a position to consider the nature and the subdivisions of *emotion*. Suppose that a person were to say: 'I am having an emotion'. Then there are two questions which it would be sensible to ask: (1) 'What *kind* of emotion?' and (2) 'Toward *what object*?'. The answer that we should expect to the first question would be: 'One of *hatred*', 'One of *fear*', and so on. The answer we should expect to the second would be: 'Towards Smith', 'Towards a ghost', and so on.

Every emotion is an epistemologically objective or intentional experience, i.e. it is always a *cognition*, either veridical or wholly or partly delusive. But every emotion is something more than a *mere* cognition. An emotion is a cognition which has one or more of the specific forms of a certain generic kind of psychical quality which we will call *emotional tone*. To be fearing a snake, e.g., is to be cognizing something—correctly or incorrectly—as a snake, and for that cognition to be toned with fearfulness. In general, to be fearing x is to be cognizing x fearingly; to be admiring x is to be cognizing x admiringly; and so on.

An emotion, then, as I have defined it, always has an epistemological object. But, corresponding to the various kinds of emotion, there are certain experiences called *emotional moods*. E.g. the mood which corresponds to the emotion of anger is crossness. One may feel cross without being angry with anyone or anything, and one may feel alarmed without being frightened at anyone or anything. I think that an emotional mood is either a pure feeling or else an emotionally toned cognition with an extremely vague indeterminate object. It might, e.g., be one's cognition of things in general or of one's present total environment. The connection between an emotional mood and the corresponding emotion is this. The pure feeling or the extremely vague cognition, which is the emotional mood, has the same kind of emotional tone as the determinate cognition which is the emotion.

CLASSIFICATION OF EMOTIONS BY THEIR CHARACTER AS COGNITIONS

Since all emotions are cognitions, we shall expect to find a division among them corresponding to the division of cognitions into intuitive, perceptual, and conceptual.

I do not think that most *purely intuitive* cognitions have any marked emotional tone. But, then, *purely* intuitive cognitions are very rare in grown persons. Intuitive cognitions occur mainly as constituents of perceptual or conceptual cognitions. Perhaps the primitive fear, which all babies are said to exhibit on hearing any loud sudden noise, such as a clap of thunder, would be an example of an emotion which is purely intuitive on the cognitive side.

Perceptions, on the other hand, are often strongly toned with emotional qualities. One may, e.g., perceive with fear an object which one takes to be a snake; and so on.

Almost any emotional quality which can qualify a perception can also qualify a *conceptual* cognition. Thus a human being can fear things or persons or events which he is not perceiving or remembering but is only expecting or believing to exist or feigning to exist. A result is that the emotions which we share with animals are felt by us towards a much wider range of objects.

There are some kinds of emotion which, from the nature of their objects, can be felt *only* by a being who is capable of conceptual cognition. Hope and anxiety, e.g., can be felt only by a being who can conceive alternative possible future states of affairs and anticipate them with various degrees of conviction. Religious awe can be felt only by a being who can think of the description of a supernatural power, either personal or impersonal, and can believe that there is an object answering to that description. And so on.

CERTAIN DISTINCTIONS APPLICABLE TO EMOTIONS

I shall now consider a number of distinctions which it is important to recognize and define in discussing emotion. They are the following: (1) *Motived* and *unmotived* emotions; (2) *misplaced* emotions; (3) *appropriate* and *inappropriate* emotions; (4) *first-hand* and *second-hand* emotions; and (5) *pure* and *mixed* emotions. I will take these in turn.

(1) *Motived and Unmotived Emotions*

One may feel an emotion towards an object without consciously distinguishing any attributes of it with regard to which one could say: 'I feel this emotion towards that object in *respect of* those attributes of it'. You may, e.g., just feel an emotion of dislike in presence of a person, without being able to mention any attribute in respect of which you dislike him. But very often one can mention certain attributes, which one believes rightly or wrongly to be present in the object, and which one believes rightly or wrongly to be calling forth the emotion which one feels towards it. You may be able to say, e.g., 'I dislike so-and-so for his ugly voice and bad manners'. To dislike a person in respect of certain qualities, which one takes him to possess, is a more complex experience than just to dislike him for no assignable reason. Presumably all the emotions of animals are of the latter kind, whilst many human emotions are certainly of the former.

I will now try to analyse these notions rather more fully. Suppose that a person feels an emotion *e* towards an object *o*, and that this *appears to him* to be evoked by his knowledge or belief that *o* has a certain attribute *p*. Then I shall say that this emotion is *ostensibly motivated*, and I shall describe *p* as the *ostensible motivating attribute*. Next suppose that a person's emotion *e* towards *o really is* evoked by his knowledge or belief that *o* has a certain attribute *p*. Then I shall say that this emotion is *actually motived*, and I shall describe *p* as the *actual motivating attribute*. Suppose, next, that a person's emotion *e* towards *o* *does not appear to him* to be evoked by any knowledge or belief that he has about the attributes of *o*. Then I shall say that this emotion is *ostensibly unmotivated.* Suppose, lastly, that the emotion *e really is not* evoked by any knowledge or beliefs which the person who feels it towards *o* has about the attributes of *o*. Then I shall say that it is *actually unmotived.*

We must now notice the following possibilities of mistake: (1) An ostensibly motived emotion may be really unmotived. I may think, e.g., that my emotion of dislike for Smith is motived by my knowledge that he is an atheist. But really it may be caused, not by this or by any other knowledge or beliefs that I have about his attributes, but by some peculiarity in his voice or appearance, which I have never explicitly noticed, but which arouses my dislike through some unpleasant association which it has for me.

(2) An ostensibly motived emotion may be actually motived, but the actual motivating attribute may differ from the ostensible one. I may think, e.g., that my dislike of Smith is evoked by my knowledge that he is an atheist. But really it may be evoked, not by this, but by my belief that he is a communist or by my knowledge that he is a successful rival in business.

(3) Even if an ostensibly motived emotion is actually motived and if the ostensible motivating attribute is the same as the actual one, it may be that the object does not really possess that attribute. I may think, e.g., that my dislike of Smith is evoked by my belief that he is a communist, and it may really be evoked by that belief. But the belief may be false; Smith may really be a conservative.

(4) An ostensibly unmotived emotion may be actually motived. This can happen in two ways. (i) I may have a number of conscious beliefs and bits of knowledge about Smith's attributes, and I may think that none of them evokes my dislike of him. But I may be mistaken. It may be that one or other of them does evoke it. (ii) Even if I am correct in thinking that none of them do so, it may be that I have certain *unconscious* beliefs or bits of knowledge about Smith's attributes, i.e. some which exist only in a dispositional form or which for some reason

I fail to notice. And it may be that one or other of these is what evokes my dislike of Smith.

An emotion which starts by being actually unmotived will very often generate beliefs about the attributes of its object. It may thus become an ostensibly motived emotion. We shall begin to believe that the object has the kind of attributes which generally evoke that kind of emotion; and then we may begin to believe that what evokes the emotion is our knowledge that the object has these attributes. At length our belief that it has these attributes may become at least a part-cause maintaining and perhaps heightening the emotion which we feel towards it. At that stage the emotion has become, not only ostensibly motived, but to some extent actually motived. The following would be an example of this process. One may start with an unmotived emotion of love towards a person. This may in part be evoked by some obscure and quite unrecognized bodily or mental quality in him. One will then be very liable to believe that he is unusually beautiful or brave or clever. One may then come to think that one loves him *because* of one's awareness of these qualities in him. And eventually one's love for him may *in fact* be maintained partly or wholly by these beliefs about his qualities. I take it that this is at any rate part of what is meant by the word 'rationalization'.

Beliefs generated in this way are often false. But they are also quite often true. One may begin with an unmotived repulsion for a person. This may generate the belief that he is dishonest, and we may often find in the end that he really is a crook. On the other hand, an emotional mood, such as crossness, may be due to purely internal causes, such as a disordered liver. Once started it is very liable to crystallize into the corresponding emotion, viz. in this case anger, towards the first suitable object which happens to be available. And then it is liable to generate quite false beliefs about that object. Jealousy is the stock example of an emotion which is specially liable to generate false beliefs about its objects and thus to provide itself with motives.

It seems to me that, when a belief about an object is generated by an emotion felt towards that object, one has generally a suspicion at the back of one's mind that it will not bear critical inspection. We tend to refuse to inspect such beliefs critically ourselves, and to feel resentment if other persons attempt to do so. In fact, beliefs about objects which are generated by emotions towards those objects are generally themselves emotionally-toned beliefs.

Emotions which are *conceptual* on the cognitive side, i.e. emotionally-toned beliefs, expectations, imaginations, etc., are, I think, generally *motived*. If one thinks of an object which one is not perceiving or remembering and perhaps could not perceive or remember, one must do so by thinking of it as the owner of such and such qualities or as a term standing in such and such relations. If one's cognition of such an object is emotionally toned, the emotion will generally be felt in respect of some of these qualities and relations. C.f., e.g., our emotions towards Charles I with those of a person like Cromwell or Strafford, who had actually met him. *We* can cognize Charles I only conceututally, viz. by thinking of him as a person who had such and such qualities, stood in such and such relationships, and did and suffered such and such things. If *we* feel emotions towards him, they must be motived by our beliefs about his qualities and relations. But some of the emotions which Cromwell, who had met Charles I and talked with him, felt towards him, might have been evoked by certain peculiarities in his personal appearance or his voice or manner, which Cromwell had never explicitly noted. So some at least of Cromwell's emotions towards Charles I might have been unmotived, even if they were all ostensibly motived; whilst all our emotions towards Charles I are both ostensibly and actually motived.

(2) *Misplaced Emotions*

An emotion may be said to be 'misplaced' if either (i) it is felt towards an object which is believed to exist but does not really do so, or (ii) it is felt towards an object which really does exist in respect of attributes which do not really belong to it. In the first case it may be said to be *totally* misplaced, in the second *partially* misplaced.

Let us first consider emotions which are *perceptual* on the cognitive side. A perception, or at any rate a *quasi*-perception, may be completely hallucinatory, as, e.g., a dream. In a dream one may have an hallucinatory ostensible perception of a man chasing one with a revolver, and this may be strongly toned with fear. Such an emotion is totally misplaced.

Again, a perception may not be hallucinatory but it may be largely delusive. There may be a certain physical object corresponding to one's perception, but one may be misperceiving it to a considerable degree. One may, e.g., perceive a certain physical object, which is in fact a tree of curious shape in twilight. One may misperceive it as a man lying in wait. The perception will then be toned with fear, but the fear will be misplaced. If one had perceived the object correctly as a tree, one would not have perceived it with fear. Of course there *are* real qualities in the tree and its surroundings which cause one to mistake it for a man lying in wait. These are certain shapes and spatial relations, certain arrangements of light and shade, and so on. These real attributes give rise to the false belief that it has certain other attributes, which it does not in fact have. And it is the false belief that it has these latter attributes which is the immediate cause of one's perceiving it *with fear*.

Let us next consider emotions which are *conceptual*. It is evident that these may be completely misplaced. For there may be nothing answering to the description of an object which one believes to exist, and yet the belief may have a strong emotional tone. Completely hallucinatory perceptions are very rare in sane waking healthy persons. But beliefs in the existence of objects which do not in fact exist are, and have always been, quite common among sane waking men. Indeed a large part of the life of humanity has been occupied in feeling strong emotions towards beings who never existed, e.g. the gods Jupiter or Moloch or Huitzilopochtli (to go no further); or towards beings who do exist, e.g. Hitler or Stalin, in respect of attributes which they do not possess. We must notice that all emotions which are felt towards other persons in respect of their supposed mental or moral qualities must be in part conceptual on the cognitive side. For one cannot literally *perceive* another person's mind or his experiences or his dispositions or his motives. One can only *conceive* them, and we are very liable to be mistaken in our beliefs about them, and thus to have misplaced emotions.

(3) *Appropriate and Inappropriate Emotions*

As we have seen, there are two aspects to every emotion. In its cognitive aspect, it is directed towards a certain object, real or imaginary, which is cognized, correctly or incorrectly, as having certain qualities and standing in certain relationships. In its affective aspect, it has an emotional quality of a certain kind and of a certain degree of intensity. Now some kinds of emotional quality are *fitting* and others are *unfitting* to a given kind of epistemological object. It is appropriate to cognize what one takes to be a *threatening* object with some degree of *fear*. It is inappropriate to cognize what one takes to be a fellow man *in undeserved pain or distress* with *satisfaction* or with *amusement*. Then, again, an emotion which is fitting in *kind* to its epistemological object, may be unfitting in *degree*, i.e. inordinate. A degree of fear which would be appropriate to what one took to be a mad bull would be inappropriate to what one took to be an angry cow.

It should be noticed that an emotion which is misplaced may be appropriate to its object, as that object is misperceived or misconceived. If a short-sighted person takes what is in fact a harmless but excited cow for a mad bull, it is appropriate for him to cognize it with a high degree of fear. Conversely, an emotion, which is veridical on the cognitive side, may be unfitting in kind or inordinate in degree. A woman who panics in presence of what she correctly takes to be a mouse illustrates this fact.

This notion of a certain fittingness or unfittingness, in kind or in degree, between emotional tone and epistemological object, is plainly of the utmost importance to ethics and to aesthetics. I think that it still awaits an adequate analysis.

(4) *First-hand and Second-hand Emotion*

This is an important distinction which arises in connection with emotions which are conceptual on the cognitive side. Let us take as an example the emotion of religious awe towards God. This would be a *first-hand* emotion, if and only if the person who felt it was really thinking at the time of the qualities and relations which constitute a description of God, e.g. a being of infinite wisdom and power, who has created and governs and maintains everything, and if he were really believing at the time that there is something answering to that description.

But most concepts which have been fairly often used have had names attached to them, and it is possible to use and to react to these names consistently and correctly without thinking of the characteristics which they connote. Now in many cases a certain name has become associated through early training with a certain kind of emotional mood. If one now hears or sees or uses that name, the associated emotional mood tends to be excited. One will then tend to think that one is feeling a certain emotion towards a certain object in respect of certain of its attributes, when really one is not thinking of the object or of its attributes at all. This is what I call '*second-hand*' emotion.

Many words and symbols, particularly those associated with religion, morality, and politics, are almost devoid of cognitive meaning for most people at most times. But they have become extremely powerful stimulants of second-hand emotions. It is obvious that a great deal of the emotions which we feel are second-hand, and there is always a likelihood of emotions, which were first-hand, becoming second-hand. A typical example is the sorrow felt by a bereaved person. It begins by being first-hand, and in the course of nature it tends to fade away after a while. But often the bereaved person cannot face this fact, and so pumps up a second-hand emotion to replace the vanished first-hand one.

It is important to remember, however, that nearly all second-hand emotion depends on the existence of a corresponding first-hand emotion in *someone* at *some* time in the past. If no one had ever believed in God with a first-hand emotion of awe, it is unlikely that anyone would now have a second-hand emotion of awe called up by the word 'God'. But the first-hand ancestor of a second-hand emotion may be a very long way back in the past history of an individual or of a race.

(5) *Pure and Mixed Emotions*

I think we may fairly assume that there is a certain fairly small number of primary species of emotional tone, just as there is a limited number of primary colours, and that the vast majority of human beings are born with dispositions corresponding to each of them. Let us call these 'primary emotional dispositions'. I should suppose that the emotional tones of fear and of anger, e.g., are certainly primary, and that the corresponding emotional dispositions are innate in the individual and common to the race. Probably some innate emotional dispositions do not come into action until certain stages of development, e.g. puberty, have been reached.

Now these primary emotional dispositions are either very specialized or very generalized in respect of the stimuli which originally excite them. The disposition to feel fear, e.g., seems to be excited at first only by sudden loud noises and by the experience of falling. So the original stimulus is here very specialized. The disposition to feel anger, on the other hand, is aroused from the first by the thwarting of *any* impulse. So here the original stimulus is highly generalized. In course of experience these primary emotional dispositions become generalized or specialized, as the case may be. We acquire, e.g., the disposition to fear snakes, to fear policemen, and to fear ghosts, in addition to fearing sudden noises and falls. Conversely, one acquires the disposition to feel angry at injustice done to others, beside feeling angry at being thwarted oneself.

I do not think that a given kind of emotional tone remains completely unaltered in quality as the objects of the emotion become extended and more subtle. No doubt there *is* a qualitative likeness, e.g., between fearing a sudden noise, fearing an interview with one's headmaster, and fearing God. They all resemble each other in a specific way, in which e.g. the experiences of fearing a sudden noise and being angry at a sudden blow do not resemble each other. But there is a difference in the emotional qualities of these various experiences of fear. This might be compared to differences of *shade* between various instances of the same colour, e.g. scarlet, rose-coloured, pink, etc. I think, then, that we must say that the various primary kinds of emotional tone become differentiated in shade as the cognitions which they qualify become more complex and more abstract.

Suppose now that one perceives or thinks of an object which has several characteristics. In respect of one of them it may excite one emotional disposition, e.g. that of fear, and in respect of another of them it may excite another emotional disposition, e.g. that of anger. One's perception or thought of the object will then be toned with an emotional tone which is a blind of the fear-quality and the anger-quality.

I think that the best way to conceive of blended emotions is by analogy with blended colours, such as purple or orange. Any shade of purple resembles pure blue to some degree and pure red to some degree, and there is a continuous series of possible shades of purple, stretching from pure blue at one end to pure red at the other. A sensation of purple is produced when the same part of the retina is stimulated at the same time by a stimulus which would produce a sensation of pure red, if it acted alone, and a stimulus which would produce a sensation of pure blue if it acted alone. In the same way there are many different shades of blended emotional tone, stretching, e.g. from pure fear without anger to pure anger without fear. The particular shade of blended emotion which is felt on any particular occasion will presumably depend on the relative degree of excitement of the various emotional dispositions, e.g. the fear-disposition and the anger-disposition.

The following remarks are worth making about blending. (i) It may be that certain primary emotional dispositions, e.g. those of anger and of fear, are *directly* linked from the first. Others become linked only indirectly in the course of experience. (ii) Probably a *grown* person hardly ever has an experience with a *pure* primary emotional tone. The notions of the pure primary emotions, like the notions of the pure primary colours, are ideal limits. (iii) Whilst some of the primary emotional qualities blend readily with each other, as do the colours red and blue or red and yellow, it may be that others will not blend. The latter would have to each other the kind of opposition which there is between complementary colours, such as red and green or blue and yellow.

Lastly, it is worth while to notice that there are certain emotional adjectives, such as 'sad' and 'cheerful', which apply to a total phase of experience as a whole rather than to any part of it. We might call such qualities emotional 'pattern qualities'. They *depend on* the qualities and relations of the constituent parts of the whole, e.g. on the emotional tones of the various experiences included in a total phase of experience. But they are not *reducible* to these. Very often superficial introspection will catch the emotional pattern-quality of the phase as a whole, and will fail to reveal the emotional qualities of the constituent experiences. One may notice that one feels sad or elated without knowing why. More elaborate introspection will reveal the emotional qualities of the constituent experiences, but it may lose sight of the emotional pattern-quality of the total phase as a whole.

Sentiments

Suppose that a certain object has been repeatedly perceived or thought of by a person. Suppose that it is complex in its nature and structure, and that this person has perceived it or thought of it in many different contexts on various occasions. These various cognitions of the object will have produced a highly complex trace, i.e. a very complex *dispositional idea* of the object. Suppose that this trace has become associated with the traces of certain names, phrases, or symbols, which have often been heard or seen or uttered in intimate connection with perceiving or thinking of this object. Lastly, suppose that, on many occasions when this object has been perceived or thought of, strong emotions have been felt towards it by this person. When he perceived or thought of it in certain situations, or when he specially attended to certain aspects of it, his cognitions of it had the emotional tone x. When he perceived or thought of it in certain other situations, or when he specially attended to certain other aspects of it, his cognitions of it had the emotional tone y. And so on. The result is that the dispositions corresponding to the emotions x, y, etc., will have become associated with his dispositional idea of this object. Henceforth anything that excites the dispositional idea of the object, e.g. perceiving of it, thinking of it, or perceiving or thinking of any word or phrase or symbol connected with it, will tend to excite all these emotional dispositions. We sum all this up by saying that this person has 'formed a *sentiment*' about this object.

When a sentiment is aroused the emotional tone of the experience will be some shade of a blended tone. The particular shade will vary according to the past conditions under which the sentiment was formed and the present circumstances which are exciting it. It is of course possible that some of the associated emotional dispositions are such that the corresponding emotional qualities are like complementary colours and will not blend. It may be, e.g., that fear and contempt will not blend; and yet a certain object may have come to arouse both of them. In that case the person who cognizes that object may have the two kinds of emotional tone rapidly alternating with each other. Or he may distinguish certain features in the object, and at the same time feel pure fear of it, in respect of some of them, and pure contempt for it in respect of others.

Sometimes a sentiment gets concentrated on one particular *symbol* for the object instead of on the object itself. Or it may become concentrated on one particular *part* of the object instead of on the object as a whole. We then say that that symbol or that part has become a *fetish*. Fetishism is a fairly common aberration of sexual sentiment.

Presumably there are no *innate* sentiments. But there are certain sentiments which practically every human being will inevitably acquire quite early in life. One is a sentiment about himself and his own powers, defects, achievements, and failures. Another is a sentiment about his parents or parent-substitutes, such as nurses, and about the members of his household in general. Another is a sentiment about the social groups, other than his household, of which he is a member. Everyone is a self;

everyone had parents, and started life as a helpless infant kept alive and trained by them or by substitutes for them; and nearly everyone grows up as a member of several social groups. It is therefore inevitable that reflective, filial, family, and other social sentiments should be formed fairly early in practically everyone.

Certain reflective emotions, such as remorse, self-approval, etc., are obviously very important to ethics. It is worth while to notice that we have emotions and sentiments, which are not only reflective, but are about our own emotions and sentiments. These may be called '*second-order reflective emotions*'. A person may, e.g., be ashamed of being afraid, or afraid of being ashamed, or afraid of being afraid, or ashamed of being ashamed. Again a person may feel angry with himself in respect of his sentiment of love for a person whom he knows to be worthless and unfaithful to him. This is just one more instance of the extreme complexity of human life and experience as compared with anything that occurs or could occur in animals. I take leave to doubt, for this reason among others, whether even an exhaustive study of the emotions of rats in mazes furnishes a very adequate or a very secure foundation for conclusions about the emotions and sentiments even of the quite ordinary human beings who pursue that study. To introspect carefully, to note sympathetically the talk and the behaviour of one's fellow-men in their intercourse with each other and with oneself; to read autobiographies and the novels of great novelists; and to study and to watch performances of the plays of great playwrights; these are the only effective ways of learning about emotion and sentiment in their specically human forms.

In conclusion there are two points worth noting about the *names* which are used in ordinary life for various emotions and sentiments:

(i) We have an enormous number of such names, e.g., 'envy', 'jealousy', 'contenpt', 'pity', 'awe', etc. But we must not rashly assume that there are different kinds of emotional quality, either pure or blended, corresponding to each of these. Two emotions which have the same quality, or two sentiments which when aroused give rise to two such emotions, may have different names because they have different kinds of *object*. 'Envy', e.g., is the name of a certain kind of emotion called forth by witnessing another person getting what one wants for oneself. 'Jealousy' seems to be the name of an emotion of much the same quality, where what one wants for oneself and what the other person gets is the affection of some third person. I do not say that there is no shade of difference in the emotional quality in the two cases; but the different names are certainly given in respect of the different kinds of *object*, and not in respect of the difference, if any, in the shade of emotional quality.

(ii) Because a certain sentiment is distinguished from others by a certain name, e.g. 'love', we must not rashly assume that the blended emotion connected with it contains any emotional constituent that is *peculiar to* it. It is certain, e.g., that the blended emotion which one feels when one is in love with a person and when that sentiment is aroused, has several factors which occur in other blended emotions connected with different sentiments. It is quite possible that there may be no single factor in this blended emotion which does not also occur in some other blended emotion. It may be that what distinguishes this emotional quality from all others is some pattern-quality due to the particular proportion in which emotional factors, each of which occurs elsewhere, are here blended.

Even when the blended emotion characteristic of a certain sentiment does have a peculiar emotional constituent, it may be that this by itself is somewhat trivial. Suppose, e.g., that lustful emotion is a peculiar constituent of the blended emotion connected with the sentiment of sexual love for a person. Suppose that every other constituent of this blended emotion can occur as a constituent of some other blended emotion. It might still be the case that these other emotional features, though less characteristic of erotic emotion when taken *severally*, were *collectively* as essential as the constituent of lustful emotion. *Mere* lustful emotion, if it should occur unblended with these other constituents, might not suffice to constitute that peculiar emotion which is felt when one is in love with a person and when that sentiment is aroused.

In such cases as these we are rather liable to give the same name (*a*) to the *blended emotional quality* characteristic of a certain sentiment, and (*b*) to any emotional quality which is held (rightly or wrongly) to be a *peculiar constituent* in that blend. The name 'erotic emotion' might be given, e.g., either (*a*) to the blended emotion which is felt by a person towards another whom he is in love with, or (*b*) to the purely lustful emotional quality which is, perhaps, the only constituent peculiar to that blended quality. If this happens and we fail to notice it, we are certain to be landed sooner or later in tiresome controversies which are really purely about words.

XIV

A REPLY TO MY CRITICS[1]

(IX) MORAL PHILOSOPHY

Under this heading come the papers by Professors Frankena, Hedenius, and Kuhn; Mr Hare's paper; and one section of Professor Blanshard's.

(A) *Professor Frankena's Questions*

In order to formulate the questions which Professor Frankena puts to me, I will begin by introducing the phrase 'moral sentence in the indicative'. This is to denote a sentence in the indicative mood, in which the grammatical subject is a name or a description of a person, an action, an experience, or a disposition (or of a class of such), and the grammatical predicate is some word like 'ought' or 'ought not', 'right' or 'wrong', 'good' or 'evil', used in its *specifically moral* sense. It would not be difficult to show by instances and counter-instances what I have in mind.

In terms of this phraseology, I think that what Professor Frankena asks me may be summarized as follows: Have I any decided opinion, and, if so, why do I hold it, on the following

[1] This selection has been reprinted from Paul A. Schilpp, editor, *The Philosophy of C. D. Broad*, La-Salle: Open Court Publishing Company, 1959, by courtesy of the publisher and the editor of the Library of Living Philosophers. It consists of Professor Broad's comments on several papers concerning his moral philosophy, which also appeared in the Schilpp volume. The particular papers discussed are William K. Frankena's 'Broads' Analysis of Ethical Terms' (pp. 537-561), R. M. Hare's 'Broad's Approach to Moral Philosophy' (pp. 563-77), Ingemar Hedenius's 'Broad's Treatment of Determinisn and Free Will' (pp. 579-96), Helmut Kuhn's 'Existence in C. D. Broad's Philosophy' (pp. 597-612), and portions of Brand Blanshard's 'Broad's Conception of Reason' (pp. 233-62). Prior to each section of his reply, Professor Broad gives a brief statement of that portion of his critic's paper to which he is answering. Thus, Broad's remarks should be intelligible even though relevant sections of his critic's essays are not reproduced here.

interconnected questions? (1) Do moral sentences in the indicative express *judgments* or not? (2) If *not*, what does the utterance of such a sentence express? (3) If *so*, do words such as 'ought' and 'ought not', etc., when used in their specifically moral sense, stand for predicates of a *certain peculiar kind*, which has been described as 'non-natural'? (4) If such words stand for predicates which are '*natural*', what account should be given of the 'natural' characteristics for which typical words of this kind stand?

Now a short answer, and a true one so far as it goes, to Professor Frankena's questions would be: No! I have no decided opinion on any of these points. But I could say the same about almost any philosophical question. The reasons which incline one to or against a certain opinion on any one philosophical question are always highly complex, and they are always bound up with the reasons which incline one to or against certain opinions on many other philosophical questions. Here, as elsewhere in philosophy, I have tried to clear up the questions and to indicate logical connections between certain answers to some of them and certain answers to others. These are necessary preliminaries to any attempt to come to a reasoned decision about them. But it does not follow that it is sufficient to enable a person to do this. So far as I am concerned, I find myself now inclined to favour one kind of alternative and now another, but never to come down decisively in favour of any. At most I feel fairly confident that some proposed answers to some of the questions are *inadequate* by themselves.

I will now try to be a little more concrete. Let us give the name 'predicative' to all theories which hold that moral sentences in the indicative express *judgments*, in which a *moral attribute* is ascribed to a person or action or experience or disposition. I will begin by mentioning and dismissing one general argument against all predicative theories, which has been thought by many intelligent contemporaries to be conclusive.

It is alleged that a sentence can express a synthetic judgment, if and only if one can conceive and describe some kind of possible perceptual situation or introspectable situation which, if realized, would tend to confirm it or to invalidate it. Now consider such a sentence as, e.g., 'Acts of promise-breaking tend as such to be morally wrong'. If this expresses a judgment at all, the judgment is certainly not analytic. But, it is said, one cannot suggest any possible perceptual or introspectable situation which, if realized, would tend to confirm or to invalidate what it expresses. So it is concluded that it cannot express a judgment. And a similar argument is applied to all moral sentences in the indicative.

This argument leaves me wholly unmoved. The account of synthetic judgments, which is its main premise, is obviously a generalization based *exclusively* on a review of *non-moral* indicatives, and in particular of statements about *physical* and *psychological* phenomena. Now there are admittedly whole classes of sentences in the indicative which seem *prima facie* to express synthetic judgments, and which are plainly *not* of that kind. Moral indicatives are important instances of them. If you first exclude all such sentences from your purview, in making your generalization about the conditions under which alone a sentence can express a synthetic judgment, and then use that generalization to show that such sentences cannot express synthetic judgments, you are simply begging the question. For the only legitimate ground for excluding these from your purview, and nevertheless holding that your generalization covers *all* sentences which express synthetic judgments, would be a *prior* conviction that *these* sentences do not express synthetic judgments.

Dismissing this kind of argument as circular, I would next remark that there are two general principles to which I should appeal in preferring one type of theory to another. They sound rather platitudinous when stated baldly; but, in default of anything better, they are not to be despised. (1) Other things being equal, a theory is to be preferred if it does not have to postulate anything of a kind which is not already admitted as a fact and found to be readily intelligible. (2) Other things being equal, a theory is to be preferred if it does not have to suppose that all men are *fundamentally mistaken* on certain matters with which the whole race is and has always been constantly concerned.

Unfortunately these two principles sometimes point in opposite directions.

On the *second* principle, taken by itself, I should be strongly inclined *prima facie* to prefer an ethical theory of the *predicative* kind to one of the non-predicative kind. The normal use of uttering a sentence in the indicative is undoubtedly to *convey information* (true or false). The fact that our moral utterances are commonly couched in the indicative mood strongly suggests that most men at most times take for granted that they are making and expressing and conveying to others *moral judgments* on such occasions. If they are in fact doing nothing of the kind, but are only e.g. evincing or evoking certain emotions, issuing certain admonitions or commands, etc., their mode of expression seems to betray a fundamental misapprehension of their situation.

On the *first* principle, taken by itself, I should be inclined *prima facie* to favour an ethical theory which holds that moral concepts are *empirical*, in the sense that they are derived from data presented in sense-perception or introspection, in the familiar ways in which, e.g., the concepts *red* or *angry* are derived, and the concepts *mermaid* or *hot-tempered* are derived. On the same principle I should be inclined *prima facie* to favour a theory which makes universal propositions of the form: *Anything that had the non-moral character n would have the moral character m* to be either (*a*) empirical generalizations, or (*b*) analytic propositions.

Now, in formulating the two principles I have prefixed to each the conditional clause 'other things being equal'. The basic requirement of a philosophic theory is that it shall do justice to *all* the facts characteristic of the region with which it deals (including, of course, 'higher-order' facts about the inter-relations of the 'lower-order' facts), and that it shall neither ignore nor distort any of them. When this fundamental condition of inclusiveness and non-distortion is taken into account, I think that the two principles point in opposite directions.

I have tried to show, in various papers quoted by Professor Frankena, that it is doubtful whether any *predicative* theory can do justice to the facts unless it admits (*a*) that the concepts of moral attributes are *non-empirical*, and (*b*) that there are universal propositions, connecting certain non-moral attributes with certain moral ones, which are *synthetic* and yet *necessary*. Now, as I have said above, the second principle would incline one to favour *predicative* theories, whilst the first principle would incline one to favour theories which do not involve either *non-empirical concepts* or *synthetic a priori judgments*.

It is plain that philosophers of two different kinds, who might agree in accepting my argument up to this point, would here diverge from each other. (1) Some are quite convinced that there *can* be no non-empirical concepts and no synthetic *a priori* judgments. They will have to accept some form of non-predicative theory, and make the best of it. (2) Others (including myself) have no such convictions. They will be in a freer position. They are not *obliged* at the next move to accept any form of non-predicative theory, but they are equally not obliged at this stage to *reject* all forms of it. They can view that type of theory sympathetically as a praiseworthy attempt to do without non-empirical concepts and synthetic *a priori* judgments in an important region of human experience. They may even offer a helping hand, as I have tried to do in certain of the writings quoted by Professor Frankena.

Those who feel obliged to accept some form of non-predicative theory will be most usefully occupied in the following tasks. (i) In trying to account plausibly, in terms of their theory, for the main outstanding facts which seem *prima facie* to demand a theory of the *predicative* type. (ii) In trying to adduce facts which seem to fit better into a *non-predicative* type of theory than into any of the predicative type. One such fact, e.g., is that the state of mind (whatever it may be) which is expressed by uttering sincerely and wittingly such sentences as 'That act would be wrong', always tends to evoke a reaction *against* doing the act in question. It might be alleged that this seems to be a *necessary* proposition, and not a mere empirical generalization about human nature. Now it might be argued that, if what such a sentence expresses is a *judgment*, one will have to hold either (*a*) that the psychological proposition in question *is* merely an empirical generalization, or (*b*) that it is a *necessary synthetic proposition* known *a priori*. The former alternative seems unplausible; and the latter is one to be avoided, if possible, in accordance with my first principle. Now it might fairly be alleged that, on some forms of the non-predicative theory, the proposition in question would be *analytic*. That would certainly be a point in favour of such forms of non-predicative theory.

Whether the non-predicativists have succeeded in these tasks or not, I think that there is no doubt that, in the course of their very strenuous efforts to perform them, they have made some valuable contributions to moral philosophy. At the time when I wrote *FTET* moral philosophy in England and the USA might fairly be described as dormant and apparently moribund. Since then, partly owing to the writings of certain predicativists (like Prichard and Ross) and partly owing to those of certain non-predicativists (like Professor Stevenson and Mr Hare), it has become one of the liveliest branches of philosophy. *Plurimi pertransibunt et multiplex erit scientia.*

There is one other topic, closely connected with those which I have discussed above, on which I will briefly comment. That is the phrase 'non-natural characteristics'. As a student at Cambridge I was brought up to believe that it is a fundamentally important proposition of ethics that moral attributes belong to a peculiar category called 'non-natural', and that there is something called 'the naturalistic fallacy', which most moralists had committed who had written before the light dawned in 1903. When I became Professor of Moral Philosophy, and had to write a course of lectures on ethics, I was unable to discover any intelligible and tenable account of the meaning of this distinction between 'natural' and 'non-natural' attributes. It also seemed to me that, unless 'fallacy' be used in the improper and question-begging sense of 'mistaken opinion', instead of in its proper sense of 'invalid bit of reasoning', there was nothing which can be described as 'the naturalistic fallacy'.

I do not propose to traverse again now this much trodden ground, but I will state briefly and dogmatically the conclusion which it seems fair to draw. *If* words like 'morally good (or evil)', 'morally right (or wrong)', etc., stand for characteristics, *then* the characteristics for which they stand differ from non-moral ones in being *dependent on the latter* in a way in which no *non-moral* characteristic appears to be dependent on others. No doubt some *non-moral* characteristics are *necessarily* dependent on others, e.g. to have a shape entails having a size. But none of these cases of necessary connection between non-moral characteristics seems to be at all like the connection between being a breach of promise and being morally wrong, which we express by saying that being a breach of promise necessarily contributes towards making an act morally wrong.

Now a non-predicativist might accept all this, and simply use it as water for his own mill. He might proceed to argue, in accordance with my first Principle, that any ethical theory which can avoid postulating characteristics of such an odd kind as moral ones would have to be, if there were such, is to be preferred (other things being equal) to one which has to postulate them. Suppose he could then explain in detail, in terms of a certain form of non-predicative theory, how it comes about that moral adjectives *seem* to stand for characteristics of this peculiar kind. Then I think that there would be a fairly strong *prima facie* case for preferring his form of the non-predicative theory to any form of predicative theory known to me.

Now non-predicativists have attempted such detailed explanations. I am impressed, if not completely convinced, by their efforts up to date; and I am inclined to think, at the moment of writing, that it is likely that the truth lies somewhere in that direction rather than on predicative lines. I could not be more definite if Professor Frankena (that kindest of men) were to hold a pistol to my head, which I cannot imagine him doing.

(B) *Moral Philosophy and Moral Practice*

The main topic which Mr Hare discusses is the bearing or lack of bearing of moral philosophy on moral practice. As regards the historical part of his essay I would make the following comments.

Mr Hare rightly mentions Moore and Prichard as the two

most influential English moral philosophers at the time when I was young and for many years afterwards. Each held that the moral concepts which he took as fundamental are not only unanalysable, but also of a unique and peculiar kind. Now anyone who takes such a view must, if he would be consistent, hold that any proposition, in which the subject is described in purely *non-moral* terms and the predicate is or involves one of these moral notions, must be *synthetic*. Mr Hare thinks that this commits such a philosopher to the particular epistemological view, called by Sidgwick 'aesthetic intuitionism'. This view he ascribes to Moore and to Prichard, and he thinks that for those who hold it moral philosophy can give no guidance to those who seek to know what they ought to do in various types of situation.

Now I do not think that a person who holds the Moore-Prichard type of theory as to the nature of moral concepts is necessarily committed to aesthetic intuitionism. The latter view may be stated roughly as follows. The only way to discover what is morally good or morally obligatory (as the case may be) in a particular situation is to put oneself actually or imaginatively into that situation, and to note what kind of value-judgment or deontic judgment one then makes. Now I do not doubt that it would be a *necessary preliminary* to giving practical guidance to others that one should oneself often have done what the aesthetic intuitionist has in mind. It would also be a *necessary preliminary* that other men should have done the like, and should have recorded the moral judgments which they then made. But at that stage there are the following two conceivable developments.

(1) Suppose a person admits (as Sidgwick certainly did, and as I imagine both Moore and Prichard would do) the possibility of necessary *synthetic* universal propositions, which can be seen to be true *ex vi terminorum*. Then it is conceivable that one might arrive by 'intuitive induction' at a number of synthetic *a priori* axioms, stating necessary connections between certain non-moral and certain specifically moral characteristics. This alternative would no doubt be rejected unhesitatingly by Mr Hare and by most of his English and American contemporaries. But in a

historical account it must be remembered that it has been held by many eminent and influential moral philosophers.

(2) Even if this alternative be rejected, there remains the theoretical possibility of *inductive generalizations*, of a high order of generality and reliability, similar in content to the alleged synthetic *a priori* axioms of the rejected view.

Now such a set of moral axioms, or of well established moral inductive generalizations, *might* be capable of elaborate deductive development, and *might* be found to entail consequences which no one could have foreseen. These consequences, together with factual information about the situation in which a particular person is placed, and about the probable consequences of this, that, or the other alternative action, *might* enable a moral philosopher to provide him with valuable (though never infallible) guidance as to how he morally ought to act.

The legitimate source of scepticism here is of course the very general conviction that none of these 'mights' is in fact realized. The first alternative would involve admitting that there are *synthetic* necessary propositions knowable *a priori*, and this is very commonly held to be an exploded superstition. The second of them, though it might be admitted to be theoretically possible, seems not in fact to be true. *Either* (*a*) there are no well-established inductive generalizations in morals; *or* (*b*) if there are, they do not (like, e.g., the laws of motion and the law of gravitation) form a system capable of elaborate deductive development and detailed application.

Passing from the historical to the other parts of Mr Hare's essay, I agree that many young persons take up the study of philosophy because they are morally perplexed and hope that moral philosophy will give them practical guidance. But I think that this attitude covers a number of different troubles and demands, and I propose to distinguish some of them.

(1) A person may have been brought up to accept as *unconditional* a number of general moral principles, as to how one ought or ought not to act in any instance of certain frequently recurring types of situation. It may be that each of these maxims, considered in isolation on its merits, still seems to him on

reflection to be obviously true. But he may become aware, either in his own life or in the lives of others, of situations in which several of these principles are relevant and it is impossible to act in accordance with one without acting against another.

Moral philosophy could help here, if it could carry out the following programme. (i) Indicate a certain more general principle, which seems on its merits to be at least as obviously true as any of the more special ones. (ii) Show that, in acting on each of the more concrete principles in the relevant kinds of situation, one will *generally* (though not invariably) be acting in accordance with this more general one. (iii) Show that, in the exceptional situations, where several of the more concrete principles are relevant but it is impossible to act in accordance with all of them, this more general principle provides a satisfactory answer to the question how one ought to act. (iv) Suggest the causes which may have made the more concrete maxims seem to be true in their *unconditional* form, when really they are true only in the majority of situations in which they are relevant. This is the kind of programme which, e.g., Utilitarianism claims to carry out; and it has allayed, or at any rate mitigated this kind of perplexity in many highly intelligent and conscientious persons, such as J. S. Mill and Sidgwick.

(2) A great many conscientious plain men and several very eminent moral philosophers, e.g. Plato, Butler, and Sidgwick, seem to hold the following conviction. *All* moral maxims are subject to a certain implicit condition. When this is made explicit, any acceptable moral maxim would take the form: 'In situations of the kind *s* one ought always to behave in the way *w*, *if and only if* such behaviour would not be in the end and on the whole detrimental to one's own interests.' Now the difficulty is that there are kinds of behaviour which seem to many of these very persons to be morally obligatory or to be morally forbidden even in situations where the condition just mentioned seems *prima facie not* to be fulfilled.

If such a person appealed to moral philosophy in his perplexity, its first move should be to clear up the many ambiguities in the phrase 'one's own interest'. Is this supposed to be confined to one's own *happiness or unhappiness*; or is it to be extended to cover the improvement or worsening of one's own character, intellect, and personality? If the latter, is it to be confined to improvement or deterioration in *non-moral* respects, or is it to be extended to cover *specifically moral* improvement or deterioration also?

So much might fairly be regarded as within the range of *moral* philosophy. But what might be demanded is an assurance that behaviour, which we all agree to be morally obligatory, but which often *seems to be to all appearances* detrimental to the agent's long-term 'interest' (however that may be interpreted), can never *really* be so, and therefore is no exception to the general principle in question. Now it seems to me that any attempt to show this would fall outside the realm of specifically *moral* philosophy, since it would turn on the nature and destiny of the human individual and the organization of the rest of the universe. Philosophy has traditionally been held to be closely concerned with such questions, but the prevalent view among professional philosophers in England and America at the present time is that that is an elementary mistake.

(3) What troubles many intelligent and conscientious persons nowadays is something still more fundamental. There is a certain view of the nature and destiny of man, which seems to have the whole weight of biology and experimental psychology behind it, viz. a 'behaviourist' or 'epiphenomenalist' view, which I will call for short 'scientific materialism'. To many people it seems that, if this view be true, the notion of moral obligation must be a mere figment, which arose somehow in the days of men's ignorance of their nature and destiny, and now survives precariously like a vestigial organ. When they contemplate the scientific evidence they cannot help accepting the materialist account of human nature. When they are engaged in co-operating or competing with their fellow-men they cannot help thinking that they have moral obligations. When they try to bring together these two convictions into one focus it seems impossible to reconcile them. They naturally, and I think quite legitimately, appeal to professional philosophers to help them.

Now philosophers might seek, and in fact have sought, to do this in various ways. One is to try to show that, when the scientific materialist view of human nature and the notion of moral obligation are both properly understood, there is no incompatibility between accepting the former and continuing to hold that men are subject to moral obligations. This type of solution will be helpful, only if it can succeed without having to give such an account of moral obligation as seems to the intelligent and conscientious non-philosopher to distort it or eviscerate it or altogether to dissolve it. Another way would be to admit the conflict, but to deny the adequacy and the ultimate coherency of the scientific materialist account of human nature, whilst granting its plausibility and usefulness in the limited context in which it has arisen. I think that the first type of answer might fairly be said to fall within *moral* philosophy, and the second only within *philosophy* in a wider sense.

It would take me too far afield to attempt to discuss adequately the 'test' for rightness or wrongness, which Mr Hare very tentatively puts forward at the end of his essay. I will consider only the following point. Mr Hare says that A will be inclined to judge it to be *wrong* for him to treat B in a certain way, if, on imagining himself to be in a similar situation as *patient* instead of agent, he finds that he would *dislike* to be treated in that way. What is not clear to me is what Mr Hare takes to be the relevance of this 'dislike' on A's part.

It seems to me that all that is *logically* relevant is that A should judge that it would be *wrong* for another to treat him as he is proposing to treat B. Whether he would *dislike* or *like* being treated in that way seems logically irrelevant.

Perhaps Mr Hare wishes to assert only the *psychological* proposition that A will be inclined to judge that it would be wrong for another to treat him as he is proposing to treat B, if and only if he would *dislike* to be treated in that way. If so, I think it is a very doubtful generalization. Perhaps, then, what Mr Hare wishes to assert is only the following. A needs to be convinced that he would dislike to be treated in the way in question, *not* in order to judge that such action by another towards him would be wrong, *nor* in order to judge (in accordance with Mr Hare's principle) that such action by him towards B would be wrong, but in order that the latter conviction should have *any practical effect* on his conduct towards B. If that is what Mr Hare means, I think it is a rash generalization about human motivation.

I am inclined to think that the only relevance of A's *disliking* the experience which he would have if he were to be treated as he is thinking of treating B is this. (i) An *important*, though neither a necessary nor a sufficient reason for thinking that it would be *wrong* to treat B in a certain way, is that B would dislike to be so treated. (ii) An *important*, and perhaps indispensable, way for A to gain a *vivid* and *practically effective* belief that B would dislike a certain experience is that A should imagine himself to be having a similar experience in similar circumstances, and should find the idea strongly distasteful. The vivid and practically effective belief thus gained is not, of course, infallible. It seems to me likely, e.g., that many soldiers do not find the experience of hand-to-hand fighting as horrible as I feel that it must be when I try to imagine myself in their situation. But, though not infallible, it is a most valuable corrective to a common tendency to perform, without any concrete realization of the consequences, actions which will produce, in those affected by them, experiences which the latter would intensely dislike.

(C) *'Ought' and 'Can'*

The relations between the former and the latter of these notions form the main topic of Professor Hedenius's paper. I would like at the outset to make the following general remark. The treatment of the whole subject in my lecture 'Determinism, Indeterminism, and Libertarianism' is extremely condensed and somewhat dogmatic. It omits much that should be included in any adequate discussion; the points raised are not sufficiently developed; and objections and counter-arguments are not considered. Such defects are inevitable when a vast and intricate subject has to be handled in the course of an hour's lecture.

Professor Hedenius draws a distinction between acts which

are morally *obligatory* and acts which are morally *imputable* to the agent. He argues that a conceivable act, which it is impossible or inevitable for an agent to do, may nevertheless be morally obligatory. But he holds that, for an act to be morally imputable, it must be at any rate what I have called 'conditionally substitutable'. I am inclined to think that any difference between us on this matter depends mainly on different usages of certain terms, which undoubtedly are used sometimes in a wider and sometimes in a narrower sense. I will now proceed to develop this suggestion.

Consider the statement that A is under an obligation to do *x* at *t*. Does this entail (1, 1) that it is *not impossible* for him to do *x* at *t*? And does it entail (1, 2) that it is *not inevitable* for him to do *x* at *t*? Next consider the statement that A is under an obligation *not* to do *y* at *t*. Does this entail (2, 1) that it is *not inevitable* for him to do *y* at *t*? And does it entail (2, 2) that it is *not impossible* for him to do *y* at *t*?

I think it is easy to show that (2, 1) can be reduced to the form of (1, 1), and (2, 2) to the form of (1, 2). In order to do this one need only note that an obligation *not* to do *y* is equivalent (subject to two conditions which I will state in a moment) to an obligation to do *something-other-than-y*. The two conditions are these. (i) It is to be understood that 'to do something other than *y*' includes, as one alterative, refraining from all positive relevant action, e.g., just *not* answering a question. (ii) It is also to be remembered that to be under an obligation to behave in *one-or-another* of several alternative ways does *not* entail being under an obligation to behave in *any particular one* of those ways. Subject to these explanations, I propose to confine the discussion to questions (1, 1) and (1, 2).

Professor Hedenius is undoubtedly right in saying that we often use expressions which seem to imply that the alleged entailment in (1, 1) does *not* hold. Here are some examples. 'He ought to have lectured from 9 to 10 a.m. yesterday; but it was impossible, since he was then undergoing an operation.' 'He ought to be lecturing now; but it is impossible, since he is now stricken with aphasia.' 'He ought to begin to lecture at 6 p.m. in

London this evening; but that will be impossible, since it is now 5 p.m. and the train in which he is travelling from Cambridge is held up by a derailment at Bishop's Stortford.'

I am very doubtful, however, whether these expressions in fact show that the entailment alleged in (1, 1) does not hold. I suggest that in each of them 'ought' is used in a certain *conditional* sense; that the condition is regarded as obvious and as nearly always fulfilled; and therefore is not explicitly stated. I would expand my first example as follows: 'If and only if he had been able (as he normally would have been) to lecture from 9 to 10 a.m. yesterday, he *would have been* under an obligation to do so. But (owing to the exceptional circumstances of undergoing an operation at the time) it was then impossible for him to do so, and therefore he was *not* in fact under an obligation to do so.' The other two examples can be treated on similar lines.

It should be noted that the collapse of a categorical obligation, through the impossibility of performing the relevant action, very often imposes on the agent a categorical obligation to perform a certain *other* action, which *is* in his power. The lecturer in the delayed train, e.g. ought, if he can, to send a telegraph to the person in charge of the arrangements for his intended lecture in London.

Let us now consider the alleged entailment (1, 2), i.e. that if A *is* under an obligation to do x at t, it follows that it is *not inevitable* for him to do x at t. Can we think of a relevant and obvious counter-instance?

The first point to notice is this. An action, such as answering (truly or falsely) a question, returning or withholding a borrowed article, etc., has to be considered in two aspects, viz, in reference to the person affected by it and in reference to the person doing it. In respect of the *patient* the important question is: Does the action *in fact* treat him as he has a right to be treated in the situation? In respect of the *agent* the important question is: Is the action done from the *intention* (*inter alia*) of treating the patient as he has a right to be treated in the situation? An action of the former kind may be called 'right-*securing*', and one of the latter kind 'right-*intending*'.

Now I think it is certain that we often use 'obligation' and 'obligatory' in such a way that an action which the agent is under an obligation to do is one that is right-*securing*, whether or not it be right-intending. If we use our terms in that way, it is obvious that an action which the agent could not help doing may be obligatory upon him. (It is equally obvious that one which he could not possibly do might be obligatory on him.)

But I think it is no less certain that we often use 'obligation' and 'obligatory' in such a way that an action which the agent is under an obligation to do must be right-*intending*. Now it seems to be that an action, which the agent *could not help* doing, might indeed be *in accordance with* an intention on his part to treat the patient as he has a right to be treated in the situation. But one could hardly say that such an action was done *from that intention* (*inter alia*). So I do not think that an action which the agent could not help doing could be called 'obligatory', if that word is used (as it often is) to connote right-intending and not merely right-securing.

Professor Hedenius says, quite correctly, that we can talk of a man being *forced* to do his duty in a certain manner, e.g. forced to repay money that he owes. I doubt, however, whether this is relevant to the issue. In the first place, 'duty' is here used in the first of the two senses which I have just distinguished. What we mean is that A is forced to do an act which in fact treats B as he has a right to be treated. And, secondly, to say that A was forced to do x is not generally equivalent to saying that it was *inevitable* for him to do x. What it generally means is that A would have preferred antecedently not to do x, but that he was in a situation where it was practically certain that the consequences to him of not doing it would be extremely unpleasant. It was open to him to refrain from doing x and to put up with the unpleasant consequences. So his doing of x was not inevitable.

Very likely I used 'obligable' in my lecture in roughly the sense in which Professor Hedenius uses 'morally imputable'. Let us assume this for the sake of argument, and use the latter phrase in the rest of the discussion. I understand that Professor Hedenius is inclined to agree, up to a certain point, with my account of the conditions which must be fulfilled if it is to be morally imputable to A that he behaved in the way *w* in a certain situation *s*. He agrees with me up to the point that A's behaving in the way *w* would not be morally imputable unless it were, *in a certain sense*, 'determined by A's ego or self'. Now I offered a certain analysis of this latter condition, and said that it seemed to me self-evident that it could not be fulfilled. Professor Hedenius offers an alternative analysis, which would not be open to that objection.

If I understand him aright, the essential features in his account are as follows. We have at the back of our minds a reference to a certain large class of persons (e.g. contemporary middle-class Englishmen above the age of puberty); and we have the thought of a certain type of personality as *normal* in that class in respect to the nature and strength and organization of a number of important conative-emotional dispositions (e.g. desire for food and drink, desire for money, sexual desire, tendency to react with hostility when thwarted, and so on). The agent is assumed to be a member of such a class of persons. We regard a bit of behaviour on the part of a member of such a class as 'determined by his ego or self', when and only when the following conditions are fulfilled. (1) The stimulus must be of a kind to which (i) all members of the class are quite often subjected, and (ii) in response to which most of them on most occasions would behave in a certain way *z*. (2) The individual in question A behaved, when so stimulated, in a markedly different way *w*.

Now I think that the distinctions which Professor Hedenius draws are important in reference to the degree of *merit or demerit* which we ascribe to a person in respect to a bit of intentional behaviour. We do not get morally excited when a person behaves rightly under circumstances which frequently occur in the lives of all of us, and in which most of us generally do act rightly. Nor do we get morally excited when a person behaves wrongly under circustances which are highly exceptional, and in which one suspects that most such persons would act wrongly and is very doubtful whether one would have acted rightly oneself.

It seems to me that all this comes fairly easily under the sense of 'ought' and 'ought not' which I described in paragraph (ii) of the Section entitled '*Various Senses of "Obligable"*' in my lecture. I said of this that 'a clear-headed Determinist should hold either that this is the only sense, or that, if there is another sense, in which obligability entails *categorical* substitutability, it has no application'. But I added that I am inclined to think that we often use 'ought' and 'ought not' in another sense, and that in this other sense they entail categorical substitutability. I think that this is most obvious when one makes judgments about *oneself*, of the form 'I ought to have done so-and-so' (which I did not do), or 'I ought not to have done so-and-so' (which I did). I cannot help thinking that a reference to what the average middle-class Englishman above the age of puberty would or would not generally do, when subjected to the stimulus to which I was subjected, would serve only as a rough measure of the degree of my delinquency, and not at all as an analysis of my conviction that *I*, under the very circumstances in which I in fact failed to do my duty, *could* instead have done it.

(D) *The 'Existential' Account of Human Personality*

I understand Professor Kuhn to be using 'existence' throughout nearly the whole of his essay in a certain technical sense, viz. to denote the peculiar kind of being which he holds to be characteristic of a *person*, and to be revealed to each of us by the reflective awareness which is an essential factor in personality. If I understand Professor Kuhn aright, what he takes such reflexive awareness to reveal to each person may be described as follows. What a person now *is* is what he has *made himself*, through the reaction of himself as active, spontaneous, and selective, upon himself as passive and malleable. Furthermore, he, as he *now is*, is actively engaged in determining and generating himself *as he will become*, by a further process of selection and action. This interest in, and self-direction towards, the *future* is particularly characteristic of a person. Moreover, each person has a unique and fundamental concern for *himself*, and this is alleged to be an essential condition of 'the absolute validity of moral obligation and moral claims in a person'.

I am willing to accept much of this, if I am allowed to interpret it as follows, and to put certain qualifications upon it. In the first place, it is certainly characteristic of human beings (as contrasted with other animals, and especially with certain insects) to be born with extremely few and comparatively unimportant *first-order* dispositions. They are born, instead, with what Professor Ducasse calls 'aptitudes', i.e. dispositions to *acquire* dispositions and to *organize* those which they acquire. In so far as statements to the effect that a person is not 'an entity fixed and bound by its own whatness' are interpreted in this way, I think that they are true and important.

On the other hand, we must not overlook the fact that what a person can make of himself, even under the most favourable conditions, *is* limited by his innate endowments. It is true that no one knows even approximately what are his own or another person's ultimate limitations. It is true too that it is generally undesirable for a person to dwell on this topic in his own case, or for his neighbours to express a confident and narrow view about it. Lastly, it is true that experience shows that a person, who seems *prima facie* to be hopelessly handicapped, physically or intellectually or morally, sometimes does (if he seriously takes himself in hand, and if others give him understanding help) achieve a development of personality which seems well nigh miraculous. But I see no reason to believe that the possibilities are in fact unlimited in any case, or that the limits in each particular case are not fixed by the innate constitution of the individuals.

Allowing that there is an important sense in which it is true that each of us is continually making and re-making himself, we must not exaggerate the part played by the *deliberate action* of the individual himself in this process. In the case of most of us it is but fitfully and for short periods that one 'takes oneself in hand' and sets out to make onself a person of such and such a kind. In the main each man's personality is moulded for him in early life by the pressures of family, of school, of business, by the newspapers, the wireless, and the films. These influences are (after occasional struggles, which leave their scars in all, and mar the personalities and wreck the lives of some) generally assimilated fairly thoroughly, though of course *in modo recipientis*. Thereafter the reactions of most men of a given social group in normal situations are almost automatic. Doubtless the power to make a hard deliberate choice, which one realizes will profoundly modify one's life and personality, remains latent in everyone. If faced with a crisis, some few of us might make such a choice. But I suspect that in most men that power has become so repressed and overlaid and atrophied in middle life that the chance of its being exercised, if a crisis should face one, is negligible.

'Existentialism', as presented by Professor Kuhn, seems to me to be an account of human nature derived from contemplating men of forceful and original character, making hard (and for themselves and those near and dear to them, at any rate) far-reaching decisions. It is certainly most important not to neglect this heroic side of human nature, and not to forget that it can and does show itself in what we might be tempted to regard as very ordinary men and women in very humdrum circumstances. But that should not make us ignore the dim and petty background (against which these cases shine forth by their rarity), summed up in the epitaph which might so fittingly commemorate most of us:

> Too bad for heaven, too good for hell;
> So where he's gone I cannot tell.

Professor Kuhn's main criticism on what I have written about human personality is that I have treated a person and his doings and sufferings as if they were exactly like a physical thing and what happens to it, and have treated voluntary action as if it were exactly like physical causation. I must admit that there is much truth in this, as regards my published works. I can, however, assure Professor Kuhn that I am not, and have never been, a 'physicalist' (as I understand that word) about human nature. I regard the differences between men and any non-human animals of whom we have knowledge, as quite fundamental, however they may have arisen in the course of evolution. And I consider that causation, as it shows itself in rational cognition, deliberation, voluntary decision, and considered action, has certain unique peculiarities as contrasted with either purely physical causation or psychological causation at the non-rational level.

The only other matter on which I will comment is this. Professor Kuhn twits me with some *obiter dicta*, which occur towards the end of *The Mind and its Place in Nature*, to the effect that the human race might possibly escape disaster by applying psychology and genetics to 'deliberately altering the emotional constitution of mankind, and deliberately constructing more reasonable forms of social organization'. He asks me what I think about that now.

My answer is as follows. It seems to me even more likely now than it did then, that, unless opportunities for organized scientific research should be destroyed in the near future, the *knowledge* and the *power* will be available to determine the kind of individuals who shall be born (or incubated), and to mould their nature at will after birth. Such knowledge or power *could* be used on a large scale at any moment only by that person or that group who then have control in a given society. They *would* be used only in so far as those in control knew of them and desired to use them, and the *ends* for which they would in that case be used would depend on the wishes and ideals of the controllers. Given all this, the scheme would be *effective* only in so far as those in control could apply it on a large scale by consent or through inadvertence, or impose it by fraud or by force or by propaganda on the rest of the society.

Plainly that would give an unprecedented power for good or for ill to those who are in a position to use it. Beyond that platitude there is little that I can say except to add the following supplementary platitudes.

(1) There is little likelihood that the scientists, who had the knowledge, would be any more than the tools, or at best the willing technical advisers, of those who had the power to apply it. (2) Even if, by some strange chance, the relevant scientists should also be in effective control, that would be no guarantee that a good use would be made of the power. There is no reason to think that the ideals of psychologists and geneticists, as such,

in regard to human nature and society, would be better (as distinct from more practicable) than those of trades-unionists, businessmen, lawyers, soldiers, or professional politicians. Nor is there any reason to think that psychologists and geneticists, as such, would be any less susceptible than other men to the corruptions of power. (3) I am inclined to believe that there is a rather strong *negative* correlation between the qualities which help a man to get and to keep power in a highly organized industrial society of the modern type (whether capitalist, social-democratic, or communist), and the qualities which tend to endow a man with high ideals of human personality and human society. I should therefore think it much more likely that the powers in question, if used at all, would be *misused* than that they would be applied to good ends. (4) On the other hand, it seems to me plainer than ever that, *unless* the emotional make-up of the average citizen throughout the world *be* profoundly modified in certain ways in the fairly near future, the chance of humanity escaping a large-scale disaster is very slender.

Existing societies are composed of persons whose emotional reactions are largely infantile or anachronistic, i.e. adapted to situations utterly different from those with which men are now faced. They are wholly dependent for their livelihood on a complex and delicate web of economic conditions, which no individual understands. They are now brought into ever closer and more irritating contact with each other, through the development of means of quick communication and the inordinate growth of population, and their emotions are continually played upon by wireless propaganda. All the conditions for an explosion are thus given. And now such persons and societies, whom a sensible parent would hesitate to trust with a popgun, are provided with atomic and hydrogen bombs, and with rockets to convey them. So there is every prospect that the explosion, when it comes, will be shatteringly destructive.

These seem to me to be reasonably probable inferences from fairly plain empirical facts, and I do not think that their plausibility is much affected by whether one holds a 'physicalist' or an 'existentialist' view of the nature of human personality.

XV

G. E. MOORE'S LATEST PUBLISHED VIEWS ON ETHICS[1]

The first six essays in the book *The Philosophy of G. E. Moore*, published in 1942 as Vol. IV in *The Library of Living Philosophers*, are devoted to Moore's ethical theories; and Moore's comments upon them occupy the first ninety-three pages of his terminal essay. I suppose that this part of the terminal essay must contain Moore's latest published pronouncements on ethical problems. As such, it is of considerable interest and importance. Of the six ethical essays and Moore's comments on them I propose to select three for discussion here, viz. those of Frankena, Stevenson, and myself. Between them they cover the following four main topics, viz. I, The distinction between 'natural' and 'non-natural' characteristics, II, The 'autobiographical' analysis of moral indicatives, III, The interconnections of value and obligation, and IV, Ethical Egoism and Ethical Neutralism. I propose to treat each of these topics in turn.

1. *The Distinction between 'Natural' and 'Non-natural' Characteristics*

It is a well-known doctrine of Moore's that the word 'good', in one important sense of it, stands for a characteristic of a peculiar kind which he terms 'non-natural'. In *Principia Ethica* he gave certain criteria for distinguishing 'natural' and 'non-natural' characteristics. The two marks of a *natural* characteristic were said to be (i) that it 'can exist in time all by itself', and (ii) that it is a 'part' of anything that it characterizes. I tried to show in my essay that these criteria are utterly unsatisfactory.[2]

[1] Reprinted from *Mind*, Volume LXX, October 1961, by courtesy of the editors.

[2] *Editor's Note:* The criticism mentioned here is found in Selection 5 of this volume ('Is "Goodness" a Name of a Simple Non-natural Quality?'), pp. 106-123.

Moore accepted that criticism; and so we may henceforth regard that part of his doctrine as withdrawn.

In my essay I suggested that Moore was almost certainly intending to deal with the same distinction (though he does not use the words 'natural' and 'non-natural') in the paper entitled 'The Conception of Intrinsic Value' in his *Philosophical Studies* (1922). I understand his doctrine there to be as follows. (1) The characteristics of a thing may be divided into (*a*) those that *do*, and (*b*) those that do *not*, 'depend solely on its intrinsic nature'. (2) Those characteristics which do depend solely on the intrinsic nature of that which they characterize may be subdivided into (α) those which *are*, and (β) those which are *not* 'intrinsic'. (3) The *non-natural* characteristics of a thing are the members of the sub-class (α, β), i.e. those which *are* dependent solely on its intrinsic nature but are *not* intrinsic. The *natural* characteristics of a thing are the members of class (*b*) and the members of sub-class (*a*, α), i.e. they are those characteristics of it which *either* do not depend solely on its intrinsic nature *or* which depend solely on its intrinsic nature and are also intrinsic.

In his terminal essay Moore points out where I was right and where I was wrong in my interpretation of his doctrine in 'The Conception of Intrinsic Value'. I was right in thinking that he was concerned there with the distinction which he described in *Principia Ethica* by the words 'natural' and 'non-natural'. But I was wrong in thinking that he would admit there to be such a class of characteristics as (*a*, β), i.e. ones which *do* depend solely on the intrinsic nature of that which they characterize and yet are *not* intrinsic. Moore says that he held that *all* characteristics which depend solely on the intrinsic nature of that which they characterize *are intrinsic*. And he held that goodness, in the fundamental sense in which he is here concerned with it, is intrinsic.

He thinks that my mistake may have arisen from the very unfortunate terminology which he used in 'The Conception of Intrinsic Value'. He admits that he there used the term 'intrinsic property' in such a way that there would be no inconsistency between the following three statements, (i) '*p* is intrinsic', (ii) '*p* is a property', and (iii) '*p* is not an intrinsic property'. For, he says, his doctrine was that goodness (in the sense in question) *is* intrinsic and *is* a property and yet *is not* an intrinsic property of a good thing.

In view of this, I think that my misunderstanding was not only excusable but also fortunate, for it gave Moore an opportunity to remove what must have been a constant source of confusion even to wary readers. Henceforth, he says in the terminal essay, he will drop this terminology. In future, if I understand him aright, he would call *all* those properties and *only* those properties of a thing, which depend solely on its intrinsic nature, 'intrinsic properties' of it. He would then sub-divide the intrinsic properties of a thing into 'natural' and 'non-natural'. And he would hold that goodness (in the sense in question) is a non-natural intrinsic property of a good thing. It will be noted that 'being an intrinsic property of a thing' is defined in terms of the notion of 'depending solely on the intrinsic nature of a thing'. The latter notion is elaborately expounded in 'The Conception of Intrinsic Value'. I did not criticize it in my essay, and Moore takes it for granted in his terminal essay; so I shall not discuss it here.

The verbal confusion is now removed, but we are left with the substantial question: What is Moore's criterion for distinguishing between those intrinsic properties of a thing which are *natural* and those which are *non-natural*? In 'The Conception of Intrinsic Value' Moore gave two criteria, and the first of these may be subdivided into two complementary parts. In the amended terminology they may be stated as follows. (1.1) A complete enumeration of the *natural* intrinsic characteristics of a thing would be a *complete description* of that thing. (1.2) An enumeration which omitted any *natural* intrinsic characteristic of a thing would be an *incomplete description* of that thing. (2) The *natural* intrinsic characteristics of a thing seem to contribute towards describing its intrinsic nature in a way in which predicates of value do not.

In my essay I confined myself to (1.1), and said nothing about (1.2) or about (2). Moore admits in the terminal essay that

(1.2) cannot be maintained as it stands. Suppose that p and π are two properties, e.g. being red and being coloured, such that anything that had p would, as a necessary consequence, have π. Then a description which included p would not be made incomplete merely by omitting π. And yet π might be a *natural* intrinsic characteristic. So (1.2) would have to be amended to run somewhat as follows: No description of a thing would be complete, if it omitted any *natural* intrinsic characteristic of it which is not conveyed by some one or some combination of its other natural characteristics. (I use the phase '*p conveys q*' to mean the same as 'If anything had p, it would necessarily follow from that alone that it would have q'.)

Moore admits in the terminal essay that he did not clearly distinguish criteria (1.1) and (1.2), on the one hand, from criterion (2), on the other. He says that he is now inclined to rely mainly on the following amended form of (2), viz. that, in one sense of 'describe', the mention of *any natural* characteristic of a thing contributes to some extent to describe that thing; whilst the mention of its *non-natural* intrinsic characteristics does not, in that sense, describe it at all. He admits that this is extremely vague, unless we can give some more definite information as to the particular sense of 'describe' which is here relevant.

I think it is fair to conclude that Moore, at the time when he wrote this terminal essay, was unable to give any satisfactory definition of, or criterion for, a 'non-natural characteristic'. But I think that we can go further. His suggested criterion, with its admitted vagueness, due to the uncertainty of the relevant sense of 'describe', is surely grist to the mill of supporters of what I will call 'non-predicative interpretations of moral sentences in the indicative'. If, as that theory holds, the word 'good' is not the name of a characteristic at all, but its use is, e.g. to express or to evoke certain emotions, then to call a thing 'good' would *not* contribute in any way to the description of it. And yet, owing to the likeness of grammatical form between such sentences as 'That is a pleasant emotion' and 'That is a morally good emotion', e.g. there might well seem to be something paradoxical in saying that the former did, and the latter did not, contribute towards describing the emotion. So one could understand why those who never questioned that moral sentences in the indicative assign a predicate to a subject, should sum up the situation by alleging that the word 'good' stands for a property of a peculiar kind, which does not contribute to describe its subject in the familiar way in which e.g. the property denoted by 'pleasant' does.

There remain two small points which are worth mentioning before leaving this part of the subject. (1) Moore says that, in his opinion, there are at least two kinds of intrinsic value, viz. goodness (in the sense in question) and beauty. But he does not hold, and never has held, that goodness, in that sense, is a determinable in W. E. Johnson's usage of that word. I must say, for my own part, that I should need a great deal of persuasion before I would admit that there is even a *prima facie* case for regarding beauty, in any sense of that word, as a form of *intrinsic* value.

(2) The other point is this. In the course of my essay I used an argument which presupposes that the pleasantness of a pleasant experience is dependent solely on its intrinsic nature. I assumed, e.g. that, in the case of a pleasant sensation, its pleasantness is always conveyed by some intrinsic pleasant-making sensible quality of it, such as its sweetness. Now Moore points out that the relation between the pleasant-making characteristics of an experience and its pleasantness is almost certainly *not* that of conveyance, but is that of *causal determination*. I fully agree with that contention, and I will proceed to develop it in my own way, in which Moore might not have been willing to follow.

The essential point is that it is perfectly conceivable that two persons, or the same person on different occasions, should have sensations which were exactly alike in all their sensible qualities, and yet that one of them should be a pleasant experience and the other an unpleasant one. It is a very well founded empirical generalization, e.g. that the vast majority of human beings, whenever they have a sensation of the 'toothachy' kind, dislike that sensation for its characteristic sensible qualities. That is why we call toothachy sensations 'unpleasant'. But there is no kind of necessity about that generalization. It is perfectly conceivable that there might be persons who, when they had a sensation of precisely the same kind, always, or on certain special occasions, *liked* that sensation for those very same sensible qualilities for which most persons at most times *dislike* such sensations. For any such person, on any such occasion, a toothache would be a *pleasant* experience. I would suggest, then, that the words 'pleasant' and 'unpleasant', as applied to experiences, often imply a well-founded empirical generalization, to the effect that the vast majority of people, on the vast majority of occasions when they have an experience of a certain kind, would like it (or dislike it, as the case may be) for its characteristic experiential qualities. But there is also, plainly, a non-statistical sense of the words 'pleasant' and 'unpleasant'. To call an experience 'pleasant' (or to call it 'unpleasant'), in this latter sense, means that the particular person, who has it on a particular occasion, then and there *likes* it, as the case may be) for its characteristic experiential qualities. There is no kind of contradiction in saying that a particular experience, which would correctly be called 'pleasant' (or be called 'unpleasant') in the *statistical* sense, occurring on a particular occasion in a particular person, might be correctly called 'unpleasant' (or 'pleasant', as the case may be) in the *non-statistical* sense.

II. *The 'Autobiographical' Analysis of Moral Indicatives*

Consider the sentence: 'It was right for Brutus to stab Caesar', uttered at a certain moment by a person who is really considering what he is saying and is not merely talking like a parrot or giving an example in an essay. What I call the 'autobiographical' analysis of this sentence is, on its positive side, that the speaker is intending to state, beside the historical proposition that Brutus stabbed Caesar, the autobiographical proposition that he himself is feeling a certain kind of emotion (viz. one of moral approval) in contemplating that historical propositon. On the negative side the theory is that the speaker is not intending to state anything else beside that historical and that autobiographical proposition and anything that may be logically entailed by them.

This must be carefully distinguished from what I have called 'the non-predicative theory of moral indicatives'. That holds that the speaker is stating nothing but the historical proposition; but that he would not have used the moral-indicative form of expression unless he were feeling moral approval towards it himself or had wanted to induce that emotion in his hearers. (The theory can, of course, take other forms, with something else substituted for 'moral approval'.) None of the essayists explicitly defends the non-predicative theory. But Professor Stevenson defends the autobiographical analysis against certain arguments which Moore had used in his paper 'The Nature of Moral Philosophy' in *Philosophical Studies*. Moore, in his reply, says that he would be more inclined to accept the non-predicative theory than the autobiographical analysis, if he were to accept either.

Before going further it is worth while to note that the autobiographical analysis might take two different forms, which I will call 'occurrent' and 'dispositional'. On the occurrent form of it, a person who says at a certain moment that x is right is saying that he is at that moment feeling moral approval for x. On the dispositional form of the theory, he is saying that he is generally disposed to feel moral approval when he contemplates actions like x. Moore distinguished those two forms of the theory in his paper 'The Nature of Moral Philosophy'. But Stevenson considered only the occurrent form, and therefore Moore also confines himself to that in his reply. This seems to me unfortunate, because the dispositional form is much more plausible than the occurrent form.

There is a matter, which seems to me quite simple, about which both Stevenson and Moore make terribly heavy weather. The essential point at issue can be put as follows. Suppose that the occurrent form of the autobiographical analysis were correct. Then A's utterance at t of a token of the type-sentence 'x is right' would be equivalent in meaning to his uttering a token of the type-sentence 'I am now feeling moral approval of x'. Similar remarks apply, *mutatis mutandis*, to 'x is wrong'. Now that makes the predicates 'right' and 'wrong' to be doubly relational, for it makes them involve a relation to a speaker and to a time. It follows that 'right' would have a systematically different meaning on every different occasion on which it is predicated, even by the same person, beside having a systematically different meaning corresponding to each different person who predicates it on any occasion. Now the word 'right' seems *prima facie* not to answer to those conditions. It seems to be used as if it could stand for precisely the same characteristic when predicated by different persons or on different occasions by the same person. Moore's arguments against the occurrent autobiographical analysis in 'The Nature of Moral Philosophy' are simply various ways of trying to exhibit strikingly certain aspects of this *prima facie* conflict between the common usage of the word 'right' and the usage which would seem to be required if the occurrent autobiographical analysis were correct.

One of Moore's arguments was concerned with the possible alteration in a person's emotional attitude towards the same action, if he should contemplate it on successive occasions. Stevenson's criticism of this argument brings out an important point about the use of tenses in such sentences as '*x is* right', '*x was* right', and '*x will* be right'. The point may be put as follows. Suppose that A says at *t* 'I now approve of *x*, but I formerly contemplated it with disapproval'. Obviously his statement may be true. Now Moore has argued that, if the occurrent autobiographical analysis be correct, A's statement would be equivalent to '*x* is now right, but was formerly wrong'. And he had pointed out that it is nonsensical to say, of *one and the same* action, that it was right at one time and became wrong later.

Now Stevenson quite justifiably challenges Moore's right to assert that the theory entails the equivalence mentioned above. Stevenson insists that the correct interpretation of the theory is as follows. If a person says '*x is* right', he means that he is *now* feeling approval towards *x*, which is *now* being performed. If he says '*x was* right', he means that he is *now* feeling approval towards *x*, which *has been* performed. The tense in the moral indicative refers only to the date of the action which is said to be right or to be wrong; and the principal tense in the autobiographical equivalent of that indicative is *always the present*.

If we accept this contention of Stevenson's, what really does follow from the autobiographical analysis, together with the fact of the change in A's attitude, is this. A can now correctly and truly say '*x* was right'; and he could, at some former time, have said with equal correctness and equal truth '*x* is (or was) wrong'. But at no time could he correctly and truly say '*x* was right at one time and is now wrong'. For that would be equivalent to uttering the sentence 'I now approve of *x*, which happened in the past, and disapprove of *x*, which is happening now'. This is doubly nonsensical, since it asserts that the speaker had, at the same time, incompatible emotional attitudes towards one and the same particular action, and it implies that one and the same action was done at two different times.

Another argument in Moore's paper on 'The Nature of Moral Philosophy' may be put as follows. Suppose that A and B contemplate the same act *x* at the same time *t*. A may say 'I approve of *x*', and B may say 'I disapprove of *x*', and both may be telling the truth. Now, if the analysis under discussion be correct, A's statement is equivalent to his saying '*x* is right', and B's statement is equivalent to his saying '*x* is wrong'. Now the two latter statements conflict logically, whilst the two former are logically compatible. Therefore they cannot be equivalent each to each.

The true account of this situation is admirably brought out by Moore in his terminal essay. It is this. If the analysis under discussion be admissible, A can correctly and truly say '*x* is right', and B can at the same time correctly and truly say '*x* is wrong'. But no one at any time can correctly and truly say '*x* is both right and wrong'. For anyone who did so would, according to the proposed analysis, be saying 'I now approve and disapprove of *x*'. Now that could not be truly said by A, who approves and does not disapprove of *x*; nor by B, who disapproves and does not approve of *x*; nor by any third person, since no one can entertain simultaneously incompatible emotional attitudes towards the same object.

This amendment, however, does nothing to diminish the force of Moore's original argument against the occurrent autobiographical analysis, viz. that, according to it, A and B do not differ in opinion when one of them pronounces an action to be right and the other pronounces the very same action to be wrong. This is recognized by Stevenson, who proceeds to meet it by making two additions to the proposed analysis.

The first is to point out that, although A and B would not differ in opinion, in the sense of holding incompatible beliefs, they would do so in the wider sense of having opposed emotional attitudes towards the same object. The second is to remind us that in such situations each person would generally seek to alter the emotional attitude of the other and make it resemble his own.

Stevenson admits that, even when due weight has been given to these two considerations, the occurrent autobiographical analysis is not wholly satisfactory. Suppose that A asks B 'Is *x* right?' A is not as a rule wanting to find out whether *he himself* now approves of *x*, but whether B or most other people would do so. Or, again, A may disapprove of *x* and may know that B approves of it, and the motive of his question may be to induce B to change his attitude. Lastly, if A asks *himself* 'Is *x* right?', he is certainly not trying to find out whether he now approves of *x*. The situation probably is that he has conflicting attitudes towards *x*, in respect of various aspects of it, and that he is seeking to straighten them out.

Moore does not seriously dispute anything that Stevenson here says. He tells us that he has always recognized that difference of 'opinion' covers opposition of emotional attitude, but that he used not to think it possible that moral conflicts could be merely of that kind. He is now inclined to think that moral disagreement *may* be nothing but opposition of emotional attitude; but he is also inclined about equally strongly to think that it involves a logical conflict between incompatible beliefs. Stevenson, he says, has given no reasons for his own alternative; he has merely shown that certain arguments against it are inconclusive. If Moore felt obliged to abandon his own theory, he would not be inclined to stop at the stage of the occurrent autobiographical analysis, but would prefer to accept some form of *non-predicative* theory. Moore says that he is, in fact, now quite strongly disposed to think that, when a person utters the sentence '*x* is right', he is not asserting *anything* that could be true or false, not even the autobiographical proposition that he now approves of *x*. But Moore says that he also continues to have some inclination to hold his old view. And he cannot say which of these inclinations is the stronger.

III. *The Interconnections of Value and Obligation*

The longest and most complex essay in the ethical part of the book is that of Professor Frankena, and the part of Moore's reply which deals with it is also highly involved. The question at issue is the connection between the fact that a state of affairs would be *intrinsically good* and a person's being under an *obligation* to seek to *bring it into existence*. Moore has made certain statements on this topic in his various ethical writings, and Frankena discusses their truth and their compatibility with Moore's characteristic doctrines that good is a simple, indefinable, intrinsic, and non-natural characteristic.

The best way to convey an idea of the discussion is to take in turn the points which Frankena enumerates in the summary at the end of his essay, and to consider, in each case, Moore's treatment of them.

Point 1. This divides into two propositions, which I will call (1, *a*) and (1, *b*). The former is the contention that, if good (in Moore's sense) be *simple*, then the statement 'I am morally bound to do *y*' cannot *mean* the same as the statement '*y* will produce more good or less evil than any other act open to me'. The latter is the contention that the same negative consequence follows from the supposition that good (in Moore's sense) is *intrinsic*, in the sense explained by him.

(1, *a*) After a good deal of discussion on alleged obscurities and ambiguities in Frankena's reasoning. Moore proceeds to state formally what he takes to be Frankena's argument on this point. I have very little doubt that this is a correct account of what was present, in a less precise form, in Frankena's mind, and so I shall adopt it. The argument may be stated as follows. The proposition that good is *simple* entails that statements of the form 'x is good' neither include nor are identical with statements of obligation. That entails that statements of the form 'x is good' are *not normative*. That in turn entails that statements of the form 'y will produce the most good or the least evil of all the acts open to me' are *not normative*. And that entails that statements of the latter form are not identical in meaning with statements of the form 'I ought to do y'.

Now Moore holds that the fundamental step in this argument is the second, viz. that if statements of the form 'x is good' neither include nor are identical in meaning with statements of obligation it follows that such statements are not normative. The validity or invalidity of this step depends on what Frankena means by 'normative', and that (Moore alleges) is not made perfecly clear in his essay. But, setting aside minor verbal inconsistencies, it seems fairly plain that what he intends is the following. s is a normative statement about an action, if and only if it follows from the very nature of that statement that that action ought to be done. If we accept this account of 'normative', we see that the transition in step 2 depends on the tacit assumption that nothing can follow from the very nature of a statement except what is identical with or is a part of what is meant by the latter. There is in fact no doubt that Frankena does assume this premise, for elsewhere in his essay he makes it quite explicit that he thinks that the two propositions '*q follows from the very nature of p*' and '*q is synthetically, though necessarily*, connected with p' are mutually exclusive. Now Moore rejects this premise, and therefore sees no reason to accept step 2 of Frankena's argument.

As this is an important point, I will state all that is to be found in Moore's terminal essay on this topic. In the first place, he gives an example taken from Professor Langford's essay in the same volume. He says that, in his opinion, it *does* follow, from the very nature of the statement 'This is a cube', that this has twelve edges; whilst the latter is *not* identical with nor part of the meaning of the former. Secondly, in another part of his essay, Moore makes the following general assertions. He says that he uses the phrase '*q follows from p*' to mean that the conjunction '*p* & not-*q*' is *self-contradictory*. But he holds that such a conjunction may be self-contradictory *without* '*q* follows from *p*' being *analytic*.

If we put all this together, we see that what Moore is maintaining is the following. Even though good be *simple*, the conjunction 'I ought to do *y*, and *y* will *not* produce as good consequences as some other action open to me' may be *self-contradictory*, in that sense (whatever it may be) in which the conjunction 'this is a cube and this has *not* twelve edge's, is self-contradictory. I should agree that this is quite possible, provided that *ought* itself is not simple, but contains *good* in its analysis. But, if *good* and *ought* were both simple, I cannot for the life of me see how the conjunction in question could be *self-contradictory*, in any generally accepted sense of that phrase. It might, however, be *self-evidently impossible*, without being self-contradictory in the formal sense, if we admit the possibility of necessary connections and disconnections which are synthetic, but obvious on inspection. I should add, perhaps, that I am extremely doubtful whether the conjunction 'This is a cube, and this has not twelve edges' *is* self-contradictory. I should suspect that what is so is the conjunction of this conjunction with certain of the axioms of three-dimensional Euclidean geometry. If so, it is not very helpful as an analogy to the ethical propositions under consideration.

Moore remarks that Frankena might reply to his criticisms on step 2 of the argument by saying that he uses the word 'include' in such a way that '*q* is included in *p*' covers *inter alia* '*q* follows necessarily but synthetically from *p*'. But that would not help Frankena's argument, since it would save step 2 only at the expense of step 1. For, if 'include' be used in this extended sense, there is no reason why the simplicity of *good* should prevent statements of the form '*x* is good' from 'including' statements of obligation.

(1, *b*) This is the contention that, if good be *intrinsic* in Moore's sense of that word, then the statement 'I am morally bound to do *y*' cannot mean what is meant by '*y* will produce more good or less evil than any other act open to me'.

Moore says that the argument is precisely the same as that in (1, *a*), with 'intrinsic' substituted for 'simple'. It therefore suffers from the same defect, viz. that the second step is unjustified, for the reasons given above. But it suffers from a further defect. For the first step, which was quite legitimate in (1, *a*), ceases to be so when 'intrinsic' is substituted for 'simple'. From the hypothesis that good is *intrinsic*, in Moore's sense, it would *not* follow that statements of the form 'x is good' neither include nor are identical with statements of obligations.

In order to discuss this, we must remember what Moore does and what he does not mean by calling a characteristic 'intrinsic'. To say that p is an intrinsic characteristic of x means that the possession of p by x depends solely on x's intrinsic nature. Now, in the first place, it does *not* follow from this definition that every intrinsic characteristic of x must be a *pure quality*. No doubt, if goodness were a pure quality, whether intrinsic or not) it would follow at once that 'x is good' could not be identical with or include any statement of obligation. For the latter would involve *relations* to an actual or possible agent. But Moore has distinguished between the 'external' and the 'internal' relational properties of a thing; and, whilst no *external* relational property of a thing could be intrinsic, there is nothing to prevent its *internal* relational properties from being so.

We may put the matter as follows. We must distinguish between what we might call 'categorical' and 'conditional' relational properties, though Moore does not use those terms. It would be a *categorical* relational property of a certain bit of arsenic to be poisoning Mr Jones at a certain moment. That property would be external and non-intrinsic; for that bit of arsenic would not be having it unless Mr Jones had existed and had swallowed it. It is a *conditional* relational property of any bit of arsenic to be poisonous, i.e. to be such that it *would* poison a man, *if* there were one and *if* he were to swallow it. This property, though relational, may be internal and intrinsic; for a bit of arsenic would have it even though there had never been any men or though no man had ever swallowed it. Similarly, if goodness be an *intrinsic* property of x, the statement 'x is good' cannot include or be identical in meaning with any such *categorical* statement as 'z ought to desire x' or 'z ought to try to produce x'. But there is nothing to prevent its including or being identical with some *conditional* proposition of the form 'If there were a person who fulfilled such and such conditions, he would be under an obligation to desire x or to try to produce x.' For x could have that property, even if there had never been any persons, or if no person had ever fulfilled the required conditions.

Whilst I admit the validity and the importance of the distinction which Moore draws here, I do think that it is rather misleading to say of even a *conditional* relational property that it 'depends solely on the intrinsic nature of its possessor'. Surely there is an important sense in which the poisonousness of arsenic depends just as much on the intrinsic nature of *a living organism* as on the intrinsic nature of arsenic. In the same sense and to the same degree the property of being such that, if there were a person and he were to fulfil certain conditions, he would be under an obligation to try to produce x, depends just as much on the intrinsic nature of *moral persons* as on that of x. No doubt arsenic would have been poisonous, even if there never had been and never will be any living organisms; but at least we can say that the very notion of poisonousness involves the notion of organisms and vital processes, and that no amount of reflection on arsenic in isolation could have supplied the latter notions.

Point 2. Frankena's second point really divides into seven interconnected propositions. It may be stated as follows. If value be either (*a*) *simple*, or (*b*) *intrinsic*, then it cannot be either (α) *normative*, or (β) *non-natural*, or (γ) *definible in terms of obligation*. And, that being so, (*c*) there is no reason to think that it is *incapable of being defined in non-ethical terms*.

It is evident that we thus have six hypothetical propositions, which arise by combining in turn each of the two antecedents (*a*) and (*b*) with each of the three consequents (α), (β), and (γ). In addition to these six hypotheticals there is the seventh proposition (*c*) ,which Frankena states in the form 'In that case there is no reason to regard value as being incapable of definition in non-ethical terms'. We may label the six hypotheticals as

(2*a*, α), (2*a*, β), (2*a*, γ), and (2*b*, α), (2*b*, β), (2*b*, γ). The seventh proposition may be labelled (2*c*).

Moore claims to have dealt with (2*a*, α), (2*a*, γ), (2*b*, α), and (2*b*, γ) in his discussion of (1, *a*) and (1, *b*). He has admitted (2a, γ), i.e. that, if good be simple, it cannot be defined in terms of obligation, since it would be indefinable. He has rejected (2*a*, α), (2*b*, α), and (2*b*, γ). It remains, therefore to deal with (2*a*, β), (2*b*, β), and (2*c*). That we will now proceed to do.

(2*a*, β). This is the proposition that, if good be *simple*, it cannot be *non-natural*. The essence of Frankena's argument is as follows. If good were simple, it would not be normative. If it were not normative, there would be no reason to think it non-natural. Therefore, if it were simple, it would be non-natural.

Now the first step has already been discussed and rejected. And, even if both it and the second step were accepted, the correct conclusion would only be that, if good were simple, there would be *no reason to think* that it is non-natural. There would be no justification for the stronger conclusion that it *would not be* non-natural.

(2*b*, β). This is the proposition that, if good be *intrinsic*, it cannot be *non-natural*. The argument is the same as before, with 'intrinsic' substituted throughout for 'simple'. The first step of this argument has already been discussed and rejected. And the argument has the same defect as (2*a*, β), viz. that of drawing a stronger conclusion than would be justified by its premises, even if these were acceptable.

Before passing to (2*c*), it will be worth while to consider for a moment the second premise, which is common to both the above arguments of Frankena's. This is the proposition that, unless good were *normative*, there would be no reason to think it *non-natural*. The essence of Frankena's contention on this topic is as follows. In his opinion, the main point of the doctrine that intrinsic value is non-natural is that it cannot be reduced to purely psychological, sociological, biological, or metaphysical terms. Now it seems to him that the only feature in moral judgments which can plausibly be held not to be so reducible is their ostensibly *normative* character, i.e. 'the fact that they seem to be saying of some agent that he *ought* to do something'. He concludes that, unless intrinsic value 'in itself possesses a normative character or obligatoriness', there is no reason to think that it is not essentially reducible to the terms ennumerated above.

(2*c*). This proposition, which comes immediately after the six hypotheticals which we have now discussed, is stated in the very obscure sentence: 'In that case there is no reason to think that good is not definable in non-ethical terms.' We naturally ask: 'In *what* case?' In the context Frankena might mean *either* that if his six hypotheticals were true that would be no reason to think that good is not definable in non-ethical terms, *or* that if their three consequents were true there would be no reason to think this. Moore does not consider the first of these alternatives, but confines his attention to the second. This is the proposition that, if good be neither normative nor non-natural nor definable in terms of obligation, then there is no reason to think it is not definable in non-ethical terms.

The phrase 'not definable in non-ethical terms' needs a certain amount of unpacking. It will be best to start from the beginning. Good might be either (1) indefinable, or (2) definable. If indefinible, it might be either (1.1) identical with some admittedly non-ethical simple notion, e.g. pleasant, or (1.2) not identical with any admittedly non-ethical notion. If definable, it might be either (2.1) definable in wholly non-ethical terms, or (2.2) definable only in terms which are wholly or partly ethical. We could lump together the two alternatives (1.1) and (2.1) under the heading 'wholly *expressible* in non-ethical terms'; and the two alternatives (1.2) and (2.2) under the heading 'not wholly *expressible* in non-ethical terms.'

Now Frankena has argued that, if good were *simple*, it would be neither normative nor non-natural nor definable in terms of obligation. And we have interpreted (2*c*) to mean that, if good were neither normative nor non-natural nor definable in terms of obligation, there would be no reason to think that it is not definable in non-ethical terms. Putting the two together, we see that Frankena is committed to the propostion that, if good be *simple*, there is no reason to think that it is *not definable in non-*

ethical terms. But, obviously, if it be simple, it cannot be *definable* in any terms whatsoever. So, in order to make sense of the above proposition, we must assume that Frankena is using the phrase 'not definable in non-ethical terms' in a loose sense which is equivalent to my phrase 'not wholly expressible in non-ethical terms'. What he is asserting is, in fact, the following proposition. If good be neither normative nor non-natural nor definable in terms of obligation, there is no reason to think that it is not *either* (i) definable in wholly non-ethical terms, *or* (ii) identical with some simple admittedly non-ethical notion. If that is what Frankena means, it may be doubted whether (2*c*) is more than a tautology; for the only attempt which he makes to define 'non-natural' seems to identify it with 'not wholly expressible in certain enumerated non-ethical terms'.

Point 3. Frankena's third point may be put as follows. If good were either (*a*) *normative* or (*b*) *non-natural* or (*c*) *not wholly expressible in ethical terms*, then (α) it would be *definable in terms of obligation*, (β) it would *not be simple*, and (γ) it would *not be intrinsic*. The third point is therefore the conjunction of the nine hypothetical propositions which arise by uniting (*a*), (*b*), and (*c*) in turn as antecedents with (α), (β), and (γ) as consequents.

Now of these nine hypotheticals the following have already been dealt with. (3*a*, α) is the contrapositive of a step in the argument for point (1, *a*), which Moore has discussed and dismissed. (3*a*, β), (3*a*, γ), (3*b*, β), and (3*b*, γ) are the contrapositives of (2*a*, α), (2*b*, α), (2*a*, β), and (2*b*, β) respectively. And these have been discussed and rejected by Moore. Again, if (3*b*, α) be granted, then (3*c*, α) becomes superfluous. For it is admitted that, if good be not wholly expressible in non-ethical terms, it is non-natural. And, if this be combined with (3*b*, α), we can infer (3*c*, α). (3*b*, α) embodies Frankena's conviction, already discussed, that the only fundamentally ethical notion is that of obligation. We are thus left with only (3*c*, β) and (3*c*, γ). These are more simply expressed in the equivalent form of their contrapositives. If we do this, and combine them, they amount to the proposition that, if good were either *simple* or *intrinsic*, it would be *wholly expressible in non-ethical terms*, i.e. it would be *natural*. This will best be treated incidentally in connection with the remaining points in Frankena's summary.

Point 4. Frankena's fourth point is that Moore has given no adequate reason for rejecting the view that 'good' is *definable in terms of obligation*.

Moore begins by admitting that he has given no *conclusive* reason. But he thinks that he can give *good* reasons. The gist of his argument is as follows. He considers three alleged definitions of 'good' in terms of obligation, which Frankena proposes. He rejects one of them on the ground that the two propositions suggested as *definiens* and *definiendum* do not even mutually entail each other. As regards the other two, he admits that there is mutual entailment between the *definiendum* and the suggested *definiens*. But he holds that that kind of logical relation can hold between two propositions without it being a case of two sentences with one and the same meaning. The test for the latter is to ask oneself the question 'Can I think of the one without *ipso facto* thinking of the other?' In each of these two cases he holds that that is possible, and therefore that there is not identity of meaning. Now, Moore says, he cannot think of any *other* plausible instances of mutual entailment between a value-proposition and an obligation-proposition. Therefore he holds that he has given sound, though not conclusive, reasons for thinking that goodness cannot be defined in terms of obligation.

I will now say something about the three proposed definitions. (1) 'x is intrinsically good' means what is meant by 'If one is capable of producing x, one has a *prima facie* duty (in Ross's sense) to do so'. This is rejected by Moore (rightly, I think), on the ground that the former proposition might easily be true when the latter was false.

(2) I am going to formulate the second in a slightly modified form of Moore's interpretation of Frankena's rather vague statement. It will run as follows. 'x is intrinsically good' means what is meant by 'The mere fact (if it were a fact) that A could do y and that y would produce x would suffice to supply *some* reason for thinking that A *ought* to do y. Moore holds that these two propositions do entail each other. But he considers

it obvious that a person could think of x as being intrinsically good, without *ipso facto* thinking of it as having this other complicated property, which is conveyed by and conveys its intrinsic goodness.

(3) Frankena quotes a certain alleged mutual entailment, which Moore gave in his *Ethics*, and asks why this should be not regarded as a definition. We need not trouble ourselves here about *this* particular alleged mutual entailment, because Moore says that he does not now think that it holds, or that the sentence quoted correctly expressed what he had in mind when he wrote his *Ethics*. Instead, we may confine our attention to the amended formula which he now proposes in its place. It runs as follows: 'x is intrinsically good' entails and is entailed by 'If an agent were a Creator, before the existence of any world; and if the only two alternatives open to him were (i) to create a world which consisted only of x, or (ii) to bring it about that there should never be a world at all; then it would be his duty to choose alternative (i), provided (*a*) that he knew for certain that these were the only two alternatives open to him, and (*b*) that he did not think it wrong to choose alternative (i)'. Moore says that it seems obvious to him (and who shall deny it?) that a person could think of the former proposition without *ipso facto* thinking of the latter.

Point 5. The main assertion in Frankena's fifth point, and the only one which Moore discusses, is the following. Frankena alleges that, even though it be *intrinsic value* which makes a thing such that it *ought* to be pursued or brought into being by a competent agent, still Moore has given no good reason why 'intrinsic value' might not be *definable in wholly non-ethical terms*.

What Frankena has in mind is no doubt this. He is alleging that there is no obvious reason why a *purely natural* characteristic, e.g. pleasantness, should not be such that the mere fact that a thing would have it would provide some ground for thinking that any agent, who could produce that thing, *ought* to do so.

In order to discuss this, let us begin by defining what Moore calls an 'ought-*implying* property', and what I prefer to call an 'ought-*inclining*' property. The sentence '*p* is an ought-inclining property' is to mean what is meant by 'The mere fact that a thing would have *p* would suffice to provide *some* ground for thinking that any agent, who could bring such a thing into being, *ought* to do so'. Now Moore admits that *intrinsic goodness* is an ought-inclining property. He holds, moreover, that the intrinsic goodness of a thing always depends on the presence in it of some *natural* characteristic or other which is what I will call 'good-making'. Let *q* be any *good-making* natural characteristic. Then anything that had *q* would, of necessity, have intrinsic goodness. And the mere fact that anything had intrinsic goodness would suffice to provide some ground for thinking that any agent, who could bring such a thing into being, ought to do so. It follows at once that *q*, though a *natural* characteristic, will also answer to the definition of an 'ought-inclining property'. And this can be generalized at once for every natural characteristic which is good-making.

There is no doubt, then, that Frankena is right in holding that there can be, and in fact are, *natural* characteristics which are ought-inclining. It is plain that he thinks that this fact entails that intrinsic goodness *either* (i) is *definable in terms of ought*, *or* (ii) is a *natural* characteristic. He thinks that, if the former alternative were fulfilled, there would be some reason to think that intrinsic goodness is *non-natural*. For, as we have seen, he regards 'ought' as *the* ethical notion *par excellence*, and as such the most plausible instance of a non-natural notion. On the other hand, he thinks that, if intrinsic goodness be *not* definable in terms of ought, then (in view of the fact that an ought-inclining property *can be natural*) there will be no valid reason for thinking that intrinsic goodness is non-natural.

Now Moore gives an argument which, he thinks, tends to show that intrinsic goodness cannot be identical with any natural property, even if it be not definable in terms of ought. The argument runs as follows.

Admittedly some *natural* characteristics are ought-inclining. But only *intrinsic* natural characteristics can be such. For a natural characteristic is ought-inclining only through being good-making. And only intrinsic natural characteristics convey intrinsic goodness. So the question reduces to whether intrinsic goodness could be identified with any *intrinsic* natural characteristic. After these preliminaries the argument continues as follows.

The number of ought-inclining intrinsic natural characteristics is, Moore asserts, certainly very great and possibly infinite. Plainly, we cannot identify intrinsic goodness with any particular one of them or with the aggregate of all of them. Moore thinks it obvious, moreover, that intrinsic goodness could not be identified with the *disjunction* of all these natural characteristics. Suppose that there were *one single* non-disjunctive intrinsic natural characteristic, which was (*a*) ought-inclining, and (*b*) was conveyed by each of the other ought-inclining natural characteristics. Then it might be be plausible to identify intrinsic goodness with *it*. But there seems to be no one natural characteristic answering to these conditions. Therefore there does not appear to be any ought-inclining natural characteristic with which intrinsic goodness can be identified. And it certainly cannot be identified with any intrinsic natural characteristic which is *not* ought-inclining. Therefore it cannot be identified with any natural characteristic whatever.

I think that this argument is valid, so far as it goes. But it would not satisfy a person who might suggest that '*x* has intrinsic goodness' means what is meant by '*x* has *some* intrinsic natural characteristic or other which is ought-inclining'. I do not know whether Moore would count this as identifying intrinsic goodness with the *disjunction* of all ought-inclining intrinsic natural characteristics. I do not think that he would. But, if he did, I should be inclined to ask: What precisely is the objection to such an 'identification'? The advantages of the suggestion are that it avoids postulating *two* indefinable non-natural characteristics, and defines the less specifically ethical one ('intrinsically good') in terms of the more specifically ethical one ('ought'). The final objection would have to be that one can think of intrinsic goodness without *ipso facto* thinking of even so indeterminate a notion as that expressed by the phrase 'some intrinsic natural ought-inclining characteristic or other'. But is that really at all certain?

Moore's latest published Views on the Connection of Good, Better, and Ought.

On pp. 606 to 611 of his terminal essay Moore formulates four very complicated pairs of mutually entailing propositions, which express the views, which he held at the date of writing, about the interconnections of 'good' and 'ought' and of 'better' and 'ought'. I am going to state them in my own way; but what I shall say is, I think, equivalent to what Moore had in mind and is perhaps somewhat easier to grasp.

I shall begin by defining certain statements. (1.1) 'p is a *good-making* characteristic' means what is meant by 'If x did have or now has or will have p, it follows that x then was or now is or will then be intrinsically good; and if x should have had or should now have or should be going to have p, it would follow that x would have been or would now be or would be going to be intrinsically good'. (1.2) 'p is a *bad-making* characteristic' is defined in a precisely similar way, with 'intrinsically *bad*' substituted throughout for 'intrinsically *good*'. (1.3) 'p is a *valifying* characteristic' means what is meant by 'p is either a good-making or a bad-making characteristic'. (2) 'p is *more strongly good-making or less strongly bad-making* than q' means what is meant by 'If x did have or now has or will have p (and *no other* valifying characteristic), and if y did have or now has or will have q (and *no other* valifying characteristic), it follows that x then was or now is or will be better than y; and if x should have had or should now have or should be going to have p (and *no other* valifying characteristic), and if y should have had or should now have or should be going to have q (and *no other* valifying characteristic), it would follow that x would have been or would now be or would be going to be intrinsically better than y'.

We can now formulate the four pairs of mutually entailing propositions.

First Pair. (i) p is a *good-making* characteristic. (ii) If there had been, or in fact was, an agent who, before any world existed, (*a*) *knew* (α) that if he chose he could create a world characterized by *p*, (β) that he could so choose, and (γ) that if he did not so choose no world at all would ever exist; and who (*b*) *did not believe* that this choice would be wrong; then it would have been, or in fact was, the *duty* of that agent to make that choice.

Second Pair. (i) *p* is a *good-making* characteristic. (ii) *p* is an *ought-inclining* natural characteristic.

Third Pair. (i) *p* is a *more strongly good-making or a less strongly bad-making* characteristic than *q*. (ii) If there had been or in fact was, an agent who, before any world existed, (*a*) *knew* (α) that if he chose he could create a world characterized by *p*, (β) that he could so choose, and (γ) that, unless he were so to choose, a world characterized by *q* and not by *p* would inevitably come into existence; and who (*b*) *did not believe* that this choice would be wrong; then it would have been, or in fact was, his *duty* to make that choice.

Fourth Pair. (i) The world is *intrinsically better* because A chose to do *y*, when he could have chosen to do something else instead, than it would have been if he had made any other choice open to him. (ii) A *did his duty* in choosing *y*.

Moore holds that in each of these four pairs the two members are interconnected by *synthetic* mutual entailment, but are not identical in meaning. If either the first or the second or the third were *analytic*, it would provide a *definition* of intrinsic value in terms of obligation. If the fourth were *analytic*, it would provide a definition of obligation in terms of intrinsic value. For the reasons given, Moore does not regard any of them as analytic, and he therefore sees no reason to think that either notion can be defined in the terms of the other.

(IV) *Ethical Egoism and Ethical Neutralism*[1]

In my essay in the *G. E. Moore* volume I defined what I call 'Ethical Neutralism' and what I call 'Ethical Egoism'. I pointed

[1] *Editor's Note:* The remarks of part (IV) constitute a revision of Broad's criticisms of Moore which appeared in Section (1) (pp. 43-57) of 'Certain Features in Moore's Ethical Doctrines' in *The Philosophy of G. E. Moore,* P. A. Schilpp, editor, New York: Tudor Publishing Co., 1942.

out that the latter might take milder or more extreme forms, but that it is in all its forms incompatible with Ethical Neutralism. I thought that Moore had claimed in *Principia Ethica* (pp. 96 to 105) to show that Ethical Egoism (at any rate in its extreme form) is *self-contradictory*. I argued that his attempt was a failure, and that all that could be proved was the tame proposition that Ethical Egoism is inconsistent with Ethical Neutralism.

Moore says in his terminal essay, that what he was really trying to prove was not that Ethical Egoism *is self-contradictory;* but that Ethical Neutralism *would entail* that Ethical Egoism is self-contradictory, and not merely that it is false. Now Ethical Neutralism is at any rate highly plausible, and to some eminent moralists it has seemed self-evident on inspection. Therefore, if this argument of Moore's were acceptable, it would be at least highly plausible to hold that Ethical Egoism *is* self-contradictory, and not merely false.

Moore admits that his argument in *Principia Ethica* is extremely obscure and confused. He now produces a new argument and it is with this that we shall be concerned. It is extremely complex and hard to follow, and I am inclined to suspect that it contains a logical fallacy. In order to try to show this as clearly as possible, I shall exibit formally what I take to be Moore's new argument.

In what follows I shall write 'p ent q' for 'p entails q' and I shall understand by this a kind of logical relation which holds e.g. between the conjunction of the premises of a valid syllogism and its conclusion. One way of describing it would be to say that the *conjunction* of p with not-q would be *impossible*, and that this impossibility does not depend on p being itself impossible or on q being itself necessary. I shall write 'p imp q' for 'p implies q', and I shall understand by this that the conjunction of p with not-q is *in fact false*. With these notational preliminaries, the argument may be stated as follows.

Let 'p' stand for the sentence 'It would *not be wrong* for X to choose y'.

Let 'q' stand for the sentence 'X does *not know* that the world would be *intrinsically worse* if he were to choose y than if he were to choose some other alternative open to him at the time.'

Let 'r' stand for the sentence 'X knows the choice of y by him would procure *for himself* a more favourable balance of intrinsically good over intrinsically bad experiences than any other choice that he could make, and knows also that this choice would be at least as favourable to the development of *his own* nature and dispositions as any other that he could make.'

Then what Moore calls 'Proposition A' is that p would follow from r *alone*, even though q should be false. So we may write 'A' for 'r' ent p, even though not-q'. Moore asserts, and I agree, that A is entailed by Ethical Egoism.

What Moore calls 'Proposition B' is that the falsity of q would not entail the falsity of p. So we may write 'B' for 'not-q ent not-p'. Moore asserts, and I agree, that B is entailed by Ethical Neutralism.

Now Moore asserts that A entails that r does *not* entail q. For, he argues, to say that r would entail p, *even though q were false*, entails that it is *logically possible* for q to be *false*, even though r were *true*. This contention of Moore's may be written

A ent not-(r ent q)

Moore's argument may now be stated formally as follows:

B ent (not-q ent not-p) (by definition)

Hence B ent (p ent q) (by contraposition) (I)

Again, A ent (r ent p) (by definition)

Therefore (A & B) ent ((r ent p) & (p ent q))

Whence (A & B) ent (r ent q) (II)

But, as we have seen, according to Moore

A ent not-(r ent q)

Therefore (r ent q) ent not-A (by contraposition) (III)

Therefore ((II) & (III)) ent ((A & B) ent not-A)

Since (II) and (III) can be asserted, we can drop them and assert what they together entail, i.e.

(A & B) ent not-A (IV)

Now up to this point the argument is valid, if we grant Moore's contention (which I shall not here question) that A ent not-(r ent q). But what he claims to have proved is that B entails that A is *self-contradictory*. Now this must be the proposition

B ent (A ent not-A) (V)

(It must be clearly understood that it is *not* enough for Moore to show that

$$B \text{ ent } (A \text{ imp not-}A)$$

For A imp not-A is simply equivalent to (not-A or not-A), which is in turn simply equivalent to not-A. So the latter proposition would merely amount to the tame conclusion that B ent not-A, i.e. in effect, that Ethical Neutralism is incompatible with Ethical Egoism.)

The question is, therefore, whether it is justifiable to infer from (IV), i.e. from (A & B) ent not-A, to (V), i.e. to B ent (A ent not-A). The answer is that this is *not* justifiable. Consider, e.g. a valid syllogism (P & Q) ent R. Suppose that you could legitimately derive from this the proposition P ent (Q ent R). Then, if the premise P were known to be true, you could drop it and assert the proposition Q ent R. That this is not justifiable can easily be seen by taking a concrete example of a valid syllogism with a premise known to be true. Take, e.g. 'All men are mortal' for 'P', 'Socrates is a man' for 'Q', and 'Socrates is mortal' for 'R'. Then, if this kind of inference were valid, we could infer from the syllogism the proposition (All men are mortal) ent ((Socrates is a man) ent (Socrates is mortal)). Then, dropping the true premise that all men are mortal, we could assert that Socrates is a man *entails* that Socrates is mortal. Now that conclusion is certainly false. The mortality of Socrates is not a *necessary consequence* of his humanity *alone*.

So, unless I am much mistaken, Moore's new argument is fallacious, and he failed to show that, if Ethical Neutralism were *true*, Ethical Egoism would be *self-contradictory*. It is a rash undertaking to accuse Moore of a logical fallacy, and it may well be that I have misunderstood his argument. On the other hand, it is very easy for the best of us to commit fallacies in *modal* logic, and so even Moore may have done so. But that consideration cuts both ways, and I myself may have commited some fallacy in modal logic in my criticism of his argument.

XVI

OBLIGATIONS, ULTIMATE AND DERIVED[1]

I shall call any sentence in the indicative mood in which the word 'ought', or any obviously equivalent word or phrase, such as 'is under an obligation to', 'has a duty to', etc., occurs as the principle verb, a *deontic indicative*. Examples are: 'I ought to go to the dentist', 'You ought not to eat peas with a knife', 'He ought to make an allowance to his old nurse', 'Persons who have borrowed money ought to repay it to the lender at the agreed date', 'There ought to be laws against cruelty to animals', and 'A fountain-pen ought not to be continually making blots'.

The first point to be noticed is that these sentences may be divided into two classes in the following way. Some of them assert of a *person* that he ought (or ought not) to *do* so-and-so. Others assert of a *conceivable state of affairs* that it ought to *be*, or of an *actual state of affairs* that it ought not to *be*. We can thus distinguish two important classes of deontic indicatives, viz. 'ought-to-do' ones and 'ought-to-be' ones. (It may be remarked that the sentence about fountain-pens falls somewhere between these two classes; for it asserts of a set of *inanimate objects* that they ought not to behave in a certain way.)

In each of these two classes of deontic indicatives we can distinguish broadly between those in which 'ought' occurs in a *specifically moral* sense and those in which it occurs in a *non-moral* sense. In the sentences 'He ought to make an allowance to his old nurse' and 'There ought to be laws against cruelty to animals' the word 'ought' is plainly used in a specifically moral

[1] Reprinted from *Festskrift tillagnad Karl Olivecrona*, Stockholm: AB P. A. Norstedt & Soners Forlag, 1964, by courtesy of the publishers.

This paper constitutes a revised version of Broad's earlier paper 'Imperatives, Hypothetical and Categorical', *The Philosopher*, Vol. 2, September 1950, pp. 62-75.

sense. In the sentences 'You ought not to eat peas with a knife' and 'A fountain-pen ought not to be continually making blots' it is plainly used in a non-moral sense. I have no doubt that there are plenty of marginal cases, between these two extremes, where one might reasonably hesitate to say whether the sense in which 'ought' is used is or is not specifically moral.

In what follows I shall be concerned wholly with *ought-to do* indicatives, in which the grammatical subject is the name of a *person* or a *class of persons*. I shall not be considering *ought-to-be* indicatives here.

I will begin with some preliminary remarks about *ought-to-do* sentences. (1) The word 'ought' in English has certain grammatical peculiarities which are not, I think, of any philosophical significance. (i) It cannot be used in the the *future sense*. But one can see that this is of no significance, if we substitute the phrase 'to be under an obligation'. One can say, e.g., 'When you become a parent you *will be* under an obligation to support your children'. (ii) When used of the *past*, the words 'ought' and 'ought not' have certain linguistic suggestions, which are also without philosophical significance. If one says 'X *ought* to have done so-and-so', there is a strong suggestion that he *omitted* to do this. Similarly, if one says 'X *ought not to have* done so-and-so', there is a strong suggestion that he *did* that action. All these irrelevant suggestions can be avoided by substituting the phrase 'to be under an obligation'. One can say that X was under an obligation to do so-and-so on a certain past occasion, without suggesting that he failed to do it; and one can say that X was under an obligation to do so-and-so, without suggesting that he did it. (iii) It should perhaps be added that, in ordinary English speech and writing, 'to be under an obligation to do so-and-so' does *not* mean the same as 'to be obliged to do so-and-so'. The normal meaning of the latter is to *have no option but* to do so-and-so.

(2) In 'ought-to-do' indicatives the grammatical complement to the word 'ought' or 'ought-not' is a name or a description of what I will call an *agibile*, i.e. a possible act of a certain kind. This *agibile* is supposed to have been, to be now, or to be going to be com-

pletely in control of the agent's will at the time referred to in the sentence. By this I mean that it is assumed that it would have been or will be enacted, if and only if the agent had decided or shall decide to enact it, and had set himself or shall set himself to carry out his decision.

(3) Kant said, truly I think, that we use 'ought-to-do' in regard to an agent only if we conceive there to be an actual or possible conflict of motives in him concerning the *agibile* in question. It always suggests that the agent may have to 'force himself' to enact a certain *agibile*; and that, unless he makes and keeps up a certain special effort, he will either do nothing relevant or will enact some other alternative which is somehow easier or more attractive or less repulsive to him. This brings out a difference between 'ought-to-be-done', even in its most strictly moral sense, and 'morally right'. No doubt there is a close connection between the two. On one interpretation of 'ought', what a person morally ought to do in any situation is what would *in fact* be morally right for such a person to do in such a situation. On another interpretation of 'ought', what a person morally ought to do is what he *believes* to be morally right, for such a person as he *believes* himself to be, to do in the situation as he *believes* it to be. But, on either alternative, it is one thing to say that he morally ought to do so-and-so, and another thing to say that so-and-so would be morally right for him to do. In making the deontic statement we imply or suggest that he has a desire to do what is right as such, that he has other desires or inclinations which may conflict with this, and that he may need to make a special effort in order to do what he believes to be right.

This point may be brought out (as Kant remarks) by noticing that, whilst we should say that God always acts rightly, we should hesitate to apply the word 'ought' to him. For we assume that in him there would be no motives or inclinations which might possibly conflict with the desire to act rightly as such.

This reference to an actual or possible inner conflict extends to cases where little, if anything, specifically moral is involved in 'ought-to-do'. Take, e.g., the case of a person who has a decayed tooth which occasionally gives him severe pain. He may consider the question simply from the point of view of his own interests in the most narrowly hedonistic sense. He may be quite convinced that it would pay him very well, from that point of view, to go to the dentist and perhaps suffer a short bout of severe pain, in order to secure permanent freedom thereafter from toothache in that tooth. Even so, it is very likely that he will have a considerable internal struggle, and will not go to the dentist unless he takes himself in hand and forces himself to do so. A man in that situation would be very likely to say to himself 'I ought to go to the dentist', and a friend would be very likely to say to him 'You ought to go to the dentist'.

There is, indeed, one circumstance which gives a moral tinge even to such sentences as 'I [or you] ought to go to the dentist'. We approve, in ourselves and in others, the capacity and the act of overcoming one's own laziness, fear of immediate pain or unpopularity, or desire for immediate passive satisfactions, in order to carry out one's more far-reaching desires and purposes. For the possession and the exercise of that capacity is a necessary condition of *all* serious achievement, whether morally good, bad, or indifferent. We are thus inclined to feel and to express a kind of qualified moral approval of it even when it issues in acts which are morally indifferent, e.g. acts of far-sighted prudence, which cost an effort. We do so even when it issues in acts which we morally condemn. That is, perhaps, what lies at the back of the paradoxical admonition: *Si peccas, pecca fortiter*.

That completes my preliminary remarks. I will now turn to a more detailed discussion of ought-to-do indicatives concerning persons. Let us say that such sentences express 'obligations of activity'. We can then begin by classifying obligations of activity on two independent principles, viz. (1) the nature of the *activity*, with which they are concerned, and (2) the nature of the *obligation* asserted.

(1) Human activities may be divided into practical and theoretical. So we have, corresponding to this division, obligations of *practical* and obligations of *theoretical* activity.

Suppose I were to say: 'You ought to try to produce as much

good and as little evil as you can' or 'You ought to keep your promises'. These would express obligations which you are under as a being engaged in the *practical* business of co-operating or struggling with others, and affecting yourself or them for good or ill by your actions. So they are examples of obligations of *practical* activity. Suppose, on the other hand, I were to say: 'You ought to accept the conclusions which follow logically from the premises which you accept' or 'You ought to proportion the strength of your convictions to the weight of the relevant evidences available to you'. These sentences would express obligations, though not perhaps specifically moral ones, which you are under as a thinking being engaged in the *theoretical* activity of exercising your intellect. So they are examples of obligations of *theoretical* activity. Of course, theoretical activities may have practical consequences, and they are often pursued primarily in view of such consequences. But that does not affect the validity or the importance of the distinction.

Now I think there is a fairly close analogy between the two kinds of obligation. We have seen that obligations of practical activity presuppose an agent who has the desire to do right as such, but also has other desires and inclinations, which may conflict with it and may induce him to enact one of the wrong *agibilia* instead of the right one. Similarly, the obligations of theoretical activity presuppose a thinker who has the desire to think reasonably, but also has the prejudices and lazinesses, which may conflict with it. These may induce him to accept one of the propositions under consideration which he is not logically justified in accepting, or to believe one of these propositions more strongly or less strongly than the available evidence logically justifies him in doing. In each case a specific effort needs to be made and kept up, if the agent is to do what he ought. The obligations of *practical* activity presuppose that it is, in some sense, within the agent's power to enact the right *agibile*, in spite of the inclinations which conflict with his desire to do what is right as such. Similarly, the obligations of *theoretical* activity presuppose that it is, in a like sense, within the agent's power to suspend judgment when the evidence is inadequate, in spite of his desire to make up his mind.

And they presuppose that it is, in that sense, within his power to proportion the strength of his convictions to the weight of the available evidence, in spite of his prejudices and his intellectual laziness.

(2) Let us now consider the classification of obligations of activity in respect of their intrinsic nature. In that respect they can first be divided into two fundamentally different classes, viz. *teleological* and *ostensibly non-teleological.*

The sentence 'You ought to try to produce as much good and as little evil as you can 'expresses an obligation which is explicitly *teleological.* One peculiarity of such an obligation is this. It contemplates a certain *possible* state of affairs, and it considers the *agibile* as a factor contributing to bringing it into existence or to prevent its coming into existence. Or, again, it contemplates a certain *actual* state of affairs, and it considers the *agibile* as a factor contributing to prolong it, or to cut it short, or to modify it in certain ways.

But that is not enough to make an obligation explicitly teleological. An essential condition is that this possible or actual state of affairs, and these possible modifications in it, are regarded from a certain point of view, viz. in respect of their *value or* disvalue, whether moral, aesthetic, hedonic, or otherwise. In so far as other aspects of them are considered, these are taken into account only as being good-making or bad-making characteristics. The ground alleged for the obligation to enact a certain *agibile* is simply and solely that it will produce or prolong or improve a good state of affairs or that it will avert or cut short or improve a bad state of affairs. And the ground alleged for the obligation to avoid enacting a certain *agibile* is exactly similar *mutatis mutandis*.

I have used the phrase '*ostensibly* non-teleological' obligations, in the above dichotomy, because some philosophers have denied that there are any obligations which are *really* non-teleological. Utilitarians hold that all ostensibly non-teleological obligations are derivative; and that they can and must be derived, so far as they are valid at all, from the one ultimate *teleogical* obligation to produce as much good and as little evil as possible. But many persons would not be prepared to take this view about such obligations as truth-speaking, promise-keeping, etc. And any honest and intelligent Utilitarian would admit that these obligations are *ostensibly* non-teleological, though he would hold that that appearance is misleading and would try to explain how it may have arisen.

I think that there is no difficulty in defining the *notion* of a genuinely non-teleological obligation, whether or not there be in fact any such obligations. I propose to take the alleged obligation to answer a question truly, if at all, as a plausible *prima facie* example. The essential point is that the obligation to act in the specified way in situations of the specified kind is alleged not to be grounded on the *goodness or badness* of the consequences which acting (or failing to act) in that way would contribute to produce. The obligation is alleged to be grounded either (a) on certain *intrinsic qualities* of such action, or (*b*) on certain of its *non-causal relations* to the situation in which it is done, or (*c*) on certain features in its consequences *other than* their goodness or badness.

Consider the sentence 'You ought to answer truly, if at all, when asked a question'. Let us suppose, as most unsophisticated persons do, that it expresses a non-teleological obligation. The sentence might, of course, be interpreted in at least two different ways. It might mean (i) that you ought to give what you think is the true answer, whether or not you think that doing so will produce a true belief as to the *quaesitum* in the mind of the questioner. Or it might mean (ii) that you ought to give an answer which you think will produce a true belief as to the *quaesitum* in the mind of the questioner, whether or not you believe that answer to be true. On the first alternative, the obligation is not concerned with the consequences of the act at all, but with a certain quality or relational property of it, viz. its being an utterance of what the answerer takes to be the truth about the subject of the question. On the second alternative, the obligation is indeed based on a certain feature of the intended consequences of the act, viz. the truth of the belief to be produced by it in the mind of the questioner. But that does not make the obligation teleological, in the sense defined above. For the question whether it is *good* or *bad* for the questioner to have a true belief on the subject of his question is held to be irrelevant to the obligation to answer in such a way as to produce in him a true belief.

Having dealt with the classification of obligations into practical and theoretical, and into teleological and non-teleological, I will now pass to another important distinction among them. An obligation of activity may either be restricted or *unrestricted* in its range of application. A *restricted* obligation is concerned with a certain specific type of situation, e.g. that of being asked a question. The deontic indicative here asserts that any person (or any person of a specific kind) who is acting in response to such a situation ought to act in a certain specific way. An example would be: 'Whenever a person is asked a question he ought, if he has the relevant information, either to return a true answer or to decline to answer'. An *unrestricted* obligation is supposed to apply equally in *any* situation in which a voluntary action is to be done. An example would be: 'Whenever a person acts he ought to try to produce as much good and as little evil as he can'. Another example would be: 'A person ought never to treat another in a way in which he would not be willing to be treated by another'. It is evident that, if there be any unrestricted obligations, they will all be extremely abstract; and that, taken by themselves, they will give a person very little positive guidance as to what he ought to do in any particular situation.

We can now consider another important division of obligations of activity, viz. into those which are *ultimate*, and those which are *derivative*, for a given individual at a given stage of his development. An unrestricted obligation of activity is *ultimate* for an individual, if it *seems evident to him on inspection* that anyone performing a voluntary action in any situation is under an obligation to act in the way specified. A restricted obligation of activity is *ultimate* for an individual, if it seems evident to him on inspection that anyone (or anyone of a certain kind), placed in a situation of the kind specified, ought to act in the way specified. An obligation of activity is *derivative* for an individual, when (*a*) it does *not* seem evident to him on inspection; and (*b*) seems to him to require, and to be capable of, being established by deductive reasoning.

A plausible example of an unrestricted obligation of activity which is ultimate for many individuals is the Utilitarian principle: 'In all his actions a person ought to try to produce as much good and as little evil as possible'. Another plausible example is the obligation of theoretical activity expressed by the sentence: 'When called upon to make up his mind as to the truth or falsity, probability or improbability, of several alternative propositions, a person ought to proportion the strength of his convictions to the weight of the evidence available to him'. The former is specifically moral; the latter perhaps is not. So far as I am aware no reason can be given for either of these alleged obligations. And to most of us no reason seems to be needed, for it seems self-evident on inspection that people are under these obligations.

Let us now consider some of the ways in which an obligation can be derived. I am inclined to think that it is a true general principle that no obligation can legitimately be derived, unless some other obligation is already presupposed as a premise. You cannot legitimately infer a deontic proposition from *nothing but* non-deontic premises; though you can (and perhaps must) use non-deontic premises, *in conjuction* with deontic ones, in your derivation. Again, I am inclined to think that a *specifically moral* obligation can be legitimately derived only from premises which include some deontic proposition asserting a *specifically moral* obligation. I would admit, however, that these impressions of mine (and especially the second of them) may be mistaken.

Leaving these general preliminaries, let us now consider the derivation of specifically moral obligations. To illustrate some of the more important types of derivation let us take as an example the proposition: A person, when asked a question, ought never to give an answer which he believes to be false. To some people this might appear self-evident on inspection. For any such person it would state an *ultimate* non-teleological obligation of limited range. But there are many people who are not in that position, and yet would accept it as stating a *derived* obligation. There seems to be at least two alternative possible ways in which it might be derived.

(i) Suppose that an individual finds self-evident the following unrestricted *non-teleological* deontic proposition, viz. A person ought never to treat another in a way in which he would not be willing to be treated by another. (This is one form of the 'Golden Rule'.) Suppose further that he knows or believes that no-one is willing to be told a lie in answer to a question. These two propositions together entail that a person ought never to give an answer which he believes to be false to a person who puts a question to him. On the two suppositions which I have made, this proposition would state, for the individual supposed, a *derived non-teleological* obligation of restricted range.

(ii) Let us next suppose, instead, that an individual finds self-evident the following unrestricted *teleological* deontic proposition viz. In all one's actions one ought to try to produce as much good and as little evil as possible. Suppose, further, that he knows or believes that telling lies in answer to questions always produces less good or more evil in the long run than telling the truth or declining to answer. These two propositions together entail that one ought never to give an answer which one believes to be false to a question which is put to one. On the two suppositions which I am now making, this proposition would state, for the individual supposed, a *derived teleological* obligation of restricted range.

It is worth remarking here that it is conceivable that one and the same individual might accept both pairs of premises, for they are not obviously inconsistent with each other. In that case one and the same deontic indicative sentence would express for him an obligation of restricted range which could be derived *both* teleologically and non-teleologically. It might even happen that such a person also found the deontic proposition under discussion *self-evident* on inspection. In that case the same sentence would express for him an *ultimate* obligation of restricted range. He would not *need* to derive it; but he might well be strengthened in his conviction by seeing that it *can be* derived, both as a teleological and as a non-teleological obligation.

Let us next consider what Kant called 'hypothetical imperatives' and 'imperatives of skill.' The former presuppose a desire which is assumed to be common to nearly all men at nearly all times, and therefore not to need explicit mention, e.g. desire for good health, long life, prosperity, etc. The latter presuppose a desire which is peculiar to a particular individual or class of individuals on a particular occasion or set of occasions, e.g. a desire in Mr Jones to kill his wife, or a desire in cooks to make an apple-pie. Two things seem plain about these deontic indicatives. One is that, if they express obligations at all, these are not specifically moral ones. The other is that they are in some way concerned with what I will call 'obligations of *consistency*'.

An obligation of consistency may be either practical or theoretical, and in neither case would it seem to be specifically moral. I would formulate the obligation of *practical* consistency as follows: 'A person who intends a certain end ought *either* to cease intending it *or* to take the most efficient means open to him to attain it. He ought not *both* to go on intending it *and* to do acts which would make it impossible for him to attain it'. I think it is important to formulate the obligation in this *disjunctive* way. For that makes it clear that the 'ought' and 'ought-not' now under discussion are concerned with consistency or inconsistency between (*a*) continuing to intend a certain end, and (*b*) acting or failing to act in certain ways which are relevant to the attainment or to the non-attainment of that end.

Let us now consider the derivation of a 'hypothetical imperative', in Kant's sense of the word. We will take as an example: A person ought to take exercise and not habitually to overeat'.

It is assumed as a factual premise that taking exercise is a necessary condition for keeping in good health, and that habitual overeating is a sufficient condition for failing to do so. From this factual premise and the obligation of practical consistency we can infer the following proposition: 'A person who intends to keep in good health ought *either* to give up that intention *or* to take exercise, and he ought not *both* to go on intending to keep in health *and* habitually to overeat'. Now it is assumed that *all* men intend to keep in good health. On that assumption, we can substitute the phrase 'a person' for the phrase 'a person who intends to keep in good health'. It is further assumed that the intention to keep in good health is a *standing* intention, which a person cannot or will not abandon, though he can and often does act in ways which he knows to be inconsistent with fulfilling it. On that assumption, the only way for anyone to be practically consistent in this department of his life is to take exercise and not habitually to overeat. So we reach the conclusion that a person ought, *in order to be practically consistent*, to take exercise and not habitually to overeat.

Let us next take what Kant would call an 'imperative of skill'. We will suppose that Mr Jones has formed the intention to kill his wife, and that much the most efficient way open to him for securing that end is to put arsenic in her tea. From these premises, together with the obligation of practical consistency, we can infer the proposition: Mr Jones ought, in order to be practically consistent, *either* to give up his intention to kill his wife *or* to put arsenic in her tea'. If he cannot or will not give up his intention, you can say that he *ought*, in order to be practically consistent, to put arsenic in his wife's tea. But it is essential to add explicitly the qualification 'in order to be practically consistent'. For it is *only* in relation to it that the obligation exists. In the moral and the legal senses of 'ought' he ought *not* to do this. He ought to give up his intention to kill his wife.

It is sometimes alleged that what Kant calls 'hypothetical imperatives' and what he calls 'imperatives of skill' do not really express deontic propositions at all. It is suggested that they are simply equivalent to non-deontic sentences expressing causal propositions of a certain kind. Thus, e.g., it might be alleged that the sentence: 'You ought, unless you give up your intention to kill your wife, to put arsenic in her tea', is simply equivalent to the sentence: 'The most efficient means available to you for carrying out your intention to kill your wife is to put arsenic in her tea'. That seems to me to be a mistaken view, though I am willing to admit that such deontic sentences *may* sometimes be used to mean more than this. But, in general, I think that the causal proposition is only the *factual ground* for a derived deontic proposition. The latter has *also* a *deontic ground*, viz. the ultimate, though not specifically moral, obligation of practical consistency. I take it that Kant would have agreed at least with the negative part of my contention. For he calls such propositions 'imperatives', and surely a mere causal proposition could not be called an 'imperative' in any sense of that word.

That brings me to the next question which I propose to discuss. As we all know, Kant gave the name 'imperatives' to what is expressed by ought-to-do indicatives about persons. How far is that nomenclature illuminating, and how far is it misleading? That question, in various forms, has been much discussed by many able philosophers in recent years. I fear that all that I can say about it here is somewhat platitudinous.

If the name 'imperatives' is taken literally, the doctrine would be that an ought-to-do indicative about persons expresses neither more nor less than what would be naturally expressed by a corresponding sentence in the imperative mood. E.g. the sentence 'You ought not to steal' would express and convey exactly what is expressed and conveyed by the sentence 'Do not steal!', i.e. an order issued by one person and received by another. Another possible alternative interpretation of the doctrine would be the following. Such a deontic indicative does indeed express or convey something which is not expressed or conveyed by any sentence in the imperative, viz. some characteristic kind of *information*, whether true or false. But it *also* expresses or conveys a command, as an ordinary sentence in the imperative would do. And its specifically *deontic* character, which distinguishes it from such other sentences in the indicative as, e.g., 'Stealing will probably land you in jail sooner or later', is bound up with this imperative function. A third alternative would be a more cautious modification of the second. Instead of saying that a deontic indicative derives its specifically deontic character from expressing or conveying a command, it might be said that such sentences *function in certain respects* in a way analogous to ordinary imperative sentences. There are unlikenesses as well as likenesses, and the likenesses are not exact. Perhaps that is all that Kant wished to imply by his use of the word 'imperatives'. And, however that may be, perhaps that is all that can be maintained. I will now make some comments on this.

(1) I think that the first alternative can be rejected at once, at any rate as regards specifically moral ought-to-do indicatives about persons. In the case of a *literal* imperative, e.g. the military command 'Form fours!', there is no sense in asking whether what it expresses is *true or false*. The only sensible questions which can be raised about a literal imperative are such as the following. Was it actually uttered, and, if so, was it meant seriously? Granted that that was so, is there any doubt as to precisely *what* was commanded? Granted that there is no doubt on that point, was the person who uttered the imperative entitled to issue orders on that subject to the person or persons whom he addressed?

Now, in the case of a moral deontic indicative, e.g. 'You ought not to give an answer which you know to be false, when asked a question', it seems obvious that we can sensibly raise a question which does not fall under any of the above headings, viz. Is it in fact *true*, or is it *false*, that a person ought never to act in that way in such a situation? Conversely, it seems plain that certain of the questions which can be raised about literal imperatives do not arise in regard to moral deontic imperatives. A person may, e.g., fully believe that he ought not wittingly to give false answers to questions put to him; and yet he may deny that anyone has actually forbidden him to do so, and deny that anyone would be entitled to issue orders to him on that subject.

(2) Among literal imperatives we must distinguish two different kinds, which may be called 'violent' and 'legitimate'. The imperative 'Stand and deliver!', issued by a highwayman at the point of his pistol to a wayfarer, is an example of the former. The imperative 'Form fours!', issued by an officer to a company of his own men, whom he is drilling, is an instance of the latter. Now there seems to be very little analogy between a *violent* imperative and what is expressed or conveyed by a specifically moral deontic imperative. On the other hand, analogies between *legitimate* imperatives and specifically moral deontic indicatives tend, for the following reason, not to throw much

light on the nature of what is expressed by the latter. A legitimate imperative is one issued by a person who has a *right* to give orders about a certain matter to certain persons; and it is issued to one of those persons who is under an *obligation* to obey him in such matters. An officer stands to his men in a certain relationship, which gives him a right to command them in certain of their actions, and places them under an obligation to obey his commands in respect of those actions. Thus the notion of a *legitimate* imperative *presupposes* the notion of rights and correlative obligations. So there is a kind of vicious circularity in claiming to illuminate the notion of moral obligation by reference to legitimate imperatives.

(3) I think that there are at least two causes which make it seem plausible to assimilate deontic indicatives to literal imperatives:

(i) There is at least one genuine likeness between the situation in which a person stands when he literally receives a command and that in which he stands when he believes himself to be under a moral obligation to act in a certain way. In both cases the act is not one which he would do simply because he likes doing it, as he might dance a jig or whistle a certain tune simply because he felt so inclined. Again, it is not one which he would do as an obvious means to securing some immediate satisfaction or cutting short some unpleasant experience, as he might eat if he felt hungry or if he were offered some food whose taste he knew that he liked. On the contrary, the act commanded and the act judged to be obligatory are often alike in being irksome or positively unpleasant in themselves. They are often alike in that they involve forgoing some immediate satisfaction, or bringing on oneself some pain or loss or unpopularity, or incurring some danger. They tend, in fact, in both cases to be acts which, as we say, 'go against the grain'. And the more they do so, the more fully does the agent realize, in the one case that he is being *commanded,* and in the other that he is under an *obligation.* This is certainly an important analogy.

(ii) For Jews, Christians, and Mahometans, at any rate, some of the most important negative obligations, i.e. duties of omission or avoidance, are formulated in the so-called 'Ten Commandments' as *literal* imperatives, issued by God, and promulgated on his behalf to men by his prophet Moses. That no doubt makes it easy for those brought up in any of those religions—and all contemporary Europeans and Moslems have been brought up in societies which are rooted in them and are still haunted by the ghosts of them—to *identify* what is expressed by a deontic indicative, e.g. 'A person ought not to steal', with what is expressed by a literal imperative uttered by God, e.g. 'Thou shalt not steal!' or 'Do not steal!'.

But, even if we were to accept the story of the alleged events on Mount Sinai in the most literal sense, the identification would be quite unwarranted. At most it might be held that the only *ground* for the deontic proposition that a person ought not to steal is the *fact* that God has issued the command 'Thou shalt not steal!'. Now that fact is not something that can be expressed by a sentence in the imperative mood; it is the alleged *historical* fact that a certain command has been issued by a certain person on a certain occasion. Moreover, it is not really possible to hold that the historical fact *alone* could be the ground for the deontic proposition that a person ought not to steal. If a similar command had been issued, e.g., by Moses on his own authority, no one would suppose for an instant that the fact that he had issued it would be a ground for the corresponding deontic proposition. An essential premise would be that the command was issued by *God*; and that we, as his creatures, stand in such relation to him that we have a *duty* to obey his orders. Unless you add this latter deontic premise, the Ten Commandments would be nothing but violent imperatives. In that case, though it might well be *prudent* to obey God's orders, in view of his overwhelming power, there would be no more question of *moral obligation* than there is in handing over one's purse to a highwayman at his command.

(4) We may note, further, the following *prima facie* differences between literal imperatives and what is expressed by deontic indicatives:

(i) A person does not literally issue orders to *himself*. But it is just as intelligible for a person to say of himself: '*I* ought to make an allowance to my old nurse' as it is for him to say of another: '*You* ought to make an allowance to your old nurse'. Attempts are sometimes made to evade this difference by representing statements of the form: 'I ought to do so-and-so' as expressing commands issued by a man's conscience or his higher self to his lower self. This way of speaking involves personifying one's conscience or one's higher self, and treating one's lower self as another person. That is harmless enough in practical life. But, if taken seriously, it is plainly mythology of a dangerously misleading kind. Here, at least, the example of Kant should be regarded as a warning and not as an encouragement.

(ii) A person does not literally command or forbid an action which he knows or believes to have already been done or to have been already left undone. But it is quite common and intelligible to say: 'A did x, but he ought not to have done it' or 'A failed to do y, but he ought to have done it'.

(5) It seems *prima facie* that certain deontic indicatives, so far from *expressing* commands, state the *ground for* issuing certain legitimate commands. Suppose I utter to someone the literal imperative: 'Pay me £2 19s 4d immediately!' Let us assume that I am not an armed robber issuing a violent command. The other man may reasonably ask me: 'Why should I do so?' Then it would seem that I should be giving a reasonable ground for my demand, if I could truly say: 'You promised to pay me that sum at the present date and time, and you know very well that you *ought* to keep your promises.'

On the whole then it seems to me that the unlikenesses between what is expressed by deontic indicatives and what is expressed by literal imperatives are at least as striking and important as the likenesses. What I think must be admitted, however, is this. A person's belief that he is under an *obligation* to enact a certain *agibile* on a certain occasion (provided that the belief is occurring as an actual experience, and is not existing merely as an unactivated disposition) does exert on him (provided he be mentally normal and that he has been subjected to a minimum of moral training) a felt impulse towards enacting that *agibile*. If we substitute the words 'refrain from enacting' for 'enact', and 'repulsion against enacting' for 'impulse towards enacting' in the above sentence, the resulting sentence is perhaps even more obviously true. Suppose, now, that the *agibile* which one believes oneself to be under an obligation to enact is in other respects distatsteful to one, or that some of the alternative *agibilia* are in other respects attractive to one. Then, I think, it must be admitted that the felt impulse towards enacting the *agibile* which one believes that one ought to enact, does resemble, perhaps more closely than anything else that one can recall, the experience which one has on receiving a command from a person, whom one recognizes to have the right to issue it to one, to do something which is in other respects distasteful.

INDEX